THE LOAN SOLDIER

ADVENTURES

OF A MILITARY MAN ABROAD

THE LOAN SOLDIER

ADVENTURES OF A MILITARY MAN ABROAD

BRUCE DUNCAN

Greenfinch Press

Published in the United Kingdom by Greenfinch Press,
an imprint of Petrospot Limited
Petrospot House, Somerville Court, Trinity Way,
Adderbury, Oxfordshire OX17 3SN, England

www.petrospot.com
Tel: +44 1295 814455
Fax: +44 1295 814466

First published in Great Britain in 2015 by Greenfinch Press

British Library Cataloguing in Publication Data

A catalogue record for this book is available from the British Library

ISBN 978-1-908663-23-8

Edited by Greenfinch Press
Book design by Franks and Franks
Typesetting and reproduction by Petrospot Limited
Printed and bound by The Printing House UK

CONTENTS

DEDICATION

I dedicate this book to my family, without whose support none of this would have been possible; to my wife, Toni, who has stood by me through good times and bad, to our sons Alex and Rorie, who have tragically predeceased us, and to our daughters, Hannah and Zoë, who have grown up to be wonderfully caring people despite having their lives turned upside down as young teenagers, and to their families.

I also owe an immense debt of gratitude to my late parents, who not only kept all the weekly diaries we sent them, but had them typed up. These have been invaluable in helping me to write this book.

The book is also a tribute to the loyalty and courage of loan service dependants; they also serve.

ACKNOWLEDGEMENTS

I owe an enormous debt of gratitude to Lesley and Llewellyn Bankes-Hughes for their painstaking work in editing my manuscript and for their meticulous attention to detail in preparing the book for publication. I particularly thank Cheryl Marshall for her skilful and imaginative work on the design and production of the book.

I also wish to thank the following people:

Bernie and Marieta Taylor, Baseline Consulting, for formatting and printing the initial manuscripts. David and Carmen Guard for reading earlier drafts and offering advice and encouragement.

General Sir Peter de la Billière KCB KBE DSO MC & Bar MSC, who, having read the manuscript, offered me a wealth of guidance and advice. I thank him, too, for his endorsement of the book.

I am indebted to The Lord Craig of Radley and Piers Morgan for endorsing the book.

I wish to thank Charles Messenger, a former RTR officer and now a military historian and author, for his advice and encouragement; Lieutenant Colonel Crispin Lockhart for confirming that the UK Ministry of Defence had no objection to the publication of the book, and to both him and Lieutenant Colonel Ed Robinson for guidance on the copyright of photographs; and Jim Daly for confirming that the Foreign & Commonwealth Office had no objection to the publication of the book and for advice on the copyright of photographs.

The following are thanked for their assistance in helping me to obtain approval for photographs: Palacio de la Zarzuela (photograph of Queen Sophia); HE Major General Aminuddin Ihsan Abidin; Lieutenant Colonel Abdur Rahim Abdul Karim; Ms Aimi Momin and Mr Sara (Brunei Darussalam High Commission, London); Ms Pua Hsiu Chin (*Brunei Times*); Mr Rasmi Shoukeirat (Embassy of the Hashemite Kingdom of Jordan, London); Mr Nat Howell (US Ambassador in Kuwait at the time of the Iraqi Invasion in 1990) (advice on White House photograph); Mr Steve Dock (*Soldier* magazine); and Ms Lorna O'Neill (Director, Public Relations, Grosvenor House).

Ms Michelle Dickson (Routledge, Taylor & Francis Group) is thanked for granting permission to use the map of Kuwait that featured in an article I wrote in the Gulf War edition of the *Army Quarterly & Defence Journal* in 1991 (the map was produced under the Director General of Military Survey, Ministry of Defence, United Kingdom, 1991).

50% of the royalties received by the author from the sale of this book will be divided evenly between ABF The Soldiers' Charity and the Royal Tank Regiment Benevolent Fund.

INTRODUCTION

I was born in South India in 1940, where I remained until I was almost thirteen. My earliest memories are of living in Trivandrum, the State Capital of Travancore (now Kerala), when my father was serving with the Indian Army during the Second World War. At the end of the war we returned to the remote and beautiful tea-planting district in the Western Ghats, known as the High Range, where my father recommenced his profession as a tea planter with James Finlay & Company of Glasgow.

Initially, my mother taught my sister, Merrilees, the eldest child, my younger brother, Hedley, and myself at home. However, in January 1948 Merrilees and I went across the hills to school in Kodaikanal, another beautiful hill station in neighbouring Madras State (present day Tamil Nadu). Presentation Convent Kodaikanal, PCK for short, was run by Irish nuns and drew children of various nationalities and religious persuasions from all over India, Indians and expatriates alike. During the war years the school had catered for boys right through to the completion of their secondary education but, by the time I joined, the age limit for boys was 13 years and was due to drop back to seven by the time I left.

Life changed for the whole family in 1953, when Merrilees and I went to boarding school in England, followed by my brother two years later. In the 1950s, travel between India and Britain was still largely by sea; the days of cheap air travel were several years away. Once sent back to school in Britain, many children never returned to India, but James Finlay did fly children out for one holiday every two and a half years. Thus we came home in 1956, when I was mid-way through secondary school, and again in 1958 when I had completed my schooling. The journey took three days each way. We flew from Heathrow to Bombay (now Mumbai) in an Air India Lockheed Super Constellation, stopping in Paris, Zurich or Rome to re-fuel and for the passengers to have a meal, repeating the process in Cairo or Beirut, before setting out overnight on the longest leg of the journey, across the Indian ocean – about eight hours from memory – to Bombay's Santa Cruz airport. The highlight of this part of the journey was being served with an in-flight breakfast! We spent the rest of the second day with kind company contacts in Bombay and then flew on in an Indian Airways or Deccan Airways Dakota to Cochin the following morning, stopping to re-fuel and take on passengers at Mangalore and Belgaum en-route. This flight was usually a hair-raising experience as the summer holidays in England coincided with the height of the South West monsoon in South India. Our aircraft could not fly above the weather and was thrown about horribly in the storm clouds. Our parents were in Cochin to greet us and drive us the 100 miles up the ghat road to our home in the High Range.

Some thoughtful soul in India had given me *Tom Brown's Schooldays* to help me prepare for what lay in store for me in an English public school. Whilst Douai in no way lived up to the terrors experienced by Tom Brown, life in England was quite a challenge for a young boy who had been brought up in an environment more at one with Kipling's *Jungle Book* than William Blake's 'green and pleasant land'. The gentle rhythm of the jungle, the excitement of a chance meeting with a panther, tiger or elephant and the rich scent of tea and eucalyptus wafting on the evening breeze were now replaced by the general clamour, hustle and bustle and tameness of post-war Britain.

Still, in my mind this was only a temporary hiatus. My intention was to follow my father's footsteps by joining James Finlay as a tea planter in India. My dreams were dashed when, just as I was about to leave school, the company stopped recruiting British tea planters, in favour of employing Indians. Though this impacted adversely on me at the time, it was absolutely the right decision. Indeed, it was the start of a highly successful handover process that was completed in the 1980s, when Tata Tea took ownership of the tea estates in the High Range, now known as Idukki.

My plans were now in ruins and I was grateful to my parents for arranging for me to take up an engineering apprenticeship at Marshall's of Gainsborough. The plan now was for me to qualify as an engineer and then apply to James Finlay for a vacancy in a tea factory in India. It soon became apparent, however, that I was not cut out to be an engineer. On the other hand, I greatly enjoyed my weekends as a Territorial Army Private in 'D' Company, 4th Battalion, the Royal Lincolnshire Regiment, coincidentally commanded by Major Marshall, the owner of Marshall's.

Accepting Major Marshall's advice and armed with his recommendation, I followed the main family tradition and joined the army. I had left school without taking the all-important Civil Service exam, which meant that I was not eligible to apply for a commission. So I enlisted into the Royal Tank Regiment (RTR) as a Trooper, with the intention of applying for a commission as an army entrant on completion of my basic training. Fortunately, I was successful, and for the rest of my military career I was very grateful for the year I spent in the ranks prior to going to Sandhurst in September 1959, as it helped me enormously to identify with the soldiers with whom I worked.

In those days the course at Sandhurst lasted two years and I really came into my own there. I was now more used to life in England and, even better, had been thoroughly inured to the self-disciplined military psyche by the tough, effective training regime of the Royal Armoured Corps (RAC) Training Regiment – 5RTR at that time – at Catterick.

I passed out of Sandhurst in July 1961 and was commissioned into the 3rd Royal Tank Regiment (3RTR) stationed in Detmold, Germany. At the time, the Cold War was at its height and tensions along the Inner German Border were giving cause for concern. So much so, that it was decided I should not attend the three-month RAC Young Officers' course at Bovington, but be posted directly to my Regiment in Germany. My arrival coincided with the erection of the Berlin Wall. After I had spent a sometimes tense, but happily uneventful, year and a bit in Germany, 3RTR was posted back to England and assumed the role of RAC Training Regiment at Catterick.

As I had come through the RAC training regime barely three years earlier, I was put in charge of the Potential Officers' Troop. This suited me down to the ground, as most of my time was spent out on the moors. However, this perhaps reawakened in me the pull of the wilds, and the wilds of the East in particular.

A tall, fair-haired Captain, Hugh Leach, had recently rejoined the Regiment in the capacity as Adjutant after a period of service with local troops in Arabia. He introduced me to the enormous possibilities for secondment that existed in the Army at the time and fired up my enthusiasm for adventure. It was not long before I was poring over the vacancies in the Army's Secondment Manual to see the positions for which I might be qualified.

I settled on Borneo and, more specifically, the Sarawak Rangers. Alas, the vacancy was restricted to the Infantry. The War Office did offer me a Regimental Signals Officer's appointment with the King's African Rifles in Nyasaland. However, at the time I did not have a 'feel' for Africa and, more importantly, whilst I did not know what my forte was, I knew that it certainly wasn't Signals. My Squadron Leader at the time, Major Dickie Everard, suggested that I ring up the Secondment Branch in the War Office and make an appointment to discuss matters with them. I took his advice and, as chance would have it, arrived at the War Office only a few days after Brunei had elected not to join Malaysia. Malaysia had responded by immediately withdrawing all support for the fledgling Brunei Malay Regiment, which was being trained by the Malaysian army at Port Dickson at the time. As Brunei was a British Protectorate, the Sultan had asked Britain to fill the void. Indonesian Confrontation had begun and, moreover, the security situation in Brunei was still a little rocky following the Brunei Rebellion in 1962. Britain was obliged to help.

The most junior officers' vacancies were in the rank of captain, of which there were two. One of these had been filled and the other had been offered, I recall, to the Middlesex Regiment. A response was required by the end of the day and I was told that if the Regiment declined the vacancy it would be offered to me, despite only being a Lieutenant and a non-infantryman at that. Luckily for me, time was of the essence. Next day I received the good news. All I had to do now was to clear the matter with my Commanding Officer, Lieutenant Colonel Carl Barras MC. He was very supportive and within a matter of days I was ready to embark on a two and a half year adventure in Borneo.

BRUNEI

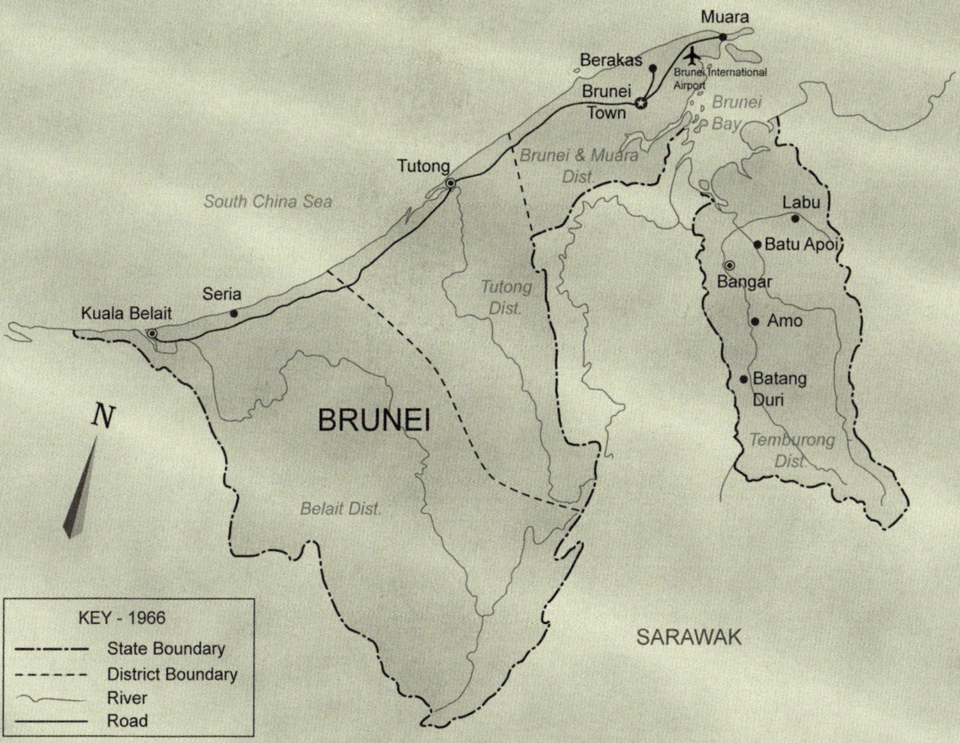
Muara
Berakas
Brunei International Airport
Brunei Town
Brunei Bay
Tutong
Brunei & Muara Dist.
South China Sea
Labu
Batu Apoi
Bangar
Amo
Batang Duri
Temburong Dist.
Tutong Dist.
Seria
Kuala Belait
BRUNEI
Belait Dist.
N
SARAWAK
KEY - 1966
State Boundary
District Boundary
River
Road

BRUNEI

Just before midnight on 17 May 1964, a Bristol Britannia of British Eagle Airways sped down the runway at Heathrow airport and soared into the night sky. I was on my way to Brunei. I cannot remember much about the first leg of the journey, the flight to Singapore, apart from the fact that we arrived just after breakfast on Tuesday morning, some 26 hours after leaving London.

My mother had been born in Singapore, and this had been her home until she married my father. She was still fluent in Malay and was able to give me a good grounding in the language during my fortnight's embarkation leave, which I spent at home.

My maternal grandfather, who was now in his 80s, had chosen to retire in Singapore. I welcomed the opportunity to visit him. He had last seen me in 1942, when he came to stay with us in India for a short while after the fall of Singapore. I was only a small child at the time and had no recollection of him. I was struck his strong resemblance to my mother; the way he spoke and his every mannerism seemed to mirror hers.

A retired electrical engineer, my grandfather expressed a great interest in my new posting and told me that he had installed the first electrical power station in Brunei Town in the 1930s. He talked nostalgically about 'home' and of my mother, whom he had also not seen since 1942. Yet he was happy in Singapore and intended to remain there for the rest of his life.

My professional contact in Singapore was the Brunei agent, Mrs De Souza. A highly efficient person, she had an admirable sense of duty towards Brunei, although she had never actually been there herself. She told me that the Brunei Malay Regiment had just moved back to Brunei, and that I was due to fly out to join it on 21 May.

After we had flown for almost two hours over the calm blue waters of the South China Sea, we landed at Kuching, Sarawak in southern Borneo. Here, for the first time, I saw evidence of the conflict I was about to join; a low intensity operation known as Indonesian Confrontation, or simply Confrontation. Anti-aircraft guns pointed to the sky, military aircraft cluttered the airfield apron, and army vehicles and soldiers seemed to be everywhere.

Within 20 minutes we were airborne again and heading northeast up the western coast of Borneo. Below me, a thin strip of glistening white sand separated the sea from the coastal plain, which in places penetrated several miles inland before surrendering to the rugged mountain ranges of central Borneo. As far as the eye could see, the land was covered by a thick mantle of jungle. Here and there, the brown veins of a river and its countless tributaries snaked their way through this green carpet on their journey to the sea. Along the banks of some of these rivers I could make out the occasional longhouse, the traditional dwelling of the Iban people of Borneo – the fearsome head-hunters of old.

Soon after leaving Kuching, the torches of flame belching from the Seria oilfields signalled our arrival over the Sultanate of Brunei. From the neat Shell settlement I could make out a road leading up the coast towards Brunei Town – the only road I had seen since leaving Kuching. Here and there, surrounded by jungle, small villages and patches of cultivation clung to the road.

As the aircraft swept over Brunei Town on its final approach, two quite different spectacles struck me. One was the most beautiful mosque I had ever seen and the other was a fascinating village perched on stilts in the middle of the Brunei River – a veritable Venice of the East. This was Kampong Ayer, meaning 'water village', and was the original Brunei Town, dating back at least to the fifteenth century.

At the airport I was met by the other volunteer captain, Roger Sherrin. Seconded from the Royal Sussex Regiment, he had arrived out a few days before me and had been appointed Adjutant of the Regiment.

Roger drove me into Brunei Town, where we stopped outside a new block of flats, known as the Tongkadeh Flats – this was to be our home until our barracks were complete. Having dumped my kit, we went to the rather dilapidated Brunei Hotel, in the centre of town. On the ground floor of the hotel was the Okay Bar, the town's only restaurant. Run by two young Chinese, Johnny and Jimmy, this was where we ate for the next few weeks.

After a delicious lunch, Roger drove me down the twisting jungle road to our camp at Berakas, about nine miles outside the town. En-route, we passed a detention centre, which still housed a number of people for their part in the Brunei Rebellion of December 1962, including the leader of the rebellion, Azahari.

A few miles beyond the detention centre, Roger turned right onto a makeshift access road rising gently towards the brow of a hill. As we breasted the rise, there spread out before us lay Berakas Camp. Overlooking the South China Sea, the beautiful deserted beach a mere 50 yards from the buildings, it looked magnificent even in its unfinished state.

We made our way down the slope and came to a halt at the edge of the barrack square. From here, we walked across to the Commanding Officer's office for my joining interview.

Lieutenant Colonel Donald Fletcher MC of the Parachute Regiment was a very fit and energetic man, who had the ability to inspire and instil confidence and self-belief in those who worked for him. Confirming Mrs De Souza's information that the Regiment had only just arrived, he told me that, apart from the advance party, everyone was still on leave until 1 June – some ten days ahead. He said that the Regiment had been placed under the operational command of 51 Gurkha Infantry Brigade, based in Brunei, and he stressed the political as well as the military importance of it becoming effective as soon as possible. To this end, 'B' Company was to become operational by 15 June, followed by the rest of the Regiment by 1 August.

Apparently ignoring the fact that I was only a 23-year-old lieutenant, albeit masquerading as a captain, and, furthermore, was not an infantryman, he told me that I was to take temporary command of 'B' Company. Rumours were circulating about subversion, infiltration by Indonesian elements and the smuggling of arms and ammunition. All these activities were designed to destabilise Brunei and make it an easy target for Indonesia, and a highly prized one at that. My initial task was to determine the veracity of these rumours and, if confirmed, the extent and the level of support they were receiving amongst the population. I was to achieve this by patrolling all the main river complexes and visiting the isolated kampongs and longhouses along their banks. Having only ten days to familiarise myself with the geography of Brunei and make my operational plan, and then a fortnight in which to prepare my men for the task, was incredibly daunting. The CO, of course, promised to give me every assistance – I just had to ask.

I felt both awed and excited by this unexpected challenge. If Colonel Fletcher was concerned, he certainly never showed it. Quite simply, he had had no choice – there was only me to choose from, and he was certainly true to his word in the support and advice he gave me.

The Sultanate of Brunei is situated on the north west coast of Borneo and embraces an area of 2,226 square miles of swamp and jungle. It is bordered by Sarawak to the north, east and south and is almost divided in two by the 5th Division of Sarawak. The larger southern 'half' of the Sultanate contains the districts of Brunei, Tutong and Belait, the latter incorporating the rich oilfields of Seria. The coastal road provides easy access to the main villages in this area, but, at the time, the only way to travel inland was by boat or helicopter. The smaller 'half' of the Sultanate, to the north of Brunei Town, comprises the Temburong District. In 1964 this was a very isolated area of thick jungle, almost entirely surrounded by Sarawak and accessible only by boat or helicopter. This was, perhaps, where the greatest threat to Brunei's security lay.

'B' Company was about 100 strong and, for the purpose of this operation, I organised it into four rifle platoons plus a small headquarters. All the men were Brunei Malays, except for the company sergeant major and one sergeant, who were both infantrymen, seconded, like me, from the British Army. I did, however, have three very capable Brunei Malay captains and it was soon apparent that the soldiers too had a very sound military grounding. Moreover, everyone in the company was immensely proud to be given the honour of being the first local troops to operate in Brunei.

My plan was to establish four bases, in Temburong, Tutong and Belait Districts and on a small island, Baru Baru, in the middle of Brunei Bay, from where we could patrol the bay and its coastline.

Some 48 hours before I was due to deploy, we received disturbing intelligence reports suggesting that subversive elements may have penetrated the Regiment itself, bringing its loyalty into question and putting all us volunteers at risk. With true British phlegm, Colonel Fletcher held a 'welcoming' cocktail party in his garden for all the 'loan service' personnel. When the party was in full swing, he briefed us on the situation and warned us all to be on our guard. Later, he made his way over to me and said that it was vitally important for us not to over-react to this situation. The political significance of Brunei's own soldiers operating in the Sultanate was immense and, thus, the Brigade Commander and he had decided that I should proceed as planned. In his view, by showing this level of trust and confidence in our soldiers, we would discredit any potential subversive elements within our ranks.

I would be lying if I said that I wasn't apprehensive when I deployed 'B' Company into its operational bases on 10 June. We had been able to requisition existing buildings and amenities everywhere except on Baru Baru. Here, we had to construct small huts, called bashas, built from nipah palm. In addition, all our drinking water had to be brought to the island by boat and we had no electricity.

We were to operate from these bases until relieved by other troops from the Regiment in early August. On 15 June we set out on the first ever patrols undertaken by the Brunei Malay Regiment in a concerted 'hearts and minds' operation encompassing the entire Sultanate. From the outset, my soldiers, who were blissfully unaware of the security drama back at Berakas Camp, were magnificent and went about their task in a thoroughly professional manner.

'B' Company was now spread over a front about 80 miles wide, making control very difficult. When I was allocated a helicopter from the Brigade I was able to visit all the platoon locations in a day. However, when, as usually happened, I had to rely on a Land Rover and outboard motorboat, it could take several days.

Initially, I spent my time visiting the bases rather than going out on patrol myself, as this would have meant I was out of contact for days at a time due to our lack of effective radio communications.

Whenever possible, the Regiment's doctor, Major John Moran, accompanied me on these visits. One of our earliest trips was to the island base of Baru Baru. By now I felt confident enough to operate the outboard motorboat myself. All went well until we were within a few hundred yards of the island. There are a number of rocks in this area and it is necessary to follow a narrow, marked channel. The sea was choppy and a strong ebb tide was running, so, to maintain direction, we kept moving fairly quickly. Relieved at having negotiated the channel successfully, I turned in towards the island rather too sharply and a wave caused the boat to lurch alarmingly, throwing me overboard, much to the amusement of the soldiers on shore. For a time, John was unaware of my absence. Realising just in time, he was able to cut the engine and allow the boat to beach gently on the shore. Meanwhile, I began to be washed out to sea. Not being a strong swimmer, and wearing full combat kit, I began to fear the worst. Luckily a local fisherman spotted me and came over in his boat to rescue me.

As I stepped ashore, the soldiers tried their best not to show their amusement, while I tried to pretend that nothing had happened. It was not my best moment.

John was the strongest string to our bow. He was always ready to ask for the assistance of a *bomo* (witch doctor) if a soldier felt that he had been put under a spell that Western medicine could not counter. I remember one instance when one of our soldiers was stung around his midriff by a jellyfish while fishing in the sea off our beach at Berakas Camp. He reported to the medical centre, but told John he had been cursed by a *bomo* for some indiscretion in his village and this was the sign. He added that he would die by midnight. John could find nothing medically wrong with him, except for a mild reaction to the jellyfish sting. The soldier's condition started to deteriorate for no apparent reason until John asked him who had cast the spell and, more importantly, who was powerful enough to remove it. Armed with this information, he secured the services of a powerful *bomo*. The soldier's 'illness' was all in the mind, but John was convinced that he would have died, but for the *bomo* lifting the spell.

John's evident concern for the well-being of the soldiers and the civilians whose trust we were nurturing made us welcome everywhere. He, himself, almost died when he contracted dengue fever. A Roman Catholic, he even received the last rites. There was great relief and rejoicing when he recovered, some even crediting the priest with similar powers to a *bomo*! John became a permanent fixture in Brunei. Long after I had departed, he left the RAMC and became Brunei's State Medical Officer, such was his standing in the Sultanate.

To patrol the rivers we used wooden boats, known as *prahus* in Malay, fitted with 40 horsepower outboard engines and painted in the Regimental colour of Port Dickson Green, a greyish green, with a red stripe at the waterline. These boats could carry a section of eight soldiers and their equipment, and they worked very well in Brunei Bay and the coastal plain areas, where the rivers were deep and sluggish. However, they were unsuitable for the shallower, faster-flowing waters of the *ulu* (upper reaches) deep inland. To operate effectively here, we had to purchase dugout canoes, known locally as *temuais*. These were powered by 15 horsepower outboard motors, had virtually no freeboard and, to the inexperienced, were alarmingly unstable.

Our soldiers were drawn entirely from the Brunei Malay population, who lived in and around Brunei Town and the settlements along the coastal road to Seria. They came largely from urban, farming or fishing stock and their boat-handling skills were more than adequate to enable them to operate on the rivers in the coastal areas and, of course, in the bay.

The *ulu* reaches of the rivers, however, posed real challenges; boatmen required different skills here. Unsurprisingly, we experienced a number of accidents, resulting in the loss of equipment and, in one case, the loss of a *temuai*. Once, the *temuai* in which the doctor, John, was travelling capsized in fierce rapids and he was trapped under the boat, almost drowning as it was swept away by the current. Two soldiers managed to rescue him, semi-conscious, some distance downstream and, thankfully, were able to revive him.

Another major problem was our lack of experience in jungle operations, be it on the coastal plain or in the *ulu*. None of us had been on a jungle warfare course – there simply had not been time. We were therefore unable to 'see through' the foliage, and incapable of moving silently through the undergrowth. I was quite certain that if we were to meet an Indonesian patrol in these early days we would stand little chance. The answer, I felt, lay in recruiting Ibans, the people of the *ulu*, to join our ranks. However, the Sultan wanted the Regiment to remain exclusively Malay, doubtless because of the religious complications that might otherwise arise. The Malays were all Muslims, whilst the Ibans worshiped the nature around them – the birds and the trees.

A sensible compromise was reached by allowing us to attach Iban police trackers to our patrols in the *ulu*. Not only were these men superb trackers, they were also experts in handling *temuais*. Over the course of the next few weeks, I got to know two of our trackers in Temburong, Yu and Angung, well. In the early days, we depended very heavily on these two men and learned from their example and guidance.

One of the first lessons these Iban trackers taught us was how to move silently through the jungle by flexing our knees slightly just before each footfall. Each foot then landed more gently, minimising the noise of snapping twigs or rustling leaf litter. They also taught us how to look through the undergrowth on the jungle floor instead of merely looking at it, thereby adding a little more distance to our field of view, perhaps crucial if one bumped into an enemy patrol. Again, they taught us to listen to the animals and the birds. These would warn us (and the enemy, of course) of people in the area.

Almost every day in Brunei it rained in the middle of the afternoon for an hour or so. Some of these showers were torrential and were accompanied by thunder and lightening. I remember patrolling up a narrow, steep-sided gully the morning after one of these storms. Pointing to the debris caught up in the trees some ten feet or so above our heads, Yu warned us of the dangers of flash floods following heavy rain and the need to plan our patrol routes accordingly.

Some skills I could never grasp, including Yu and Angung's ability to maintain direction in the jungle. They seemed to know exactly where they were at all times. Our maps were pretty basic and we were rarely able to see more than a few yards in any direction. I was quite unnerved on one occasion, when we came across a stream that appeared to be running in the wrong direction according to my map. I was the only non-Bruneian in the patrol and the security situation within the Regiment was still unclear. I voiced my concern about our location to Yu, the tracker. He could not read my map, but advised me to put it away! He assured me that we would reach our destination, a longhouse on another river near the border with Sarawak, before nightfall. Only if this did not happen should I doubt him, he added. To my amazement and relief, at about four o'clock we reached the banks of the river and there, barely 100 yards upstream of us on the far side, was the longhouse. I never doubted Yu again.

Another difficulty that the soldiers faced was visiting the Iban longhouses – a fundamental requirement in our 'hearts and minds' operations in the *ulu*. After all, if there were to be an incursion across the border by the Indonesians, the *ulu* people would be the first to be contacted, and so it was essential for us to win their confidence. To our Malay soldiers, the Ibans were not only savage former head-hunters, but they reared pigs for eating and allowed dogs to roam about the longhouse. This was offensive to Muslims soldiers and, understandably, they were therefore reluctant to dwell in a longhouse. Remembering that the spark that ignited the Indian Mutiny had been forcing sepoys to bite the tips off their cartridges, which had been smeared in a protective coating of grease made from pig and cow fat, I was certainly not going to force this issue. The solution was simple: to operate from temporary jungle bases, making regular visits to the longhouses, often with the doctor, to win the Ibans' confidence.

My first visit to a longhouse was a great experience. We had travelled for about an hour up the Temburong River from our base in Bangar when we rounded a bend and Yu pointed to a group of naked boys playing at the water's edge 100 yards upstream. Some were jumping into the strong current and swimming back to the bank, whilst others were being taught how to paddle *temuais* by older children.

Downstream of the children, women wearing colourful sarongs were either washing or fetching water for the evening meal. The women took fright at seeing us and hurried back to the longhouse. The children, on the other hand, were full of curiosity and gathered on the bank to watch us land. They were very shy and tried to hide behind one another, taking a quick peek at us when they thought we weren't looking.

Yu led us up the steep path to the longhouse. This was Long Amo, his home. The longhouse is a unique structure and I cannot imagine a better example of community living. The concept of the building stems from three reasons. First, the jungle is thick and it is much easier to clear a limited area and build a single, long dwelling than to clear the bigger area required for a village. Second, a single building is easier to defend from attack than a village. Third, with everyone living under the same roof, the aged, sick and widowed people of the community are more easily cared for and are never allowed to feel lonely or unwanted.

Longhouses are always built beside or within easy access of rivers, which are the roads of the *ulu*. The building itself is a wooden and nipah palm structure raised on stilts. The space under the house incorporates chicken runs and pig sties. At each end of the building is a door up against which a tree trunk, with steps hewn out of it, leans to provide access. Inside, a large central corridor runs the length of the building. At the centre of the corridor, some longhouses have a raised dais upon which the *Pengulu*, or headman, seats himself on festive occasions, or to hold court. In effect, this is the community hall of the longhouse, where all social events take place and where visitors bed down for the night. To the landside of this corridor, a series of doors leads to the private rooms of each of the families in the community – one room per family. On the riverside of the corridor there are a number of openings onto a veranda, which also runs the entire length of the longhouse. Here, the inhabitants can hang out their washing and also do their cooking.

When I was in Borneo, I was told the largest longhouse was in Sarawak and was about half a mile long. None that I visited in Brunei was anywhere near as big. Longhouses are never referred to by their length but by the number of doors they have; the doors being an accurate indication of the number of families living inside. So you would speak of a longhouse of 53 doors, rather than one of 600 feet.

Yu led us to the foot of one of the tree trunk stairways giving access to the Amo longhouse. The *Pengulu*, wearing a shirt and trousers and flanked by a number of other similarly attired men, stood in the doorway above. He beckoned us to join him. Yu indicated for me to climb the staircase first. At the top I greeted the *Pengulu* with the requisite limp handshake and subservient bow of the head.

Yu followed me into the longhouse, but the soldiers remained on the ground below. A number of other men then joined us who were dressed in a combination of shirts or vests, and trousers or sarongs. The *Pengulu* bade us all to sit in a circle on the floor. He was an old man with a gentle expression on his face, but many of his colleagues were rather fierce-looking and, like him, heavily tattooed. Some of these tattoos were merely decorative but others bore considerable significance. Warriors were identified by the tattoo of a hornbill on their throats. The bird faced outwards, head uppermost, with the body centred on the man's Adam's apple and with the wings spreading outwards round the neck towards the line of the shoulder. Some warriors had heavily tattooed fingers, purportedly indicating that they had taken a head; one for each finger tattooed.

After we had all sat down, two young girls approached. They were dressed in brightly coloured sarongs and wore bead necklaces. One carried a kettle filled with tea and a tray of glasses, while the other held a bunch of rather overripe bananas. Shy but poised, they awaited the *Pengulu's* almost indiscernible gesture to start serving. Yu told me that this was the traditional welcoming ceremony. It was now time for me to distribute my gifts: a bottle of brandy and hundreds of cigarettes for the men and sweets and balloons for the children. These were well received and, with the formalities over, the central corridor of the longhouse was soon full of men, women and children chatting noisily. As we sipped brandy and the very potent Iban rice wine called *tuak*, some of the men began traditional Iban dances to the haunting ring of Iban gongs, combined with the hollow-sounding beat of bamboo striking bamboo. As night fell over the jungle, the women brought in trays heaped with rice and curry, which we all tucked into with our hands.

The soldiers, who had set up a defensive position on the riverbank by our *temuais*, seemed rather concerned when I told them I intended to sleep in the longhouse. In truth, I, too, was a little apprehensive, but to show trust and respect in this way was an essential part of the 'hearts and minds' process. Bedding down alone in the corridor, I enjoyed a good night's sleep and I was woken at dawn by the cocks crowing and the pigs grunting just below me.

As the sun started to lighten the eastern sky, women made their way down to the river to collect water, whilst the men started to prepare their equipment for another day's fishing, hunting or tending their fields. The crop they were growing was hill padi. This differs from the usual padi one sees growing in flooded padi fields in that it grows on dry land on the hillside. Each year, the Ibans clear just enough jungle on a rotational basis to plant their crops. After the harvest, the jungle is allowed to reclaim the area until it is required again, perhaps ten years later.

The Ibans were expert hunters. Their quarry comprised monkeys, sloths, deer and wild boar. Whilst they hunted for the pot, the killing of wild boar also served to protect their crops from being destroyed by these animals. In days of yore, they used the blowpipe to kill game. In the hands of a skilled user, this weapon has a range of about 25 yards. Many blowpipes had a metal spearhead attached with rattan (home made twine) to the far end of the pipe, rather like a rifle with a fixed bayonet. This enabled the weapon be used as a spear to despatch a wounded animal – very necessary if confronted by a pig in a 'death charge'.

During the 1950s, the shotgun took over from the blowpipe and by the mid-1960s, when I was in Brunei, the requisite skills to manufacture the blowpipe seemed to have died out, at least in that country. Indeed, the only blowpipes I saw anywhere in Borneo were those being sold in curio shops, where they commanded a terrific price. Following the Brunei Rebellion in 1962, the Sultan ordered all firearms in civilian hands to be impounded. Whilst this was a necessary measure it presented the Ibans with a problem; they were no longer able to defend their fields against marauding wild boar. Moreover, without any control of their numbers, the wild boar population rapidly increased, thereby exacerbating the plunder meted out on the Ibans' crops. In 1965, the Brunei government sought to ease the situation by allowing the Iban police trackers to cull the wild boar population in the vicinity of the longhouses at regular intervals.

During my last few days in Brunei, Yu and Angung invited me to take part in a wild boar hunt at Long Amo, an offer I readily accepted. Once supper was over, the hunting party prepared their equipment. Apart from Yu and Angung's shotguns, this comprised a number of small hurricane lanterns, each with a highly polished brass dish attached behind the glass windshield to act as a reflector. When all was ready, we set out, splitting into two groups at the jungle's fringe. The lanterns threw a dim light over the ground a few feet ahead of us. The flickering flame caused faint shadows to play tricks on us in the half-light; weird shapes would appear around us only to disappear again as we moved slowly forwards. My mind started to wander in this eerie atmosphere, so that when I felt a firm hand on my shoulder I almost jumped out of my skin.

Yu had heard the sound of something moving in the undergrowth. Bringing the shotgun very carefully up to his shoulder with one hand and stretching the lantern out in front of him with the other, he began to search the area ahead. The lantern soon picked up the blood-red eyes of a wild boar. Yu carefully lined up the shotgun, squeezed the trigger, and the stillness around us was shattered by the gun's deafening report. The jungle awoke into a chaotic cacophony: terrified birds squawked as they flew blindly into the air, monkeys shrieked their alarm in the tree canopy high above, while all about us the sound of animals crashing through the undergrowth was evidence that we had stumbled across wild boar. I was scared stiff, but Yu had experienced this many times before. He stood silent and motionless and gestured for me to do likewise. After what seemed an age, but in reality must have been no more than a minute or two, calm was restored to the jungle. Yu moved forwards and there, less than ten yards from where we had been standing, lay a fine boar, its tusks glinting as the light of the lantern fell upon them. Yu marked the spot so that we could retrieve the animal later and then we moved on.

Every nerve in my body tingled with excitement as the full thrill of this escapade began to sink in. Minutes passed before Yu froze again on seeing another boar's eyes reflecting back at us. Just as he prepared to fire, we heard a boar moving through the undergrowth very close to our left. We both swung round to face the danger, whereupon the animal Yu had first spotted beat a noisy retreat, spooking the rest of the sounder and revisiting pandemonium upon the jungle. The hunt continued in similar fashion well into the night, Yu bagging another boar. Angung, too, met with success. We returned to the longhouse in the small hours to grab 40 winks before dawn heralded in a new day, when, over breakfast, Yu and

Angung recounted our night's adventures.

The Tutong area of operations included, in my opinion, the most beautiful and romantic place in Brunei. This was Lake Merimbun, a shallow expanse of water fringed by reed beds and grassy banks in the midst of the jungle in *ulu* Tutong. Home to many species of bird, I regarded it as a picture of gentleness and tranquillity, especially at dawn, when a thin mist rose from the still, warm waters. A tiny community lived on the southern shores of the lake, their *kampong* (village) comprising just three small wood and nipah palm huts. The peaceful setting was, perhaps, a little misleading; the lake and surrounding area was also home to numerous crocodiles and pythons.

Our base in the Belait area was some 35 miles further down the coastal road south of Tutong. We would drive down to the oil-rich area of Seria. Here, turning inland, we travelled along an unsurfaced road for about five miles to our camp in a *kampong* called Badas, on the banks of the Belait River. Alternatively, we could take the narrow gauge train that ran between Seria and Badas – the only railway in Brunei. The Belait region contained the largest and most influential longhouse in Brunei. Known as Mengilas, its *Pengulu* was looked upon as the leader not only of the neighbouring longhouses within Brunei, but also those across the border in Sarawak. During the Brunei Rebellion, this powerful *Pengulu* had assembled all his men before leading them down the Belait River in a show of force to offer his assistance to the Sultan. When I was in Brunei, Mengalis still had bronze cannons 'guarding' its approaches, although by then their function was purely ornamental.

My soldiers, particularly those operating in the Tutong area some 30 miles south of Brunei Town, seemed very fond of bringing 'pets' home from their patrols for 'Tuan', as I was known. The first of these was an abandoned baby monkey, a long-tailed macaque, which I called 'George'. At first it was very nervous but, after a day or two, it began to eat from our hands.

However, without warning, or the slightest provocation, it would suddenly sink its needle-sharp teeth into you. Not only were these bites painful, they posed a potential rabies hazard. So 'George' was returned to the jungle and, I fear, an uncertain fate.

Another 'pet' was 'Alfred', a beautiful young python about eight feet long. When I saw him he looked so miserable cooped up in a small cage, so I released him back into the wilds. Finally, there was 'Sad Eyes', and I got quite a fright on our first meeting. Having been out on patrol, I was pleased to be back at our base – a rather nice wooden house in Tutong. I was wet, tired and hungry. All I wanted to do was to wallow in a cool bath, get something to eat and then turn in. However, it was clear that the soldiers in the camp did not want me to enter the bathroom at all, let alone have a bath. Imagine my surprise when I found a small crocodile lying in the bathtub! The soldiers explained that it was the only place to put the poor creature, but I assured them that he would be a lot happier in the river outside.

Six weeks after deploying on operations we handed over our responsibilities to two other companies of the Regiment and returned to Berakas Camp, where my company was given the task of constructing a jungle rifle range just beyond the camp gate. The main requirement was to make a 100-yard range with a clear field of fire for eight people firing from a static firing position towards targets placed at the butts at the far end. Importantly, the jungle canopy had to remain intact as far as was possible to retain the lighting conditions that exist in the jungle.

Clearing some 1,100 square yards of jungle was hard work, especially as we were only equipped with *parangs* (knives). The butts had to be built up with hundreds of sandbags, each one filled by hand from sand taken from the beach about half a mile away. To the left of this range we also constructed a jungle lane range. This comprised a narrow twisting lane through uncleared jungle, with pop-up targets positioned to either side along its course. These targets were activated by hand-operated wires. A single firer at a time would move slowly down the range, rifle at the ready. Meanwhile, an instructor following a few yards behind would activate targets for a few seconds at random. Some of these targets would only be a matter of feet away from the firer.

The jungle lane was designed to sharpen our reactions, and it brought home the need for soldiers on patrol to be alert at all times. This sounds obvious, but is difficult to maintain in practice; patrols might operate for weeks and months at time without making contact, but at the instant contact is made he who reacts first survives. During my two and a half years in Brunei, we only had one contact with the enemy, but often bumped into civilians living and working in the jungle; obviously you had to be able to identify instantly friend from foe.

It was on this range that I had two brushes with nature. The first occurred when we were taking a well-earned rest during the construction of the range and I was leaning against a tree. Suddenly, the soldiers in front of me jumped back yelling, "*Jaga baik, Tuan, Ular*!" By now I knew enough Malay to know that this meant, "Look out, Sir, snake!" They seemed to be looking at the tree behind me and on a level with my head. I slowly eased myself away from the tree and turned round. There, on a branch, was a Wagler's Pit Viper. Bright green in colour, its triangular-shaped head was only inches away from my face. It did not show any aggression, but had clearly been disturbed by our activity and wanted to move to a quieter location. This is quite a poisonous snake and, before I could stop him, Sergeant Emran dispatched it with his *parang*.

The second encounter was much more frightening. I have a real fear of spiders and I think that the soldiers had noticed this. We had just finished firing on the range for the day and, while the soldiers picked up the empty cases, I checked that the cardboard ammunition boxes were empty before throwing them on the fire. I had checked several boxes when my hand closed around something soft and hairy in one of them. Looking down, I found myself holding the largest spider I had ever seen. The soldiers had been waiting for this moment and I did not disappoint them. Letting out an involuntary shriek, I hurled the spider away as they doubled up with laughter. After we had all recovered our composure, they told me that they had killed the spider and had put it in the box to see my reaction. My performance had exceeded their expectations!

Trying to regain the initiative, I decided that we should take the spider back to camp for identification. It looked like a giant tarantula, but, in the end, we decided to send it back to the Natural History Museum in London. However, we failed to preserve it properly before dispatch. Several weeks later, I received a letter from the museum, informing me that this was a bird-eating spider. Thought to be highly venomous, the museum had been unable to confirm just how toxic it had been, due to the poor state of the specimen by the time it reached them. The letter went on to say that there was reason to believe that this might be a new species of bird-eating spider and asked us to send them another specimen, if possible. The letter ended by including instructions on how to prepare this next spider for dispatch. Happily for me at least, I never came across another of these spiders during my time in Brunei.

Another, far less frightening, encounter occurred on a jungle patrol, when a snake literally flew across in front of me at a height of about ten feet. It was about three feet long with a wide, flat ribbon-like body. Appearing to 'swim' through the air, it was stunningly beautiful with glistening dots of red, green and yellow all over its body. It landed in some bushes a few feet from me and disappeared from view. I later identified this creature as the aptly named Paradise Flying Snake – a 'jewelled' snake if ever I saw one. It is a slender snake with the ability to flatten its body to form an aerofoil, thus enabling it to glide considerable distances. A rear-fanged, only slightly venomous snake, it doesn't pose a threat to humans.

Towards the end of September 1964, the Company Commander designate, Major Rogers, arrived to take over 'B' Company. Although sorry to be losing my command, I had known all along that mine was a temporary appointment and I was just grateful to have been given this unbelievable experience.

It was at about this time that the Sultan said that he wanted the Regiment to add an armoured car troop to its inventory. As I was a member of the Royal Tank Regiment, Colonel Fletcher gave this task to me. At the time, 4RTR had a troop of Ferret Scout Cars deployed in Brunei and the Sultan wanted the Brunei Malay Regiment to be similarly equipped. My initial task was to achieve this, and so I sent a telegram (signal, in army parlance) to the Crown Agents in London with a request for four Ferret Scout Cars and ancillary equipment. In due course, I received their reply stating that the lead-time on my order was about two years. This was totally unacceptable. Colonel Fletcher told me to signal back stating that we were on active service and the vehicles were an urgent operational requirement. If the UK was unable to meet our needs then we would be forced to look elsewhere. We reminded them that Brunei was still a British Protectorate and said that we would await their considered reply before informing the Sultan. That did the trick, and we received a telegram stating that our order would be with us in about six months' time.

In the meantime, 4RTR kindly helped out by giving selected soldiers some familiarisation training on their vehicles. Luckily, the Regiment had a number of trained mechanics within its ranks, so our immediate maintenance concerns were addressed. What we desperately needed was to send a cadre of soldiers on a driving and maintenance course. Malaysia seemed the obvious choice – mainland Malaysia was only a couple of hours away by plane and our soldiers would not have to contend with any cultural or language difficulties. However, understandably, Malaysia was still smarting at Brunei's decision not to join their Federation and so declined our request. The UK was an option, but it was a long way to go and it would take time to lay on a purpose-built course.

The Australian Armoured Corps School, situated in Puckapunyal some 35 miles north of Melbourne, came to our rescue. It was willing to run a special eight-week course for six of our soldiers almost immediately. The school asked that I accompany the soldiers to act as the liaison officer and interpreter. By now, I had attended the five-week Malay language course run by the British Army in Nee Soon Camp, Singapore, and this, combined with my previous experience, meant that I was quite fluent in the language.

We left Brunei in February 1965 and spent two days in Singapore sorting out visas and buying the soldiers some suitable civilian clothes for the cooler weather in Australia. On the evening of the second day we boarded the overnight BOAC Comet to Sydney, via Darwin.

I began to appreciate the sheer size of Australia when the flight from Darwin to Sydney took almost as long as the flight from Singapore to Darwin. In Sydney, we had to move across to the inter-state airport, from where we caught a Trans Australia Airlines Viscount to Melbourne, where an officer from the Armoured School met us. He escorted us on the army coach for the final stage of our journey to Puckapunyal, where we arrived late in the afternoon.

After the humid, claustrophobic confines of the jungle, the vast open spaces of the Australian bush and the fresh scent of eucalyptus pervading the clear, dry air filled us with excitement. It was towards the end of summer and, although the nights and early mornings were decidedly chilly, by mid-morning it was really quite warm and there was precious little shade.

To a man, the Australian soldiers went out of their way to make us welcome. Never once was I, nor any of my soldiers, allowed to kick our heels in camp over a weekend; we always found ourselves invited to people's homes.

The course itself was enormous fun. We first had to grasp the general mechanics of the vehicle and then show ourselves to be reasonably proficient at driving along the dirt roads on the training area. Following months of dry weather, the dust thrown up by the vehicles was quite amazing. Driving goggles were essential, and even then the dust managed to find its way into our eyes and every other conceivable nook and cranny. The soldiers at Puckapunyal boasted that their dust was the finest in the world, and I had no reason to doubt them! The biggest hazard we encountered on these roads came from kangaroos with little or no road sense. Seeing these strange creatures for the first time was a marvellous experience.

Midway through the course we were deemed safe enough to take to the public highways, and over the next four weeks we travelled the length and breadth of Victoria. The scenery was varied and, in places, spectacular, encompassing rolling grasslands and forest-clad mountains, stretches of water that sparkled like sapphires in the folds of the bare, boulder-strewn mountains of the Dandenong Range. Crystal clear torrents cascaded down mountainsides and the peaceful creeks and rivers reflected the beauty surrounding them.

Our travels took us to a gold mine as well as a nature reserve, where we saw koala bears and an echidna. An anteater, this creature looks a little like a small porcupine and is an egg-laying marsupial mammal. Perhaps only the platypus beats it in the world's league table of strange animals. What struck me most about the wildlife in the area was the beauty, variety and sheer abundance of birds. Cockatoos, parrots, parakeets, lorikeets, kingfishers and many others became such familiar sights that I started to take them for granted.

At the end of the course, the soldiers returned home to Brunei. However,

Colonel Fletcher kindly suggested that I should take a couple of weeks of my annual leave to see something of the rest of Australia before going back. I did not need any persuading.

I spent a few days in Canberra and then moved on to Sydney, where I met up with a friend, Rory Collins, from my school days at Douai, and his Australian wife, Fran. They took me sailing in Sydney Harbour, a wonderful experience that included spectacular views of the Harbour Bridge and the Sydney Opera House, which was still under construction. They advised me to visit Katoomba, a town in the heart of the Blue Mountains, about four hours by road from Sydney. Nearby is the awe-inspiring sight of a deep, sheer-sided valley. Leaning over the rails of one of several vantage points, the ground falls away from your feet to the valley floor about a quarter of a mile below. On one side the valley is flanked by three gigantic pillars of rock, known as the Three Sisters, and on the other, by a single pinnacle called Orphan Rock.

I planned to return to Brunei via Perth, but discovered only just in time that the onward flight from Perth to Singapore was via Jakarta, the capital city of the country whose forces we were opposing in Borneo. So I cut my losses and flew back from Sydney after a memorable two and a half months down under.

As I entered Berakas Camp I was stopped at the Guardroom and told the Colonel wanted to see me immediately. My heart sank into my boots. Had I overstayed my leave? Had something happened at home? It was long after normal working hours and many thoughts raced through my mind as I drove straight up the hill to Colonel Fletcher's house overlooking the camp.

I relaxed when he opened the door. He was smiling and invited me to come in and sit down. The conversation went something like this: "Bruce, old chap, I've got yet another new challenge for you, one that promises to be really very interesting, albeit rather tricky. How do you rate your Malay now?"

I told him that I had coped reasonably well as an interpreter on the course in Australia.

"Good," he said, "I thought you would say that. In this new job you'll need to be pretty fluent. The Sultan wants a military ADC (aide-de-camp) and has asked the British government to provide him with one. They have accepted the commitment and the MoD has instructed me to nominate one of my officers for the role. You're the only chap available."

He continued: "I want you to keep the Recce Troop (Ferrets) for the time being, but train up a Bruneian officer to take over from you as soon as possible. Meantime, if the Sultan accepts you, you'll have to hold down both jobs. I don't know anything about this new appointment, but we have an audience with HH at ten o'clock tomorrow morning and we'll both know the score after that. Welcome home!"

As I returned to my bungalow, my emotions were all over the place. I was very apprehensive, but at the same time I could hardly believe my luck; this must surely be the most rewarding and interesting job in Brunei.

Next morning, I made my way with the Colonel to the Istana (palace), situated at the top of a hill overlooking the Brunei River and the picturesque village of Kampong Ayer. A palace attendant ushered us into the rather dark, but cool, entrance hall. A deep pile red carpet covered the floor and a splendid chandelier hung from the ceiling. From the back of the room, a staircase led up to the private apartments.

We had been in the building only a few minutes, when a small straight-backed man came down the stairs. He was wearing an open-necked check shirt, khaki trousers and highly polished black boots, and around his waist a stout leather belt supported a holster containing a Smith & Wesson .38 revolver. He had dark, wavy hair and a friendly smile lit up his youthful-looking face.

This was His Highness, Sir Omar Ali Saiffudin KCMG, the twenty-eighth Sultan of Brunei. He shook us both by the hand, before leading us through to an adjacent room, where my new appointment was discussed over tea and biscuits.

In essence, my responsibilities were to be threefold. First, I was to become the Sultan's bodyguard, so, together with the Special Branch and the Police, I would be responsible for the safety of His Highness both at home and abroad. Second, I was to be responsible for the security of the Istana. Finally, I would be required to brief His Highness on military matters with which he was involved and would also assist the Civil ADC in the numerous civil functions and ceremonies that took place throughout the year.

His Highness wanted me to start work at once. However, he fully understood the need for me to continue training up the Recce Troop. In barracks, the Regiment worked a five-day week and it was agreed that I should divide my time between the Istana and the Regiment by spending two full days and three afternoons each week at the Istana. This left me with three mornings to train up the Recce Troop – in barracks the afternoons were reserved for sport and recreation. This proved to be a very busy time, as our four Ferret Scout Cars arrived within a few weeks of our return from Australia, just as I was trying to get to grips with my new responsibilities at the Istana.

My office in the Istana was yet to be built. In the meantime, His Highness said I could work in the magnificent office he had just vacated for new premises in his private apartments upstairs. This was the grandest office I would ever occupy throughout my army career. I sat behind a great mahogany desk beside a highly polished walnut table and around 20 matching chairs – no doubt the scene of many a State meeting. Pictures of the British Royal family looked down from the walls, including an old and faded portrait of Queen Mary that was greatly treasured by His Highness.

Over the next few days, I became acquainted with all His Highness's staff working in the Istana. Foremost amongst these was Mrs Marianne Lloyd Dolby, who was married to the manager of the Government's rubber plantation at Gadong. She had a dual role as His Highness's private secretary as well as lady in waiting to Her Highness, the Raja Isteri. An intensely loyal and efficient person who helped me enormously, Mrs Lloyd Dolby was greatly loved and trusted by all members of the Royal Family.

The Civil ADC, Pehin Sungga Mara Data Abbas, welcomed having a colleague to share the demanding, protocol-governed workload. As a token of our joint working status, he presented me with one of a pair of vicious 'tiger claw' fighting knives, keeping the other for himself. Fifty years on I am still reminded of him, and the happy working relationship we enjoyed, whenever I see it amongst the souvenirs in my 'den' at home. Of the numerous other members of staff, including the Grand Chamberlain, the confidential secretary et al, the other person I had most to do with was His Highness's driver, Ibrahim, or Songkok as he was affectionately known. Not only did he drive the Royal car, a venerable 1953 Daimler, but he kept it, and all the other cars in the Royal garage, gleaming in showroom condition.

As the Sultan's bodyguard, I was required to be armed whenever I accompanied him on duty. The Sultan ordered me a spring-clip, quick draw shoulder holster, and chose a beautifully engraved silver-plated Walter PPK pistol from his collection with which to arm me. Being left-handed, all my uniforms had to be modified to include a hidden opening behind the box pleat of the right hand breast pocket to give me ready access to the weapon. I was also required to practice drawing and firing it every day on the 25-yard range in the palace grounds. I still have the holster, but had to surrender the pistol on relinquishing my privileged appointment.

My first job was to tighten security at the Istana. Since the Brunei Rebellion, a high protective wall had been built around the palace grounds, and flood lighting had also been installed. However, there was virtually no control over visitors to the Istana. His Highness had always been very close to his people and even the humblest of his subjects was free to see him at any time. Whilst this was laudable in principle, in the unsettled days of Confrontation, not to mention the possibility of subversion within Brunei itself, this presented an unacceptable security risk. After consulting with His Highness, I arranged for identity cards to be issued to everyone who enjoyed unrestricted access to the palace or its grounds, and these had to be produced on demand. In addition, only vehicles displaying an Istana windscreen sticker were permitted to enter the grounds. Members of the public were still welcome to see His Highness, but had to obtain a temporary pass at the guardroom.

Finally, the Brunei Malay Regiment was now responsible for providing the Istana Guard. The publicity that accompanied the introduction of these measures helped to ensure that they were accepted with a minimum of resentment or inconvenience. The Sultan was immensely popular with his people and they wholeheartedly supported any action taken to safeguard him and the Royal Family. Although now regulated, the daily flow of visitors to the Istana was still considerable. I was the final 'gatekeeper' for anyone from the general public entering the Istana.

Within a fortnight of taking up my duties, His Highness informed me that he had to go to London for talks with the British government and he asked me to make the necessary arrangements. Luckily, he was a seasoned traveller and a tried and tested routine was already in place. We would take a scheduled Malaysian Airways flight to Singapore and then join the QANTAS flight bound for London. While in London, His Highness and his entourage would stay at the Grosvenor House hotel, on Park Lane, where he always occupied the same suite of rooms.

Using existing procedures, I was required to make special arrangements with Customs and immigration officials, so that the Royal party could move directly from the aircraft to the hotel. The only real problem I experienced with this, and all subsequent trips, was trying to determine the actual size and composition of the party and its luggage, a fact that gave many a government, airline and hotel official ulcers, not to mention the frantic ADC.

On this first visit, our aircraft was scheduled to fly via Tehran, where my sister, Merrilees, was living with her husband, Michael. The Sultan readily agreed that I should send them a telegram about our fleeting visit and include an invitation for them to join us at the airport. On our arrival, the Shah's VIP building was made available to His Highness and his entourage, and in the main lounge several tables groaned under the weight of bowls laden with fruit, mainly strawberries, and caviar – a rather odd mix. It was late, perhaps 3.00 a.m., but there amongst the officials gathered to greet His Highness, it was wonderful to see Merrilees, Michael and their six-month-old baby son, Dominic.

The only problem we encountered on this visit occurred when the Metropolitan police were told that I was armed. Understandably, they wanted to impound my pistol for the duration of our stay, but His Highness was adamant that I should retain the weapon. Sir Dennis White, a former High Commissioner in Brunei and then Brunei's representative in London, who was at the airport to meet us, brokered a sensible compromise. Having pointed out to the police that I was a professional soldier who could be trusted with a firearm, it was agreed that I could carry the weapon provided it was kept out of sight, was not cocked and the safety catch was applied. Moreover, I was authorised to use it only as a very last resort to save the Sultan's life. Under no circumstances could I use it to save my own life. This seemed entirely reasonable to me; after all this was Britain in 1965, when gun crime was virtually unheard of.

In the Grosvenor House, I occupied the room next to His Highness's suite. My responsibilities included accepting all incoming telephone calls, fielding visitors and arranging private audiences with the Sultan. I did not participate in official meetings with the British government, but was expected to act as the interpreter during private audiences at the Grosvenor House. This was quite a challenge, because the Sultan talked very quietly and also, although reluctant to speak in English, he had a very good understanding of the language. Thus, if I did not quite get the nuance of what he was saying, he would step in, very gently, and correct me.

His Highness was a modest man who rarely spent money on personal luxuries but who did enjoy shopping for others. Sometimes, especially if time was of the essence, he would ask me to telephone a store in advance so that he would be afforded VIP treatment on arrival. Usually, however, he preferred to arrive unannounced and took great pleasure in being able to move about unnoticed among the crowd. Sometimes, he sent me out alone on specific errands. One such occasion concerned the purchase of a new State car to replace his aging, and increasingly unreliable, Daimler.

For the next State car, he wanted a black Daimler limousine fitted with a landaulet body, and I was asked to place the order. I duly set off to Stratstone in the Cromwell Road in my Sunday best and carrying an official-looking briefcase. Initially, the sales executive in the showroom gave me a rather frosty reception; on reflection, I was very young and clearly the cars on display were of little interest to people of my age, or means. However, his attitude changed dramatically when I told him who I was representing; in no time at all I was in the manager's office and working on the details of the order.

On another occasion, His Highness asked me to buy him a second-hand genuine London taxi for around £200. He wanted it to be in good mechanical order as he intended using it as an amusing personal runabout back in Brunei. He had a great sense of humour and hoped that a British expatriate might absent-mindedly hail him while he was driving in Brunei Town. Eventually, I tracked down a dealer in second-hand taxis and spent a very amusing hour or so with the Cockney salesman. I told him that I was buying the taxi for somebody living in Brunei, which was part of Borneo.

At first, his reaction was flippant, but when I told him it was for the Sultan of Brunei he quickly changed his tune. "That's like a king in'it?" he said, " 'ave to be a real good 'un then. Cost you 'bout three hundred nicker."

I said would get back to him and, having discussed the matter with His Highness, confirmed the sale despite not having seen the vehicle – the salesman was going to search for a "real good 'un" and I believed him. I left Brunei before it arrived but, true to his word, the taxi that was subsequently seen being driven around Brunei really was in excellent condition. (The State Daimler also arrived in Brunei after I had left the Sultanate.)

Perhaps the most nerve-wracking aspect of my life on these visits to London was looking after the Sultan's wellbeing at night. He would delight in going for walks along the deserted streets in the very early morning without telling me. The solution was to go to bed fully clothed and arrange for the night porter to call me as soon as he saw His Highness in the hotel lobby. I would then dash downstairs and the night porter would tell me the direction in which he had set off. Eventually, the Sultan would look round and see me following some 20 or 30 yards behind, smile and then walk on alone for about an hour before returning to the hotel.

We happened to be in London on New Year's Eve in 1965. His Highness wanted to see in the New Year in Trafalgar Square and asked me to accompany him. I had never experienced this before and was quite looking forward to the occasion. However, I had not bargained on the seething mass of boisterous, high-spirited people that packed into the square as the bewitching hour approached. We began to feel quite crushed – His Highness was barely five feet tall – when an enormous fair-haired man, a Scandinavian I think, saw the Sultan squeezed up against him. "You'll never see anything from down there," he said, and, with no further ado, picked him up, held him aloft and they both disappeared into the crowd. It was about an hour before I found the Sultan. By this time, the crowd had started to disperse and he was standing by one of the fountains watching revellers dancing in the water. He was soaking wet, and soon after went down with a severe chill, but he had had a marvellous evening. As for me, I was just grateful that, eventually, all was well; I counted my blessings.

Our visits to Britain often took us out of London to events such as firepower demonstrations by the Royal Armoured Corps at Bovington and the Royal Artillery at Larkhill. Indeed, at Larkhill a radio-controlled drone went berserk during a display. We were all asked to take cover under benches as it whizzed about overhead, eventually crashing several hundred yards down range. Our hosts were quite concerned, but the Sultan put them at their ease, saying that the experience had added to the enjoyment of the day.

We also visited the Royal Military Academy, Sandhurst, where his two eldest sons, including the current Sultan, His Majesty Hassanal Bolkiah, were enrolled as officer cadets in January 1966.

On the only occasion that Her Highness, the Raja Isteri, accompanied His Highness to London, the Sultan paid my family the greatest compliment by asking to visit our house to see what a typical British family home looked like. My parents lived in the hamlet of Taston, some 20 miles north of Oxford, and the two Daimler limousines had great difficulty negotiating the narrow, unsurfaced lane that led to their small Cotswold stone cottage. His Highness was enchanted by the blaze of colour in the garden, the uninterrupted view over the surrounding countryside and, especially, the quaint cottage with its low ceilings and heavy wooden beams. My mother served a traditional English tea, including cucumber sandwiches, strawberries and Cotswold cream. After about two hours His Highness made his farewells and our convoy set off back to London.

Quite the most interesting trip I made with His Highness was the visit to the World's Fair in New York during July 1965. In the event, this turned out to be a mini-world tour, taking in New York, London, Nairobi, Rome and Hong Kong in the space of ten days.

During our time in New York we stayed at the Waldorf Astoria; the most opulent hotel I had ever been in. Our apartments were on the fifty-second floor and His Highness's suite was like an extravagant film set. The floor of the spacious entrance hall was polished marble and an enormous chandelier lit up the room, its beauty reflected a thousand times by two enormous mirrors positioned opposite one another. The whole effect was enhanced by an extravagant display of fresh flowers at the far end of the room.

On entering the suite, the door to the left led to the dining room. Richly decorated in green and russet hues, it contained a dozen matching chairs around a magnificent walnut dining table, upon which stood two gleaming silver candelabra. The door at the far end of the entrance hall opened into the spacious sitting room, which was luxuriously decorated in shades of blue and filled with glorious sprays of fresh flowers. A window across almost the entire length of the outer wall gave spectacular views across New York. A further door led to the luxurious en-suite bedroom.

Throughout our stay everyone in His Highness's party took meals in his dining room, where a silver service was provided. The other rooms occupied by our party were normal en-suite bedrooms; all, that is, except mine. I had been registered as His Highness's ADC/Bodyguard, and I was accommodated accordingly. Just outside the entrance to His Highness's suite of rooms, my room had no windows and was just big enough to take a single bed – nothing more. Across the corridor, on the other side of the entrance to the main suite, I did, at least, have my own bathroom facilities.

Visiting the World's Fair was an eye-opening experience. Today, the displays would seem to be very ordinary; in 1965, they represented the cutting edge of the world's technology and we could barely do it justice in the two days we had available. As was his way, His Highness dismissed the cars so that we could walk amongst the crowds and soak up the atmosphere as we moved from pavilion to pavilion. General Motors had attached a fleet of their latest convertibles to a moving roadway to transport people in complete comfort through a Disney wonderland. General Electric had constructed a moving auditorium that revolved around three stages, each of which comprised life-like robots representing 'the typical American family' spanning the last hundred years. In another pavilion, Du Pont demonstrated the manufacture of nylon from its raw materials, and we watched, spellbound, the apparently magical colour changes in various liquids.

An entire pavilion was devoted to the life and times of Sir Winston Churchill, who had died earlier in the year. This was an immensely popular and emotionally charged venue; many people wept as they listened to recordings of his wartime speeches.

We also watched an impressive water skiing display, examined the Aston Martin used by James Bond in 'Goldfinger', rode on a Swiss ski lift and Japanese monorail and, at meal times, sampled food from around the world.

Unfortunately, we could not prolong our stay in New York, as His Highness was due back for more talks in London. So, within three days of our arrival in the 'Big Apple', we flew back across the Atlantic. His business in London was completed earlier than expected, but His Highness was not one to let the grass grow under his feet. He had an open invitation to visit his old friend and former British High Commissioner to Brunei, The Right Honourable Malcolm MacDonald, who was now the British High Commissioner in Kenya. So he decided to leave London a day early and visit Nairobi on the way back to Brunei.

A quick phone call and we were all invited to lunch the following day! We flew overnight to Nairobi in the luxury of a BOAC VC10, arriving at Embakazi airport just after breakfast. Mr MacDonald, who was at the airport to meet us, took us to the New Stanley Hotel in town, where there was just time for us to have a quick wash and brush up. We then set off for a brief glimpse of the Rift Valley. This was a fascinating sight: it seemed as if, in the distant past, a giant sledgehammer had struck the land with such force as to cause it to fall many hundreds of feet below its normal level. Looking into the valley, I could just make out the valley floor through the heat haze; the brown savannah grassland was tinder dry and interspersed with wide-branching acacia trees. Here and there I could see small villages, thin wisps of smoke curling lazily into the still air from the clusters of mud huts. It looked so peaceful down there, almost as if I was looking into another world, a refuge from the tumult and pressures of life in 1965!

There was just time to drive down to the valley floor, before we headed back to Nairobi and Mr MacDonald's residence. Here we enjoyed a long drink before sitting down to a cold lunch beside the swimming pool at the bottom of the garden. The atmosphere was relaxed and informal, and the food delicious – just what was needed on a blistering hot day.

After lunch, we paid a visit to the Nairobi game park, just outside the city. At the entrance to the park a large sign warned people to remain in their cars at all times. This seemed pretty obvious advice, especially as no sooner had we passed through the gates than a troop of baboons 'invaded' our little convoy, pinching the High Commissioner's pennant from the flagstaff of his car and pressing their faces against the closed windows. Everywhere we looked we could see game: gazelles bounded through the long grass, herds of zebra and wildebeest grazed steadily, whilst giraffes lolloped away with their characteristic slow-motion gait at our approach.

I was beginning to enjoy myself when my ADC responsibilities brought me back to earth with a bump. Someone in the other car had run out of film and all the spare rolls were apparently in our car. "Captain, please take some film to the other car," the Sultan asked, to which I replied, rather unconvincingly, "Certainly, *Duli Tuanku* (Your Highness)." Our two vehicles were about 15 feet apart, but to me they seemed more like fifty. Not wishing to appear a coward, I got out and sprinted across to the other car, ready to thrust the film through a window. Unfortunately, all the windows were firmly up and it seemed an age before the occupants within worked out how to lower them. I then had to wait until the used spools of film were gathered up for me to take back. I must have been away from the sanctuary of my car for barely a minute or two, but to me it seemed like an eternity.

While this drama was unfolding, Mr Macdonald had noticed a number of vehicles going to a spot some 300 yards ahead of us. As soon as I was in the car, we went to join them, and there, yawning lazily as he stretched out in the grass, was a large male lion. He had just finished gorging himself on his kill – probably a waterbuck – and was now lying down beside it. He seemed totally unconcerned about the cars surrounding him, although he did roar a warning at one vehicle that tried to get a little closer. We all sat and watched him for ages, the softening rays of the evening sun highlighting the russet tints of his handsome mane. Was he on his own, I pondered, or was the rest of the pride nearby; indeed, had they been nearby when I was darting between our vehicles? Perish the thought!

We flew overnight to Rome, arriving on Sunday morning, and we were due to depart for Hong Kong that same evening. His Highness told me that he was going to rest in our hotel, but said I was welcome to do as I pleased. Although very tired, I was determined to make the most of this opportunity (I have yet to return!). It was a glorious summer's day and richly tanned people in casual summer clothes thronged the streets, or sat in open-air cafés sipping long, cold drinks and eating ice creams. After attending Mass in one of the many beautiful churches, I made my way to Saint Peter's Square in the Vatican along with hundreds of other people; the sounds of their carefree chatting and laughter heightening the atmosphere. We were all here to see His Holiness, Pope Paul VI. As he came out onto his balcony at midday to bestow his blessing on us, all the noise fell away. In the deep silence, you could have heard a pin drop, in sharp contrast to the resounding cheers and hand clapping afterwards, as the Pope stood waving to us for a few more moments.

That evening we joined the QANTAS flight bound for Hong Kong. The descent into Kai Tak airport was an exhilarating experience. The final approach was marked out by a series of red lights on top of the skyscrapers of Kowloon, and the aircraft seemed to skim uncomfortably close to some of the loftier buildings. As it approached a chequered board positioned upon a mound, the aircraft banked steeply to the right, the starboard wingtip seeming almost to touch the buildings. Then it levelled out and touched down on the runway, a thin strip of man-made land running out to sea.

The Governor, Sir David Trench, met us at the steps of the plane. He escorted us to the airport's VIP lounge, where he hosted His Highness until our baggage was collected and loaded into a van. We then made our way to the Mandarin Hotel, arguably the finest hotel in South East Asia at the time. The car we travelled in was a magnificent Rolls-Royce of about 1950 vintage. The hotel's car, it had been put at His Highness's disposal for the duration of his short stay.

We were here for only one night, but after spending most of the day shopping, everyone seemed ready for bed. Although I, too, was tired, I felt I had to seize this opportunity. With the Sultan's blessing I departed for the bright lights after supper. It was dark outside, but Hong Kong was alive. Countless people jostled their way along the pavements and the streets were crammed with cars. I made my way to the area known as Aberdeen, where the lights of the famous floating restaurant danced prettily on the gentle swell and lit up the many junks riding at anchor, their aging timbers creaking and groaning under the strain. I then made my way up to the top of Hong Kong's peak to survey the captivating view from Lookout Point. A million lights twinkled below me, the lights of vehicles mapped out the many streets in red and white pencils of light, several ships, their outlines etched in coloured lights, dotted the harbour and, here and there, moving lights traced the paths of junks criss-crossing the harbour. By contrast, it was all peace and solitude up here at Lookout Point, and I was alone with my thoughts.

Early the following morning we returned to the airport, where we boarded a Cathay Pacific Electra bound for Brunei. The three Hong Kong Chinese air hostesses looked after us in true Oriental style and we were landing in Brunei in next to no time.

All the State officials were at the airport to welcome His Highness. Prayers were said in thanksgiving for his safe return, following which he shook hands with everybody before getting into his State car and returning to the Istana.

Once I had checked that all the baggage had been delivered to the Istana, I made my way back to Berakas Camp, my mind full of the memories of a quite extraordinary experience. But I did not have to get down from cloud nine; life in Brunei with the Sultan was a unique experience and every bit as fascinating.

To mark the successful completion of its first year on active service, His Highness honoured the Regiment with the title 'Royal' at an impressive parade at Berakas Camp. We were now the Askar Melayu Diraja Brunei (Royal Brunei Malay Regiment). At the same time, His Highness began wearing the uniform of a full colonel in the Regiment. From now on he was very much our Colonel-in-Chief, taking a great interest in everything we did. Over the coming months he added a flight of three helicopters, a flotilla of three coastal patrol craft and a hovercraft to our inventory, making us, at the time, the only Regiment in the world with a genuine land, sea and air capability.

On one of our visits to London he placed an order for one of the most sophisticated warships of the day. A gas turbine-powered gunboat capable of 60 knots, *Pahlawan* (Warrior) was destined to be the fastest vessel in the South China Sea. His Highness very kindly invited me to its launch ceremony at Vosper's yard at Portsmouth on 5 December 1966, although by then I had completed my tour in Brunei and was preparing to rejoin my Regiment in Germany.

The Sultan would regularly visit the Regiment to discuss matters with Colonel Fletcher, or to attend training exercises. Once, after watching a tactical exercise by the Recce Troop, he commanded one of the Ferrets on the 12-mile trip back to the Istana. At the Istana itself, he would occasionally participate in the physical training sessions which I ran for the soldiers on Istana guard duties. Never once on his visits to the Regiment did he expect special treatment; all he wanted was to be able to meet and talk to his soldiers. As you may imagine, this did wonders for morale.

He endorsed Colonel Fletcher's plans to use the helicopters, not merely to move soldiers about, but also to set up a flying doctor service in the *ulu* regions as part of our 'hearts and minds' operations. Initially, the landing zones at the various longhouses were prepared and maintained by our soldiers, but as the impact of the flying doctor service became evident, the local inhabitants took on this responsibility. His Highness also made good use of the helicopters to visit our soldiers on operations in the *ulu*, who were steadily growing in confidence as they became more familiar and effective on jungle operations. In my opinion, these two initiatives contributed most to the Regiment's success during Confrontation.

The Sultan also used these opportunities to visit his people living in the *ulu* regions, who might otherwise not see him from one year to the next. Usually these visits would start with the headman delivering a welcoming speech to which His Highness would respond. Then the villagers would put on a short display of dancing and singing, followed by refreshments.

However, when the Sultan visited a very remote longhouse called

Supon Kechil, in *ulu* Tutong, we were treated to a genuine Iban welcoming ceremony. Two beautiful girls in their teens stood at the foot of the steps of the longhouse to greet us. Their ceremonial sarongs were richly decorated in Malay dollars and their breasts were pressed close to their bodies by tightly fitting cross bands. At the top of the steps stood the *Pengulu*, resplendent in his ceremonial feathered headdress, his *elang* (ceremonial sword) held in his right hand.

As we entered the longhouse, we were invited to sit on straw mats on the floor in the communal corridor. Once we were all seated, the *Pengulu* went into one of the rooms and returned holding a chicken, the unfortunate bird protesting noisily at being held upside down by its legs. Uttering prayers to the gods, the *Pengulu* then held the bird over the heads of all the guests, starting with His Highness. He then disappeared into the room again and a few seconds later a squawk signalled the end of the chicken. When he next appeared, the *Pengulu* was holding the bird's tail feathers, soaked in blood, in his right hand. He asked us all to hold out our hands, palms uppermost, while he smeared them in blood with the feathers, while uttering prayers.

As the blood dried on us we were joined by the men of the longhouse, each of them in their ceremonial costumes. They made a splendid sight. Moments later the young women, no less spectacular in their tribal costumes, came forward with dishes of rice and Iban delicacies, which they placed before us. Then two young girls came forward, each carrying a serving bowl, which they offered in turn to the guests. Our task was to select the choicest morsels from the food laid before us and place them in these bowls. Once the guests had made their contribution the girls handed the bowls to whosoever the *Pengulu* nominated. I was one of those so honoured, or, rather, His Highness delegated his place to me. The girls then led the two of us away to a room filled with rice sacks and instructed us to bury our bowls in the sack of our choice. I later learned that this was a peace offering to the gods, designed to stave off their wrath and ensure a plentiful harvest in the coming year.

Once we had returned to our positions on the mat, the *Pengulu* delivered his welcoming address to which His Highness responded in glowing terms. The *Pengulu* then proceeded to demand a speech from each of the guests; no easy task when one is ill prepared, but we all passed muster. The formalities over, the girls served tea and *tuak* (a very potent rice wine) while the visitors and the men tucked in to the delicious feast spread before us.

Not all my experiences during this time were joyous ones. On 6 September 1966 one of our helicopters crashed when the tail rotor drive failed just after takeoff. One of two old Whirlwind helicopters we had had on lease, it came down in thick jungle about half a mile from the entrance to Berakas Camp at 7.20 a.m. I was one of the first at the scene and was confronted by a raging fire amongst the twisted wreckage. All that was left of the helicopter was the tail rotor, one of the main rotor blades and a float, all of which had been ripped off the aircraft as it crashed down through the trees. There was no sign of the pilot and I feared that he might have been lost in the inferno.

Our other lease aircraft was soon overhead and I signalled to the Colonel standing in the doorway not to lower a line. The helicopter then turned in a wide sweep to return to camp, but passing over an open patch of *lallang* (grass about six feet high) the badly burnt pilot was spotted. The helicopter landed in the clearing to begin the rescue, but on takeoff, the *lallang* wrapped itself around the floats and caused the aircraft to somersault. Miraculously, nobody was hurt in this second crash and the would-be rescuers quickly beat down the grass to enable a British Army helicopter to land and take the injured pilot to hospital. It had not been our greatest day.

About a fortnight later, we lost a very promising young Bruneian officer,

Lieutenant Abu Bakar. He was swept away and drowned when leading his platoon across a swollen river in an attempt to intercept an enemy patrol. He belonged to 'B' Company, the one I had commanded, and I was amongst the mourners at his funeral in Tutong. The cemetery lay in the shade of some giant trees in a thin strip of jungle by the edge of the town's *padang* (green). The Iman started the proceedings with some prayers, and the man's body was brought forward to the graveside, wrapped in a shroud and carried in a wicker stretcher. After more prayers, the body was gently lowered into the grave and the wicker framework removed. The Regiment's firing party then fired a salute and a lone bugler sounded the Last Post, followed after a minute's silence by Reveille. This incident hit us all hard and morale was only partially restored when the Indonesian intruders were captured a few days later, fittingly by a patrol comprised entirely of Brunei Malays.

I found Brunei to be a land of festival, where Muslim, Christian and Chinese holidays were celebrated in almost equal measure. For example, our 'weekend' was Friday and Sunday. The two biggest celebrations were Hari Raya Puasa (Eid al Fitr), the feast that signals the end of the Muslim fasting month, Bulan Puasa (Ramadan), and the Sultan's birthday. The Hari Raya Puasa celebrations spanned two days. This was the time to show hospitality to the wider family, neighbours and, indeed, total strangers. In every household, delicious food and soft drinks were offered to whosoever called. Over the two days, I visited many a soldier's home, as well as those of my colleagues in the Istana. To do otherwise would have caused great offence; far better to offend one's own digestive system!

The Sultan's birthday called for much more overt celebrations. Brunei Town was transformed with exotic decorations to become a kaleidoscope of colour by day and a fairyland of twinkling lights by night. The main highway into town was spanned by numerous arches, the builders vying with each other to win the coveted street arch competition, and the town *padang* became a fairground.

The day's celebrations began with a combined military and civil parade in the centre of town with His Highness taking the salute. Within an hour of the parade finishing, VIPs took their seats in the throne room in the Istana for the Sultan's birthday honours investiture ceremony.

The throne room – or Singgasana – seated around 200 people. Protected from direct sunlight to keep it cool, it was illuminated by several beautiful chandeliers. The entire floor was covered in a rich yellow carpet, yellow being the Royal colour. At the far end of the room there was a raised dais upon which the elaborately carved thrones of the Sultan and the Raja Isteri were placed.

Everybody dressed in their national costumes for this event. The vast majority were Malays, their colourful sarongs exquisitely decorated with pure gold and silver thread. Together with the glittering decorations and medals worn by most of the guests, the spectacle was a feast for the eyes.

When all was ready I informed the Sultan, who then processed into the room with the Raja Isteri and a sizeable entourage. The Royal couple were preceded by two courtiers dressed in scarlet; one, representing the army commander in bygone days, shouldered an enormous antique brass blunderbuss, while the other, representing the Commander of the former Royal Guard, carried a full length shield in one hand and a sabre in the other. Behind the Royal couple came the Royal umbrella holder, shielding the couple with a gold-coloured umbrella. Next, in line abreast, came the civil ADC, the lady-in-waiting and myself. Bringing up the rear were two men dressed in black, one carrying a spear and the other a sabre, both representing the former Palace Guard, plus a further man, also wearing black but carrying tobacco, representing the former palace servants. As I processed up the aisle in the throne room I felt immensely privileged to be participating in what was a centuries' old Bruneian Royal ceremony.

After speeches and presentations to His Highness, the investiture ceremony got underway, the awards being presented by His Highness in descending order of precedence. Those receiving an Order were accompanied by a number of 'warriors', half of whom wore scarlet and carried spears and the other half dressed in black and carrying sabres. This was symbolic of ancient times when the Sultan would reward heroes by giving them so many members of the Palace Guard in recognition of their services. As I recall, those being awarded the First Class of an Order were accompanied by 32 'warriors', a Second Class recipient by 16, a Third Class by eight and a Fourth Class by four.

The colourful costumes, the dignity displayed by those who wore them and their historical relevance to the proceedings captured my imagination. Lost in my daydreams, I was brought back sharply to reality at hearing my own name called out. His Highness had very generously chosen to appoint me to the Order of the Crown of Brunei (Third Class), Brunei's equivalent of the Royal Victorian Order (MVO). This was a tremendous honour and totally unexpected. As Brunei was a British Protectorate, Her Majesty Queen Elizabeth II had graciously granted me unrestricted approval of the award. This meant that I could wear it with pride for the rest of my army career, which I did, albeit self-consciously at times, as it was a very impressive neck decoration.

The afternoon was given over to two competitions. First, a colourful and ingenious float procession through Brunei Town, where participants competed for honours in two categories, vehicle-mounted or bicycle-mounted. The second competition was a regatta that took place on the Brunei River at Kampong Ayer, again comprising two racing categories, speedboats and war canoes.

The day's celebrations ended with an enchanting lantern procession in the evening, followed by a Royal banquet at the Istana for upwards of 800 guests. The banqueting hall could only seat 300 people, so the remaining 500 were seated on the palace lawn. The seating plan for these banquets was a nightmare for the civil ADC and his team. Everybody had to be seated according to their status, not merely by table, but by their position on the table. Even some of the expatriates became very conscious of their status.

I can remember one occasion when somebody took exception to being seated on a lower table than another expatriate whom he considered to be his junior. The fact that the 'junior' was a member of the Privy Council and was thus correctly seated at the Privy Councillors' table cut no ice, and the complainant took great offence and excused himself from the banquet. As he was a prominent British businessman, I was invited to explain myself to the High Commissioner the following morning. Luckily, he accepted my explanation, but nevertheless gave me a rocket for not having handled the situation better. As I left the room, smarting slightly, he said, "Here's a bit of advice someone once gave me. Provided you have done your level best, those that matter don't mind and those that mind don't matter." I have taken that advice to this day, as often as not when I, myself, have been tempted to stand on my dignity.

The celebrations in Brunei Town completed, over the next few days the Sultan attended day-long festivities in the districts of Belait, Tutong and Temburong. The highlight of all these district celebrations was a tug-of-war competition against the Sultan's team. The team captains decided upon the number of participants beforehand, 20 per team being the norm. It was mandatory that His Highness and I, both small, light men, had to be part of the Sultan's team; weight was not a consideration. Everyone was allowed to sit down and seconds even prepared the ground by digging footholds to give their men greater purchase. Apart from these changes, the normal tug-of-war rules applied and the result was determined by the best of three pulls.

We enjoyed a fairly easy time of it against the teams from Belait and Temburong, but in 1965 the Tutong team lived up to their fearsome reputation. The Sultan's team won the first pull after a struggle lasting 26 minutes. Exhausted, the teams changed ends for the second pull. Strain as they might, neither team was able to make any headway. Day was overtaken by night and still we pulled, seconds pouring water over us and dropping segments of orange into our mouths. Eventually, Tutong won the pull; it had taken one hour and 13 minutes. Everyone was now on their chin-straps. The officials called a hurried meeting and, much to everyone's relief, it was agreed to postpone the final pull for a week. In the event, the third pull turned out to be a massive anticlimax, the Sultan's team winning in a mere 40 seconds. However, Tutong had laid on another delicious feast and cultural show, so everyone went home a winner.

There were two Royal weddings during my tenure as military ADC. The current Sultan, His Majesty Hassanal Bolkiah, who was then the Crown Prince, married his first wife in early August 1965, and his sister, Her Highness Princess Masna, was married in September the following year. Both weddings gave rise to joyous, extended celebrations throughout Brunei. In ancient times the wedding celebrations for the heir to the Sultanate spanned a period of 100 days, but Crown Prince Hassanal Bolkiah's celebrations lasted some 40 days. The description that follows covers his wedding. The celebrations for Princess Masna's wedding were similar until brought to a premature close after 19 days due to a cholera outbreak in the Sultanate.

Before the Crown Prince's wedding, I moved from Berakas Camp to live at the Istana so as to cope with the heavy workload. My prime responsibility centred on the security of the Istana, but I was also required to offer the civil ADC whatever support I could. Official ceremonies took place almost every day and the grounds of the Istana were thrown open to the public until 11.00 p.m. every night, the attractions including fairgrounds, variety shows, cultural dancing and firework displays. Once the public had left I had to make a final check of the grounds with members of the guard before I could turn in. At 5.00 a.m. every morning, I was awakened by the trumpets and drums of the Gadang Jaga Jaga (ceremonial musicians), positioned just outside my window; another day of celebrations had dawned.

The first official function to which guests were invited was the engagement ceremony, which took place in the absence of the happy couple. In the case of the Crown Prince, the Sultan, seated with his guests, sent emissaries to the bride's father, seeking permission for the Crown Prince to marry his daughter. Later, the emissaries returned bearing a letter of consent from the bride's father.

Another ceremony was held for the Sultan to receive the bride's dowry from her father. I was surprised to see that a small child, beautifully dressed and adorned and borne aloft on the shoulders of an old woman, was part of the dowry. I later learned that this was purely symbolic; a representation of a custom in ancient times whereby a young slave, with many years of life ahead, was included in the dowry.

The first ceremony involving the bridegroom saw Crown Prince Hassanal Bolkiah seated on the Royal throne in the Singgasana facing the assembled guests. One by one, those guests specially chosen by him came forward, dipped the fingers of their right hand into various colourful liquids, before daubing his hands with the mixture. The Imam conducted the next ceremony in the main mosque. This was the actual marriage, although, in keeping with custom, only the bridegroom was present. This was followed by the Berinni – the symbolic cleansing ceremony attended only by the bridegroom's close family.

Arguably the most colourful and openly joyous ceremony of all was the grand procession through the streets of Brunei Town, the entire route lined by cheering crowds. The motorcade moved slowly, as the ceremonial palace guards escorting the Royal car were on foot. The car itself had been transformed into a fairytale coach, by the imaginative use of plywood and the artistry of many brushstrokes.

After the procession, the bridegroom and his bride spent three days with her family before returning in triumph to the Istana as man and wife; the occasion marked by a lavish banquet and firework display for 800 guests.

My tour in Brunei came to an end in mid-October 1966, barely a fortnight after Princess Masna's wedding. The Sultan very generously awarded me the SLJ (Third Class) – an award roughly equivalent to the MBE – which, once again, the Queen graciously gave me unrestricted permission to wear.

I was desperately sad to be leaving after what had been a unique and fascinating experience. Saying goodbye to the Sultan, my colleagues in the Istana, the soldiers in the Recce Troop and Johnny Yong, the 'fixer' in Regimental headquarters, was really quite an ordeal. Never before or since have I found myself so emotionally involved in my work. I suppose it was because I was a bachelor and these people were my extended family; a family that had accomplished so much from scratch together.

Luckily, there was still something to look forward to; another adventure beckoned. The Brunei government was responsible for the cost of my return journey to Britain and the travel agent it used was the Borneo Company. The manager told me that I could make as many stopovers as I wished on the flight home without incurring any extra charge, provided I continued to travel west. I would, of course, have to pay for my accommodation. As I had three months' leave, I decided to visit Nepal, India, Pakistan, Afghanistan and Iran on the way home.

I craned my neck to get a last glimpse of Berakas Camp as the Borneo Airways Fokker Friendship soared into the air on its short hop to Jesselton in Sabah, where I boarded a Malaysian Airways Silver Kris Comet bound for Singapore. On arrival, I was taken to the Prince's Hotel Garni in Orchard Road for the night. Time was precious; I only had a few hours left in the Far East. As soon as I had dumped my kit, I left to wander about Singapore, joining the thronging crowds in the streets, breathing in the rich aromas of the East and soaking up the atmosphere to store as a treasured memory. Next morning there was just time for me to say a final farewell to my grandfather – he was gathered unto his fathers about a year later – before heading to the airport to catch the flight to Calcutta (now known as Kolkata). Here I was put up in a smart hotel in town for all of four hours, from midnight to 4.00 a.m., before returning to the airport to catch the plane to Kathmandu.

The first part of the journey took me over the flat cultivated lands of the Ganges delta and the Brahmaputra flood plain – a jigsaw puzzle of fields, criss-crossed by irrigation channels. Suddenly, the scene below changed, and we were now flying over a maze of steep-sided hills and valleys clothed in a thick verdant mantle of jungle. Here and there, a small torrent twisted and turned as it made its escape to the plains below. This was Nepal. The aircraft started to lose height and I felt that I could almost reach out and touch some of the loftier peaks and then, almost as suddenly as they had appeared, the hills vanished once more and we were flying over the neat, cultivated fields of the Kathmandu valley.

Unexpectedly, the British Embassy had kindly sent someone to meet me at the airport and take me to the newly opened and ultra modern Hotel de l'Annapurna next to King Mahindra's palace.

After a wash and brush up, I went for a stroll round Kathmandu. In the recently constructed areas of the town the streets were designed to accommodate vehicles, but elsewhere they were narrow, cobbled walkways bordered by quaint buildings leaning at crazy angles. As well as providing access, these thoroughfares also appeared to serve as sewers and the sight and stench of the filth everywhere took me by surprise.

At dinner that evening I met a Parsee couple who were on a world tour. They had hired a car and invited me to join them on a tour of the valley next day; a very kind gesture that I gladly accepted.

We spent the day sight-seeing in the valley. Highlights included the village of Patan, about five miles from Kathmandu, where the pagodas around the Durbah Square were decorated with erotic carvings in celebration of mankind's fertility.

Another highlight was a visit to a large Tibetan refugee camp, again only a few miles from Kathmandu. Here the people still wore long black robes and clung to their national identity. They lived in a very close community and, in order to maintain their independence, had started a thriving textile industry. The women, singing happily, worked their fingers at incredible speed to produce eye-catching rugs and carpets with traditional designs. In addition, shawls, scarves, boots and a wide variety of Tibetan curios were on sale in the little shop nearby. Looking at these seemingly happy people it was hard to believe that they had endured the treacherous journey across the Himalayas when fleeing from the Chinese only a few years earlier. I greatly admired their resolve and was inspired by the way they simply embraced their lot without the slightest hint of self-pity. Tough people!

I was fortunate to be in Kathmandu during the Festival of Dashain, Nepal's equivalent of Dussehra, which celebrates Lord Rama's slaying of the demon Ravana; the victory of Good over Evil. Along with countless others, I made my way to the Durbah Square at dawn on a chilly October morning to witness the animal sacrifice ceremony, about which I had heard so much. I found a ringside seat on the balcony of one of the buildings lining the square. From here I looked down upon the officers and men of the Nepalese army gathering below. The Colours of each Regiment were positioned at various points around the square. In front of each stood a wooden post within a star marked out in white chalk upon the dusty red ground. The posts stood about three feet high and had a hole drilled through them about six inches from the top. At the base of each post there was either a block of wood or sheaf of straw to serve as a chopping block. To one side of each post was an array of coloured powders, herbs, flower petals and liquids which a Brahmin priest used to perform 'pooja'; blessing the post, the kukris and other items connected with the ceremony.

When all was ready, a Nepalese soldier dressed in a vest and shorts stepped forward and picked up the standard-sized kukri lying beside the Colour of the senior Regiment on parade. He accepted the melon offered to him by the Brahmin priest and proceeded to split it in half with a single blow of the kukri. Next, a young kid goat was brought forward. The priest performed 'pooja' over it, sprinkling it with water mixed with various ceremonial ingredients. The animal shivered and shook its body as the cold water fell on it, the reaction being interpreted as meaning that it was ready to be sacrificed. The creature was quickly placed on the chopping block; there was a flash as the kukri fell and then blood spurted out of the lifeless body as the head rolled in the dust a foot or so away, its mouth opening and shutting several times by reflex action. The carcass was then dragged around the post, encircling it with a ring of blood.

This was the signal for all the Regiments to begin making their sacrifices. Melons were the first items to be sacrificed, then came chickens, followed by kid goats. At first I found the scene so sickening – kukris flashing, blood spurting and carcasses being swung round the posts spraying blood everywhere – that I tried to detach myself from the gruesome reality by looking through the lens of my camera.

Eventually, all the goats had been sacrificed and it was now the turn of the buffaloes. A specially selected soldier stepped forward and picked up the larger of the two kukris lying beside the Colour of the senior Regiment. This was a two-handed knife almost the size of a sword. The blade was angled like that of the standard kukri, but the top end broadened out considerably to act as a weight. After the now familiar 'pooja' ceremony and the animal's inevitable 'acceptance' of its fate, the buffalo was placed astride the chopping block. A rope was tied around its neck and the loose end was passed through the hole in the post and pulled taut by a soldier. A third soldier got hold of the poor creature's tail and pulled in the opposite direction. Thus the buffalo's neck was stretched to the limit. The 'executioner' sized up his target, the weapon held high above his head. Then, in the blink of an eye, the blade was in the chopping block, a fountain of blood spurted from the wound and the head rolled on the ground. So swift did death come that, for a split second, the headless animal stood upright, before crumpling to the earth. In a flash, the soldier who had been holding the animal's tail grabbed its hind legs and swung its limp body violently round the post splattering blood everywhere. Numerous buffaloes then suffered the same fate.

Following each sacrifice onlookers rushed forward carrying receptacles fashioned from leaves or paper. These they filled with blood which they either drank or bespattered those around them. I had been forewarned about this and had taken the precaution of wearing a plastic mac, which was covered in blood by the end of the ritual.

Each of the animals had to be despatched with a single blow, otherwise the 'executioner' and his followers – the Regiment in the army's case – would suffer a year's bad luck. I must have witnessed over 100 sacrifices that morning and in not one instance was a second blow required.

I was due to fly to the tiny settlement of Pokhara, some 150 miles west of Kathmandu, at noon that same day. As soon as the ceremony was over, I discarded my plastic mac, collected my things from the hotel and sped towards the airport, arriving just after 11.00 a.m. Here I was told that my aircraft would leave sometime during the afternoon. Time appeared to be of no consequence. The airport building did not boast a lounge or restaurant and time began to drag. After about two hours I decided to go outside on the airside of the building. As I did so, a siren began to wail. I dashed inside again thinking that I was about to be arrested, but nobody seemed interested in me. A few minutes later a Dakota landed and taxied up to the building. The siren had been the signal for the herdsmen to clear the runway of their goats and buffaloes!

Just after 4.00 p.m., the tannoy announced that our aircraft was ready to depart. As we walked across the apron towards our Dakota I noticed that all my travelling companions were from the east, apart from one person. This was Joe, an American Peace Corps volunteer.

As we clambered aboard the aircraft, I was surprised to see that there was nothing but the bare shell of the fuselage; no carpets and no trimmings. The seats, which were in pairs either side of a central aisle, were made of tubular steel and canvas and there was one seatbelt for each pair of seats. Joe shared his belt with me. A young Nepalese boy in a pair of crumpled grey slacks and a rather grubby white shirt was handing out sweets. This was our flight attendant. The engines coughed into action rather reluctantly and we taxied down the runway.

As soon as we were airborne the young Nepalese boy asked me if I was Captain Duncan. On admitting to the fact, he told me rather sternly that the Captain wanted to see me. What could I have done, I pondered, to be summoned by the Captain? As I entered the cockpit the pilot greeted me with a broad grin. He was alone. An Indian, he had been flying Dakotas almost all his life. He was sitting on his seat with one leg tucked under him, smoking a cigarette. He beckoned me to sit in the co-pilot's seat, saying that I would be more comfortable here than in the back. During the flight, he told me most of his passengers were Communist Chinese engineers engaged in constructing a road from Tibet to Kathmandu. He felt uneasy about them and the road they were building.

We flew over steep hills and plunging valleys. Incredibly, they were almost all terraced and under cultivation – the result of endless years of toil. Rivers flowed along the deep gorges, their ice blue colour betraying their origin as melt water from the Himalayas, which remained hidden behind a thick blanket of cloud. Midway through the flight we passed over the little settlement of Gorkha, which lends its name to the legendary soldiers from these wild hills, who have served the British Crown with such distinction for 200 years.

After about 40 minutes we started to lose height and the pilot pointed to a few low buildings at the edge of a small lake nestling amongst the hills. This was Pokhara, but I could not see any sign of an airport. Then, as we flew over a lush green field, I noticed two herdsmen chasing their livestock to one end. We circled once more to make sure the 'runway' was clear and then came in to land, coming to rest beside a large tree that served as the air terminal. Many people had gathered to greet us; the arrival of the daily aircraft from Kathmandu was quite an important event in the lives of the inhabitants here.

Pokhara 'town' comprised a series of dilapidated mud dwellings and stores that bordered one side of the runway. It also boasted a single, rather primitive hotel, which was run by Tibetan refugees. The refugee camp was the largest I had seen in Nepal. Situated between the town and the lake, it consisted of a jumble of temporary shacks and tents and seemed to evoke a sense of real hardship and suffering. Yet the inhabitants appeared content with their lot; they had experienced far worse.

I was due to spend just under a week in Pokhara, but had been unable to make any accommodation arrangements before my arrival. As it happened, Joe invited me to stay with him. The only Westerner in the area, he welcomed my company. For the past year or so he had been living with a Nepalese family about two hours by foot further up the valley, helping to run their smallholding, whilst teaching them and their neighbours about basic hygiene and sanitation. Five months earlier, he had left for Kathmandu to be debriefed at the end of his assignment in Pokhara and be given a new task, but had fallen seriously ill. Now well again, he was returning to Pokhara to collect his belongings before moving to yet another isolated settlement

I accepted Joe's invitation and only realised that he was living with a family of lepers when I arrived at their house! Despite the lateness of the hour Joe was given a tremendous welcome and even I, a complete stranger, was greeted like a long lost friend.

As I looked about this humble, rather dirty dwelling, I marvelled at Joe's selfless humanity, but he made light of the difficulties he had faced and was at pains to assure me that the form of leprosy with which his host family was afflicted was not contagious. Indeed, he had become so accustomed to living with them that he had completely forgotten to tell me about their illness.

I bedded down on the floor of Joe's room and drifted off to sleep. Next morning I awoke early. The air was crisp and clear, and sunlight streamed in through the open window. The sight that met my eyes was awe-inspiring. There, in all its splendour stood Machapuchare – the Fishtail mountain – its twin peaks appearing to touch the sky. Its snow-covered surface was dazzling white in the glancing, early morning light.

This is Nepal's sacred mountain and, as such, it was out of bounds to mountaineers. Indeed, it would lose its mystical attraction if man were ever permitted to 'conquer' it. Behind Machapuchare were the peaks of the Annapurna range, themselves rising majestically to over 26,000 feet. I stood in wonder at the open window, feasting my eyes on the scene before me. However, within half an hour the clouds rising from the valley below drew an impenetrable veil across this magnificent spectacle and once again

I was conscious of the squalor all about me. Indeed, the Himalayas were only visible for about an hour every morning throughout my stay, but I made sure I was up and about to see them.

While Joe tidied up the loose ends of his project I spent my time walking and fishing in and around Pokhara. One of my haunts was the picturesque Fewa Lake. On still, cloudless days I am told that the sight of Machapuchare reflected upon the lake's surface is magical. Unfortunately, I was denied this experience, but even so I often found myself taking in the scenery instead of paying attention to my rod and line. I fared better in the stream running through the gorge far below our temporary home, usually managing to bring something home for the pot.

Within a few days Joe's work in Pokhara was complete. I helped him to load all his belongings onto a bullock bandy, a cart drawn by one or more buffaloes or oxen, which is the humble man's transport throughout the Indian subcontinent. After saying our farewells, we made our way down the valley to Pokhara, where we treated ourselves to a Tibetan meal in the hotel. We then made our way over to the terminal tree and lay down in its shade to await our aircraft. At last, the siren heralded its imminent arrival, whereupon we joined our fellow passengers in clearing the runway of live-stock to enable it to land. Back in Kathmandu, Joe and I parted company; he to his new village and myself to Agra.

In Agra, I stayed at Laurie's, a charming, unpretentious little hotel on the outskirts of the town. It was surrounded by trees in which numerous parakeets carried on an endless, rather noisy, and yet endearing conversation. At the entrance, two snake charmers invited passers-by to see their wares. For a rupee you could drape a python round your neck and for two rupees you could see cobras dancing before the snake charmer's swaying pipes – or you could buy the pipes, germs and all! For about five rupees you could witness a fight to the death between a mongoose and a cobra.

This was obviously a favourite with tourists, but having been brought up in India, I knew it to be far from reality and very cruel. The snake is usually very lethargic and is sometimes even milked of its poison, rendering it defenceless. Just as the mongoose is about to administer the *coup de grâce* the snake charmer usually steps in to stop the contest, like a boxing referee stopping a one-sided fight, in the hope that the snake might recover for just one more fight.

When I was a child growing up in India, snake charmers used to clear our garden of cobras about twice a year, releasing them into the tea fields some distance from our bungalow. So for old time's sake, I opted for the two rupee snake charming display but, because I had been born in India, I was given the honour of watching with the python draped around my neck at no extra cost – some perk!

I had read a lot about the Taj Mahal and thought that I might be disappointed by the real thing. However, its beauty is spell-binding. The complex Koranic texts and intricate floral designs which decorate the marble surface are so perfect that rosebuds appear almost lifelike and even the veins in the tiniest leaves are included; all inlaid with semi-precious stones. I was able to visit this magnificent mausoleum both by day and by moonlight and felt greatly enriched by the experience.

The next stop on my journey was Peshawar – the gateway to the North West Frontier – which I reached via Delhi and Karachi. Several of my relatives had served on the North West Frontier and I had always been intrigued by stories of this rugged territory that was still under tribal rule; *Keepers of the Khyber* by Arthur Catherall had been one of my favourite books as a child.

Peshawar could have changed little since its days as a British Indian Army garrison town. People still talked of the 'cantonment' and most of the roads bore the names of famous battles or revered generals. I spent the night in Dean's Hotel. This was a collection of bungalows clustered together within a small compound. One of the bungalows was larger than the rest and served as the hotel's public rooms. The décor and furnishings were faded now, but the whole place exuded the atmosphere of yesteryear. I was constantly aware of the great social functions that must have taken place within these walls less than a quarter of a century earlier. But times had changed. The waiters far outnumbered the four guests who sat down to dinner that evening, and I was the only foreigner. In 1966, Dean's was a very quiet place and I wondered how long it would survive.

The manager of Dean's confirmed that there was a daily bus service between Peshawar and Kabul via the Khyber Pass. He advised me to go to the Afghan Consulate in Old Peshawar to get more information. I was there at 7.00 a.m. next morning and was told that the bus left daily between 8.00 and 10.00 a.m. Indeed, I could travel on today's bus if I wished. I duly produced my booklet of traveller's cheques, but the Afghan official brushed these aside with utter contempt when I tried to buy my ticket. A Pakistani standing nearby told me that the official wanted proper money, not coloured pieces of paper. No banks were open at this hour. My only option was to get back to Dean's to change my traveller's cheques.

The Pakistani offered to look after my kit, while I rushed out of the Consulate and hailed a Vespa scooter taxi. Dean's readily changed my cheques, but I could not get the Vespa driver to understand that I needed to go back to the Afghan Consulate. Before I knew it we had left Peshawar and were heading towards the Khyber Pass! It was after 9.00 a.m. before I finally got back to the Consulate, but, luckily, the bus was still there. My kit, however, appeared to have vanished, along with the Pakistani gentleman. I cursed my stupidity, but then another stranger tapped me on the shoulder and pointed to my suitcases, which were strapped onto the roof of the bus along with all the other baggage.

My fellow travellers all appeared to be Afghans and largely male. Each wore a cloak or blanket over a loose fitting smock and trousers and turbans round their heads to ward off the autumn chill. They had wonderfully chiselled faces, unruly beards and piercing eyes. Being the only Westerner, I was the centre of their attention. As they were unsmiling and spoke in such stern tones, I was unable to determine their mood towards me, which made me feel rather uncomfortable. I decided to go right to the back of the bus and make myself as inconspicuous as possible. Just before the bus set off, an old man, who was clearly unwell and in a lot of pain, was helped onto the bus and guided down to the bench seat at the back. I gave up my seat and helped to make the ill man a makeshift bed. When they had got him settled, the helpers got off the bus. As they departed one of them turned to me and said: "Look out him. He bad!" At first I panicked, but then realised that I had been asked to look after the sick man. That made me even more concerned; what if he died en-route? I looked at the poor man. His faced was etched in pain, yet he never uttered a sound and never once complained. I learnt later that he had just undergone an abdominal operation in Peshawar, but had insisted on returning to Kabul straight afterwards.

The bus headed out of the town, stopping outside a prosperous looking house on the outskirts. Here, a refined man followed by two women got on the bus, while several other men loaded their luggage onto the roof. The man was dressed in a smart European suit and tie, while the women both wore all-enveloping black *abayas* with only a tiny mesh window for their eyes. Once these new passengers were seated, the bus set off along the dusty road that leads across the plain towards the jagged mountain barrier that forms the North West Frontier, separating Pakistan from Afghanistan.

As we drew nearer to the Khyber Pass I could clearly see the slit trenches that used to form the last line of defence. Deeper into the old defended area, mud forts and earthworks became a common sight. We were now in the foothills of the frontier, a maze of red, stony outcrops and sharp ridges with sheer drops. I wondered at how people could have fought in such terrain.

Rounding a particularly sharp bend, the bus came to a sudden stop, a moment of agony for my sick patient. To our right there was an impressive mud fort, which might have been taken straight from the pages of a storybook. At its base, a large mud archway spanned the road and across this, written in bold white letters, were the words, 'Khyber Pass'. I leapt out of the bus, camera at the ready to record the scene, but was immediately confronted by the fiercest warrior I had ever set eyes on. He was swathed in bandoliers of ammunition and pointed an ancient rifle rather menacingly straight at my chest, while growling orders that I did not understand. Still clutching my camera, I raised my hands, whereupon he swung his rifle round to point out a tiny sign at the roadside that said 'No Photography' in what I assumed to be Urdu, Pushtu and, crucially, also English.

I made a gesture of apology and walked backwards towards the bus. My 'captor' followed and sat down beside me. I could see that under his arsenal he was wearing a long grey smock and baggy trousers that seemed to be made of hessian. His rifle was a single shot breach loader and a wire binding held the foresight in place. This was a soldier of the legendary Khyber Rifles, that famous force of tribesmen charged with policing the wild hills of the North West Frontier.

The barrier lifted and the bus entered the pass. Jagged hills crowded in upon us on all sides, practically every pinnacle being crowned by a watch tower, and, where the ground permitted, great mud forts dominated the surrounding countryside. Some of these were still occupied by men of the Khyber Rifles and their Regimental flag fluttered proudly from the mud bastions. The surrounding hills bore the badges of some of the famous Regiments that had served on the North West Frontier, each etched out with stones: Doograhs, Gurkhas and even Leicester's. Save for the bus and the metalled road upon which we were travelling, we had gone back over a 100 years in time. Indeed, in many places, the rough track that for centuries had formed part of the old Silk Route could still be seen. I can still picture this untamed landscape in my mind's eye but, alas, have no photographs.

Halfway up the pass we arrived at the village of Landi Kotel, where the Khyber Rifles soldier gestured a farewell and left the bus, which then climbed on to the top of the pass. Only then did it dawn on me that I had not been under arrest, but this soldier had been our escort until this point on the pass. What a relief!

We now looked down on the desolate plains of South Eastern Afghanistan and began our descent towards the border control point of Torkham. Here we all had to get off the bus to go through Customs and have our passports stamped at the immigration control office. Initially, the authorities insisted that the sick Afghan also had to leave the bus – there were no exceptions to the rule. It took me some time, with the help of some of the other passengers, to convince an official to enter the bus to complete his paperwork. Only then was I able to go through the system myself and, being the only Westerner in the group, this took ages. As I left the building, I saw, to my horror, that the bus had departed. I rushed back inside, where an official told me to sprint down the road through 'no man's land' to try to catch up with the bus at the Afghan control point. I arrived exhausted, just in time, but still had to get my papers stamped. As I entered the bus I received a formal 'rocket' from the driver that was then endorsed by almost all the passengers. Feeling suitably, albeit unfairly, admonished I got back into my seat just in front of the sick Afghan, whose pained eyes also appeared to condemn me. Nevertheless, I had an overwhelming sense of relief at not having been stranded at this remote outpost.

We were now in Afghanistan and our route took us across a flat, desolate and uninteresting wasteland. After about two hours we arrived at the bustling little community of Jalalabad. We stopped here to let everyone stretch their legs and get a bite to eat. Chastened by my experience when I had last left the bus, I chose to stay with the sick Afghan. I asked someone to bring him a cup of coffee. He was obviously suffering cruelly, and the arduous journey was beginning to take its toll, but he remained stoic and uncomplaining.

At 5.00 p.m., the driver entered the bus and was relieved to see that I was present. He then sounded the horn to warn everyone that he was about to leave. Within a few minutes all the passengers were back on board. We had been joined by a group of really fearsome looking men; magnificent examples of the uncompromising land which had fashioned them. They were all very noisy and one, in particular, appeared to have a great sense of humour, keeping the bus in stitches throughout the three-hour journey to Kabul.

An hour out of Jalalabad, we arrived at another awe-inspiring mountain barrier. I could see no way through, but the bus made for a tiny gap in the hills, barely wide enough for the Kabul River and the thin strip of tarmac following its course. We had entered the Kabul gorge. The gorge became narrower and the mountains seemed to lean in upon us, blotting out the evening sun. To my horror, I then saw our road snaking its way up the near vertical cliff ahead of us in a series of hairpin bends. Some of these were so acute that the road had been built out from the mountainside to enable vehicles to negotiate them.

As we edged our way up, the view from my window became ever more spectacular, yet alarming. It would not do to make a mistake here! There was a little mosque at the top where we stopped, some to pray whilst others stood and admired the incredible view: the gaping depths of the gorge and the thin ribbon of road that twisted and turned its way up one of its seemingly insuperable flanks.

Ahead of us the road passed through a tunnel onto the Kabul plateau. We were now at an elevation of about 6,000 feet and nearing the end of our journey. Night had fallen and there was a distinct nip in the air that chilled us all to the bone. The cold gripped the sick Afghan who began to shiver uncontrollably. I put my jacket over his chest and shoulders and a member of the fierce group from Jalalabad took off his cloak and wrapped it around him.

It was just after 8.00 p.m. when the bus came to a halt on the square outside the Kabul hotel. After a ten-hour journey, we had finally arrived.

On our arrival, friends and relatives of the sick Afghan boarded the bus to take the brave man home. As he was carried past me he uttered the word "English" and held out his hand in gratitude for the minimal help I had given him during what must have been one of the toughest days in his life. This was the first time I had heard him speak and I was greatly touched.

Within minutes everyone had departed, except the man dressed in the European suit and the two women with him. Now he approached me and asked where I was staying. When I told him I was booked into the Spinzer Hotel, he said that it was not far away, but would be difficult to find in the dark. He insisted on taking me there. We said our farewells at the entrance to the hotel and he disappeared into the night and out of my life – yet another person who had helped me on my way for no reason other than I was a stranger in his country.

I was only in Kabul for three days and wanted to make the most of the opportunity. Next morning I was up early and after breakfast set off to explore my new surroundings. The city was hemmed in on all sides by bare rocky hills of a reddish hue. The buildings in the centre of the city were quite modern, but the mud dwellings that clung to the hillsides all about would not have looked out of place in biblical times. The inhabitants, too, seemed to have been unaffected by the passage of time. All the men were turbaned and dressed in loose-fitting robes, while the women were shrouded in black from head to toe. Wild-looking men on horseback galloped down the streets, their flowing robes making for a very romantic scene.

Almost every third shop sold antique firearms at very low prices. I was spoilt for choice and ended up buying one of the smaller, lighter weapons purely because I was already laden down with baggage. It was a flintlock with a modified curved stock, beautifully inlaid with bone. This, together with a leather powder horn plus a locally made tool to fashion flints, set me back the equivalent of £5.00. On my return to England, an antique dealer told me the gun was a Tower flintlock and bore the stamp of the East India Company and the date 1806. In all probability it had been lost in a skirmish on the North West Frontier and had fallen into Afghan hands. Rather fittingly it was now back in British Army ownership, and still hangs from a beam in our cottage.

During the afternoon, I climbed up the hill behind the hotel, passing through a cluster of mud dwellings. Here I caught a glimpse of life in the hills. There was no water or vegetation of any kind up here. Everything had to be carried up from the shops in the valley below. The villagers filled goatskins from taps in the city and then carried these home on their backs up the steep hillside, along with all their other supplies. I climbed further up the mountain, well above the last mud buildings and was now quite alone in this harsh landscape. From where I stood I could see the entire city of Kabul, the sandy plateau on which it stood and the snow-capped mountains beyond. I was, however, conscious of a baying sound that seemed to be coming from further up the mountain. I scanned the rocky terrain, but could see nothing. Every time I moved forward the baying started and seemed to be growing in volume. When I stopped, so did it. I was not sure if there were wolves in these parts, but that is what the noise sounded like. So I decided that discretion was the better part of valour and made my way back to the hotel. There I was told that I had, indeed, been listening to wolves and had been wise not to continue my climb.

At supper I met an Afghan man who was a lecturer at the recently established Kabul University. He spoke perfect English and next day took me sight-seeing around Kabul and its environs. The place that enthralled me most, however, was the Afghan room in the Spinzer Hotel itself. The décor represented an Afghan desert tent and we sat on cushions on the floor. In the far corner sat three Afghan tribesmen, their faces full of character. One was an old man, whose weather-beaten face was carved with deep furrows and encased in an unruly snow-white beard. Another was middle aged, his proud face heavily lined and his thick, jet-black beard beginning to grey at the edges. The third man was a youngster who did not wear a beard but sported an impressive moustache.

The two older men played different string instruments, the likes of which I had never seen before (or since). While these two picked out the tune and recited traditional folk stories in song, the young man beat out the rhythm on two bongo-like drums. So skilled was he that he could beat out the sound of a single horse trotting, cantering or even galloping. His *pièce de résistance* was to represent the sound of an entire army of horsemen charging into battle – each of his fingers seemingly beating out a different rhythm. With the storytellers also reaching a crescendo, the effect was intoxicating. I could picture the scene: horses with nostrils flaring, riders leaning forward, sabres glinting in their hands and their robes streaming out behind them.

Next morning I made my way to the airport to catch my flight to Tehran, innocently carrying my newly acquired antique gun. Here, at passport control, I was asked for the certificate of authority to take the weapon out of the country. Apparently this had to be obtained from the museum in Kabul, but no one had informed me, least of all the vendor. I was about to surrender my prize when the officer addressing me suddenly changed his demeanour from authoritative official to that of an uncertain minion who told me to step aside and wait. Looking over my shoulder I saw two very large men in uniform approaching the desk. I took them to be Russians, but never discovered if I was correct. As luck would have it, my plane was called as the official attended to their problem and I was able to walk out and board it still clutching my musket.

The flight to Tehran took about two hours and for almost the entire time we flew over inhospitable country, ranging from barren desert to red, rocky mountains. Minutes before our arrival in Tehran, the scene to starboard changed to reveal the impressive Elburz mountain range, the highest peaks dusted with the first snows of the coming winter. Beyond and stretching to the horizon, lay the Caspian Sea, its waters glinting in the sunlight; the lush green margin around its shores in marked contrast to the parched desert below.

As we lost height, I could make out numerous holes on the desert floor set at regular intervals, almost like a grid system. Later, I discovered these to be access vents to a vast system of ancient man-made underground channels carrying water from the mountains to all parts of the country – an incredible feat of engineering.

I planned to spend three weeks with my sister and her family in Tehran, but was in for a rude shock at the immigration desk. Here, the only mistake the Borneo Company in Brunei made in my complex itinerary came to light. Apparently, if one travelled from Brunei to Tehran no visa was required, but I had broken my journey on several occasions and certainly did require a visa.

The plan was to send me back to Kabul, where my visa was no longer valid and I might be in trouble over the gun I had bought. My brother-in-law, Michael West, a lawyer in the Oil Consortium, had come to the airport to meet me. Luckily, I could see him through the windows in the wall dividing the controlled section from the public area. Using sign language I managed to communicate the problem to him. Amazingly, he was able to redeem the situation and after a tense hour or two I was issued with a visa at the airport. A much-chastened traveller shook him heartily by the hand and hugged my sister and her two little ones, Dominic, now 22 months old and his eight-month-old sister, Sue, who I was seeing for the first time. I was no longer on my own and had a really happy time staying with them in their home in a quiet Tehran suburb.

One afternoon we all went for a drive out to the hills near the Caspian Sea. From a distance, the barren hillsides looked brick red. Once amongst them, however, although the predominant colour of the stones was indeed red, others reflected almost all the colours of the rainbow. Some stones were a single colour, but most were a mixture of strata in various combinations of red, brown, yellow orange and green. As my Regimental colour was green, I picked up a green stone as a keepsake, and still have it today.

Towards the end of my stay in Iran, I took the opportunity to visit Isfahan, an ancient city famous for its magnificent mosques, covered market and the beautiful carpets that bear its name. I was not disappointed. Quite the most spectacular mosque, in my opinion, was the Masjid-i-Shah, which stands at the far end of the main square. Its tall arches and impressive minarets are decorated in the most exquisite, intricate mosaic designs. The craftsmen who achieved this degree of excellence, not just here but on numerous other mosques in the city, were truly gifted.

At the other end of the square I watched for ages as another set of skilled craftsmen, blacksmiths in this case, fashioned beautiful trays from beaten copper, the rhythmic ring of their hammers pervading the whole square.

The covered market, also on the perimeter of the square is, I understand, one of the largest and oldest in the world. A labyrinth of narrow corridors lined with tiny shops selling all manner of wares, it is quite the most extraordinary shopping centre I have ever been in. You could buy virtually anything here, from the sublime – gorgeous Persian rugs and intricately worked gold and silver jewellery – to the mundane – kitchen utensils, clothes and groceries. In 1966, prices, too, were unbelievably low. I bought a 'silver' cigarette box ornately engraved with a Persian design for less than £1.00. It may not have been sterling silver but, nevertheless, it has stood the test of time.

The shop that most caught my attention was one in which an artist was painting miniature Persian scenes depicting hunting, polo playing and community living. I sat and watched him for about an hour. So fine was some of his work that one of the brushes he used was just a single cat's whisker. Naturally, I ended up buying a set of his pictures, which are admired to this day.

The most treasured souvenir I bought in Iran was an Isfahan rug. It cost much more than the remaining money I had, but the shopkeeper was keen to get hold of hard currency so agreed to sell it to me for the $84 I had left.

My time in Tehran came to an end all too quickly. My sister, Merrilees, who was pregnant with her third child, seemed very tired throughout my stay. I accepted this to be quite normal for a mother with two very young children and another on the way. As I bade her farewell I did not know that this was the last time I would see her.

On arrival at Heathrow, I made my way to the UK citizens' passport control desk, only to be told by the immigration official that I was in the wrong queue. He advised me to join the queue signed, I seem to remember, 'Aliens'. This was in the days when Enoch Powell was beginning to raise the spectre of racial tension within the United Kingdom, which culminated in his notorious 'Rivers of Blood' speech some 18 months later. I thought nothing more of it, but when I reached the immigration official dealing with the non-British citizens I was in for a shock. He asked me for my work permit, which, of course, I did not possess. Then he asked me where I intended to go, to which I replied, "Oxford". The questioning continued: "Why are you going to Oxford?", to which I replied in all innocence: "Because my parents live there." His reaction to this was unexpected; he appeared to lose his composure and said: "My God, all you aliens have parents in Oxford!" and without further ado decided to refuse me entry to the country, recommending, instead, that I be deported! Quite frightening stuff.

I was interviewed by another official to whom I explained I was a member of the British Army returning from a secondment overseas. I added that I was due to rejoin my Regiment in Germany in six weeks. Luckily, I was able to produce a posting order to back up my story. In the end, I was allowed to enter the country "for six weeks" and was required to report to my local police station to make them aware of my presence. I thought no more about it and, just after Christmas 1966, duly rejoined my Regiment in Germany. However, in the following Spring the problem raised its head again. The Regiment had reached the final of a rugby competition and the match was due to be played in England. I was in the team, but when the ferry docked at Dover, I was told that I could not go ashore. The captain of our team pleaded my case and undertook to guarantee my return to Germany within 48 hours. He presented the official Regimental Part One Order with my name on the team list as evidence.

On my return to Germany, I sent my passport back to the passport office in London, enquiring why I had been refused entry into Britain. It transpired that the problem related to the times when I had accompanied His Highness, the Sultan of Brunei, to England. His entourage did not pass through Customs and immigration, but went straight from the plane to the hotel. Our passports were gathered up by an official beforehand and returned to us later in the hotel. I was usually the only British person in the party, but my passport had been processed, along with all the others, as if I were a Bruneian, and stamped accordingly. The fact that I had been born in India and that my passport had been issued by the British High Commission in Brunei had helped to cause the confusion. The matter was resolved by issuing me with a new passport.

So ended an extraordinary chapter in my military career. My wife Toni and I returned to Borneo on holiday in early summer 2013, timing our visit to Brunei to coincide with Armed Forces Day on 31 May. I wanted to show Toni where I had first volunteered for loan service almost half a century ago. The country was far more advanced than when I knew it; His Majesty, Sultan Hassanal Bolkiah, having made good use of the country's oil revenues to benefit all his subjects. Roads now link most of the outlying villages and settlements, although you still have to travel by boat to the northern enclave of Temburong, where the virgin rainforest remains virtually intact. Here I was reunited with my marvellous tracker, Yu. It was great to see him. Like me, he was an old man now, but still as fit as a fiddle, and we shared a glass or two of *tuak* for old times' sake as we reminisced about the past.

The single Regiment in which I had served had now grown into very efficient and well equipped separate army, navy and air force entities, totalling some 8,000 men and women.

We were treated like royalty: given VIP seats at the Armed Forces Day Parade, allocated a liaison officer throughout our stay and were even invited for an audience with His Majesty in his magnificent Istana Nural Iman. It was a truly wonderful experience.

1. Brunei Town from the air, showing the strikingly beautiful Omar Ali Saifuddin Mosque and Kampong Ayer (1965) (Crown copyright)

2. Omar Ali Saifuddin Mosque (1964)

3. Brunei Airport (1964)

4. Berakas Camp nearing completion (1966)

5. Temburong District. An example of the terrain in which we were operating (Crown copyright)

6. A Royal Brunei Malay Regiment (RBMR) *tamuai* patrol on the Temburong River (by kind permission of *Soldier* magazine)

7. Long Lamaling, showing a typical entrance to a longhouse (Crown copyright)

8. Inside the first house in Amo village, with Yu (right foreground), Angung (fourth from left with baby) and me (in the centre at the back) in October 1966 (Crown copyright)

9. The RBMR Recce Troop on the beach at Jerudong (1965) (by kind permission of HM Sultan Hassanal Bolkiah) (Crown copyright)

10. The Civil ADC, Pehin Sungga Mara Darta Abbas (1965) and me (by kind permission of HM Sultan Hassanal Bolkiah)

11. The Inauguration Parade, Berakas Camp, 31 May 1965. HH Sir Omar Ali Saifuddin, accompanied by the CO, Lt Col DM Fletcher MC, with me one pace behind, inspects the Regiment after according it the title 'Royal' (by kind permission of HM Sultan Hassanal Bolkiah)

12. HH Sir Omar Ali Saifuddin, Colonel-in-Chief RBMR, and officers of the Regiment at Istana Darul Hana on 31 May 1965. Lt Col Fletcher is seated fourth from the left; Major John Moran is standing fifth from the left, and I am to his right (by kind permission of HM Sultan Hassanal Bolkiah)

13. HH Sir Omar Ali Saifuddin, wearing army uniform and accompanied by the British High Commissioner, HE Mr Fernley (Max) Webber CMG MC TD, and me, is given a traditional welcome on a visit to a remote settlement. Major Dedrick Wright, Second in Command RBMR, can just be seen behind

Mr Webber (By kind permission of HM Sultan Hassanal Bolkiah) (Crown copyright)

14. HH Sir Omar Ali Saifuddin and me about to board our helicopter at the end of an up-country visit. I am caught in the act of securing my holster's safety strap (by kind permission of HM Sultan Hassanal Bolkiah)

15. RBMR Sea Wing's flotilla in Brunei Bay (1965) (official Royal Navy photograph (Crown copyright))

16. HH Sir Omar Ali Saifuddin greets my parents at a reception at Grosvenor House, Park Lane, London (1965) (by kind permission of Grosvenor House, which holds the copyright, and HM Sultan Hassanal Bolkiah)

17. Ceremonial palace officials

18. Ceremonial palace guards

19. Tug-of-war – a traditional event to celebrate HH Sir Omar Ali Saifuddin's birthday. His Highness is at the centre of the picture wearing dark glasses, and I am just in front of him (by kind permission of HM Sultan Hassanal Bolkiah)

20. An early morning sighting of Machapuchare – the sacred 'Fish Tail' mountain – taken from Joe's house near Pokhara, Nepal, in October 1966

21. Kabul, November 1966

22. The last photograph I took of my sister, Merrilees, with her husband, Mike West, and their children Dominic and Sue (Tehran, November 1966). Merrilees died on 22 April 1967

23. Meeting up again with Yu at his house in Batang Duri on a visit to Brunei in June 2013

24. Being presented to HM Sultan Hassanal Bolkiah at the Armed Forces Day celebrations at Bolkiah Garrison, Bandar Seri Begawan, Brunei on 2 June 2013. Toni can just be seen behind me, and a picture of the late HH Sir Omar Ali Saifuddin hangs on the wall (by kind permission of the *Brunei Times*, which holds the copyright, and HM Sultan Hassanal Bolkiah)

1

2

3

4

5

6

7

8

10

9

11

12

13

14

15

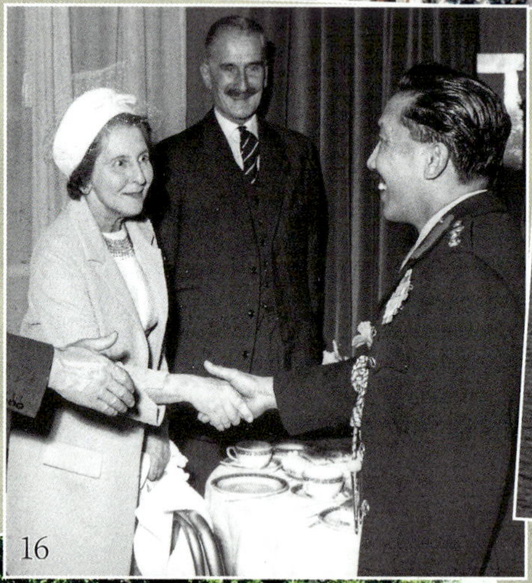

16

17

18

19

20

21

22

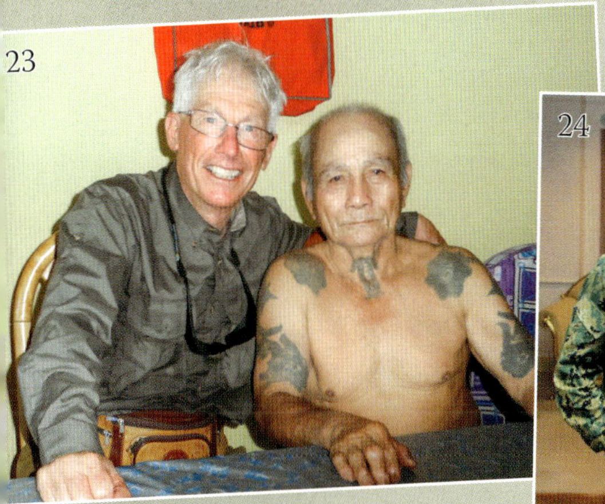
23

24

SUDAN

LIBYA
EGYPT
Wadi Halfa
Dunqunab
Red Sea
Port Sudan
Suakin
Dongola
Nile
Haiya
Ed Damar
Meroë
CHAD
SUDAN
ERITREA
Omdurman
Khartoum
Kassala
Jebel Marra
Wad Medani
Geneina
El Fasher
El Obeid
Sennar
Dinder
Zalingei
Nyala
En Nahud
El Jebelein
Ed Damazin
Kadugli
ETHIOPIA
N
CENTRAL
AFRICAN
REPUBLIC
Wau
Pibor
Post
Bor
SUDAN - 1982
Juba
Yei
Nimule
ZAIRE
UGANDA
KENYA

SUDAN

PRELUDE

Some five months after I left Tehran, Merrilees died along with her unborn baby, leaving Michael to care for two young children. She was just 28. The cause of death was liver failure, apparently caused by a condition that had lain dormant within her since her childhood in India. Her death was a dreadful blow to all of us; Merrilees had been a wonderful daughter, sister, wife and mother. It was to her that my brother and I used to turn when we were separated from our parents during our schooldays in England, and our dear, gentle sister never failed us.

At the time of her death, I was the adjutant of my Regiment, 3RTR. In this capacity I received all compassionate telegrams concerning bereavements affecting members of the Regiment. I would then break the sad news myself, or find an officer closer to the unfortunate man to carry out this cruelly painful task. I knew Merrilees had been ill, but had just finished reading three air letter forms from home, marked on the outside, 'Good News', 'Better News', 'Even Better News', all telling me that she was on the mend, when the Post Corporal handed me a telegram. Then my eyes fell upon its contents and I read my own sad news. In a way I was grateful to be alone, rather than having to pretend to be brave in front of someone else.

I busied myself in my work and for the next few years my army career followed along conventional lines. I served with my Regiment in tanks in

Germany and armoured cars in England and the Middle East, attended the Staff College, Camberley, and completed tours with both the Ministry of Defence (MoD) in London and Headquarters, British Army of the Rhine (BOAR) in Rheindahlen, Germany, after which tour I was appointed MBE. However, two events during this time helped to shape my future life.

First, on 17 March 1968, St Patrick's Day, I met the girl of my dreams at a tea party cunningly arranged by my mother. When she told me she had guests for tea on Sunday I was not amused. I was home for the weekend with a large assignment of work to complete for the following Monday. However, Toni changed all that; suddenly there was more to life than paperwork! The relationship blossomed to the point where I dared to 'pop the question', and to my delight I received a positive response.

At the time, officers under the age of 25 were required to seek their Commanding Officer's permission to get married. Although I was 28, etiquette demanded that I, too, seek permission, purely out of courtesy. Of course, my request was granted, but my Commanding Officer stressed the importance of the step I was about to take. An armoured car squadron from the Regiment was on the point of being deployed on a nine-month unaccompanied tour to Sharjah in the Arabian Gulf, and he felt it would be a good idea for me to join it, "to give me time to reflect upon my decision."

Naturally, Toni and I were upset, but it did prove to us, at the outset, that it takes a very special spouse to marry into the army. In the event, I was utterly enthralled by the desert; its uncompromising harshness, its austere beauty and tranquillity. The people who lived in this unforgiving environment were equally intriguing; their dignity, pride and spirituality seemed to come from another age.

At the time, Sharjah was little more than a collection of mud dwellings on the perimeter of a joint Army/RAF military base. Dubai was not much different and the only building of note in Abu Dhabi was the whitewashed mud fort. The souk in Sharjah had a number of craftsmen working with gold and silver. One in particular made exquisite gold and silver filigree jewellery. The British servicemen knew him affectionately as Robin Bastard – a corruption of robbing bastard! He enjoyed our good-natured banter and traded very successfully on the name. He made the beautiful gold bracelet I gave Toni as a wedding present, as well as all the other gifts I brought home. In marked contrast to his nickname, his prices were entirely reasonable and his craftsmanship utterly superb.

The military forces in Sharjah were also responsible for helping to keep the peace in northern Oman, as most of the Omani armed forces were engaged in fighting the Dofar war in the south of the country. So I was able to see Oman when it still only had about ten miles of black top road and when the gates of the capital, Muscat, were closed from dusk until dawn.

Two events during the Omex Patrol, as our routine deployment into northern Oman was called, made a lasting impression upon me. It was mid-August and the weather was so hot that we were unable to operate the vehicles during the heat of the day. The routine was to set out at first light and motor until about 10.00 a.m. We would then leaguer up and 'make shade' until about 4.00 p.m., before moving on until forming a night leaguer at last light – about 6.00 p.m. (As it was important for our presence to be known, we had to operate during daylight.)

It was while 'making shade' one day that I met my first Omani. We were in a barren area of desert when he suddenly appeared out of nowhere. His loose-fitting white robe, known as a dishdasha, fluttered in the wind. At his midriff he sported a *kunja* – the distinctively curved Omani dagger – attached to a belt around his waist, and slung across his body was a bandoleer loaded with bullets. These were for the Martini Henry rifle he held in his hand. His *shemagh* – headdress – was worn like a turban and one end was drawn across his face to give some protection from the driving sand. His bearing and demeanour exuded utter confidence and certainly showed that he was not about to be daunted by a squadron of armoured cars; he was the master in this, his desert domain.

My crew was brewing up at the time and tucking into some hard tack biscuits and jam, which we squeezed out of toothpaste-like tubes. He readily accepted our invitation to join us and seemed to like our rations, particularly the jam. So when he made to leave we gave him some packets of biscuits and tubes of jam to take away with him and thought nothing more of it. At last it was time to push on in the relative cool of the late afternoon. I was in my vehicle with my head and shoulders protruding from the cupola, when I felt a tap on my shoulder. Turning around I was astonished, if not a little alarmed, to see the Omani. In his right hand he held three fresh spring onions, which he insisted on giving to me. Where on earth had he got them from in this seemingly barren wasteland? Then with the typical Arab gesture of farewell, he dismounted and disappeared back into the dunes.

A few days later my vehicle blew its engine. At the time the squadron was skirting to the south of the Bahla oasis. The squadron leader had no option but to leave me with a small REME (the army's vehicle mechanics) detachment to make my own arrangements for recovery or repair with our base in Sharjah. It was two days before help arrived and in the meantime we ran short of water.

The date palms of Bahla oasis shimmered in the heat haze some two miles to the north, their fresh green colour in marked contrast to the yellowish-white glare of the surrounding desert. Rising above the palms was a sizeable, but crumbling mud fort, around the base of which, hidden amongst the palms, were the many mud dwellings of Bahla's inhabitants. I did not know it at the time, but in those days Bahla was known throughout northern Oman as a place of sorcery and mystery – a place that strangers should avoid.

The shade and the cool breeze rustling through the palms immediately struck me as I entered the oasis. Then I spotted the clear water running along numerous channels, known as falages, throughout the settlement. At the centre, there was a pool of water where camels were drinking thirstily, tended by a number of men dressed similarly to the Omani we had met a few days earlier. This was just how I had imagined an oasis to be. The men's bearded faces stared at us as we dismounted from our Land Rover and started to walk towards them, arms outstretched in a gesture of peace and a jerrycan in each hand clearly indicating the purpose of our visit.

Although very reserved, they showed no hint of hostility. Instead, they offered us the usual Arabic greeting, *"As salaam alaykum,"* and, like true desert dwellers, gestured for us to fill our containers. I responded by giving them a packet of 200 cigarettes and, our task completed, we headed back into the searing heat of the desert. I got the distinct impression that our presence there had been tolerated rather than welcomed. This made me want to learn this people's language so that I could get to know them better.

A Wessex helicopter brought out our replacement power pack. We were on a gravelly piece of desert rather than sand, which enabled the pilot to use his helicopter as a crane to lift out the damaged power pack and position the replacement. As far as we could tell this had not been done before and, in any event, was an excellent example of joint service cooperation, not to mention skilful flying. The repair completed, I eventually rejoined the Squadron near Muscat.

Toni and I faced yet another taste of what army life had in store for married couples when my return from Sharjah was delayed slightly 'due to the exigencies of the Service'. My future father-in-law was not at all happy when he had to alter the date of our wedding at rather short notice. Having arranged similar celebrations myself in recent years, I can now understand why!

Several years passed and I had slotted into the routine life of a 'married pad', as army families were known. Then, early in 1980, when I was on the staff at the Royal Military Academy, Sandhurst, I was telephoned by my postings' branch and asked if I would like to go on a two-year secondment to the Sudan – on promotion. Despite being in a highly prestigious and rewarding appointment at Sandhurst, I felt the pull of the desert, but thought it only fair to ask my family first; by then we had four young children. Toni had been a volunteer with Voluntary Service Overseas (VSO) in Mali when I was in Brunei, so knew the challenges we were likely to face in Africa better than I did. She leapt at the opportunity, as did the children. Within a few months, and with a ten-week Arabic course under my belt, we were on our way.

I was to be the Armoured Advisor in the Sudanese Armoured Corps School, and went ahead of the family to take over my new appointment from my predecessor, who was also in the Royal Tank Regiment. Daytime temperatures were such that it was uneconomical for planes to fly in and out of Khartoum during the day; all activity therefore took place in the small hours of the night. However, when I stepped out of the aircraft at 2.30 a.m. it was as if I had been hit by the heat from a blast furnace. If it was this hot now, what was the temperature likely to be at midday, and how was I going to be able to cope?

My initial impressions of Khartoum were not favourable. Apart from the avenue along the southern bank of the Blue Nile, where the evaporation from the river and the shade took the edge off the searing heat, Khartoum was a stiflingly hot, dirty, dusty sprawling urban complex. All the roads were heavily pot-holed and in many districts a thick layer of sand covered the crumbling tarmac. The basic essentials, such as water, electricity, petrol, gas, and even food, also presented real everyday challenges for the inhabitants.

Our house was much bigger and better than the one my predecessor had occupied for almost his entire tour and, importantly, had a small, shady garden in which the children could play. But it was built of concrete and thus acted like a storage heater. At least it had air coolers in two of the bedrooms and the dining room. An air cooler blows air through a damp hessian screen into the area to be cooled. A pump draws water from an internal reservoir to keep the screen damp. When passing through the screen, the air is not only cooled, but is also moistened, making conditions in the room very pleasant. However, during power cuts these coolers were rendered useless and the house heated up like a stone.

When I arrived, raw sewage was leaking from the upstairs bathroom's waste pipe and trickling down the stairs. Moreover, we had been without electricity for almost three days and the food in the freezer was beginning to defrost. I was amazed when my predecessor dismissed these problems as 'minor inconveniences'; the electricity would return before the food had fully thawed and, as for the leaking sewage, I should not use the upstairs toilet and merely walk up the other side of the stairs until the problem was rectified. He had been in the Sudan for two years and, in time, we too learned to put things into perspective – it was the only way to survive here.

Meanwhile, I felt this was not the place to bring the family, at least not until I had been able to sort out the basic essentials. There was a telephone in the house, but it was not connected to the outside world and remained inoperative throughout our time in Khartoum – although I was once sent a sizeable bill for its hire that was subsequently withdrawn. To telephone home I had to go to the General Post Office in the centre of town and join the queue. When my turn came, I handed my number to an operator, who then made the connection and directed me to one of a bank of telephone booths. I then competed with all the other callers to make myself heard and to hear what was being said in reply. I told Toni of my concerns, but luckily she was made of sterner stuff and a fortnight later she and the children joined me.

The British Army Training Team (BATT) that I had joined comprised about ten men and their families. It is fair to say that we all struggled for the first three months; Toni, toughened by her previous experience in Mali, was perhaps the only exception. Indeed, in his first meeting, held about a month after our arrival, the Team Commander, Colonel Blundell-Hollingshead-Blundell of the Grenadier Guards, told us all that if we wanted to return home, we could do so with his full support and without shame. However, if we chose to stay we (and our families) were to stop whingeing and make the most of our time here. Nobody left, and in the end nobody regretted staying – quite the reverse!

Our house came with two resident cats. Mister Green was a large vicious feral male and was quick to scratch. With rabies prevalent in Sudan and our four young children vulnerable to attack, I had no option but to put him down. Lucy was a smaller, jet black female, with an exposed canine giving her an evil appearance. We called her the witch's cat. She, too, was temperamental, but after discussing the problem with the vet, we elected to have her spayed rather than put down. Once the decision was made, he carried out the deed there and then, on our dining table, with our two young boys – eyes popping out of their heads – trying to watch! Lucy bonded with our youngest child, Zoë, and at night always slept at her feet.

Because everything was in such short supply in Khartoum, each family had to bring out a two years' supply of the basic commodities, ranging from tinned foods and powdered milk, through essential First Aid items (including malaria prophylactics) down to such necessities as washing up liquid and loo rolls. This, in itself, was a major challenge. Imagine being able to go to your local supermarket only once every two years; what would you buy, and in what quantities? Luckily, the NAAFI, the Services' domestic suppliers, had some useful guidelines to help us. Our order included two seven-pound tins of Marmite! In addition, we were given six ten-man army ration packs to be used only in the event of a real emergency, such as a coup, curfew or serious food shortage. Long before our tour ended we had eaten the lot!

We bought our vegetables from a 'donkey man', who passed by the house on a regular basis. He had all manner of fresh produce in large sacks slung across his donkey's back, as well as an all-important set of scales. If you bought carrots he would weigh these out first to determine the cost, then cut off the tops and feed them to his donkey. In this way the customers paid for the donkey's fodder, but nobody minded as we valued the service and liked him and his donkey.

Other donkey men stopped by the house selling rope, plastic containers and even milk, which they carried in large metal churns and measured out with a ladle. However, we did not buy our milk in this way, as it was of doubtful quality, and instead we bought it from the Belgravia Dairy. Started by an Englishman with a herd of Friesian cows many years earlier, this dairy was on the banks of the Blue Nile in North Khartoum. It supplied milk in green bottles and if we put our empty bottles out before 10.00 a.m. they would be replaced by full ones about half an hour later. The fresh milk had to be taken indoors as soon as possible, and put in the fridge or (if the electricity was out) under a wet towel. Even this milk had to be boiled before we could use it.

Milk was in short supply and it was quite an achievement to get onto the Belgravia Dairy's milk round. So I got quite a fright when I went to pay our bill one day to find we were not included in the ledger under Duncan, Toni or Bruce. The accountant asked to look at my cheque book and then, with the satisfied sigh of one who has solved a problem, reached for another ledger, reserved for businesses, and triumphantly pointed to the entry: 'BAC Dun Can Co. Ltd' – a company making cans for dun(g), no less! My rank, Lt Col, had been mistaken for Co. Ltd. I knew better than to point out the error as it would probably have resulted in us being removed from the milk round and being asked to re-apply. I therefore kept my peace and happily paid my bill – the dairy continued to supply us with milk throughout our time in Khartoum.

We did the bulk of our food shopping in the local souk. Fruit was usually in good supply, and the grapefruits were a particular favourite. They were small, thick-skinned and full of pips, whilst the flesh was pink, tart and juicy. These became a staple food at breakfast. Limes were also a family favourite. These were pressed and mixed with sugar and water to make a delicious, refreshing drink called 'limoon'.

Fresh meat was either hung or laid out in the blazing sun and was always hidden under a thick black blanket of hungry flies. These swarmed up in clouds when disturbed by the butcher, who used a large tree trunk as a chopping board. This was no place for the squeamish! If you wanted mince, he could do this for you on the spot, provided the electricity was on. If not, we had to do it at home, using the hand-operated mincer supplied by the army; the only army quarter in which we were ever issued with such culinary equipment.

Bread was an essential staple food and was often in short supply. As such, it was never on display. Instead you kept an eye on your local bakery, and when a queue started to form you knew that bread was on sale. The bread was sold through a small hole in the bakery wall, for one *piasta* a piece. We all took one of these small, squashed baguette-like 'breads', spread with Marmite or marmalade, to school or work every day as our mid-morning snack.

Eggs were sold by the dozen and came loose in polythene bags, making it almost impossible to avoid breakages on the bumpy journey home. They looked like bantams' eggs and were lost in our eggcups. In any case, after finding that several of them were almost ready to hatch, we decided not to serve boiled eggs so as to avoid any unpleasantness at the dining table; it was safer to serve them poached or scrambled. This, at least, kept the nasty surprises in the kitchen!

The electricity was very unreliable, and I cannot remember a day when we did not experience a cut. Indeed, during our first two weeks we had a total of only 19 hours of electricity. Usually these cuts lasted only a few hours, but once or twice they persisted for a day or more. At such times we covered the freezer with a wet blanket to keep the contents cool – and we hoped for the best.

As the house was so hot, we slept outside as a family on our balcony throughout the year, except for the months of December and January, when the nights were chilly. Even during the 'rainy season' – July to September – we would sleep on the balcony until it started to rain, and then roll up our mattresses, go indoors and spend the rest of the night on the floor; no mean feat with four children ranging in age from nine down to four years!

Two entries in the diary we kept at the time illustrate the problems posed by our unreliable supply of electricity:

Saturday 16 May 1981

Well over 100°F today and 33% humidity. Electricity off when we arrived home – no hardship as we sleep outside ....

Then two days later:

Monday 18 May 1981

Still no electricity – the house is like a furnace and we're beginning to worry about the freezer....

Because we were unable to rely on electricity, we were supplied with a Calor gas cooker as a back-up. Calor gas, however, was also prone to shortages. When a bottle ran out (we were supplied with two) we then had to wait for a gas delivery at our local petrol station. Then it was a matter of queuing and hoping that sufficient gas bottles were delivered. This task usually fell to Toni. Once the gas arrived and the manager had determined the number of bottles delivered, he would let people know if it was worth their while continuing to queue. You could have been queuing for two hours in the boiling sun by this point, and on one occasion, poor Toni was number 84 in the queue when 80 bottles were delivered. As she noted in our diary, *"If you can't take a joke....!"*

Sometimes, we found ourselves without electricity or gas and had to resort to cooking with charcoal, using a Sudanese 'barbecue', known as a *mangat.* Made from an old kerosene container, this resembled a large biscuit tin with perforations around its sides and a loosely woven tin mesh across the top to provide a cooking surface. It was very efficient, but had to be used outdoors. Once there was an absolute dearth of power or fuel of any sort; no electricity, no gas and no charcoal. I had to go and forage for rubbish in the streets to fuel our *mangat.* This incident drove home to all of us just how tough it was for many people to survive in Khartoum on a daily basis. Our 'crisis' had lasted only a few hours, straddling a single evening meal.

Petrol was not expensive – about 50 pence a gallon when we arrived in 1980, rising to about 80 pence by the time we left in 1982. It was, however, of very poor quality and very scarce. When it was available, taxis were allowed three gallons per day and private cars between three to five gallons every three days, depending on engine size. The entitlement for our Land Rover was five gallons every three days.

Obtaining petrol was quite an operation and usually involved waiting hours in a queue. It was therefore prudent to go armed with a thermos of water and a book, or, if unclassified, work-related material. A two-hour wait in a petrol queue would be considered normal, but on at least two occasions I spent nine hours in a queue; in one of these instances the pumps ran dry while filling up the car immediately ahead of me, severely testing my patience. Sometimes we had to wait over 48 hours before being served. During such times, we would leave our car in the queue overnight and take turns sitting in it during the day (when petrol was really in short supply, queuing for it took precedence over work).

On the rare occasions when petrol was reasonably plentiful, the petrol attendants sometimes agreed to fill your tank to capacity. We would then siphon off as much as possible into the 40 gallon drum and spare jerrycans we all kept in our garages and then try to fill up again three days later. This enabled us to store fuel to cater for prolonged 'petrol famines', as well as for recreational trips into the desert and to run the team's ski boat – a recreational facility provided by the Nuffield Trust to mitigate the testing conditions under which we lived. The longest period we experienced without being able to buy petrol was six weeks.

Apparently, during a prolonged period without fuel some four years earlier, the BAAT Commander at the time, then Colonel Peter de la Billière, got on a bicycle and cycled all over Khartoum in the searing heat visiting every member of the team to see how they were coping. The Sudanese were hugely impressed by this and still sang his praises.

Another phenomenon we had to get used to were the *haboobs,* or dust storms, that used to envelop Khartoum on a regular basis throughout the hot summer months, coating everything with a thick layer of dust. The first indication of an approaching *haboob* was seeing a 'mountain' on the horizon where no mountain existed. If you had time, this was when you tried to seal every window and door from the impending storm. When it arrived, visibility was cut to a few yards and, during the day, the sky took on an intense, flame-orange hue, transforming one's world into a weird, alien environment.

On one occasion, a group of us were caught in a *haboob* just before nightfall when camping on the banks of the Nile. We were eating supper and I just had time to lash our canvas awning to the side of the Land Rover to form a windbreak. However, we were unable to clear up before the storm struck. We put our two young daughters to bed inside the Land Rover, while we and the boys slept outside behind the windbreak. We spent a restless night with the *haboob* raging almost until dawn, but awoke to a bright new day. Our campsite had been transformed. Everything, including ourselves, was covered in a thick mantle of fine sand. Most of the smaller items of equipment, such as plates, cutlery, our torches and, crucially, my Silva compass, were lost and all our food had been spoilt by sand. After a quick brew, we all cut our losses and returned home.

Anyone reading this account could be forgiven for thinking that life in Khartoum was unbearably miserable. Certainly it was challenging, but once we were 'conditioned', we all took it in our stride, and the friendships forged through the relative adversity of this experience have proved to be enduring. When conditions are generally harsh, the benefits of any 'positives' are magnified tenfold; and we had several of these experiences. First and foremost among these were the people themselves. They were wonderfully friendly and hospitable. Early on in my tour, I remember going round to complain about the noise coming from a neighbour's house late one night. I was met at the door by an enormous Sudanese, who gave me the warmest of welcomes and insisted I join the party – a wedding celebration! I did not have the heart to say why I had called, but instead stayed long enough not to cause offence and then meekly made my way home. In a land full of hardship, the Sudanese still found cause to party and everyone was welcome.

Another plus was that we had a considerable amount of help in the house. Salbatori was our official cook-come-cleaner. He had been employed for seven years by BATT to support the Armoured Advisor. With Toni and I both working and because so much time was spent queuing for everything in the souk, not to mention cleaning the house after every *haboob*, we felt the workload was too much for one person. We therefore took on Gedaye, an Eritrean refugee, to do the washing and ironing, and to assist Salbatori in cleaning the house. She also used to baby-sit for us. We shared a gardener, Ibrahim, with three other families, and were also assigned a night watchman (known as a *gaffier* in Sudan) called Yussef to protect us at night.

Salbatori was a southerner. A very hard and willing worker, he was small, dark-skinned and blessed with a charming manner. We were surprised when he did not arrive for work one morning, but we had to go off to school and work before we could determine what had happened. When Toni and the children returned from school that afternoon, there was Salbatori. The poor man was in a bad way, having been hit by an army lorry and a car while cycling into work that morning. He had spent eight hours being checked out in hospital and questioned by the police. We had paid Salbatori his week's wages the day before, and when he was found to be in possession of a relatively large sum of money, the police became suspicious and confiscated the money, along with his bicycle and his keys. At the hospital he had been x-rayed, given a prescription for medication and told to go home. No attempt had been made to clean the dreadful grazes and cuts he had suffered and so Toni bathed these herself.

When I arrived home, Toni met me at our gate to tell me what had happened. My army driver agreed to accompany Salbatori and me to the police station to assist me in clearing Salbatori's name and reclaiming his possessions. The policeman on duty could not have been less helpful; southerners counted for nothing in northern Sudan. I was glad that I was in uniform and accompanied by a Sudanese soldier, as things became very heated before I finally got my way.

We would have preferred to look after Salbatori at home, but quite understandably, he wanted to return to his family. I was quite appalled to find that he lived in a slum on the outskirts of Khartoum, where hundreds of people lived cheek by jowl in shelters made from scraps of corrugated iron sheeting, cardboard, plastic sheeting – anything they could lay their hands on. There was no sanitation and no running water and the narrow paths between the countless shacks were running open sewers. This was my first experience of a real slum and it shook me. But to Salbatori this was home and this is where he wanted to be. We visited him on a number of occasions during his convalescence. It was three weeks before he was well enough to return to work.

Salbatori had never been out of Khartoum before and told us that he would like to see the desert. So one weekend we took him camping a few miles from the city, arriving just in time to make camp and have a meal before nightfall. When we awoke next morning we noticed Salbatori standing on his own staring at the horizon and so we went to see if all was well. He was captivated by the bleakness, the wide open spaces and the silence. All he could say was "No people! Where the trees?"

Gedaye was a gem and the children loved her. She had been a refugee in Sudan for 25 years and, in addition to working for us, worked as a volunteer in the Eritrean Office for Refugees in Khartoum. After about six months, the demands of her dual responsibilities started to take their toll, particularly when she was covering for Salbatori following his accident. She became more and more exhausted and we began to be concerned for her health. Eventually, she told Toni that her heart was in helping her Eritrean countrymen and so she wanted to stop working for us. She did, however, promise to find us a replacement.

And so Olga came into our lives. Wonderfully wide about the hips and missing an eye, her appearance confirmed her reputation as something of a tartar. When she was baby-sitting, she used to carry a thin little stick and woe betides anyone who dared get out of bed to go to the loo! Indeed, we had to ban her from using the stick when we learnt that she used to rap the children on the back of their legs to maintain order! An Ethiopian

Coptic Christian, she was dubbed 'Olga the Ogress' by the children, who nevertheless all took to her.

The only person who really let us down was Yussef, the night watchman. About three months after our arrival he was joined by a much younger man whom, he said, was his son. The idea was for them to share the night watchman's duties and the attendant salary. A few days later, I got out of bed on the balcony during the night and was surprised to see all our holdalls and Toni's handbags strewn about the bathroom floor. A quick check confirmed my worst fears – we had been burgled. Among the items stolen was our shortwave radio – our link with the outside world – as well as Toni's engagement ring, which she had taken off to play tennis the previous evening, and the beautiful gold filigree bracelet from Sharjah that I had given her as a wedding present.

Having roused Toni, I went out to see Yussef, who was sleeping soundly outside our garden gate. There was no sign of his 'son' and he never did return. We got the distinct impression that he and Yussef were in league with one another. To add to our woes, when Toni went to take the children off to school, she found the Land Rover had a flat tyre. It was 3 November 1980, my fortieth birthday!

The police came next day, but any confidence I had in them evaporated when they told me that it was too windy to take fingerprints. We never did recover any of the stolen items.

Barely four weeks later, we were invited out to supper at short notice. Gedaye was unavailable, but Salbatori kindly agreed to baby-sit for us. Because he had to be up early next morning to prepare breakfast, we agreed that he could go to bed, provided he slept on the balcony outside the children's rooms, rather than in his own room downstairs at the back of the house.

When we arrived home we were met by a very agitated Salbatori, shouting, "*Harami, Harami*" ('Thief, thief' in Sudanese Arabic) at the top of his voice. It transpired that he had fought off two burglars single-handedly after they climbed up onto the balcony. In the scuffle, the intruders leapt off the balcony and fell through the roof of the covered way below, but got away. A Sudanese girl next door heard the commotion and called the police, whilst Salbatori went to find Yussef. Needless to say, he was sitting outside our garden gate fast asleep. Of course, he had seen and heard nothing, so next day we parted company. Naturally, we were not going to tell the children what had happened, but we were amused by their reaction at breakfast next morning. Alex, our eldest, and five days short of his tenth birthday, spoke for them all when he said: "We all like Salbatori, but we don't want him to baby-sit again, because he has some very noisy friends!"

We replaced Yussef with Abdul, another Eritrean refugee. He was a very sincere man, but could be absolutely maddening at times. He told me that he had some mechanical experience and could help look after the Land Rover. However, on our first joint maintenance check, I had to caution him for smoking whilst I was putting fuel into the vehicle, whereupon he flicked the ash towards the fuel intake, which was still open. Later, I was just in time to stop him topping up the battery levels with petrol! After that, we agreed that it was best if he left the vehicle alone.

In terms of the facilities in town, the Sudan Club, set in the heart of Khartoum, was a real 'oasis'. Here you could get a meal, sip a cool beer or limoon, have a swim and sit in the shade on the lush green lawn. We spent most of our afternoons there. There were also three hotels that offered a measure of luxury. The Grand Hotel on Nile Avenue was a relic from the days when the British were in Sudan. We used to go there in the early evening and sit on the terrace sipping limoons, while watching the egrets coming home to roost in the trees outside. The Hilton and The Friendship Palace were modern, luxury hotels, and we used to treat ourselves to breakfast at one of them on a Friday – my day off – about once every two months.

Another huge bonus was the BATT ski boat, fuel and engine serviceability permitting. This was moored at the Sudan Yacht Club on the Blue Nile. The clubhouse was actually the *Melik*, one of the British gunboats that saw action at the Battle of Omdurman on 2 September 1898. We used to take the ski boat up to the Green Village, a mile or two upstream from Khartoum. There was no village here, nor any greenery, just a deserted sandy beach where young children could play in safety. It was also an ideal spot for skiing. But you shared the water with some pretty impressive monitor lizards, themselves an attraction when basking on the rocks on the opposite bank. Another wonderful sight was the colony of weaver birds in the acacias overhanging these rocks; their brilliant yellow bodies and shiny black heads in marked contrast to the drab, dusty grey/green of the trees.

All our children went to the English-run primary school, Clergy House. Due to staff shortages, Toni was seconded as a teacher for the top class, Class 6, and found herself teaching Alex. The school occupied a grand old house in Khartoum quite close to where we lived. It had a large garden with some mature trees, which made an excellent, albeit dusty, playground with plenty of shade. Unfortunately, the lease on this building expired in early 1982 and was not renewable, so Clergy House closed down on 26 February 1982 and opened as Khartoum International Primary School (KIPS) in new buildings three days later on, 1 March. As interested parents, we lent a hand in moving all the furniture from Clergy House into the new school.

KIPS was situated beside Khartoum International Airport's runway in the midst of the desert, without any shade and nothing but scorching hot sand for a playground. It also lacked an access road, which meant that in the rains you needed a 4x4 vehicle to get to it. Luckily, our daughters,

Hannah and Zoë (and, of course, Toni), only had to endure its blisteringly hot conditions for three months. Our time in Khartoum came to an end before the infrastructure needed to support the school in the long term had been put in place.

We knew all along that our two sons, Alex and Rorie, would have to return to school in England after our first year in the Sudan. They joined Worth School in East Sussex in September 1981, so finishing their schooling in Sudan without having to endure the rigours of KIPS.

Certainly the departure of the boys dampened our spirits and I could understand why my mother said that 'the magic had gone out of her life in India' when her children left for school in England. At least our boys were able to rejoin us for all the school holidays, which made things a little easier.

The British Army Training Team (BATT) had taken over from the Soviets a few years earlier. Most BATT members, or Batmen as we were known, were employed as directing staff or team administrators at the Sudanese Command and Staff College in Omdurman. One or two of us, however, were posted as advisers to our particular Arms' Schools. I was our sole representative at the Sudanese Armoured Corps School at Shajara, about five miles south of Khartoum. Shajara means 'tree' in Arabic, but if it was still there, I did not see it.

My office was at the end of a single-storey office block bordering the tank park. The office was equipped with a desk and a chair and, most importantly, an air cooler; an absolute godsend when the electricity was on. There was a small opening in the wall next to the tank park, protected by wooden shutters. This allowed light to pour into the room when the shutters were open, as well as sand, of course.

The other offices in the block were occupied by my support team of three

English-speaking southern Sudanese soldiers: Sergeant Constantino, the Chief Clerk, and Privates Albino and King Henry. They were a marvellous team – Sergeant Constantino was an excellent Chief Clerk, serious and efficient, while the two youngsters could be infuriatingly inefficient at times, but they meant well and were always full of fun. After returning from his annual leave towards the end of my tour in the Sudan, King Henry burst into my office brandishing a spear and went into hysterics as I leapt up to defend myself. He then sprang to attention, saluted and handed me the spear, plus two others, and a serval skin – his tribal costume – so that I would remember him "when you go home to Ingerland".

When I got home that afternoon, I was pressed upon to dress up in the serval skin and pose, spear in hand, for my family and some friends who had dropped in. Unfortunately, the serval skin fell victim to moths some years later, but the spears still adorn a wall in my study and are a happy reminder of Private King Henry and our time in the Sudan.

As NATO and the Warsaw Pact were still locked in the Cold War, I found it strange to be working almost exclusively with Soviet armoured equipment. Sudan's main battle tank (MBT) was the Russian T55, and almost all the wheeled armoured vehicles were from the Soviet Union. We also had a number of Chinese T62 tanks, a smaller and much lighter copy of the T55, plus a handful of French Panhard armoured cars, which had a tendency to flip over if the main armament was fired broadside. The only British vehicles were some Daimler Ferret Scout Cars, the most reliable of the wheeled vehicles.

I was impressed at the reliability of the poorly maintained T55 and T62 tanks. However, this admiration was matched only by my apprehension when operating in them on live-firing exercises. The main armament ammunition was stowed on the inside of the turret wall all around one's head and, in the heat of the desert, became almost too hot to handle. I found this unnerving; how stable was the ammunition at such temperatures, I wondered? I had been used to tanks in which the ammunition is stowed out of the way below the turret ring; a much safer option.

While in barracks, the working day was from 6.00 a.m. to 2.00 p.m., and we worked a six-day week, Saturday to Thursday, with Friday being our day off. As a Catholic, I was keen to go to Mass on Sundays. This was never an issue with my Sudanese colleagues. On the contrary, they insisted that I attend Mass before coming to work on Sundays, saying: "It is important for all of us to practise our religion."

The army Land Rover taking me to and from work would arrive at any time between 5:30 a.m. and 7:30 a.m., meaning that I had to get up at 5.00 a.m. Breakfast at the camp was at 9.00 a.m. and, as a rule, I would return home about 2:30 p.m. for a late lunch. I usually took a Marmite sandwich and cold water to work with me for breakfast, but quite often was invited to join the Sudanese for breakfast in the headquarters mess.

The table would be laden with Sudanese delicacies and I used to stick to the things I could recognise: beans, usually swimming in oil, and small pieces of meat and fish, that we ate with our hands. One breakfast, however, was a special one in the Commandant's house in Omdurman, to celebrate the birth of his daughter. Here the usual breakfast fare was set before us, but with one frightening addition, a large bowl of Sudanese delicacies. The only ingredient I could recognise was sliced raw onion in the purple-pink mixture which also contained white semi-cylindrical chunks that resembled sea anemones.

As the only non-Sudanese in the gathering, I was made guest of honour and the Commandant accorded me the privilege of sampling the 'mystery' bowl first. I took what I thought was a marshmallow and an onion ring. As I bit into the 'marshmallow' it exuded air with a faint hiss. Next, I tried the white 'sea anemone', which was really rubbery and tasteless, and took an awful lot of chewing before I could get it down. After that I tried to ensure that my plate was laden with 'normal' breakfast fare, but the 'mystery' dish came my way at regular intervals and I was not allowed to pass it on without first savouring its contents.

On the way home, I asked Lieutenant Colonel Omar, my Sudanese opposite number at the Armoured School, what was in the special dish. When he told me that it was raw sheep's liver, lungs and small intestine my stomach did a double somersault! To cap my day, Toni had prepared a special treat for lunch. Her diary note reads:

> *With perfect timing, I had chosen liver and onions for lunch and he just couldn't face it!!!*

My main role at the Armoured School was to update or write training manuals, pamphlets and courses, which the clerks would type up. I would then take these to Colonel Omar in the adjacent office block to be translated into Arabic for use in the school. In addition, I would occasionally be asked to write and deliver a three- to five-day course in English for middle-ranking officers – senior captains and majors – to prepare them, for example, for the Command and Staff College entrance exam.

It was in the Armoured School that I got my first taste of local politics. Junior officers were required to pass the Troop Leader's course before they became eligible for promotion to the rank of captain. All instruction in the school was in Arabic. This placed the southern Sudanese officers at a disadvantage as most had only a limited grasp of Arabic, English being the common 'foreign' language in the South. Sudan had only recently emerged from a civil war between the largely Arab, Muslim North and the African, largely Christian South. One day two young southern Sudanese officers approached me. Both had been former rebels in the civil war. They said that they were having problems understanding both the courseware and instruction on their all-important Troop Leader's course, as they were not Arab speakers.

Naively, I gave them English versions of the relevant pamphlets. Next day the General commanding the Armoured Corps called me to his office and told me that it was army policy that all instruction in the various training schools, both written and spoken, was to be conducted in Arabic. After all, it was quite possible that southern officers might find themselves commanding Arab speaking soldiers, he explained. I took the point, but said that if the southern officers and soldiers felt penalised it could well trigger another civil war. The General responded by saying, "Bruce, don't get involved with politics", and that was the end of the matter. Two years later, Colonel John Gurang, a southerner, reignited the civil war.

When I deployed for the first time on an armoured exercise, we worked well from first light until about 10.00 a.m., and then formed a leaguer to await the arrival of breakfast/lunch. I imagined that we would soon be tucking into a meal prepared in barracks, but when the truck arrived, I was surprised to discover that our rations comprised two live goats and a sack of rice! The soldiers displayed remarkable skill and efficiency in slaughtering, skinning, butchering and cooking these animals and the resultant meal was delicious. But this all took some time!

Two high profile events marked out my time as the armoured adviser. The first of these was the Armoured Corps Day celebrations on 31 January 1981, at which President Nimeiri was the guest of honour. I had put forward a series of activities for consideration, expecting one or, at the most, two to be selected. I was hoist by my own petard, however, when they were all accepted. Accordingly, I was required to lay on an equipment display, a tank obstacle course, build a 3-D scaled sand table of an actual piece of ground for use on indoor training exercises and conduct a musical ride with Ferret Scout Cars *à la* Royal Tournament.

The musical ride proved to be the biggest challenge. Nothing like this had ever been seen before in the Sudan. We had to overcome some considerable hurdles concerning fuel shortages and vehicle serviceability in addition to observing tribal sensibilities when selecting the team. We also had to prepare a suitable piece of desert in which to conduct the display. By dint of hard work, determination and enormous good luck we pulled it off. The following extracts from the diary I kept at the time sum up the atmosphere of the day:

> *The musical ride was magnificent and the crews certainly had kept their best performance for the Day. Once the crowd got over the shock of seeing the first crossover, they went wild, whooping their appreciation at every manoeuvre and giving the team a standing ovation at the end. Senior officers had tears of pride in their eyes. I tried to get through the throng to congratulate the team, but was unable to do so because of the numerous well-wishers from Private soldiers to Brigadiers who all came up to hug and kiss me.*
>
> *The soldiers, their tails well and truly up, now raced across to the next stand – the tank obstacle course. Many rode on vehicles, including the Ferrets that had just completed their display, but the majority of them actually ran round the three-kilometre course, keeping pace with the tanks. Toni and the children were ushered into a Land Rover and, at one point, found themselves travelling abreast of the President.*

Toni and the children were then greatly honoured by being invited to the strictly all male celebratory breakfast, while I went to check on the next two stands. Unfortunately, as they made their way to breakfast they passed right by the ceremonial killing of a cow at the very moment the deed was being performed. Toni shielded the girls from the scene, but the boys saw it all, which naturally put them off their breakfast – a fact spotted by President Nimeiri, who passed a note down to Toni to tell the boys to eat up!

The equipment display after breakfast went well, as did my presentation to a select military audience in the grandly-named Combat Decisions Room, with the sand table. This faithfully represented a 3.5 square-mile piece of ground near Kassala (subsequently doubled in area) and had taken six weeks to make. Being made to scale meant that it could be used to give accurate grid references and make and execute proper tactical plans, using model vehicles. It was also wired up so that users communicated by radio, as if they were in their vehicles. So all in all, this was an excellent, cost-effective training aid. Imagine my dismay when, some six months later, I saw a heap of coloured sand outside the room and discovered that my model had been destroyed, on the orders of the School Commandant, because the room was required for a meeting. When I registered my protest, I was told that I could remake the model next day, as the meeting would not take long! One had to get used to frustrations such as this and adopt the Sudanese approach of saying *"ma'a leish"* – it doesn't matter – and move on.

The second event that defined my time with the Sudanese Armoured Corps was when we were required to stage a mounted parade of our vehicles down Nile Avenue in the centre of Khartoum as our contribution to Armed Forces Day on 25 May 1981. The occasion coincided with an official visit by President Sadat of Egypt, who was to be the guest of honour at the parade.

The Sudanese wanted to put every serviceable armoured vehicle on parade. I had reservations about this. If a tank broke down on the route, it could, at worst, disrupt the parade and at best leave a gap in the ranks. I suggested placing a number of recovery vehicles and tanks in reserve at strategic points along the route out of sight of the saluting dais. My suggestion was dismissed; it was to be all vehicles on parade. We must put our faith in Allah, I was told, and not show doubt by deploying reserves.

The Armoured School looked after me particularly well on the day, inviting not only me but all the family and allocating us seats in the stand reserved for senior Sudanese officers, right next to the saluting dais. We felt a little self-conscious because all the Ambassadors and other dignitaries were seated behind us! The following extract from my diary gives the flavour of the occasion:

At the appointed hour of 7.30 a.m., a huge cavalcade of police cars and motorcycle outriders, sirens blaring, heralded the arrival of President Nimeiri and his guest, President Sadat. Then the fun began; for the next two hours we were really entertained. Contingents from all elements of the Armed Forces, plus the Police, Prison Service and Civil Defence, headed by the Royal Guard, marched past. The Physical Training Corps then put on an impressive Kung Fu display, with a terrific vocal accompaniment that must have been little different from the war cries of the Khalifa's Army at the Battle of Omdurman. Interspersed with the marching troops there were several flypasts by Air Force jets, transport aircraft and helicopters. One flight of eight helicopters each carried a girl dangling from a rope and waving to the crowd. Another helicopter and, quite separately, two fighter aircraft put on impressive aerobatic displays. In the interval between these displays, mortars on the opposite bank of the Nile fired 'bombs' into the air that exploded at about 500 feet to deploy the Sudanese flag and flags bearing the picture of President Nimeiri.

This was followed by the Armoured Corps' mounted parade, comprising in excess of 100 vehicles, including tanks, armoured cars, Scout Cars and recovery vehicles from America, Britain, China, Czechoslovakia, France and Russia. They were all beautifully turned out and thundered by the saluting dais in perfect order. Bringing up the rear of the parade were motorised floats representing all the regions of Sudan as well as the country's industries. We were greatly impressed and I cannot but feel that President Sadat was too.

Because my advice concerning vehicle breakdowns had been summarily dismissed, I attended the parade with fingers crossed. However, as can be seen from our diary account above, Allah certainly smiled upon us that day.

Less than five months later, President Sadat was assassinated while taking the salute at a military parade in Egypt, marking the eighth anniversary of the Yom Kippur war with Israel. What a tragedy this was, not just for President Sadat's family and Egypt, but for the prospects for lasting peace throughout the troubled Middle East.

When I was there, Sudan was the largest country in Africa and arguably the most diverse geographically, ranging from the Sahara desert in the north, through bush and swamp in the centre to tropical forests in the south. It was not the sort of place to waste time luxuriating in the artificial, air-conditioned world of the Hilton or Friendship Palace hotels in Khartoum; there was far too much to see. There was also the time and opportunity, because Sudan celebrated all the Muslim and major Christian festivals. So we seized every chance to explore as much as we could of this fascinating country.

The largely unspoilt battlefield of Omdurman (known as Kerreri to the Sudanese) lay on our doorstep. As a family, we visited it on numerous occasions, spending hours walking over the ground where the major actions had taken place and picking up pieces of shrapnel, which were constantly being unearthed by the shifting sands. Once, when I was there on my own, I was approached by an old man riding a donkey. At the time I was looking at the memorial to the 21st Lancers in the *khor* (dry river bed) in which many of their number had been hacked to pieces by the Hadendower tribesmen, led by Osman Digna, arguably the Kalifa's most able general.

When I told my new companion that I was learning about the battle, he said that his father had taken part in this particular action. He then led me to where his father had stood and fought during the 21st Lancers' charge. He had been taken there many times as a small boy. I was both amazed and thrilled to meet somebody with such a personal, direct link with the battle.

I became sufficiently knowledgeable about Omdurman to give talks on it in the Staff College and Armoured School and also to help in setting the military history paper for the Command and Staff College entrance exam in 1982. I was also fortunate enough to find an old Hadendowa sword tucked away behind some sacks of grain in the Omdurman souk. It was beautifully engraved in Arabic with the words, *'If Allah is with us, who can stand against us'*, sentiments that also appear in the Bible. It bears the Muslim calendar date 1240 (about 1825) and thus, in all probability, was used in the battle. The vendor was happy to sell it to me, especially as its scabbard had almost totally rotted away. It cost far less than the newer, stronger swords fashioned from old vehicle leaf springs that he had for sale.

Hugh Leach, who had inspired me to volunteer to go to Brunei on loan service, was now in the Foreign Office and, as luck would have it, working at the British Embassy in Khartoum. He had rented a farm on the banks of the Blue Nile at Butri, about an hour's drive south of the city and kindly invited us there on a number of occasions. We loved Butri, especially sleeping outside at night, when the breeze wafting over us was cooled by the waters of the Nile. Hugh was something of an eccentric and used to sound Last Post and Reveille at the appropriate times, standing on the river bank dressed in his white dishdasha.

Many of the attractions, such as the Sabaloka Gorge – the Sixth Cataract on the Nile – and the dam at Jebel Auliya on the White Nile, were within a couple of hours' drive into the desert from Khartoum. We would visit one or other of these places of interest, or would simply relax in the desert about once a month, spending the night under the stars – we never used a tent. Almost invariably we teamed up with other BATT families, as it was unwise to venture deep into the desert on one's own.

The amount of planning and preparation needed for one of these trips was considerable. First, it was necessary to collect enough fuel for the vehicles. As mentioned earlier, this was an ongoing task throughout our tour, and we all became adept at siphoning petrol from our vehicles to maintain reserve stocks at home.

About a week before setting out we would make ice and store it in the freezer and would also freeze plastic containers of water. On the day before departure, Toni prepared the first day's lunchtime picnic and the evening meal. We always took watermelons to give us extra fluid – these were really cool and refreshing, even on the third day of a trip. Finally, there was the camping gear and our personal kit to prepare – no small task with four youngsters to cater for. Just before setting out, we filled *charguls* with more drinking water. I first came across *charguls* in Sharjah, where they were standard army issue. They are small water containers made of canvas coated with wax. Just enough water seeps through the canvas to evaporate on the outer surface, thereby cooling the water within. We slung the *charguls* on our vehicles' wing mirrors as our ready drinking water supply.

One of our longer trips took place over the Easter weekend of 16-18 April 1981. Four BATT families accompanied Phillip Gordon, an expatriate budding tour guide, on an expedition to Meroe, situated on the east bank of the Nile between Shendi and Atbara, about 100 miles into the Sahara, north of Khartoum. For the first 30 miles we had the benefit of a pot-holed black top road, but thereafter it was into the sand.

The Kushite sites in and around Meroe date back to 200-300 BC. One of the attractions at Meroe itself was the enormous ruined temple, complete with the king's and queen's thrones, a sacrificial altar with runnels to drain away the blood, and a slab of stone covered in Meroitic hieroglyphics, that, at that time at least, had yet to be deciphered. In one particular spot, you could see ancient tiled flooring some six inches below the sand.

The main attraction, however, were the pyramids nearby. Numbering about 20, these were all much smaller than the famous pyramids at Giza, the largest standing only about 50 feet high. The larger pyramids housed the remains of the kings and queens and stood atop two low hills, giving them a commanding view of the surrounding flat desert landscape. The remaining pyramids at the base of these hills housed the remains of ministers and other important dignitaries.

Sadly, the top third of every pyramid had been destroyed, the rubble lying around the base of each of them. The blame for this act of vandalism is thought to rest with an Italian adventurer, Guiseppe Ferlini. One account claims that he actually did discover treasure – gold and jewellery – in the apex of a pyramid in Meroe in 1834. Another account, however, states that he suspected that the pyramids held hidden treasure and so he planted some in one of the pyramids and, after 'finding' it, encouraged others to help him look for more. Whichever account is true, after Ferlini 'struck gold' no further treasure has ever been discovered in Meroe.

We made camp amongst the pyramids and went to sleep under a star-studded sky. Next morning, we awoke to find that we were being observed at a respectable distance by some bedouin. Once we were up and about they moved in to sell us beautifully made local food covers and bowls made of straw. We spent the first part of the morning exploring the pyramids and the surrounding area, during which time we spotted two caves in a nearby *jebel* (mountain in Arabic). These turned out to be the ancient quarries from whence the stone for the pyramids and temple had been hewn. It was fascinating to see the marks left by the chisels more than

2,000 years before.

Mid-morning saw us grinding our way through the sand looking for the ruins of Musarurarat to the south of Shendi. Here, the Lion Temple had been beautifully restored in recent years, apparently by a German archaeologist. It had some marvellous Egyptian-style wall carvings of gods, kings, queens and, to our surprise, elephants – an indication that this area of barren desert was once forested. Nearby, there was another very large temple, with numerous elephant carvings and also an enormous walled courtyard with ramped walkways, which some archaeologists believe was used as an elephant training arena. We made camp here for the night.

Next day we headed further south for the settlement of Naga. Here, a well, which we were told was over 200 feet deep, gave succour to a few hardy desert dwellers and their livestock. The wellhead, which was unprotected, was at the top of a shallow man-made dome. Camels and donkeys were used to draw the water from the well by walking down the slope from the wellhead, pulling ropes made from strands of leather to which leather buckets were attached. At the wellhead, people tipped the water down runnels into numerous troughs from which camels, donkeys, goats, sheep and cattle quenched their thirst. Looking around, we could see animals making their way out of the surrounding desert from all points of the compass to drink at this veritable fountain of life.

Nearby, there was a very small, picturesque ruined temple known as the Kiosk. Displaying both Greco-Roman and Egyptian architectural styles, it featured on the back of the Sudanese one pound note. A few yards away stood another temple, similar in style to the temple at Meroe.

Our route back to Khartoum took us through an area of desert littered with petrified wood. In places we could identify complete trees, lying on the ground. There were examples of hardwood trees as well as palm trees – evidence that this area was once verdant woodland and even a little marshy.

On one of the Muslim Eids we teamed up with the Whites (Mike was the BATT adviser at the Infantry School) to visit Kassala on the Ethiopian border. We had the option of driving in a huge loop of several hundred miles on the black top road, or braving the track across the desert shown on our maps – a distance of less than 200 miles. We chose the latter, but to our dismay the track disappeared about 20 miles east of Khartoum.

Before going to Sudan, I had bought a vehicle-mounted compass in an antique shop in Fowey, Cornwall. Apparently, it had originally been fitted to a Second Word War German Afrika Korps artillery piece in the Western Desert, but was now mounted on top of the dashboard in my Land Rover a little further south in that same desert. Mike and I both carried hand-held compasses as well. After a short discussion, we agreed to drive on a compass bearing towards a very prominent mountain on our route, Jebel Qeili, about 120 miles away!

This done, we set off over the horizon, passing through dry grasslands and stony desert and some enormous waterholes, where goats, sheep, cattle, donkeys and camels gathered in their hundreds. We had to make a detour to cross the Atbara River and by mid-afternoon had reached an area of abandoned cultivation that appeared to stretch for miles in all directions. Our bearing took us across the grain of this hard, broken ground and the going soon became almost impossible for our Land Rovers. Just as we were about to call a halt, we saw the faintest of outlines of Jebel Qeili on the horizon. We therefore decided to drive north following the lie of the land, but keeping Jebel Qeili in view to try and escape this impassable area. Our luck was in; within three miles we came across a well-worn track that took us straight to Jebel Qeili and beyond.

It was now about 5.00 p.m. and we had barely an hour's daylight left. We were still some distance from Kassala, so would have to camp out in the desert. However, we were in the most desolate of areas, the ground was as flat as a pancake for as far as the eye could see. The surface was hard earth, rather than sand, with small patches of short coarse grass. There was nothing for it; we turned off the track for about 200 yards (we did not want to be mown down by a souk lorry in the middle of the night) and set up camp. It was our 11th wedding anniversary, and Mike and Anne had kindly brought along a bottle of wine to celebrate!

The night was bitterly cold and we were all up with the sun at 5.30 a.m. Our two boys, Alex and Rorie, went off on what is known as a 'shovel recce' in the army, but our girls and Felicity White kept yelling out mischievously, "We can still see you!" Indeed, they could; there was not the slightest fold in the ground or bush to afford the barest modicum of privacy. It was just as well that we were all good friends!

We set out after breakfast and within a couple of hours could see the extraordinary outline of the Taka *jebels* at Kassala. It was as if a giant had picked up a dozen or so gigantic, smooth pebbles and placed them on end side-by-side in the sand. No one would try to portray mountain scenery in this way; it looked so alien, so unearthly.

We stayed three nights in Kassala, basing ourselves at the government rest house. We were looked after royally by the Provincial Governor, the Army Commander and the Commissioner of Police. The latter even provided a police car and two escorting officers to give us a day-long tour of Kassala – the Sudanese always went out of their way to be hospitable to strangers. When the time came to leave, we decided not to press our luck and returned to Khartoum via the much longer black top route.

Later on in our tour, we, together with the Whites, retraced our steps along this rather boring road to Kassala and then pushed on a further 180 miles or so to the village of Erkowit in the Red Sea Hills. At an elevation of over 3,000 feet it enjoys an almost Mediterranean climate and was a much favoured resort by the British during the time when Sudan was an Anglo-Egyptian Condominium (1898/9-1956).

We based ourselves nearby at the Sudanese Infantry Training Wing at Gebeit, a former British Army camp. The surrounding *jebels* were decorated with the badges of numerous Regiments that had been stationed there in the past, including the Scots Guards, Ox and Bucks, and South Staffords. Some Sudanese Regiments had carried on the tradition, making this a living memorial. We spent a night on the coast visiting the deserted town of Suakin, where we certainly needed our sunglasses. All the buildings were made entirely of coral, the brilliant white glare from which was quite dazzling. The coastline beyond Suakin was rugged and absolutely deserted and could have seen very few visitors in the quarter of a century or so since the British left the area.

We camped on the beach in a sheltered cove and spent two days snorkelling in the calm waters of a coral reef. The marine life in this part of the Red Sea was quite outstanding; fish of all hues, shapes and sizes, and the various corals, sea anemones and giant clams all seemed to be vying with each other for the prize of being the most beautiful exhibit in the sea. The result was an unbelievable kaleidoscope of colour in the silent world below the crystal clear waters of the reef.

Once or twice we broke the rule about taking a minimum of two vehicles into the desert, but only when we knew we were travelling on well-used routes and having left our itinerary and timings with friends. One such trip was to the oasis of Umm Inderaba, some 70 or so miles west of Khartoum. At about the midway point, Qoz Abu Dula challenged the traveller. This was an enormous, low sand dune, over three miles wide in places and running north to south for about 100 miles. Our Land Rover was well equipped, including sand trays and an inflatable jack, which could be used effectively in loose sand to deal with punctures. Nevertheless, the journey across the dune on a compass bearing was quite tough and the engine was overheating badly by the time we were through to the other side, forcing us to stop and make camp well short of our objective. We had not met another vehicle all day!

In the morning, we were reassured to see a number of souk lorries grinding their way across the barren landscape barely half a mile north of us in the direction of Khartoum. Help was at hand after all if we needed it.

We breakfasted on bacon and baked beans and were on our way again by 8.00 a.m. Gradually, the desert began to take on a greener look, and we began to see more and more bushes and trees on the horizon. We were now passing by groups of sheep, goats, donkeys and camels, all heading in the same direction as ourselves. Here and there, scattered amongst the bushes, we spotted mud dwellings protected by thorn bush *zaribas* (barriers) to prevent the goats from eating their straw roofs.

A little further on in the midst of some trees were small buildings, including a little white mosque, its minaret rising defiantly above the trees. This was Umm Inderaba. Dotted amongst the trees were little centres of industry, including blacksmiths, carpenters and charcoal sellers, as well as literally hundreds if not thousands of animals – sheep, goats, donkeys, camels and cows.

Having no surface water, this was unlike any oasis we had seen before. However, the numerous wells were evidence that just ten or so feet below the sand there was water aplenty. Umm Inderaba was a thriving little community deep in the Sahara. The locals had not seen many *hawajas*, meaning teachers – the word by which all white people were known in Sudan – and they made us very welcome. I was invited by some of the village elders to take a glass of tea under the baobab tree near the mosque, while Toni and the children were joined by some of the women and their youngsters.

All too soon we had to be on our way back to Khartoum. We elected to take a more southerly route, which took us to the dam on the White Nile at Jebel Auliya and then along the black top road back to Khartoum. Quite apart from taking in the dam at Jebel Auliya, Qoz Abu Dula was narrower at this point. Even so it proved quite difficult to cross. The movement of the vehicle, as it swayed from side to side and pitched to and fro, was not unlike that of a small boat in a choppy sea.

On reaching Jebel Auliya we were safely out of the sand. With Khartoum only a few miles north along the black top road, we could now afford to relax a little and watch the fisherman at work around the lake behind the dam. Some were in boats, while others stood on the dam wall or around the lake shore. They used various methods to catch fish – rod and line, and circular nets, which were cast out to form a graceful ring as they struck the water before the fisherman drew them back in. Others used nets resembling the butterfly nets of old to scoop fish out of the water.

In March 1981, we spent ten days in southern Sudan. The visit did not get off to the best of starts as our flight was delayed for over nine hours and we arrived in Juba just before dusk, minus our luggage – it had been too hot when we left Khartoum for the aircraft to carry any baggage in the hold. It caught up with us next day.

Colonel Kamal, the Commanding Officer of the local Armoured Regiment, met us off the flight and took us to the British Overseas Development Agency (ODA) compound, which was to be our base during our time in Juba. He left us to settle in, but returned a couple of hours later to take us to supper at the Officers' Club on a hill near the town. We had our meal out on the tennis court listening to the captivating rhythm of African drums drifting up on the cool night air from the valley below.

Over the next few days we saw just how different southern Sudan was from the north of the country. Here, in place of the desert, the landscape ranged from typical African bush to dense forest. The people looked and dressed like Africans rather than Arabs and, in the main, lived in round straw huts known as rondavels, rather than the more substantial buildings found in the north.

The Sudanese army kindly put a Magirus-Deutz lorry and an escort of six armed soldiers at our disposal, and, in addition to showing us around Juba, arranged for us to visit Yei, some three hours down a bumpy dirt road to the south west towards the border with the Democratic Republic of Congo (DRC) and Nimule in the extreme south on the border with Uganda.

As a woman, Toni had to travel in the cab of the lorry, while the children and I travelled with our escort in the cargo bay at the back. This had no seats, but the floor had been covered with a layer of straw with mattresses on top to make things more comfortable. There was no canopy, so we were open to the elements, not to mention overhanging tree branches – a new experience.

In Yei we stayed in the local army barracks. Our accommodation was a mud building under a straw roof, comprising two rooms and a veranda, on which there was a stone jar for drinking water. The 'facilities' consisted of a 40 gallon drum and bucket for washing, while the loo was a wooden plank with a hole in it at the top of some steps. The house was enclosed behind a high straw fence, which afforded us complete privacy.

Yei was a delightfully picturesque settlement comprised almost entirely of straw rondavels around a bustling souk. Here you could buy local produce and contraband cigarettes, but little else. The road was lined with mango trees, while numerous blue and pink jacarandas, magnolias and flame of the forest trees, all of which were in full bloom, provided a truly magical backdrop. There was also an experimental pineapple farm, which produced an abundance of delicious fruit. However, the area lacked the infrastructure needed to transport the mangos and pineapples outside the immediate vicinity of Yei.

The only substantial building was the massive Catholic church, built in 1978, where we attended Mass on the Sunday. It was a truly joyous experience with numerous lively hymns accompanied by the thunderous beat of two large African drums positioned near the altar. At the most solemn part of the Mass, the consecration, the congregation broke into spontaneous applause, as if to acknowledge the Lord's arrival into our midst.

The journey to Nimule took over five hours, again in the back of the Magirus-Deutz lorry with our armed escort. The dirt road took us through some dramatic scenery with rugged mountains, rushing streams and dense bush. At about the halfway point we made a welcome stop at the tiny settlement of Kit, to stretch our legs and have a bite to eat. The final stretch to Nimule included a hair-raising descent down into the White Nile valley in the failing light. The track was very narrow, steep and had an uncertain verge. The drops were enormous and some of the corners were impossibly tight. We prayed a lot!

We arrived at the army outpost in the pitch black of an African night with a storm building. The setting was straight out of the pages of history – six or so straw rondavels around a single mango tree, the whole encircled by a straw fence. There was no light and, at first, apparently no one at home. Then, quite close by, a voice boomed, "Hello, who are you? I am Captain Hitler and I am in charge here!" I all but jumped out of my skin!

Although he had been given no warning of our arrival, Hitler (he told us that he had a brother called Mussolini!) was not thrown; he was used to dealing with the unexpected. He took us up to the small government resthouse nearby, which kindly opened its doors to us. The accommodation was spartan yet spotless. Someone went into the village and bought a gallon of black market fuel to start the generator to give us some light, whilst the cook rustled up a meal of tinned pilchards and rice.

First thing next morning I went to see Hitler. He commanded a platoon of about 30 soldiers with responsibility for patrolling the border in the Nimule area. Amazingly, he had not received any instructions from his headquarters in Juba or Khartoum for over three months and neither he nor his men had been paid during that time. They had not been issued with any rations and his Land Rover, parked under the mango tree, had not moved since running out of fuel three months before. Yet he led his soldiers with pride and had somehow continued to motivate them sufficiently to carry out their patrolling duties. Surprisingly, morale appeared high. All he asked of me was to remind Juba and Khartoum of his continued presence in Nimule, as they seemed to have struck his unit from their records!

I was full of admiration for the man. Here was a true and loyal soldier, a born leader, and I knew I could not have done half as well in his shoes. Of course, on my return I sang his praises with the army in both Juba and Khartoum, and made them aware of his situation. I hope my protestations had the desired result.

The tribes in the Nimule area were essentially Sudanese, but lived astride the border. Showing commendable pragmatism, the Ugandan authorities had positioned their control point several miles short of the border. Thus Hitler was able to take us across the bridge over the stream that formed the border at this point, allowing us to set a foot, quite literally, in Uganda, much to the children's delight.

Food was very scarce in Nimule. The resthouse seemed to have an endless stock of tinned pilchards and rice, but nothing else. We noticed rolled up straw mats in the branches of many trees. Hitler told us that these were beehives – honey was a very important commodity here and the local people would barter with it. We bought some (it was really delicious) and occasionally had it with our rice instead of pilchards. We also bought some very small bony fish off a fisherman for a real treat of grilled fish and rice for one meal.

The main attraction in Nimule was its defunct nature reserve, incorporating both banks of the White Nile, including the beginning of the Fula rapids. Our lorry was able to take us around the northern part of the reserve down to the start of the rapids, an awe-inspiring spectacle of thunderous, white surging power, as the White Nile forces its way through a narrow gorge. En-route we came across various species of birds, antelope and monkeys, as well as a large python that was trying to wrest a catfish from a fishing net. A pod of some 20 hippos was cooling down in the calmer water above the rapids, while on the bank a herd of about 70 elephants was ravaging the vegetation. We wondered how long it would be before they had to move on in their quest for food and possibly come into conflict with humans. As we were down wind, we dismounted and moved to within a few yards to photograph some of these marvellous animals.

To reach the southern sector of the park, we crossed the White Nile in a tiny boat that threatened to sink under the weight of its passengers. This was quite an experience. First, the boat had to be paddled upstream, hugging the northern bank, for about 100 yards. Then the boatmen turned it into the current and paddled like fury to reach our destination virtually opposite our starting point, below which the Fula rapids and, in all probability, a watery grave awaited the unsuccessful! Once on dry land, we walked amongst the game, including various antelopes and warthogs, but luckily nothing dangerous; the only hazard being the journey back across the river.

After three nights in Nimule it was time for us to leave. We went to say farewell to Hitler. Somehow he had managed to acquire a kid goat, which he pressed upon us as a farewell gift. Sudanese generosity is legendary, they have virtually nothing and yet they will willingly share their last cup of water with a complete stranger. We stopped again at Kit, where the soldiers made short work of dispatching the unfortunate animal and conjuring up a really delicious meal, with some vegetables and bread we had bought in a tiny wayside souk.

While we were waiting for our meal I met a very dignified middle-aged man whose bearing and clothing made him stand out from everyone else in the village. He turned out to be a Ugandan refugee, a lieutenant colonel in the Ugandan Army who had been forced to flee Idi Amin's regime two years earlier. He was now living in exile in very modest circumstances, but showed no bitterness or self pity – just a longing to return to Uganda one day. My heart went out to him – he and I were the same rank, but our circumstances were so very different.

On our last evening in Juba we noticed scores of Dinka men and women in tribal costumes streaming down the road. The men wore monkey skin loin clothes over boxer shorts and either leafy foliage around their heads and shoulders or feathered headdresses. All carried either a club or a spear. Some were riding bicycles, the tails of their monkey skins flying out behind them making for quite a comical sight. The women wore short skirts and colourful beaded tops, the backs of which extended well above their necks. Their faces, arms and legs were daubed with a white paste, giving them a ghostly appearance.

Everyone looked in festive mood, so we decided to follow them out of town for about one and a half miles into the bush. We were then privileged witnesses to a wonderful spectacle of impromptu tribal dancing to the relentless beat of dozens of drums. Men and women in separate lines jumped up and down in time with the drums and then wove in and out, whole lines moving forward like giant snakes. Now and again, a group of men broke out of the general mêlée and hustled the girls into the centre, and in this way we found ourselves caught up in the middle of the dance, which was both exhilarating and a little unnerving. The dancing went on well into the night, a full moon giving the dancers ample light, making this a truly memorable climax to our visit to southern Sudan.

Next day we flew back to Khartoum...eventually! Another 6.00 a.m. start, followed by delay after delay, and a final takeoff at 3.00 p.m. minus luggage – it mirrored our outward journey perfectly.

A group of us, including Toni's sister, Anni, and a Sudanese friend, Anis Hajjar, saw in the New Year (1981/82) in Dinder National Park, situated on the Ethiopian border, two days' drive south east of Khartoum. We arrived just before nightfall on 30 December, Alex's tenth birthday. The park had only just re-opened after a two-year closure and we were its first guests. We were housed in a delightful collection of straw rondavels set around a clearing about the size of a football pitch on the banks of the Dinder River.

For protection, the compound was surrounded by a straw fence with a gap of about 20 yards at the entrance. This was guarded at night and if the lions threatened to enter the camp a gong would be struck once to sound the alarm. This was the signal for the men to be prepared to stand at the openings to their rondavels (there were no doors) and shout if necessary to scare off the intruders! A constant sounding of the gong meant that the lions were in the camp and we had to take up our stations immediately.

The guides were particularly concerned that we had brought a lamb with us, which we intended to slaughter and barbecue on New Year's Eve. At first we all thought this was just a bit of hype to get us excited. Not for long. Next morning on our first game run we saw small groups of animals almost all the time; many types of antelope, monkeys, giraffes, plus three lions. So the guides were not joking – there were lions here.

On the afternoon game drive our vehicle was attacked by African bees, a really horrifying experience. I was driving at the time and, although a number of passengers were on the roof of my Land Rover, the African guide sitting beside me told me to drive as fast as I could to escape the swarm. There was nothing for it but to yell for everyone to hold tight as I put my foot down. Once clear, I stopped so that we could deal with the bees on us, and we had to get out of the vehicle in the very area in which we had seen the lions that morning. Our Sudanese guide was excellent, even extracting a bee from inside the ear of Anni. Meanwhile, I had to run into the bush to catch Zoë, aged six, who was trying to run away from the bees stinging her.

That night we celebrated the New Year feasting on our barbecued lamb, followed by Scottish country dancing to the strains of music provided by a tape recorder. No sooner had we gone to bed, however, than the gong was sounded, followed by the growls of several lions. They remained at the entrance for about two hours, but withdrew as dawn broke. We saw three of them less than half a mile from the camp as we set out on our game drive next morning. That day we also saw a flock of around 30 ostriches and several giraffes.

'Our' lions returned about 10.00 p.m. in the evening and seemed a little bolder, prowling up and down and growling at the entrance at regular intervals all through the night. The gong was sounded on three occasions and none of us got much sleep, but luckily the lions baulked at entering the camp. It was a weary, but well contented group that set off next morning on the two-day drive back to Khartoum.

The most ambitious trip we undertook was to Jebel Marra, during the 1982 Easter holidays. Jebel Marra is an extinct volcano in west Darfur near the Chad border. For this expedition we joined forces with the Moores, an expatriate family living in Zalingei near the base of the *jebel.*

We flew from Khartoum to Nyala, the capital of Darfur, where we landed on a cleared strip of sand for a runway and were intrigued to see that the refuelling wagon was a cart drawn by a pair of horses and carrying two 40 gallon drums. We really seemed to be 'out in the sticks' here.

We spent the night in the local resthouse, before setting out for Jebel Marra very early next morning in a Land Rover kindly provided by the army. The army had also provided us with an escorting officer and a driver. We all had to travel in the back, which did not have seats and, moreover, we had to share the space with all our luggage, a second spare wheel and a leaking plastic container of fuel. More worryingly, the vehicle had no brakes. But, hey, we had transport and were on our way!

After travelling 25 miles along a sand track we reached Kas, in the midst of a raging dust storm. A tiny settlement halfway to our destination, Torra Tonga, high up on Jebel Marra, Kas was little more than a collection of thatched mud huts and a wayside souk. We stopped here for breakfast in the local eating house – an open-sided shack with a corrugated iron sheeting roof – where our meal of scrambled eggs, liver, tomatoes and greens was cooked on an open fire before our eyes and tasted absolutely superb.

We then started the hair-raising climb up the *jebel* to Torra Tonga. The route could be identified at first, but then deteriorated into a boulder strewn animal track and, finally, into a dry water course. At one point we even had to drive up the smooth rocks of what would become a waterfall during the rains.

We reached Torra Tonga at 1.00 p.m., having taken six hours to cover the 50 or so miles from Nyala. Our friends, the Moores, had arrived half an hour earlier. Phase I of our expedition had been accomplished.

Torra Tonga was unlike any other place we had seen in Sudan. Situated at about 7,000 feet, the thatched stone rondavels looked out of place amongst the pine trees that covered the mountainside. But for them, we could have been in Germany! The village stood right on the edge of the mountain, affording spectacular views of the desert wastelands far below. Here there was also a memorial to the passengers and crew of a plane that had crashed into the mountain some years earlier.

The volcanic crater that was our final objective was only two and a half miles from here as the crow flies, but the intervening ground was a tortured mixture of fissures, rocky outcrops and a mini Grand Canyon, an insurmountable obstacle to all but man and beast. Accordingly, Charles Moore had arranged to hire a dozen donkeys to carry our supplies and the younger children on this final leg of our journey. A quick check with the village headman confirmed that everything had been arranged as planned.

After a snack lunch we set about filling our ten water jerry cans and water bottles. To do this we used a spring down a steep gully about a third of a mile from the village. It was hard work and took some three hours to complete. Even so, this allowed us only a gallon of water per person per day, barely sufficient in daytime temperatures around 40°C. Therefore, this water was solely to be used for drinking and cooking; we would have to use the water from the volcano's lake for all other purposes.

Ringing in my ears all the time was the advice of our Medical Sergeant in Sharjah to combat heat illnesses: "Keep an eye on the colour of your pee; if it's like water, you're all right, if it's like neat whisky, start drinking water, and if it's but a puff of steam, call a priest." It would be very serious to succumb to heat illness whilst in the crater and we were beyond any medical assistance up here.

Just before nightfall, the donkey boys and their animals arrived, but there were only nine of them. We cut down on our kit as much as possible, but could not sacrifice any of our water – the heaviest element of our baggage. All the children, therefore, would have to walk, or be carried by us, and we all had rucksacks.

We planned to load up before dawn and set out as soon as it was light, so that we could reach the crater before the sun caused temperatures to soar. However, the donkey boys had other ideas and did not turn up until almost 8.00 a.m., and then only after been chivvied by us. By now the sun was already warming the mountain. To make matters worse, there were now only seven donkeys, two having gone lame.

Toni and Jane Moore set off with the children as soon as possible, accompanied by one donkey carrying a jerrycan of water and our breakfast. Charles Moore and I remained behind to load the other six donkeys, but it soon became apparent that their number was insufficient for our needs. At last, I got away with the six laden donkeys, whilst Charles remained behind to await the arrival of a replacement animal.

I caught up with the leading group at our breakfast stop just below the entrance to the outer crater – the caldera – and after a bite to eat, we moved on together. Soon we reached the rim of the caldera and there, a few hundred feet below us, was a tree-studded savannah plain with a shallow lake at its centre. On the far side we could see the rim of the inner crater, beyond which lay our destination. Semi-wild horses and donkeys, as well as cattle, roamed the savannah, while numerous birds flocked on and around the lake – a scene that, but for the heat, conjured up images of the Garden of Eden.

There was an anxious moment once we descended the outer rim and set foot in the crater, when the donkey boys decided they had gone far enough. We still had almost a mile of open ground to cover under a now burning sun, and there was no way we could get our equipment and supplies to our intended goal without the donkeys. Luckily, I succeeded in persuading the donkey boys to honour their commitment to continue on, and so the crisis was averted. I have an enduring memory during that final leg of our journey of Zoë, willing herself to keep trudging on through the hot volcanic ash, dragging her teddy behind her; she was only six years old. She still has that much loved, battered old teddy today!

The final hurdle was to get up and over the inner ash cone, but our reward was the sight of a beautiful circular lake, about 600 yards in diameter, shimmering in the sunlight. The ash cone plunged straight into the lake all the way round its circumference, except for one small fissure that offered us not only a way down, but just enough space for a campsite at the water's edge. It was 3.00 p.m., meaning that the walk in from Torra Tonga had taken us six hours.

As soon as the donkeys were unloaded, their handlers set off back to Torra Tonga and we all cooled down with a swim in the chilly, foul-tasting mineral waters of the lake. Charles arrived with the last donkey at about 6.00 p.m., just as the light began to fail. The little donkey boy with him was only nine years old, so we decided it best to keep him and his donkey with us for the night. In the event, he elected to stay with us throughout our stay.

We camped for three nights in this idyllic, remote site. Our days were spent swimming in the lake of the inner crater, exploring the outer crater and generally having a carefree time. The nights turned out to be bitterly cold, with ice forming on any water left in mugs and cooking pots. To combat the cold, we ate our evening meal around a roaring campfire before climbing into our sleeping bags. Quite apart from the cold, we had to keep the fire burning through the night to ward off the unwanted attentions of a troop of baboons that shared the area with us.

We had one visitor during our stay – a Sudanese school teacher who had trekked up to the crater alone on 3 April 1982. He requested a cup of water and, while sipping this, asked if we were British. On learning that we were, he said very gravely, "You are at war!" "Who with?" we asked. He did not know, but said he thought it was with South America, and without further ado set off in the direction of Torra Tonga. We asked him to remind the headman to send us the donkey boys next day. It was days before we learnt that we were at war with Argentina over the Falkland Islands.

Meanwhile, selfishly one might say in hindsight, our main concern was whether or not our donkey boys would return, and it was with much relief that we saw them making their way over the crater rim just before nightfall the following evening. They joined us for supper and afterwards we had a really enjoyable singalong around the campfire. The donkey boys stole the show with a fine display of African drumming, using our saucepans and jerry cans as instruments – wonderful stuff!

Next morning, the donkey boys were their uncooperative selves again and so Toni, Jane and the children were forced to go on ahead to try to get across the open plain of the caldera before the heat of the sun, reflecting off the crater rim, turned it into a cauldron.

The donkeys were not carrying so much weight now, as most of our water and rations had been consumed. It was therefore possible for the children to take turns in riding part of the way. However, our tactics in motivating them to keep walking on the journey into the crater now worked against us. None of them wanted to ride, being determined instead to walk all the way back to Torra Tonga. We had to force our daughters to ride, something they still continue to remind us about!

The trek back to Torra Tonga took us five hours and we believe that we set a record for the largest group (four adults and seven children) to camp in the inner ash cone on Jebel Marra. The villagers came out to welcome us on our return and we were relieved to see that our army escort was amongst them.

We were all pretty exhausted and Jane Moore was suffering from minor heat exhaustion, but at least we had plenty of water here. After a good night's sleep and a lie in the following morning we all felt as right as rain again. After breakfast, we struck camp and loaded our two vehicles, putting all the baggage in the army Land Rover so that everyone, except myself and our Sudanese escort, could travel in the greater comfort and safety of the Moore's vehicle. Then we bade farewell to the friendly people of Torra Tonga and made our way to the Moores' house in Zalingei, arriving an hour after sunset.

Zalingei was a quiet little backwater way off the beaten track. Charles Moore was managing an agricultural project in the area. Their bungalow was very basic; for example, their water supply was two 40-gallon drums situated on the roof, which had to be replenished by hand. A fire would be lit under one of these drums to provide hot water. Electricity was provided by a generator, which only ran for limited periods of the day. The family kept two donkeys, Noddy and Big Ears, which they used to get about the village.

What struck me most about Zalingei were the enormous trees – a type of acacia, I believe – that provided excellent shade. Crops grown under them yielded 50% more produce than those grown in the open, and when their fruit ripened in the wet season, it became a highly nutritious animal feed.

After two nights with the Moores it was time to head back to Nyala. We decided to return via Gollol, a picturesque village with a beautiful little waterfall – an unusual sight in Sudan – on the southern slopes of Jebel Marra. Here, quite by chance, we became involved in a wild celebration where women with painted faces waved shiny objects, such as tin trays and mirrors, in the air, while the men brandished spears and beat drums. Everyone was singing. The centre of attention appeared to be something covered by a blue shroud atop a highly decorated camel. I gestured with my camera to see if they minded being photographed and much to my amazement and delight they responded with great glee, whipping away the blue shroud to reveal two young children, each carrying a sword. We could not tell if they were boys or girls, but understood this to be some sort of 'coming of age' ceremony.

In the pine wood near the waterfall we had another stroke of luck, coming across a fine old man carving a Sudanese throwing stick. This weapon is roughly similar to the Australian boomerang – except that it does not return to the user! The hunter throws it about two feet above the ground to bring down game, such as antelope, by breaking their legs. They were also used effectively at the Battle of Omdurman against the horses of the 21st Lancers.

A beautifully weighted, finished example with very sharp edges lay at the man's side. He was happy to be photographed and, when we made to go, he offered me the finished hunting stick. I tried to decline, suggesting that he offer me the less-impressive unfinished one instead. He misunderstood me and must have thought me very greedy, because he then gave me both and would not allow me to return them. Luckily, I had some Sudanese money on me, which I gave him, using sign language to explain I could not take his gift without offering something in return. Both hunting sticks are now on the wall in my study, alongside King Henry's spears.

Once back in Nyala, I went to confirm our seats on the flight back to Khartoum the following day, Easter Sunday, and received some troubling, even incomprehensible, news. Our seats with Sudan Air were indeed confirmed, but not on tomorrow's flight, nor any flight up to and including 31 May – more than six weeks away! Indeed, I was told that we might have to wait until September if the six of us wanted to fly back together. I went to the railway station, where I was informed that there were no seats available until 1 July. In the souk I was told the only way we could get back to Khartoum at the moment was in the back of a souk lorry – a journey of six to eight days across open desert. "But," added the helpful official, "it will be too hot and your children will die!" We were in a bit of a fix.

Next morning, we packed up the Land Rover, went to Mass and then on to the airport, on the off chance that we might be able to get on our booked flight – one could never be certain about anything in Sudan. Alas, we were unsuccessful. However, we did meet a Mr George Calderbank of Hunting Technical Services and he undertook to radio Khartoum to advise people of our predicament.

On hearing our news, my boss, Colonel Dermot, was unfazed. With the sangfroid so typical of a Guardsman he sent back a message telling me not to worry, but to establish a temporary BATT wing in Nyala, until we were able to return to Khartoum! However, the children had to get back to school (including the boys, who were then at Worth School in England) and Toni's head teacher was unlikely to be amused if she did not get back in time to teach her class. In the meantime, the army in Nyala kindly put a Land Rover at our disposal and suggested we see a little bit of Darfur, while they tried to resolve the problem.

Although we made the most of the Land Rover, I went into the army headquarters every day to see if there was any chance of getting back to Khartoum. Three days went by and we were running out of rations and money to buy food – we had no means of drawing money in Nyala. Then, on the fourth day, I was told that President Nimerei was visiting Nyala that afternoon. As a consequence, the scheduled Sudan Airway's flight was being re-routed to omit El Fasher on both the outward and inward flights (I believe the plane was carrying the President – hence the change of route). This meant that those passengers booked to go to El Fasher could not travel.

The Army had acted promptly and reserved us seats on the plane. Our relief was tempered by the knowledge that our luck was someone else's misfortune.

We arrived at the 'airport' in good time and bade a heartfelt farewell to all the soldiers who had looked after us so well. Despite the long wait, there was much to see. Huge crowds were gathering to greet the President. These included fierce-looking tribesmen (Baggara, I believe) armed with swords and spears, mounted on horseback or riding haughty camels with elaborately decorated saddles – a truly thrilling spectacle.

We were almost sorry to see our plane touch down, but were very relieved once we were safely on board and en-route to Khartoum. We had had quite an adventure.

As I re-read our diaries to write this account, I had an overwhelming sense of sadness that many of the people who provided us with such an exhilarating experience in 1982 may now be amongst either the perpetrators or the victims of the utter brutality and abject misery that is the humanitarian catastrophe of Darfur. Our daughter Hannah spent 13 months in Kas and Nyala between May 2004 and July 2005, in very different and dangerous circumstances from our carefree days in 1982, working as a volunteer with Médecins Sans Frontières (MSF). Torra Tonga was by then a janjaweed stronghold and the children she had once played with there were now amongst those bent on doing her harm.

Despite the challenges of living in Khartoum, generally speaking we all remained remarkably healthy throughout the two years we were there. However, we did have the benefit of the Khartoum Clinic for emergencies, something we were more than grateful for on three occasions.

One evening, Zoë slipped on the wet floor and split her head open on the stone steps leading upstairs. It was hard to believe that so much blood could flow from such a tiny body. I was out at a meeting at the time and had taken the Land Rover, but luckily a fellow batman, John Caiger, had just dropped by to see me when the accident happened. He bundled Toni and Zoë into his Land Rover and rushed them to the clinic. Thankfully, Zoë had not fractured her skull and, after having three stitches in the wound, was allowed home, where she proudly showed me her bandaged head.

Hannah's accident was more serious. She was being driven home in the dark from a birthday party by Robin and Barbara Corpe, school teacher colleagues of Toni's, when their car was struck by a train on an unmanned level crossing and dragged several hundred yards down the track. Fortunately, the train, which was delivering aviation fuel to the airport, was travelling very slowly. Barbara Corpe and Hannah took the full brunt of the impact. Barbara was more shocked than physically injured, but Hannah had taken a blow to the right side of her face and a spring from the back of the front passenger seat had been driven into her cheek just below her right eye, which was completely closed. She was just five days short of her seventh birthday. A passer-by brought them both to our house (Robin Corpe had to stay at the scene of the accident) and Toni took them to the clinic. By chance, a Finnish eye specialist was visiting Khartoum at the time and happened to be at the clinic when Toni arrived. She examined Hannah and, to our relief, found that her eye was undamaged and her cheekbone intact. She had got away very lightly.

Our most serious incident concerned our son, Rorie, who was ten-years-old at the time. A group of us had decided to walk the length of the Sabaloka Gorge (the Sixth Cataract on the Nile), a distance of about eight miles. We did not have the benefit of a map, but I had previously reconnoitred the northern end, while Phillip Gordon, the budding guide, had done likewise at the southern end. In both cases, we found the path to be well defined and flat, making for easy walking. Neither of us had seen the central section, but had no reason to believe that it would be any different. We were horribly wrong; here there was no path and the *jebels* plunged directly into the river.

The night before our walk, we camped at the southern end, so that we could set off at dawn and complete the walk in the cool of the early morning. We then planned for John Caiger, Phillip Gordon and me to return, collect our vehicles and drive round to link up with the others at the northern end. We had not been walking long before one of the group started to feel unwell. John elected to return with him and suggested that both should then drive round to the other end so that nobody had to return on foot. This probably saved us from disaster. Midway along the gorge, the path disappeared and the going got really tough, requiring us to scramble up and down loose scree for almost three hours. At one point, we had to edge our way along a narrow ledge with a sheer drop of about 20 feet to the swirling waters of the Nile. There was no merit in turning back, as our help would now be at the far end. The sun was now well up and its heat was being radiated from both banks of the gorge. At last we made it, but several of us were suffering from heat exhaustion.

Rorie was the worst affected and once back in Khartoum ended up in the Khartoum Clinic. At first, the doctor was convinced he was suffering from malaria. I had to fight for him to be treated for heat stroke – by this stage he had stopped perspiring and his temperature was 40.5°C. Luckily, I had my army Heat Illness First Aid *aide memoire* from my days in Sharjah, which gave me the confidence to challenge the initial diagnosis and insist that Rorie be treated for heat stroke. Apart from a saline drip, this entailed packing him in ice to bring his temperature down, and ice was not the easiest commodity to find in Khartoum. We got what we needed from the Hilton hotel. Meanwhile, he was also tested for malaria, the results proving negative.

At a later stage, Rorie pleaded for me not to leave him, although I hadn't moved from his side. We asked for his temperature to be taken and found it to be below 39°C. My First Aid *aide memoire* said that the ice should be removed from around the patient when his temperature fell to 39°C. I therefore asked the nurse to remove the ice but, understandably, she said only the doctor could authorise such an action and he wasn't at the clinic. In desperation, I said it was my ice and our son, so I would remove the ice and we would be responsible for what happened. Happily, after three worrying days, Rorie made a full recovery and was allowed home. Never before or since have I challenged a doctor, but these were desperate times. We all realised just how lucky we had been, not to mention how foolish! The experience drove home to me that one must never assume anything in the unforgiving environment of the desert. From then on we were much more careful.

Our terms and conditions of service in Sudan included a mid-tour break of 51 days, the bulk of which had to be taken in a temperate climate. We chose to take our leave in England, apart from a ten-day break in Egypt en-route. In Cairo, we stayed with General Fiky and his family, whom we had met in Khartoum when the General was the Egyptian Military Attaché. Their house was tiny and, much to our embarrassment, they vacated their bedroom for us and camped in the sitting room while we were there. Although it was Ramadan, Madame Fiky insisted on preparing and serving us normal meals, despite our protestations. Slaving over a hot stove in Cairo in July, without being able to take so much as a sip of water, must have been real torture, yet she was always smiling and relaxed.

We took the opportunity to visit Luxor, travelling overnight in the brand new Messerschmitt 'bullet' train. This was fully air-conditioned (bitterly cold for us) and the service included 'airline-style' meals. It was also very expensive, so we booked only two cabins (three seats in each that converted into two bunks) between the six of us. The boys bagged the top bunk and Toni shared with Zoë, whilst I did likewise with Hannah, who kicked me out of bed in the middle of the night and so I ended up sleeping on the floor!

We were not keen on staying in one of the many characterless luxury hotels in Luxor, so a very helpful tourist policeman took us to the El Salim hotel near the Nile and close to the station. Here, we had a spotlessly clean room with five beds (the girls shared) and a fan rather than air conditioning, which we preferred as we found the latter too cold after a year in Sudan. The en-suite facilities included a Western-style loo with a shower. All this cost the princely sum of five Egyptian pounds per night – roughly £1 sterling!

Later that morning we took a horse-drawn carriage to see the ruins at Karnak and spent the afternoon in a *felucca* (sailing boat) on the Nile visiting Banana Island, a very peaceful place where one could wander in the shade of numerous fruit trees.

The main purpose of coming to Luxor was to visit the Valley of the Kings. When he briefed us in Khartoum, Hugh Leach had said that the only real way to capture the atmosphere of this amazing place was to travel by donkey.

"Go down to the river and ask for Mohammed, the donkey boy," he had said. So we did. Everyone knew to whom we were referring, but Mohammed was now a man and a successful businessman at that, having swapped his donkeys for a fleet of taxis. However, we met up with another young lad, also called Mohammed, who had a string of four donkeys, one each for the boys, while the girls rode with us (much to their annoyance!).

Hugh was right; ambling along the dusty road, past the Colossi of Memnon, sitting in splendid isolation in an open field, and into the Valley of the Kings was a unique experience, lost to those who whistled past us in their hermetically sealed luxury air-conditioned coaches. This was even more the case when, on leaving the Valley of the Kings, we scaled the *jebel* and traversed along the edge of a yawning precipice before descending to Queen Hatshepsut's magnificent limestone temple in the next valley. We returned to the ferry via the complex of Ramesseum, the round trip of seven hours leaving us content and saddle-sore in equal measure.

On our return to Luxor, we just had time to sip an ice cold limoon by the Nile, watching the sunset, before catching our 'bullet train' back to Cairo. After a relaxing day, the Fiky's took us to Old Cairo and its ancient souk during the evening. Here, all our senses were assaulted: the vivid colours in the cloth shops, the glitter of gold and silver, the rich smell of leather, numerous spices, hubble bubbles and Arabic coffee, the cacophony of sound and the general buzz of activity took us back in time to the days of the *Arabian Nights* and *Ali Baba and the Forty Thieves*.

The following evening, England seemed quite tame by comparison, but it was good to catch up with family and friends – and, importantly, catch up on our sleep – the main reason why we had to spend most of this leave in a temperate climate!

We were keen to visit Ethiopia, the roof of Africa, before our time in Sudan came to an end. As we wanted to make this trip with all the family, we waited until the boys flew out for the 1982 summer holidays. At the time, a civil war was being waged in the north of the country, where Eritrea was fighting to gain independence from Ethiopia. As a consequence, Ethiopia was not a popular tourist destination and obtaining permission was quite an achievement in itself. Our flight to Addis Ababa, via Asmara, the provincial capital of Eritrea, gave us an insight into the conflict. Virtually nobody disembarked here, while more people wanted to get on the flight than was possible. Meanwhile, the plane was surrounded by soldiers and those of us flying on to Addis Ababa had to remain in our seats.

Financing the trip was also very difficult. We had to make a private arrangement with a British firm with offices both in Khartoum and Addis Ababa. Under the arrangement, we paid their Khartoum office a sterling cheque for all our travel and accommodation expenses plus our spending money, and we were to be given the equivalent in Ethiopian currency (Birr) from their Addis counterparts on our arrival. Unfortunately, the plan fell through as the manager in Addis went on holiday without briefing his staff about the arrangement. We faced the severe embarrassment of being unable to pay the Forship Travel Agency, with whom we were booked, with the probable consequence of being put in jail! Our tour guide, Yellma, was blissfully unaware of the situation and did not query our request to go to the British Embassy the next morning, before setting out on the planned tour of the city.

At first, the staff in the Embassy were not at all sympathetic, stating that I should not have come without making proper financial provision. My response that I thought I had done just that fell on deaf ears. It dawned on me, not for the last time, just how privileged diplomats were to be sheltered from the trials and tribulations faced by ordinary people like us when living in certain countries abroad. After much discussion, I was allowed to cash a personal cheque for our 'spending money' and was asked to return to the Embassy at the end of our stay to obtain the funds I needed to pay the Forship Travel Agency. In the meantime, the Embassy would contact our Embassy in Khartoum, confirm my identity and, subject to verification, arrange the transfer of the necessary funds. I had been given a flea in the ear, but at least the problem had been solved.

Armed with some local currency, we headed straight for the market to buy suitable clothing. Not only had we arrived during the rainy season, Addis is 7,000-9,000 feet above sea level and was decidedly cold compared to the scorching heat of Sudan. We all needed warm, waterproof anoraks, items we could not get in Khartoum.

Travel outside the capital, Addis, was very strictly controlled and

Yellma had yet to succeed in obtaining the permits required for our intended itinerary by the time we arrived. Thankfully, he overcame this remaining hurdle towards the end of that anxious first day.

Early next morning, we clambered into an old VW camper van, driven by Yellma, and set off for Awash National Park in the Rift Valley, a two-day drive from Addis through beautiful countryside. On the first day we stopped for lunch at Hora Lake, a haven for birds, including black geese, sacred ibis, pelicans, avocets and, most strikingly, 5,000 or more flamingos that painted the far shore a brilliant salmon pink.

We spent the night in the town of Nazareth based at the Adarma Ras hotel. This was sheer luxury – a two-storey quadrangle with an outdoor swimming pool in the centre, surrounded by the most striking bougainvilleas, ranging from deep purple through red and orange to bright yellow. Amazingly, we seemed to have the place to ourselves.

At Awash, we were the only visitors in Kereyou Lodge, the park's campsite, which was situated, quite literally, on the edge of the impressive Awash River gorge, the muddy waters of the river being some 500 feet below us. Small game abounded here and the birdlife was exquisite. There was also a pod of hippos in the river. However, the highlight of the visit was, perhaps, sharing breakfast with some all too bold Hamadryas baboons. One male was especially impressive, his magnificent silvery-grey and white speckled mane giving him the appearance of a small lion. The baboon that won the children's sympathy, however, was a rather sad-looking, one-eyed female that sat patiently on a nearby rock hoping to be thrown a few scraps. She was not disappointed.

On the return journey to Addis we stopped at To Sodere. Here, a hot spring served an outdoor Olympic-sized swimming pool right out in the wilds. We spent a relaxing hour swimming here, whilst a troop of green monkeys rifled through our clothes looking for titbits. We were interested to see that they had yet to learn how to drink Pepsi Cola from a bottle, preferring instead to pour the contents onto the grass and then suck it up.

Our main reason for coming to Ethiopia was to see Lake Tana, the source of the Blue Nile (known as the Abbay in Ethiopia), the river that had given us so much enjoyment in Khartoum. So, the day after we returned to Addis from Awash we flew in an Ethiopian Airways Dakota to the tiny township of Bahr Dar on the southern shores of the Lake. (Some people argue that the true source of the Blue Nile is a spring in the surrounding hills that feeds into the Lake, an area that was out of bounds due to the tense security situation prevailing at the time.)

For the entire flight we flew at only about 2,000 feet above the ground and we felt as if we could reach out and touch some of the higher mountains. The Blue Nile gorge was an amazing sight – being very deep and steep-sided, it is virtually inaccessible throughout its long journey through Ethiopia. The river, like all the other rivers and streams we flew over, was mud-red in colour, evidence of the precious silt being carried downstream to enrich the fields along its course through Sudan and Egypt.

After a flight of some two hours, we touched down on the grass airstrip at Bahr Dar, where the pilot kindly took the children in to see the cockpit as our luggage was unloaded. Then we made our way to the Ghion Hotel, situated at the end of the runway on the shores of Lake Tana.

Just under 20 miles east of Bahr Dar is the village of Tiss Abbay. Nearby, the Blue Nile crashes over the Tis Issat Falls, a spectacle that rivals the Victoria Falls on the Zambezi in size and grandeur, but one that is far less well known. Indeed, when we visited them in 1982, we had to pass through no fewer than three armed checkpoints, manned by an assortment of men in uniform and tribal dress. We had to leave our vehicle at the second checkpoint and make our way on foot along a narrow, boulder-strewn and very muddy mountain track.

After about half a mile, this descended into a gorge and across a raging torrent via a stone footbridge, reputedly built in the 7th century to link the kingdoms of Gonder and Bahr Dar. The third checkpoint was at the bridge and our venture almost foundered here when the guards refused to allow us through. Apparently, this was a high risk area. It was maddening to be so near and yet so far. Luckily, our Ethiopian guide from Bahr Dar was unwilling to take no for an answer. Eventually, a compromise was reached and we were allowed to proceed in the company of an armed escort, wearing tribal dress rather than uniform, whose orders we were to follow without question. We agreed and gratefully set off up the other side of the gorge.

On reaching the top, the rumble of the falls and the sight of fine mist rising into the sky ahead started our pulses racing. A few hundred yards further on, we breasted a rise and there the falls were, slightly below us. Spanning several hundred yards, they comprised three main falls and countless smaller ones. The waters, which had the appearance of frothing chocolate, plunged down into a deep chasm at the base of the mountain-side. Being entirely on our own in this wild landscape made us feel very privileged, albeit a little nervous. All too soon our escort signalled for us to retrace our steps. Clearly, it was unsafe to linger here, particularly as the sun was getting low in the sky, and we reluctantly obliged, such was the pull of the spectacle before us.

We awoke next morning to sunshine and showers. Undeterred, we spent the day in what was described as a 'luxury launch' – in reality, a tiny rust bucket with virtually no protection from the rain – visiting various monasteries on Lake Tana. We arrived at what we considered to be the most impressive of these just as the sun came out after a heavy squall. Called Ura Kidane Mehret, it was situated on top of a hill at the tip of a remote peninsula, rather than on one of the many islands.

Disembarking, we found ourselves in a tropical paradise. Several papyrus boats, the design of which had not altered for millennia, rested amongst the rocks and grass by the shore. Our guide led us up the hillside along a narrow path through dense vegetation, steam rising from the wet foliage. Exotic birds flitted to and fro, and monkeys, signalling our arrival, chatted excitedly in the branches above us. Here and there, tiny paths branched off from the main track leading to grass and reed huts set amongst the trees.

Some of the locals came out to look at the odd group of strangers in their midst. They were unthreatening, but kept their distance. At the top of the hill we came upon the Coptic monastery, a collection of circular buildings several hundred years old, built almost entirely of wood, and mud mixed with straw and cow dung. At the entrance to one of these buildings, a centuries-old, hollow stone bell was suspended from the rafters on leather thongs. It was sounded by striking it with a small round stone, the result being a pleasing mellow tone that resonated all around the monastery compound.

In another building, the surface of the inner walls was covered in beautiful religious paintings depicting scenes from the Old and New Testaments, including Moses and the burning bush, Abraham about to sacrifice his son, Isaac, the Last Supper and the Crucifixion, as well as a huge painting of the Virgin Mary.

Priests clothed in beautiful robes and carrying crosiers adorned with intricately carved Coptic crosses showed us some of the monastery's treasures. These included exquisitely illustrated bibles, a black velvet vestment elaborately decorated in solid gold thread and three brass crowns.

On leaving the island, we asked the skipper of our launch if we could see the point at which the Blue Nile flowed out of the lake on its long journey to the Mediterranean. Not only did he agree, but he took us a little way downstream, a thrilling experience made all the more so when a hippo unexpectedly rose up beside us from the murky waters to see what all the commotion was about. As we made our way back to Bahr Dar, we were intrigued to see cormorants diving around the launch to catch the fish disturbed by our passage. We were lucky enough to get an excellent sighting of one swimming at great speed underwater alongside us in pursuit of its prey.

Out time in Bahr Dar flew by and all too soon we stood on the grass airstrip watching our Dakota make its descent from a watery sky. When the plane came to a halt, the pilot got out and unscrewed a cap on the underbelly of the aircraft. Liquid immediately poured out, whereupon he cupped his hands to collect and taste some and then spat it out. He did this several times before replacing the cap. Out of interest, I asked him what he was doing. He replied that all the seals on the plane had perished and no spares were available. As he had flown through rain, water had found its way into the fuel tanks. This gravitated to the bottom and simply needed to be drained off. It was not a problem, he assured me, but I wish I had not asked, especially when it rained all the way back to Addis.

We left Ethiopia with mixed feelings. On the one hand, we had enjoyed a unique experience, not only visiting some breathtaking places, but having them all to ourselves. Throughout our time there we did not come across a single other tourist. However, the repressive regime of President Mengistu meant that we were always under a certain amount of tension. For example, we could not admit to any link with the armed services, something we coped with splendidly, except on one occasion when we passed a burnt out Soviet armoured vehicle on the road and the boys identified it incorrectly as a tank. I instinctively corrected them, saying it was a BRDM, much to the consternation of the family who admonished me as one with the word 'D'! – the children's name for me, derived from 'D' for daddy. Yellma appeared not to notice this ill-advised exchange.

In Addis, the Russian influence was everywhere to be seen. Hammer and sickle signs adorned most doors and billboards in the streets proclaimed, 'The inevitable success of socialism'. The people did not appear to be as friendly as the Sudanese, but this was because nobody knew whom they could trust. How could you confide in people if you were unsure whether or not they were informants or members of the Secret Police? One person, when we were alone, summed up the situation to me very succinctly: "Socialism promised everything, but now we weep for our mistake."

Three weeks after our return to Khartoum, my successor arrived. Our first meeting was not auspicious. There was a power cut at the time and I was sitting on our porch steps trying to repair the cistern to the downstairs' loo. Next morning, he was even more horrified when he saw my sand-swept office in Shajara. Casting my mind back to my own misgivings when I arrived two years before, I empathised with him; living and working in the Sudan was an acquired taste.

However, the overwhelming friendliness and generosity of the people more than compensated for the hardships we all endured, and it was with truly heavy hearts that we roared down the runway and into the night sky above a largely blacked out Khartoum.

With the benefit of hindsight, would I have accepted this posting? Unquestionably, yes, as would the entire family. We were rewarded in so many different ways and the country and its people made such an impression on us that several years later two of our children returned there as aid workers with MSF. In 2012, we co-hosted a reunion for those who shared the experience with us 30 years earlier. It was quite amazing how strong the bond between us still remained.

1. Our sleeping arrangements on our balcony – I took the photograph on a timer. Rorie was the only other person awake. Note: Lucy always slept on Zoë's bed.

2. Salbatori using our charcoal-burning iron

3. With my Sudanese counterpart, Lt Col Omar, at the Armour School, Shajara (Crown copyright)

4. Major Ali 'Tattoo', leader of the Ferret Scout Car musical ride (Crown copyright)

5. A northern Sudanese NCO – Red Wing leader in the musical ride (Crown copyright)

6. A southern Sudanese NCO – Blue Wing leader in the musical ride (Crown copyright)

7. The complete musical ride team (Crown copyright)

8. Alex, Zoë, Toni and Hannah on the Kerreri Heights overlooking the Omdurman battlefield. The River Nile can just be seen in the background

9. The pyramids at Meroe

10. One of the Sudanese custodians of the Meroe site

11. A Greco-Roman ruin, known as 'The Kiosk', near Naga in the desert north of Khartoum

12. The extraordinary *jebels* at Kassala

13. Animals gather around one of the many wellheads in the Umm Inderaba oasis

14. Toni with our children and Sudanese army escort on the Ugandan border at Nimule. Captain Hitler is on the far right

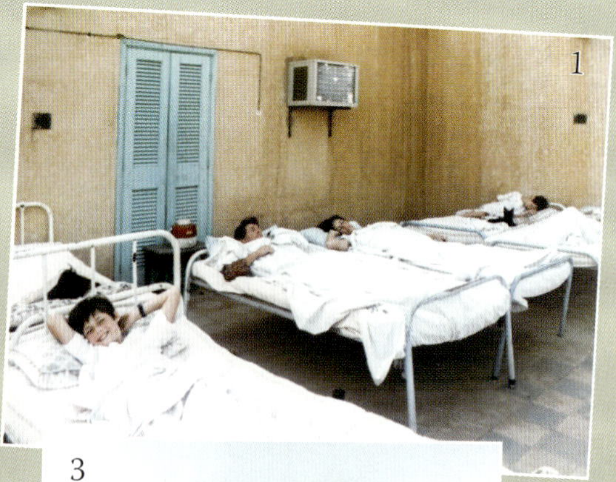
1

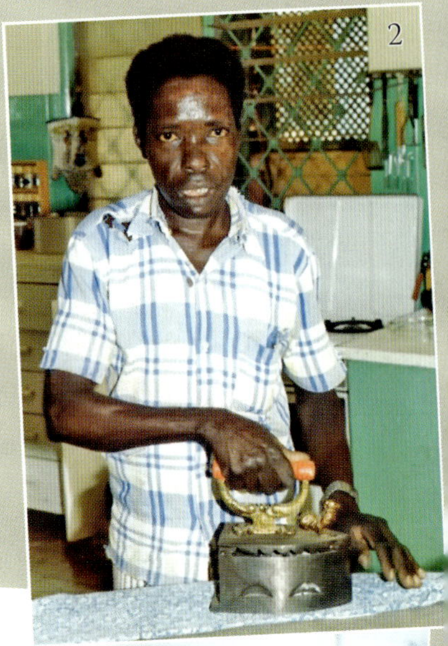
2

3

4

5

6

7

8

9

10

11

12

13

14

15

16

17

18

19

20

21

22

23

24

15. Toni and the children crossing the White Nile, Nimule

16. Toni outside our rondavel in Dinder game reserve

17. An aerial view of the caldera at the summit of Jebel Marra. The inner crater, in which we camped, can be seen at middle left

18. Zoë at the edge of the inner crater lake

19. Crossing the *jebel* from the Valley of Kings to reach Queen Hatshepsut's temple in the adjacent *wadi*. We were walking at this point as the track was on the edge of a cliff with a daunting sheer drop

20. Queen Hatshepsut's temple

21. Tribesmen near Awash, Ethiopia

22. Toni's photograph of the children and me amongst reed boats on Lake Tana, Ethiopia

23. Toni's photograph of the children and me, plus our local guide and armed local militia escort at the Tis Issat Falls (1982). Queen Elizabeth II was photographed with Emperor Haile Selassie in exactly the same spot in 1965.

24. My photograph of Toni and the children with the pilot of 'our' Dakota at Bahr Dar airstrip

NIGERIA

NIGER
CHAD
Lake Chad
Sokoto
Katsina
Kaura Namoda
Kano
Maiduguri
Rijau
Zaria
Jaji
Kaduna Airport
Kaduna
BENIN
Bauchi
Gombe
Jos
Wawa
Minna
Bida
Kafanchan
Yankari Game Reserve
Abuja
NIGERIA
Makurdi
Benin City
Lagos
Owerri
CAMEROON
N
Gulf of Guinea
NIGERIA - 1983

NIGERIA

PRELUDE

On leaving Sudan I was posted back to the United Kingdom to the Army Personnel Selection Centre (APSC) at Sutton Coldfield. With apologies to everyone from the Birmingham area, I have to confess that I had never heard of Sutton Coldfield, but, unsurprisingly, we soon grew to love the town and the surrounding area.

The job entailed heading the unit through which all potential male soldiers passed to be tested, evaluated and, if successful, placed in one of the hundreds of trades available to people joining the Army. We functioned very much like the proverbial sausage machine, processing some 400-500 applicants a week. Potential recruits would arrive on Monday to be assessed on Tuesday and Wednesday. As they left on Wednesday afternoon, a second batch would take their place and the cycle would be repeated. Women who wanted to join the Army attended a separate selection centre, with which I had a liaising responsibility.

The APSC had a wing in Edinburgh for the selection and placement of all Scottish male applicants. I had to visit this wing on a regular basis and when I did so I was occasionally accommodated in Edinburgh Castle. I found it quite thrilling to be living in such an iconic building and, as I looked out across the city from my bedroom window, it was hard to believe that I was being paid for the privilege.

Two events during my time at Sutton Coldfield jolted me out of the complacency which comes with working in a thoroughly predictable, routine environment. The first of these was the miners' strike in 1984/85. For much of the time, our barracks became a key base for the police responsible for maintaining law and order in the Midlands' coalfields. We accommodated up to 600 police all week, every week for several months. The resultant pressure on our facilities was huge, particularly in the cookhouse. Not only did our cooks have to prepare three square meals a day for our potential recruits, they also had to feed the police, preparing haversack rations for them to take out on duty, as well as serving evening meals late at night and early breakfasts at around 2.00-3.00 a.m. In short, they were working in shifts round the clock. One young policeman tried to cheer up one of the cooks by remarking on how much he must be making on overtime, and was amazed to learn that there was no such thing as overtime in the Armed Forces.

Occasionally, there was time for a bit of healthy 'inter-service' rivalry. One such instance was a football match against the Sussex Constabulary. By half-time we were three goals up, but before the second half got underway a number of police, dressed in riot gear, reinforced their side's 18-yard box! Unsurprisingly, the 'match' ended early in an amicable three-all draw.

In the late summer of 1984, we were placed on a very high state of alert in the face of a potential IRA attack. On going to bed one evening, the phone rang – it was the duty officer informing me that there was a suspect package in the guardroom. It was addressed to me and he felt sure I would like to come and see it. That was probably the last thing I wanted to do, but duty called. Certainly the package looked suspiciously like a bomb. It was the size of a large loaf of bread, tightly bound with sticky tape and addressed in poorly formed block capitals to: 'THE COMMANDING OFFICER'. It was in a mail sack that had been delivered earlier.

I moved everyone from the building and then did something that I now know was very foolish. Reasoning that the package had been moved about in a mail sack, I felt it safe enough for me to remove it from the building and place it in the centre of the cricket pitch (being careful to avoid the wicket!) where it would cause no harm if it exploded. I then notified the authorities and requested a bomb disposal team be sent to deal with the situation.

The Army's bomb disposal unit had no one available, so the task fell to a police bomb squad based in Aldershot. Their expert arrived on the scene just after 2.00 a.m. and asked me to brief him on the incident. Then, positioning me behind a low wall at the edge of the playing fields, he went out to the 'bomb'. Seconds later, I felt a tap on my shoulder. "If I should go, do you know enough to describe this bomb in detail?" asked the policeman. I had to reply that, in all honesty, I did not. I had no measurements, did not know if it had been addressed in biro or ink, or whether the writing was dark blue or black, etc. So he invited me to accompany him out to inspect the package and he described it to me in great detail. He then asked me to retreat behind the wall once more.

An age went by before there was another tap on my shoulder. The policeman was pale and drenched in perspiration, but was clearly relieved. "Do you want a cigar or a bar of chocolate?" he asked, his face breaking out into a broad grin. The 'suspect package' was crammed full of cigars and chocolate!

Ever since the days of the Raj, the British Army has been followed around the world by a most loyal band of brothers from the subcontinent – Indians, Pakistanis and Bangladeshis – who set up canteens serving 'tea and wads' in the most unlikely places.

Known as Char Wallahs, they are the very offspring of Kipling's Gunga Din, and every bit as appreciated by the Army for the service they provide. The 'suspect' package had been sent to me by the Char Wallah at Moscow Barracks, Belfast. It included a letter thanking me for sending him so many recruits, thereby greatly increasing his profits! Of course, I wrote back expressing my appreciation for his generosity, but I explained to him that I was only doing my job and advised him against sending me any more presents, as I was not permitted to accept them.

I ended by saying I was deeply touched by his generosity, especially as I was a 'cousin brother', having been born in India, and hoped his canteen would continue to prosper.

As my tour at Sutton Coldfied entered its final chapter, I was contacted by the personnel department in the Ministry of Defence to discuss my next posting. The officer was most concerned that, in the interests of my career, I take a high profile desk job either in the Ministry of Defence or in Headquarters United Kingdom Land Forces (HQ UKLF), Wilton. I had already undertaken two 'funnies' (secondments) in Brunei and Sudan, and he felt it important that I now got back into mainstream soldiering. Therefore he was looking to place me in the south of England.

Barely a month later he phoned me to say he had got just the job for me in a place called Kaduna. "Where on earth is Kaduna?" I asked, to which he replied, "Nigeria". I reminded him of his advice that my next posting should be in the south of England. He delighted in telling me that Kaduna was on the Greenwich Meridian directly south of England! Then, adopting a professional tone, he began to talk up the appointment – I would be one of the Directing Staff at the Nigerian Command and Staff College, an elite appointment and certainly not a 'career foul'.

I broke in and said that I would seriously consider the post, but what was the catch? It transpired that we were in the process of handing over our responsibilities to the Nigerians and so the posting would only be for 15 months at the most, possibly less; not good in career terms, nor ideal for family stability. The Nigerians had insisted that we supply them with an Armoured Corps officer, as the current team was lacking in that respect. There were no volunteers for the post, but somebody had said that I would say "Yes". I was assured that, if I accepted the appointment, steps would be taken to ensure that my career would not suffer. I was asked to give my response within 72 hours.

Unbeknown to me at the time, Toni's father had served with the West African Frontier Force (WAFF) during World War Two and had been stationed in Kaduna for much of the time. So we had a link with the area. Although three of our children were now at boarding school and, once again, we would have to endure the sadness of separation if I accepted this posting, we reached a unanimous decision. At least the school holidays would be exciting! I duly informed my posting's branch that we were willing to go.

It was now April and I was due to leave at the beginning of June. Amongst the wealth of information contained in the theatre brief was the fact that the only suitable vehicles with support in Kaduna were Land Rover, Peugeot and Mercedes. As I owned a Citroën Familiale, it was evident that one of the main items we needed to purchase was a car.

Under our conditions of service, the UK government would only pay the cost of shipping for a new, or nearly new, car from one of these three manufacturers. As time was so short, I decided to write to each of the companies asking if they had a cancelled order or demonstration car that I could buy. My preference was a Land Rover. Our Land Rover in Sudan, purchased second-hand after spotting an advertisement placed in *The Lady*, of all magazines, had been a tremendous success and I was keen to repeat the experience.

Ignoring my request for an existing vehicle, Land Rover wrote back saying that they could provide me with a new one ready for shipping early in the New Year if I placed an order immediately. This meant that I would be without a vehicle for almost my entire tour. Clearly, a Land Rover was a non-starter. Peugeot was little better, stating that they could provide me with a new vehicle in Nigeria by the end of the year, again provided that I placed my order there and then. Mercedes wrote back stating that I had just missed the latest build programme, but that within a week they would supply me with a list of cancelled orders from around Europe from which to choose a suitable vehicle. Of course, they warned, I would be unable to alter the specification of any of these vehicles. I was duly sent a selection of vehicles, together with an undertaking that the company would arrange for the vehicle of my choice to reach Nigeria within weeks of my arrival.

Mercedes was the most expensive of the three vehicles. It was also the least practical, given its low clearance and the poor roads in Nigeria, particularly the unsurfaced bush roads. On the plus side, however, Nigerians regarded it as a status symbol and thus it had the best resale value of the three. In any case, I had no option. Securing a bank loan, I placed my order for a very smart, white 130 TE.

Our small tri-service group, numbering just over 20 families, was housed in the grounds of the National Defence Academy (NDA) – Nigeria's equivalent of the Royal Military Academy, Sandhurst – situated on the northern outskirts of Kaduna. It comprised a Royal Navy Advisory Team (RNAT) of five, including one Royal Marine and commanded by Captain Peter Broadbent, a British Army Advisory Team (BAAT) of about a dozen, including the support staff, commanded by Colonel Graham Holland for most of my tour, and a Royal Air Force Advisory Team (RAFAT) of four, commanded by Group Captain Peter Le Marquand. Together, these teams made up the British Advisory Teams (BAT). The BAAT Commander was in overall command as the Senior British Officer (SBO).

The married quarters were a mixture of bungalows and duplexes. The latter were small two-storey blocks, each accommodating two families. We shared duplex Number 7 with the Royal Marine's family, the Wards, who were wonderful neighbours.

Apart from a small kitchen, the ground floor of the duplex comprised a large 'L-shaped' dining/sitting room leading onto a lovely covered patio. Upstairs, however, was rather cramped for a family of six with just two small double bedrooms, a bathroom and a tiny, narrow bedroom-cum-study that would otherwise have been the upstairs landing. This became Hannah's and Zoë's room, their small beds squeezed in end to end.

Everyone enjoyed the privacy of a generously-sized garden, and we had access to tennis and squash courts. We also all enjoyed the luxury of being allocated a cook, housemaid, gardener and night watchman, as were all our Nigerian colleagues. John, our cook, was a well-built, efficient young man with a rather serious demeanour. A good cook, he acted as head of the house staff. Our housemaid was a sweet-natured girl called Lisa, while Christopher, our gardener, was a very capable young man with a beaming smile and a strong work ethic. He had ambitions of becoming an officer in the Nigerian Army. Indeed, several years after we left Nigeria, he contacted us to say that he had joined the army as a soldier and was being posted to the Nigerian High Commission in London. Unfortunately, we were abroad during his entire tour in Britain.

Night watchmen, known as 'Magardies', tended to come and go. Theirs was a soulless task, sitting outside the house from 6.00 p.m. to 6.00 a.m. every day. As we lived in a restricted military area they were unlikely to experience anything out of the ordinary to break the monotony of their nightly vigil. An over-zealous, newly-appointed Magardy, however, did succeed in hitting Lisa over the head one evening, when she tried to enter the house whilst we were out. Our cook John was all for taking the law into his own hands and it took several days to smooth ruffled feathers and restore calm.

Despite the undoubted luxury of house staff, life could become very frustrating when basic facilities, that we took for granted in Britain, were either unreliable or non-existent. For example, only the team commander had a telephone in his house. While we were allowed to use this to contact family back home in a real emergency, we had to go to the Nigerian External Communications public telephone exchange in the centre of town to make routine calls, a process that might take well over an hour and then end in failure.

Our electricity was provided by the National Electric Power Authority (NEPA), but the supply was unreliable, subject to surges that damaged electrical equipment as well as frequent, often prolonged power cuts. "*NEPA dunquench*" soon became a well used part of our vocabulary – *dunquench* being the Nigerian expression for something that was broken.

To minimise the impact of these power cuts each duplex shared a generator, a marked improvement on our circumstances in Sudan. However, the generators were extremely noisy and during power cuts the reverberations of several of these machines bouncing off the walls of our houses were quite deafening. Consequently, there was a general agreement not to start them before 7.00 a.m. or to run them after 11.00 p.m. to allow families, especially those with young children, to get some sleep. Each duplex also shared a freezer. In our case, this was in the Ward's house, whilst we had the generator – quite a good incentive to keep on good terms with your neighbour!

During the hot dry season, occasional water cuts added to our frustration, but we kept two jerrycans of drinking water in reserve for just such emergencies.

From time to time, particularly in the wet season, we were visited by the 'Mossie Man'. He carried a noisy machine and spray tank on his back and would fumigate our house and garden with a choking chemical cloud, probably DDT, to keep down the mosquitoes. At other times, he would attack the cockroaches and I remember watching in amazement as a seemingly endless 'river' of the creatures left one of our drains after such a treatment to seek refuge elsewhere. It was hard to believe that we could have provided a home to so many.

A less disrupting monthly visitor was our barber, a marvellous old man who walked with a limp. He knew how to give you a proper military haircut – very, very short back and sides – but nothing else. It transpired that he had joined WAFF – the same organisation to which Toni's father was attached – during the Second World War. On completion of his training in Ghana, he had been sent out to Burma to fight the Japanese. Wounded there, he was evacuated to a British military hospital in Madras, where he was trained as a barber as part of his rehabilitation. On his return to Nigeria, he served for 16 years in the Nigerian Police and then did a stint as a security guard at a hospital in Kaduna before falling back on his hair-dressing skills during his twilight years.

Various vendors also visited us at regular intervals. One of these was Yacoub, the vegetable man, who brought his wares in huge baskets balanced on his head. Each time he went through the same ritual of unpacking his scales and weighing out vegetables in kilos. The bill was usually the equivalent of £20, about four times as much as one would have paid in England, but more or less the 'going' price of the markets in town. But our favourite trader was Rufus. He lived in Ibadan, over 500 miles away, and would arrive carrying a suitcase crammed full of quaint little wood carvings depicting local people and scenes from everyday village life. By Nigerian standards his goods were inexpensive – a four-inch figure would cost about £3. Considering his return bus fare was £80, he must have done a fair bit of business to make his trips worthwhile.

Kaduna itself offered very little by way of recreational facilities. Some of us joined the expatriates' amateur dramatics society and the local 'Hash', while our children were lucky enough to be lent a pony called Bilbo during some of the school holidays. The British High Commission in Lagos had a Consulate in Kaduna headed by the Deputy High Commissioner, HE Mr Dick Best. He and his staff were very good to the BAT team and we attended many functions there. Our main source of relaxation, however, was the TGIF (Thank God It's Friday), an American Embassy facility which the Americans kindly allowed us to use on Fridays. It comprised a swimming pool, tennis court and a tranquil sitting out area.

Midway through our tour, a delightful restaurant opened just outside Kaduna. It was called the Jacaranda Out, there being another Jacaranda in town. Originally, the Jacaranda Out had been a pottery owned and run by the Mamma family on their farm. Dr Mamma was a Nigerian married to an English woman. Mrs Mamma ran the pottery and, initially, started serving refreshments to visitors. The idea for a restaurant grew out of this small beginning, the enterprise being run by their son, Andy.

The site chosen was adjacent to the pottery, which made excellent business sense, and commanded glorious views out across the bush. Customers sat outside, shaded by thatched canopies dotted about a lush green lawn tastefully decorated with clusters of earthenware pots. Beyond the grassed area the land fell away towards the bush. This slope was beautifully landscaped with rocks, shrubs and flowers, through which an artificially constructed stream tumbled under a wooden bridge and into a lily pond. The quality of the food matched the beauty of the surroundings and the scenery, making this a very special place to come and relax.

On one of our visits we noticed that Andy had placed about a dozen baby crocodiles in the stream and pond. I believe they had been confiscated from poachers by the police and Andy was giving them a temporary home. They were delightful little creatures, no more than a foot in length, and so helpless at this stage; their soft skin and their enormous eyes making them vulnerable to attack from large birds.

Mercedes (UK) was true to its word and, within a month of our arrival, I was informed that my car had arrived in Lagos docks and was ready for collection. We had been warned that importing a car into Nigeria was a tedious process, which could take anything from one to three weeks to complete and demanded heroic levels of tact, patience and stamina.

Leaving our youngest daughter, Zoë, with friends (our other three children were at school in England), Toni and I flew down to Lagos, where we stayed with the defence attaché.

Since an attack during an Embassy reception in Lagos some years earlier, security was at a higher level than we had ever experienced before. Not only was Toni not allowed out of the compound alone, but we noticed that there was a steel grille from floor to ceiling at the top of the stairs to the first floor. Before retiring to bed on our first evening, we were given a briefing by our host. The defence attaché and his wife's bedroom was on one side of the landing, whilst we were on the opposite side. The grille at the top of the stairs was locked at night to prevent intruders gaining access to the landing. If we heard any unusual noise at night we were to leave our room at once and run across the landing into our hosts' room, which was equipped with emergency supplies and a radio and could withstand attack for several hours. Not much privacy for them when they had guests!

My task for the next few days was to obtain the signatures of various officials, both in the relevant government departments in Lagos and in the docks, in a precise order of sequence. If just one official was not 'on seat' (away from his desk or, as likely, unwilling to see you), you were unable to proceed further. Of course, if you were prepared to pay 'dash' – offer a bribe – life would be made much easier for you. But we were British government employees and thus, quite rightly, forbidden to offer bribes.

Dressed in uniform, we relied on our tact, patience and perseverance to get us around this obstacle course.

Initially, I met with considerable success and looked set to secure the release of our car in record time. However, the penultimate official was not 'on seat' and I was thwarted. Midway through the following week I finally had all the signatures I required. Clutching the precious papers in my hand, I made my way to the Customs' compound at the docks, where I set eyes on our car for the first time. Mercedes had done us proud and the frustrations of the previous ten days evaporated as I drove the car out of the docks and back to the defence attaché's house.

Just after daybreak next morning, Toni and I set off on the arduous journey back to Kaduna, a distance of around 600 miles. This was a potentially hazardous undertaking, as armed hijackings were commonplace. In the interests of security, I had to wear uniform and we were under strict orders not to stop anywhere en-route, except to refuel; hence the need for two drivers. We were, of course, required to stop at police checkpoints, but had to be alive to the fact that any of these might not be what they seemed.

In the event, we found that we had no option but to stop at the numerous checkpoints we came across, as the police were armed and the road was blocked by planks of wood bristling with nails. Our diary at the time stated that we found the police manning these checkpoints in the south of the country to be:

> *rude, belligerent and hostile and made us feel like criminals. My army uniform didn't seem to help. However, the further away from Lagos we travelled, the mood gradually changed and we were greeted more and more with smiles and salutes.*

The first hazards we encountered, however, were the state of the roads and the standard of driving. The scariest bit was the Benin Highway, a dual carriageway just outside Lagos, on which the central reservation was an unforgiving solid concrete barrier. The road was still under construction and without warning we came across holes big enough to swallow a car, where the surface had yet to be laid. Then, all of a sudden, our carriageway would disappear and we would be diverted onto the oncoming carriageway for several miles. The only problem was that nobody travelling in the opposite direction seemed to realise that this was now a two-way road. After one or two near misses, we drove gingerly along with our headlights blazing and hazard warning lights flashing to warn oncoming traffic of our presence.

Just north of Benin we were waved down by a very polite policeman who asked if we could give his young, uniformed colleague a lift to Kaduna. We readily agreed, although when we reached Kaduna we were told that we had been rather rash as this might so easily have been the prelude to a hijacking. However, in our case, it proved to be a masterstroke as we were waved through every police checkpoint from then on. It transpired that the young police corporal, whose name was Moses John, was in the Criminal Investigation Branch (CIB). He was attending a course in Ibadan in the south of the country, but had to travel back to his post in Sokoto in the very north west of Nigeria every month to receive his pay; an extraordinary imposition for him, but we could hardly have acquired a better escort.

We dropped Moses John just outside Kaduna at about 5.00 p.m. and, having been reunited with an ecstatic Zoë, were back in our own home an hour later. The journey had taken us eleven and a half hours.

Even in and around Kaduna the risk of hijacking was very real. Because of this, coupled with the appalling standard of driving, team members were not allowed to drive outside the town at night, and had to drive in convoy with at least one other car linked by radio when travelling anywhere outside the environs of Kaduna in daylight.

Whilst the Mercedes was a prestigious car, it was not the prime target for hijackers. This doubtful honour fell to the Peugeot 505, as it was the most popular car in Nigeria and made an excellent taxi. During our time in Kaduna, one team member lost his car at gunpoint in broad daylight in the town, while another managed to fight off would-be hijackers on his way back from Lagos after having collected his car. Both had Peugeot 505s.

There were no traffic lights in Kaduna. Busy junctions were controlled by traffic policemen. Dressed in immaculately pressed uniforms of dark blue trousers, saffron shirts and dazzling white gloves, these 'Yellow Perils', as we called them (the locals referred to them as 'Yellow Fevers'), were remarkably adept at maintaining the flow of traffic and made a true art of their trade. The Yellow Peril who manned the junction at 'our' end of town was particularly skilful and clearly enjoyed playing to the motorists he served. He appeared almost to break dance at his post and would signal not just with expressive hand gestures, but a quick flick of a foot or deft jerk of his head.

Apart from a small administrative team that manned the central facility in camp, the men all worked at Jaji, some 45 minutes north of Kaduna along a truly terrifying road littered with potholes and abandoned crashed vehicles. Whenever possible we travelled to and from work in the army bus. Staff Sergeant Alidue was a good driver who had ferried the British team members to and from Jaji ever since it had been established in 1976. Travelling in a large vehicle also gave us a greater sense of security, albeit a false one in all probability.

Like most of the team, I was a member of the directing staff assigned to the Nigerian Command and Staff College. Other members of the team worked in the junior division of the Staff College, or in the Nigerian Army School of Infantry (NASI), both of which were also in Jaji.

As the team was being wound down, I took over the roles and responsibilities of two of the departing members. About a month after my arrival, however, the Command and Staff College closed for the summer recess and so I had plenty of time to settle into my new role and get to grips with life in Kaduna.

The year-long Army Staff course was modelled on the Camberley course and was divided into six terms, each five to eight weeks long. These terms covered staff duties (ranging from basic letter writing, through minutes and reports to producing operational orders), administration and logistics, low intensity operations, conventional warfare, operations in support of the civil authorities and, finally, joint service operations, when the students from all three services worked together for a 'purple' term.

The students were placed in syndicates, each comprising about ten people, headed by a member of the directing staff, which included a mix of Nigerian, Ghanaian and British (referred to as Baturi) officers.

Life was, indeed, demanding for the teaching staff, who taught, guided and facilitated their syndicates throughout the working day and then had to prepare for the next day and complete any marking required once they returned home. To ensure a uniform standard of instruction across the syndicates, the team commander would drop in unannounced to observe directing staff running their syndicates, and would also review the marking of the students' exercise papers. These checks and balances were essential but they increased the pressure on the teaching staff to the extent that there was very little opportunity to enjoy a social life whilst in this role. In recognition of this, it was normal to alternate between teaching and writing duties every term. However, as the team was running down I once had to teach for three consecutive terms, which proved to be quite a challenge.

Briefing drivers and other supporting soldiers on outdoor training exercises was an added pressure. Whilst the officers all spoke good English, this was not always the case with the soldiers. I soon learned that 'the day after tomorrow' was expressed by saying 'next tomorrow' and that 'the day before yesterday' was 'last yesterday'. When ordering a vehicle to meet you somewhere out in the bush, it was very important to get these things right!

I should stress that all the exercises conducted at the Command and Staff College were TEWTs, that is Tactical Exercises Without Troops. We were therefore able to operate in the general countryside without causing any inconvenience to the local population, instead of confining our activities to designated training areas.

I once went out to 'recce' an assault river crossing TEWT on a river called the Turbo, near the small village of Bukuru. The scene either side of the river was captivating; women washed clothes, men fished and children splashed about at the waters' edge. Both banks were under cultivation, with tomatoes, peppers, oranges, lemons and grapefruit being grown, while birds – 'living jewels' – flitted amongst the vegetation.

I was also given a demonstration of just how to cross a river. A man came down the opposite bank carrying an enormous calabash on his head. On reaching the waters' edge, he simply lay on the calabash and propelled himself across using his arms and legs. Later on I saw fishermen using the same method to check their nets.

One of the unwritten responsibilities of a teaching staff's family was to throw a party for their students at the end of term. Bearing in mind that we had house staff to help us, these parties were great fun and Toni and I regarded them as true highlights. We always served Nigerian food at these celebrations, the main ingredients on the menu being yams and meat. It was important to ensure that the meat was tough and chewy; tender, soft meat was regarded as being 'off'.

To help people relax, we always asked the students to come in their national dress and I would wear my kilt. The students would all arrive a few minutes before the appointed hour and one could hear them whispering a little nervously outside. Then, bang on time, the door bell would ring. As I opened the door, they invariably fell about laughing at 'the man in a skirt' – the ice was broken and the scene was set for a relaxed and enjoyable evening. At one of these parties, a Tanzanian student came dressed as a 'white' big game hunter, complete with a solar topee, and stole the show. Good for him!

In addition to my paid job, I also took on the 'extra-mural' task of 'BAT Booze Officer'. Every member of the team had a catalogue from the wine and drinks merchant Saccone & Speed. My job was to collate the orders of individual team members on a quarterly basis and send a consolidated order to Saccone & Speed in London. When the consignment eventually arrived it was delivered to my garage and I would let people know when their orders were ready for collection. The consignment would, of course, pass through Customs in Lagos before being transported up to Kaduna and, very occasionally, items went missing. Once, I received a delightful note from a Customs official, written on a scrap of paper placed in an opened box containing orange juice cartons. It read: 'I have sampled the juice because I was very hot. It was very nice. Thank you.'

Toni wasn't allowed to be a 'lady of leisure' for long! Within a few days of our arrival in Kaduna, she visited the newly established Aisha Mohammed International Primary School to see if they would accept Zoë for the last few weeks of term. A delightful little school, it was run by an English head teacher, Mandy Cooper, who readily agreed to take Zoë, but also invited Toni to become one of her teachers. The school buildings were a number of bungalows and houses surrounding a shady courtyard with a duck pond at its centre. There were about 100 pupils at the school, ranging in age from three- to ten-years-old and drawn from 17 different countries. On her return from settling Zoë into school in England, Toni became a Second Year (six-year-olds) class teacher at the school in October 1985.

In Victorian times, West Africa was known as the white man's grave and days before we were due to fly to Nigeria we were given a sharp reminder of this. A horse belonging to one of the families had apparently died of rabies and we were asked to take out the vaccine required to inoculate the people most at risk. Malaria, however, was a greater threat. Indeed, on our arrival, we heard that a Nigerian brigadier had just died of blackwater fever, a serious complication that can occur in patients suffering from malaria. We also learnt that one of our own officers was down with a bad dose of malaria.

To reduce the risk of this disease, everyone in the team was required to take Palludrine daily and Chloroquine weekly, but despite this I, too, suffered a nasty bout of malaria just a few months after our arrival.

At the time, the treatment of malaria was simple and usually quite effective. At the onset of the 'shivers' one took four pills (I do not know their name), followed by three doses of two of the same pills at intervals over the next 24 hours. One treatment was usually all that was required. However, in my case, the malaria hung on tenaciously and even a second treatment failed. I was therefore given an impressive injection in my backside, which, according to the diary I kept at the time, "sent me into another world". Toni was back in England at the time settling Zoë into school, so I had driven myself to the clinic and had great difficulty driving home – I had to pull over several times to regather my wits. It took another few weeks, plus a repeat of that dreadful injection, to get the malaria out of my system. Since then, however, I occasionally get malaria-like symptoms.

The climate in Kaduna was divided into definite seasons. January was relatively cool and dry, too cold in fact to swim. Indeed, jumpers were needed during the first part of the morning and after sundown to keep off the chill. By March, the temperature was beginning to creep upwards and the air became increasingly more stifling and muggy until the first storm broke about mid-April, heralding in the wet season. For the next few months, daytime temperatures averaged between 35-38°C, dropping only slightly at night.

Between storms the sun shone most of the time. However, all this could change very suddenly; angry clouds would darken the sky and, amidst really spectacular electrical storms, empty their contents onto the land, sometimes almost with the intensity of a waterfall. The thunder and lightning could be quite unnerving at times, with no interval between the flash and bang and the 'crackle' of the lightning.

I well remember one storm catching us unawares as we picnicked by a lake. All the children had wandered around the shore to a point opposite us when the storm broke. To our horror they took to the water to swim back, a distance of some 300 yards. Zoë was only nine at the time but, luckily, they all made the crossing with ease and could not understand why I was so agitated.

These storms cleared the air and, once they had passed, the atmosphere was fresh, cool and filled with the aroma of Africa's rich red soil. However, this didn't last long; conditions soon grew steadily more muggy and stifling in the build up to the next storm.

At the onset of the rains, the bush country surrounding us burst into life and the general olive drab of the vegetation took on a vibrant green hue. Best of all, the flame trees that graced Kaduna (we even had one in our garden) came into flower, adding vivid splashes of red and orange to the invigorated landscape.

Towards the end of October, a dry, hot wind started to blow down from the Sahara, filling the air with a dust haze. This was the Harmattan. In colonial days it was sometimes referred to as 'The Doctor's wind', as it dried up all the stagnant water in which the mosquitoes bred, thereby reducing the risk of malaria. Indeed, the wind was so desiccating at times that we needed lip salve to prevent our lips cracking and moisturising cream on exposed skin. Occasionally, the dust – tiny particles of desert sand – was sufficiently dense to blot out the sun, causing the temperature to drop a little, as well as cutting visibility down to 50 yards or so. Once we even had to cancel an outdoor training exercise, as the students were unable to see the ground over which they were operating. When out of doors in such conditions, the dust would get into one's eyes and ears, up one's nose and down one's throat, making life pretty uncomfortable.

Although the Harmattan continued blowing until about March, as memory recalls the attendant dust haze died out by the end of the year and, in January and February, the wind became cooler, leaving the air clear, crisp and dry.

Our gardens were a haven for wildlife and provided us with the opportunity of many a practical natural history lesson. Once we were all treated to the sight of a lizard laying her eggs – seven elongated white leathery packages. Another time we spotted a very fat praying mantis. I thought she was pregnant and very vulnerable; an inviting meal for any passing bird. So I picked her up and placed her in the safety of our meat safe, together with some foliage from the bush she had been on, and then put it out in the garden. The meat safe was a wooden box with fine wire mesh sides designed to keep meat fresh and aired, but protected from flies. After days of apparent inactivity, we were delighted one morning to find the safe literally teeming with tiny miniatures of their mother. The babies were about half an inch long, light brown in colour and perfectly formed. We opened the safe and placed it under a dense bush to give the tiny creatures some protection when they emerged. By the end of the day they had all started out on life's big adventure.

The trees in our garden were all interlinked with the thick, yellowy orange silk strands of numerous orange orb web spiders. The spiders themselves could be seen either in the centre of their webs, or lurking near a tree at the edge. Coloured black and yellow, these rather sinister looking creatures could be quite large – about three inches in diameter. The silk they produced was strong enough to trap a small bird, although the spiders were not bird eaters. Walking into one of these webs, particularly at night, was unpleasant, as it took some time to break clear and you did not know where the owner was. Another favourite place for them to spin their webs was high up in the angle of the perimeter fence around the tennis court. Often a ball would lodge in the mass of silk and it was a brave person who retrieved it!

Other undesirable creatures in our garden included mosquitoes, the tumbu fly and ants. The danger presented by mosquitoes needs no elaboration, but we had not come across the tumbu fly before. This insect laid its eggs on washing hung out to dry. If clothing was left the slightest bit damp, the eggs would survive and then would hatch when in contact with your warm body. The larvae then penetrated into the skin and the result was a nasty sore that took ages to heal. Both Toni and I experienced this after taking socks off the washing line and going off to play tennis. The remedy to avoid this hazard was simple enough; everything had to be thoroughly ironed with a really hot iron, including underwear, socks, towels and washing up cloths. This killed the eggs, thereby eliminating the hazard.

Ants were not really a problem, more of a spectacle, when, during the wet season, myriads of flying ants would take to the skies to mate. When this occurred, the locals would come out in force to catch as many of the creatures as they possibly could. Even on the main roads through Kaduna it was prudent, at such times, to allow pedestrians priority as they rushed headlong into the traffic to collect their booty. These ants provided a rich source of protein, were free and, when roasted or fried in palm oil, apparently made a tasty meal.

The trees and shrubs in the garden attracted a lot of birds. We came across a coucal's nest one day with a clutch of three eggs. Coucals are oddly shaped birds related to the cuckoo. The one in question was a Senegal coucal, with russet wings, a black head and tail and an off-white front. After a few days, the eggs hatched and, although the parents were very attentive, I was able to take a peek inside and photograph the chicks. They looked like miniature hedgehogs, as their feathers were still little more than so many grey spikes. Eventually they all fledged and the mother started encouraging them to fly, much to the fascination of our cats. She seemed to accept us and even appeared to come and show off her brood to us, allowing me to come within a few feet to take photographs.

One afternoon we heard quite a commotion in the garden. Looking out, we could see that one of the fledglings had fallen off our wall and was floundering in a flowerbed with our cat, Horace, taking an unhealthy interest in it. Meanwhile, the mother was squawking away and doing her best to keep Horace at bay. Then, she did something extraordinary, flopping down in front of Horace, apparently in distress and dragging a wing. Horace thought his luck was in and pounced. With the timing of a mongoose, the mother jumped about two feet out of the way, taking Horace away from her chick. She continued with this ploy until she had led Horace to the other side of the garden. At the same time, one of the children rescued the stricken chick and placed it back on top of the wall. Her job done, the mother then flew back to reassure her youngster.

We had owned our two affectionate cats, Horace and Elsa, from kittens and they were much-loved pets. As we drew close to the end of our tour, the Deputy High Commissioner, Dick Best, and his wife agreed to give them a home, so we invited them round to supper to introduce them to the cats. That very day, Horace was nowhere to be seen, but Elsa stole their hearts and so all was well.

Two days later, we thought we heard Horace calling in the garden. I went out to investigate and realised he was in the untended wasteland on the other side of the wall. When I finally reached him, I found to my horror that his left forepaw was caught in a fearsome gin trap. He seemed to have dragged the trap all the way back to our wall. The vet tried to save Horace, but the paw became gangrenous and he had to be put down. Soon afterwards, Elsa became ill and died, apparently the victim of rat poison from an unknown source.

There was virtually nothing in the way of organised entertainment in Kaduna. We played a lot of tennis – an awful lot of tennis! I also enjoyed taking part in the Hash, as did the children during the school holidays. Many of the families, especially those with young children, had invested in above ground portable swimming pools. As the purchase of our car had 'broken the bank', we had decided against this additional expense. However, a few months into our tour we were able to buy one second-hand from a departing naval family. This was a really great boon, especially on hot, sticky days, and was also a valuable reserve of non-potable water. Other than that, we made our own entertainment in the natural adventure playground of the African bush that surrounded us, as well as taking full advantage of experiencing the numerous, very colourful, tribal and religious festivals in central and northern Nigeria.

The bush country around Kaduna offered us endless recreational opportunities. There were lakes and waterfalls to visit, excellent bird watching – some of the birds in Nigeria are quite exquisite – and gigantic granite rocks, known as inselbergs, to climb. The literal translation from German – island mountain – of these amazing rocks is really apt, as they seem to rise as black, isolated land forms several hundreds of feet above the surrounding flat 'sea' of the bush.

The nearest inselberg to Kaduna, and the easiest to climb, was called Kujama. The rock hyrax that inhabited its lower slopes added interest and we all loved watching them scurrying to safety as we approached. Halfway to the top of this inselberg, the route passed through a dense area of long grass and bush for about 50 yards. At the end of this swathe of vegetation there was a sizeable pool of standing water, making this an ideal habitat for puff adders, which were common in the bush. These large, highly poisonous vipers are slow to get out of one's way but, should you be unfortunate enough to tread on one, its strike is like lightening and the bite often fatal. Therefore, when walking in the bush we always carried our 'snake sticks', sturdy sticks about six-eight feet long which we used to beat the ground ahead of us, especially when we were unable to see our footfalls in long grass, to urge snakes to move out of our way.

Bugai was another inselberg. It rose abruptly from the bush near a tiny village and we often saw peregrine falcons in the area. Indeed, on one occasion we witnessed the amazing speed these birds can reach whilst diving towards their prey, one flashing past us at what must have been well in excess of 100 miles per hour.

For a real adventure, the boys and I once camped out on the top of Bugai for a night. After cooking and eating our evening meal, we took it in turns to keep the fire alight all night and to watch out for any unwanted visitors that might cause us problems. I was particularly concerned about puff adders; they hunt at night and could easily have been drawn towards the warmth of our bodies as we lay by the fire. Happily, the night passed without incident, although we weren't alone; as dawn broke we found ourselves surrounded by a very inquisitive troop of monkeys. However, they departed as soon as we began to stir, leaving us in peace to cook and enjoy our breakfast as the sun rose into the sky, warming us and chasing away the darkness. Aged 14 and 13, this was the first time the boys had been responsible for the safety of others whilst spending a night out in the bush. It was an adventure that lived long in the memory.

Ludo was perhaps the most spectacular and daunting inselberg we used to climb. In profile, it resembled a steep ramp soaring several hundreds of feet towards the sky. The front and sides of this massive rock fell away almost vertically to the bush below. The ridge up which we climbed was like the back of a giant animal sitting on its haunches. Watching people climbing Ludo from afar, it was easy to see that to veer just a few paces to the right or left of centre would spell disaster. However, provided one kept to the centre of the ridge, the climb was quite safe. Thanks to the convex shape of the curve, we could not see the sheer drop to either side and were thus spared the dreadful sense of vertigo that might otherwise have gripped us. Coming down the inselberg was a little more nerve-wracking, as we had a clearer idea of the ground falling away all around us.

Another attraction near Kaduna was a lake near the Nigerian Air Force base, known as NAF Lake. We often came here as a team for breakfast picnics, the air being cooler at that time of day. Indeed, we enjoyed a memorable Australia Day breakfast picnic here on 26 January 1986, organised by one of the BAT wives, Maur Huskissson, an Australian, during which we learned to throw a boomerang out over the lake.

A favourite site during the summer holidays was Bernin Gwari, a river in the midst of a defunct wildlife park about two hours' drive from

Kaduna. There were excellent picnic spots on the river bank, deep pools for swimming and mini waterfalls that acted as natural waterslides for the more daring to plunge down. While the younger children swam, we tied a vehicle tow rope across the tail of the pool and adults kept watch to prevent anyone being washed down the rapids. The only real concern was snakes. Once, when we were all playing in our favourite swimming hole, a young python dropped out of a tree and joined us in the water. Needless to say the pool was vacated in record time, by both us and the poor snake! Thereafter, Bernin Gwari lost some of its appeal!

Jos, the administrative capital of Plateau State, was a wonderful place in which to take a break. Almost exactly in the centre of Nigeria and at an elevation of just over 4,000 feet above sea level, it enjoys a cooler climate than the rest of the country. The British discovered large deposits of tin in the area in the early 1900s and by the 1950s there were some 2,000-3,000 miners, mostly Scots, living in and around the town. So strong was the Scottish presence that they had built a huge Caledonian Hall, the like of which would find few equals in Scotland itself. Known as the Fowley Hall, it was about the area of a tennis court, and beautifully decorated with the Scottish Saltire, Scottish coats of arms, clan crests and tartan drapes. This became the venue for the annual Caledonian Ball for the whole of Nigeria. When the Scottish expatriate community was at its height in the late 1950s you had to be a Scot to attend the ball, but by the time we were there, provided you knew how to perform the dances on the dance card, anyone was welcome.

Even in the mid-1980s, the Caledonian Ball was arguably the most prestigious social occasion on the expatriates' calendar in Nigeria. British Caledonian Airways supported the event, providing a piper and flying out an excellent dance band.

As members of the Kaduna Branch of the Caledonian Society, we attended the Caledonian Ball for the first time in 1985. By this time there were barely two dozen kilts in evidence amongst a gathering of some 300 revellers. The following year I was one of only three men wearing the kilt, the majority of the dancers being Danes from the local brewery. Nevertheless, the Caledonian spirit was still very much alive and kicking.

Preparation for the ball started early. The dance committee in Lagos would agree and distribute the list of dances to all the various branches dotted throughout Nigeria by early September. The individual branches would then practice and perfect these dances in readiness to declare their members ready for the ball to the overall committee in early November. Branches that found themselves wanting at the actual event risked being refused admission to next year's ball. We in Kaduna were extremely lucky to be coached by a real expert, Lynette von Kaufmann, who was elevated to being a Chieftain at the 1986 ball, despite being both female and English!

The countryside around Jos was absolutely beautiful and we took every opportunity to explore it whenever possible. The following extracts from our diaries written at the time give a flavour of what we experienced.

Outing to the Shere Hills, 24 July 1985

The Shere (pronounced 'sherry') Hills, high on the plateau near Jos, was a lovely area of rolling bush country broken by swathes of grass and rocky outcrops. Within its folds were two lakes which served as Jos's water supply.

Toni packed a picnic lunch and we set off for the first lake. It nestled in a little grassy depression and cattle were grazing on the slopes right down to the water's edge. We stopped here to drink in the scenery and to photograph some Red Bishops, a beautiful bird a little smaller than a sparrow and sporting a scarlet head. Then we moved on along the disintegrating tarmac strip of road until we reached a wide expanse of grassland, manicured by cattle, with a large shade tree in the centre. In the background was a spectacular twin-peaked outcrop formed by enormous rocks balanced crazily upon one another and known to the expatriates as Gog and Megog. The birdlife here was superb; Red Bishops, Splendid Sunbirds, Glossy Starlings, Fire Finches and a lovely blue bird, which I could not identify, flitted about and filled the air with their music.

At the edge of the grassland, and hidden behind a formidable living cactus hedge, was a tiny settlement of straw-covered mud huts. A fine old man was sitting in the doorway of his home next to the settlement's granary, the mud walls of which were embedded with animal skulls – obviously 'juju' to deter would-be thieves.

Our boys found a termite hill and, with the help of some local children and their pickaxe, set about unearthing the queen. Meanwhile, our elder daughter, Hannah, and I tried to find a safe route up Gog and Megog, but the grass near the top was too dense and high for us to see our footfalls and, as we had been warned about snakes in the area, we decided that discretion was the better part of valour and retraced our steps.

When we had regrouped we drove down a very twisty bit of track to the other delightful little reservoir, which Hannah and I had spotted on our climb. But for the absence of heather, this could have been a Scottish loch and we could see why the Scots of bygone days felt so much at home here. The outlet from the reservoir was a gushing torrent and its grassy bank, shaded by trees, offered us the perfect spot upon which to feast as much on the scenery as on our picnic.

We then set out along the bund holding back the waters to walk around the reservoir. The bund was less than ten feet across at the top and fell away sharply on both sides. We were only part way across it when we disturbed two enormous snakes, which I think were puff adders. Luckily, they took to the water and we moved on, only to encounter another, smaller snake a few yards further along. Again we decided that enough was enough and gave up our idea of a walk. In this remote area a bite from a poisonous snake, such as a puff adder or cobra, would almost certainly prove fatal.

Kurra Falls, 22 August 1986

We headed for Kurra Falls, where we had spent such an enjoyable camping trip last December in the dry season. This is a wild area comprising a series of lakes set amongst rolling, grass-covered hills which, for all the world, looked just like the Scottish highlands. The weather was not as hot as it had been on our previous visit and clouds overhead and on the horizon threatened rain. The rocky slope that fell away from the outlet to the main lake, which had been bone dry on our earlier visit, was now a beautiful cascade of sparkling white water, resembling the train of an enormous wedding dress.

Arriving at our previous camping spot, the men soon had the fires roaring. Meantime, the young were busy looking for scorpions – the area was full of small brown ones – whilst the women unpacked the 'goodies' for our slap up feast: steaks, plus the last of our bacon and the final tin of baked beans brought out from England – a real treat. Who would have thought that we would clamour for baked beans!?

If we had been allowed to make only one trip outside Kaduna, undoubtedly we would all have chosen Yankari Game Reserve, located in Bauchi State, north eastern Nigeria. At the time, Yankari was a little-known and somewhat loosely controlled facility, which made it all the more exciting, if a little dangerous. Visitors were accommodated in functional African-style chalets at a camp well inside the reserve. Known as Wikki Camp, it was situated on the slopes above Wikki warm spring, which formed a large natural swimming pool at the head of a jungle stream. Although the near bank had been concreted, the far side retained its natural covering of dense forest.

With a constant water temperature of around 31°C, this was the ideal place to relax. Although we could visit the spring 24 hours a day, we had to bear in mind that this was a game park, without a barrier of any kind to prevent wild animals entering the area. Indeed, one evening when the children were down at the spring, we heard the roar of a lion very close by and started running to fetch them back to the relative safety of the camp. They, too, had heard the lion and immediately made a hasty retreat for home. Next morning, we saw a lion's pug marks on the small man-made beach at the tail of the pool, just opposite the access path. There were no moonlight dips after this!

Our nearest and constant neighbours were baboons. These creatures seemed to know that there were rich pickings to be had in occupied chalets and were quick to find their way in at every opportunity. On one occasion, after hearing a commotion, we found Zoë in a tug of war with a young baboon over a sack of charcoal. We had to yell for her to let go before things turned nasty. The youngster ran off with his prize, but ditched it as soon as he discovered its contents. Baboons would also come worryingly close when we were cooking or eating, so that somebody had constantly to remain on guard at such times.

The baboons would often join us whilst we were swimming in Wikki Springs, taking delight in diving into the warm water from tree branches overhanging the pool. Usually, they seemed quite happy to share the pool with us. However, one afternoon we got a sharp reminder that these were wild animals, and potentially very dangerous ones at that. Hannah and Zoë were down at the pool with me enjoying a quiet swim, when we were joined by a large troop of baboons. All seemed well for a time, but then a number of adolescent males started to become very boisterous. We decided to leave, but as soon as we emerged from the water the baboons became very aggressive towards us.

Baring their fearsome teeth and screaming at the tops of their voices, the baboons rushed at us from different directions, stopping just short when we screamed back and lashed out with our arms at them. I grabbed a nearby dustbin lid to try to ward off their grasping arms and gnashing teeth, hitting one as it tried to grab hold of Hannah. At one stage, a large male got behind us whilst several smaller animals rushed us from the front in a combined attack. The large animal was screaming into my right ear and I could feel its hot breath on my neck. It seemed that at any moment he would give me the *coup de grâce.* Despite being almost frozen with fear, I lashed out behind me with the dustbin lid and managed to hit the animal in the face, bringing an end to that particular assault.

Knowing that an adult male baboon's jaws are strong enough to crush a leopard's skull, I realised that if the baboons persisted in their attack we were in serious trouble. Worryingly, they seemed in no hurry to let up. Just as things started to look desperate, a group of Nigerian women heard our shouts and came to the rescue. Amazingly, the baboons backed off a little as the women approached and calmly tucked the girls into the folds of their skirts. They then gathered round me as we started to move off, because they felt that our white skins had provoked the attack. Several of the adolescent male baboons were still keen to continue the fight, one even jumping on to a branch overhanging the access path to bar our exit. Screaming at us at eye level, he was unceremoniously put in his place by a defiant lady with a hefty swipe of her handbag! Our ordeal was over and our gallant rescuers melted away almost before we could thank them. We never discovered who they were.

The morning and evening game drives followed the same route and each lasted about two hours. We invariably saw game but, except for elephants, which were present in huge numbers, these sightings were not as prolific as in East Africa. However, some encounters, especially in thick jungle, were every bit as exhilarating and included being mock charged by elephants on three separate occasions. The following extract from our diaries includes our most frightening wildlife encounter:

Tuesday 15 April 1986

The air conditioning kept going until about 3.00 a.m., when the electricity failed. Soon our 'hut' became unbearably hot and stuffy, despite opening all the window slats (we could not open any of the windows themselves because of the baboons). We were all awakened from our fitful sleep at 6.00 a.m., when a baboon landed on our roof with a loud thump. Next minute, the Hollands' car alarm went off, triggered by another baboon. By now we were all wide awake and very sticky. Fortunately, we had filled the bath overnight, so were able to plunge in to cool down – a trick we had learnt in Sudan. We lit the barbecue to make a cup of tea and then made our way to the camp office to join the queue for the 7.30 a.m. game drive.

No diesel so no truck but, after a delay of 30 minutes, two long wheelbase Safari Land Rovers turned up and those of us who had waited managed to squeeze in and off we went. We had almost completed our run, being bitten to death by tsetse flies and having seen nothing of real interest when our guide spotted a magnificent lion and lioness very close to our vehicle in thick bush country. The lioness leapt up into a tree on the edge of our track, clambering to a height of 15 feet or so in next to no time – so no use climbing a tree to escape a lion, we pondered! She was now on a branch overhanging our way forward. Meanwhile, the male took up a position on the track beside the tree. We had ample opportunity for photographs, but had to 'shoot' through the vehicle's windscreen, because every time we poked our heads out of the side windows the animal came charging at us, snarling angrily. Clearly he felt very protective of his mate.

Eventually, it was time to move on, but we had to get past the lion and then drive under the lioness. The lion took great exception to us moving forward. Leaving the track he crouched facing us in the grass, snarling, lashing his tail and twitching his rump. Then, with a chilling roar, he took off at a rate of knots and sprang at the vehicle, hitting it just above the rear wheel arch on the side Toni and our son, Rorie, were sitting, but mercifully missing the window. The British Caledonian manager, who was with us, captured the whole incident on video. [We have a copy of the video and can hear Zoë urging the driver to "*Go! Go! Go!*" and also the thud of the lion hitting the vehicle. Fortunately, the lioness remained in her tree.]

We had hardly recovered from the excitement when, a few miles further on, we came across a herd of elephants peacefully browsing in a patch of thick bush. They seemed so calm and disinterested in us that Alex and I got out of the vehicle to photograph them – it was difficult to get good pictures from inside our closed vehicle. The animals were all around us and some were no more than 10-15 yards away.

Having since visited a number of established, internationally recognised game reserves, we now realise just how foolhardy we were. At that stage we had not experienced the mock charges to which we were subjected on later trips to Yankari.

The next day we were on the back of a lorry with a group of Nigerians when we came across 'our' two lions again, instantly recognisable by the bad tempered male. We persuaded our guide to keep our distance; he had not seen the activities of the previous day. The lion appeared to start stalking, but we couldn't see its intended prey. From time to time we lost sight of it, but each time it reappeared it was closer to us. A Nigerian standing next to me turned and asked, "Can this thing," pointing to the lorry, "run faster than that mighty beast?" When I replied "No," he responded by declaring fatalistically: "Then soon we will not be this number because he is coming and surely he will catch one of us!"

At this, a state of panic took hold, and everyone started to shout for the driver to go. Indeed, the lion was really quite close now and there was a fearful look in his eyes. Without warning, the truck lurched forward and a young Nigerian woman lost her balance and almost fell over the back. Luckily, two of her colleagues grabbed her and unceremoniously pulled her to safety as the vehicle sped away with the lion in hot pursuit. Thankfully the animal, having successfully dealt with the threat to his mate, soon gave up the chase.

Another interesting trip we undertook was to the Gurara Falls, near Abuja, about two and a half hours down the Lagos road from Kaduna. This used to be heralded as Nigeria's premier tourist attraction in bygone days, but was rapidly being reclaimed by the bush when we visited the area. Expensive road-making machinery lay abandoned and rusting by the track and the hot dog kiosk had long since closed and was falling down.

The falls, however, lived up to our expectations, although they cannot be compared to Victoria Falls or the Tissisat Falls in Ethiopia. At this point, the Gurara River makes its way down a shallow depression about 200-300 yards wide, at the end of which is a vertical step of about 90 feet, over which the river tumbles to quieter, but swift waters below. When we visited in late August 1986, the river was in full spate and the roar, the spray and its awesome power were truly impressive.

We returned to Kaduna via Abuja, which is now the capital of Nigeria but at that time was little more than a small village. As we approached it from the South, our road seemed to be straddled by an enormous inselberg, similar in shape to a miniature Ayers Rock (Uluru) – an amazing sight. This is the Aso Rock, which stands over 1,000 feet high and is over half a mile wide.

Abuja, itself was quite eerie. There, out in the midst of the bush, wide roadways were laid out, but nothing else. Some of these were surfaced, whilst the majority had merely been graded. These were the arteries and veins, the conduits, which would later provide the means of circulation for people and commodities around the city.

To get a real flavour of the culture and traditions of Northern Nigeria we travelled to Katsina in the north to witness the festivities marking the Muslim feast of Eid al-Adha (known as Eid al Kabir in Northern Nigeria) that commemorates Abraham's willingness to obey God's command to sacrifice his son Ishmael. This is one of the two most important Muslim Eids, the other being Eid al-Fitr that marks the end of Ramadan. Literally thousands of people from the surrounding villages flocked to the dusty town square to demonstrate their allegiance to the local Emir, or ruler. These festivals are known as durbars or sallahs.

26 August 1985 – Katsina Durbar

Hundreds upon thousands of people paraded around the square, some on foot, others on horseback, singing, dancing and mock fighting. Some of the men were brandishing fearsome-looking spears and small round shields made from elephant or rhinoceros hide. Everyone was dressed in the most spectacular national robes, whilst most of the horses were decked out as medieval horses of old.

One Juju *man was carrying a cluster of snakes, but I could not identify them. The whole kaleidoscope of colour, the pageantry, the cacophony of tribal chanting, drums and horns was all quite breathtaking. This went on for about an hour, as endless streams of people came to pay their respects to the Emir, who was yet to make an appearance!*

Eventually the Emir arrived, escorted by his bodyguard, which comprised 'foot soldiers' in the van carrying ancient muskets which they fired into the air at random. Two troops of cavalry carrying fearsome-looking spears brought up the rear, one dressed in loose-fitting blue robes and the other troop in scarlet tunics. The Emir, dressed in sparkling white robes, was on horseback, accompanied by a huge, bare-chested eunuch, who rode a pace behind and sheltered the Emir with a huge umbrella.

As luck would have it, we were positioned just beside the place where the Emir took up his position. Immediately, groups of horsemen took it in turns to gallop full tilt up to the Emir, brandishing spears, swords and ancient firearms. They stopped just feet away from the Emir, rearing up in clouds of dust by way of salute. At this stage, Toni wisely gathered the children closer to her, as excited horses and horsemen manoeuvred within feet of us to clear the arena for the next charge, which was already underway – all very exhilarating, if a little dangerous.

We also attended similar durbars in Sokoto and Kano.

Another truly exhilarating taste of Nigerian culture was provided by the end of year celebrations (Wasa) at the Command and Staff College – a spectacular display of vibrant tribal dancing to the incessant beat of many drums, by men and women in vivid costumes – a photographer's paradise!

Juju (witchcraft) was very much part of the culture in Nigeria, especially in the rural areas, where we came across market stalls selling all manner of potions – powders, herbal concoctions and animal parts.

Indeed, *juju* was not simply the preserve of the people living out in the bush, but seemed to be in the psyche of even some of the most educated Nigerians. A case in point concerned a Nigerian friend of ours who found some blood on her doorstep one morning. She wiped it up, thinking that one of her children had cut himself. The next morning the family again saw blood, this time just inside the door. Over the next few days the smears of blood crossed their sitting room and climbed up the wall until one morning it had splattered their wedding photograph. At this point they asked their local priest, an Irishman, to say Mass in their house. The result was no more blood.

Who had been responsible? They never discovered the culprit. It is quite possible that a member of the family had upset somebody, who had then gone to a *juju* man to place a curse on them. Of course, the trail of blood didn't appear by magic. In such circumstances, the victim invariably has to find another source of 'magic' (usually another more powerful, and more expensive, *juju* man) to remove the curse. In a country where religion and witchcraft seem to coexist, the priest was powerful enough to 'break the spell', or, rather, to deter the culprit from terrorising the family any further.

The day after the Katsina celebrations we had opted for a leisurely start, given the excitement of the day before. Thus we were barely up when the doorbell rang at about 7.30 a.m. Imagine my surprise when I opened the door to be told that Nigeria was in the midst of a coup. We were to remain in our houses and listen to the news. We tuned into the BBC World Service which opened with: *"Reports are coming in of a coup attempt in Nigeria..."* We switched to Radio Lagos, where a British Military Band played a bizarre selection of music – Rule Britannia, the Royal Air Force March, The British Grenadiers and light opera from Gilbert and Sullivan.

Every half hour, the music was interrupted by one Colonel Joshua Dogonyaro, who told us that he had seized power 'for the good of Nigeria' from the President, Major General Buhari, who himself had seized power in a coup some 20 months earlier. We were to stay calm and observe a strict dusk to dawn curfew. All ports, airports and borders were closed.

After a quiet day at home, all the BAT members congregated at the BAT Commander's house to be briefed on the situation. This had been a bloodless coup, and General Babangida, an Armoured Corps officer, had been sworn in as the new President of Nigeria. (Strangely enough, Toni had shaken hands with him at a parade in Lagos whilst I was trying to get our car released from Customs.) We were to observe the curfew and there was to be no unnecessary movement outside the married quarters' complex until the situation returned to normal. He finished by saying that the Command and Staff College was to reopen at 9.00 a.m. the following morning and all of us working there were to travel on the army bus.

Luckily all the children were out with us for the summer holidays, but this must have been a worrying time for our parents; there was no means of letting them know we were fine. Indeed, apart from the curfew and restricted movement outside the quarters' area, life went on pretty much as usual. We certainly weren't in any danger.

Within a few days life got back to normal. But then came the military purge. Within weeks of the coup, some 40 officers, including General Buhari, were compulsorily retired. Amongst the others was a Lieutenant Colonel Chris Ojokwe, a really likeable man who was my team leader at Jaji. Apparently he knew General Buhari and, by an unhappy coincidence, had visited him as a friend just days before the coup. Despite the fact that he was actually teaching a syndicate on the Staff course at the time, he was removed immediately; a rising star one minute and a penniless nobody the next.

Another victim of the purge was Colonel Coord (Coordination) at

Headquarters, the Command and Staff College. His place was taken by Lieutenant Colonel Moses Effiong, one of the key officers on the Directing Staff to whom we were in the process of handing over our responsibilities. This supposed elevation in status was to cost poor Moses very dearly later on.

Some ten days after the coup it was time for the children to return to school in England. As Zoë was to join Hannah at boarding school, Toni had arranged to accompany the children back to England and remain there for a while to settle her in.

Our point of entry and exit from Nigeria was the airport at Kano, some three and a half hours north of Kaduna on that dreaded road. We travelled in the army bus whenever possible, this being considered the safest option. The wisdom of this decision was reinforced when we were involved in two minor accidents on one particular airport run.

On another occasion it was freak weather, rather than the atrocious driving, that caused our hearts to flutter. We were about half an hour from Kano when an enormous black cloud started to move rapidly across the sky, blotting out the sun and plunging us into an eerie half-light. Suddenly I noticed the guinea corn about 200 yards ahead of us being flattened by an unseen force. An instant later, two cyclists were thrown off their bicycles in front of us before we, too, were blown quite literally off the road by a fearsome wind. Our driver, Sergeant Alidue, did magnificently. Fighting for control, he kept the vehicle out of the guinea corn and got it back onto the tarmac just as the heavens opened. We had never experienced rain like it; it was if we had driven into a waterfall but could not come out the other side. Then, almost as quickly as it had struck, the storm moved on to wreak its havoc elsewhere, leaving us to continue our journey, shaken but unharmed.

We flew to and from Britain with British Caledonian and 'our' particular aircraft were *Mungo Park* and, occasionally, *Robbie Burns* and *John Logie Baird*. The flight usually arrived and departed just before midnight. The excitement we felt as we watched *Mungo Park* make its descent into Kano with our children onboard was intense but, within a matter of weeks, this was followed by sadness as the same aircraft departed for England, whisking them away again. Knowing that we had to return to Kaduna on that perilous road, the children never settled at school until we telephoned to say that we were safely home. Given the unreliability of NET, the Nigerian external telephone service, it was sometimes several days before we could get through.

As we were not allowed to travel on the roads by night, trips to the airport entailed staying overnight in the Central Hotel in Kano. This was a large, somewhat rundown facility, but the best the town had to offer. The public rooms were located in one block, whilst all the accommodation was contained in several blocks across an unlit open patch of grass. After dark, this grassed area was patrolled by 'ladies of the night' who we called 'night fighters'. They were very brazen and persistent in their attempts to entertain male guests. On one occasion, I was intercepted and declined, stating that my wife was waiting for me in our room. Unfazed, the young lady retorted, "They all say that!" So I said she was welcome to come along and see for herself. Thankfully, she ran off when Toni opened the door.

Whenever possible, we crossed the courtyard in groups and always ensured that our children were accompanied by an adult.

Like anywhere else in Nigeria at the time, the Central Hotel suffered its share of power cuts and plumbing problems, but these were par for the course and we took them in our stride. On one occasion, however, we endured a unique experience when a swarm of bees entered the room occupied by Toni and the girls via a disused air conditioning vent. Miraculously, they weren't stung, but had no option but to vacate the room to the intruders and join myself and the boys for the rest of the night.

Meanwhile, back at Jaji, replacement Nigerian directing staff began to arrive and the plan for the British team to hand over their responsibilities and depart by the middle of the following year was confirmed. As a result, we were kept busy running the current staff course, whilst at the same time training up the new directing staff. The aim was for the Nigerians to assume full responsibility for running the next staff course, starting in August 1986, with just one or two advisers to oversee proceedings and act as back-up if required until the end of the year.

Midway through the morning on our last working day before Christmas 1985, I had almost completed handing over part of my responsibilities to a Nigerian colleague. At the morning break, I left the office and joined a group of other officers in the courtyard, whilst my would-be successor remained behind to review his notes. A few minutes later, I noticed a Nigerian Army major wearing a red beret enter my office, whereupon my colleague immediately leapt to attention – odd, I thought, as he was senior to the visitor. But I also knew that the visitor was a military policeman, by virtue of his red beret. After the minimum of discussion, the two officers left the room together. I asked my Nigerian colleagues what was going on. They all looked concerned and told me to keep talking and take no notice. I never saw my would-be successor again.

Over the next few days, almost all the Nigerian directing staff were removed from their posts and, after Christmas, their British counterparts had to pick up the pieces, including stepping in to keep the current staff course running smoothly. Apparently, the powers that be in Lagos had uncovered a plot, thought to have been hatched in whole or in part by directing staff in the Command and Staff College, to overthrow President

Babangida's fledgling government.

Amongst the Army Directing Staff who were apprehended were two of Nigeria's most promising army officers, Lieutenant Colonels Mike Iyorshe and Moses Effiong. Both these officers were graduates of the British Army Staff College, Camberley and, in my opinion, both could have more than held their own in any country's army. They were greatly liked and respected by all their colleagues at the Command and Staff College.

Just before this drama, our BAT Commander, Colonel Graham Holland, fell ill and had to return to Britain for treatment. In his absence, the position of Senior British Officer (SBO) was assumed by the Commander of the RN Team, whilst I represented the Army Team at BAT meetings.

A few days after the 'Nigerian officer cull', my Nigerian boss, Brigadier Ibrahim, asked to see me. A very approachable, pleasant and compassionate man, we had something in common, both being armoured corps officers. He was concerned about one of my former DS colleagues in particular, Lieutenant Colonel Jimmy Akor of the Nigerian Signal Corps, who had been suspended along with many other officers.

Jimmy was a quiet, conscientious officer, and somebody I would rate as totally honest and loyal. The Brigadier was convinced that he had nothing whatsoever to do with the coup attempt and asked if I could vouch for his movements over the past few weeks. Jimmy and his family lived in the NDA compound, but their house was quite some distance from ours. Whilst I was able to account for his time during office hours, sadly I could not do so for his off-duty time, particularly at night. In reality, nobody could, apart from his immediate family, and their testimony was invalid. This unfortunate scenario must have applied to a number of other officers as well.

In the event, as far as I know, no charges were brought against Jimmy. Despite this, I understand that he was dismissed from the service, without a pension, and he and his family had to vacate their army quarters immediately – another good man and his family thrown out onto the dusty, unforgiving Nigerian streets. I certainly never saw him again.

Rumours of how the coup was to have been executed soon started to spread. One of these suggested that it was to be launched by an air assault on NDA – the very camp in which we were all housed. This was to be a diversionary attack and, because it was where most of the Command and Staff College directing staff lived, it was considered to have the added benefit of deflecting suspicion away from anyone working at the College. The idea was to wait until Lagos deployed forces to deal with the situation at NDA before launching the actual coup in the capital. Whether this plan was true or a product of the rumour machine we may never know. But had such a plan been carried out, our lives would have been very much at risk.

As we entered into the Christmas school holiday period, the atmosphere, as far as our professional interests were concerned, was tense and uncertain. At home, however, we tried to carry on as normal so as not to either spoil the holiday for the children or worry them in any way about the security of our situation in the longer term, when they were back at boarding school.

Colonel Graham arrived back on 4 January 1986 and I was able to brief him about the alleged attempted coup, the officers who had been removed from the Staff College and the implications for us as a result. Clearly, it was now highly unlikely that our handover to the Nigerians could proceed as planned – we had virtually nobody to whom we could handover anything! For the second time in four months we were left to pick up the pieces again to keep the show on the road.

Whilst all this was going on I had noticed that my Adam's apple seemed to be growing rather large. Indeed, I was beginning to find it difficult to wear a collar and tie when the occasion demanded. So when Colonel Graham returned and we were more or less back on an even keel, I decided to pay Dr Smith a visit. He thought that there was something awry with my thyroid gland and recommended that I return to Britain for examination. So, in mid-February, Toni and I flew back home and I was admitted to the Queen Elizabeth Military Hospital (QEMH). Toni, too, was given a bed in the hospital's own hostel so that she could be with me.

It transpired that I had a tumour on my thyroid and needed surgery to have it removed. The 'op' was carried out there and then. Thankfully, the tumour was found to be benign and, even though I had lost half my thyroid, tests indicated that the bit that was left was still producing sufficient thyroxin, thus obviating the need for me to take any supplements. I had got away with things very lightly; something that was reinforced in stark manner during my recovery.

Whilst I was recuperating a nurse came to seek my assistance. She had discovered that I had served in the Sudan and told me that there were two badly injured Sudanese officers being treated in the hospital. They were far from home and very lonely, and she felt that a visit from me might lift their spirits. She warned me that they had one leg between them. I am not best suited to such tasks, but, of course, agreed to visit them straightaway.

Full of fear and trepidation, I knocked on the door of their room and went in. Both men's faces lit up with delight as I greeted them in (rather poor) Arabic, but almost immediately they started to look concerned. Then the older of the two grabbed his glass of orange juice and offered it to me. Their sole concern was that I was their guest and they had no gift with which to greet me – such is the legendary hospitality of the Sudanese people. Certainly, these two patients did not appear to have an ounce of self pity. The younger man was a newly commissioned lieutenant in the infantry, who had had his legs blown off in an unmarked minefield. The other man was the Regiment's doctor, who had bravely gone into the minefield to treat the casualty and had also trodden on a mine. Their lot was immeasurably worse than mine, and I enjoyed my daily visits to them during my week's recuperation.

A day or two after my operation, a fellow RTR officer from the BAT Team, Major Paddy Bangham, also returned to QEMH for medical treatment. When he dropped in to see me I asked him how things were back in Kaduna. Judging that I looked strong enough to take bad news, he told me that ten of the attempted coup suspects, including our friend, Mike Iyorshe, had been found guilty of treason and had been executed by firing squad on 5 March. At the news, I slumped into my chair and almost lost consciousness.

Moses Effiong had been spared the firing squad, but had been sentenced to life imprisonment. Whilst there was no evidence to link him to the plot, he was Colonel Coord – the person who had to have his finger on the pulse regarding all the activities in his area of responsibility – in the very establishment in which some of the alleged plotters had worked. As such, it was felt that he must either have known about the plot, or been criminally negligent in his duties – a no-win situation if ever there was one.

What made Moses' circumstances even sadder was that a few years later his delightful and wonderfully supportive and loyal wife, Christina, was tragically killed in a traffic accident on that notoriously dangerous Kano road. She had been on her way to visit Moses in Zaria prison. Years later, I was delighted to read that Moses had been released in 1993, having served seven years of his sentence.

I was not allowed to fly for three weeks after the operation, which meant that we would get back only just in time for the children's Easter holidays. In the event, Toni returned to Nigeria alone a few days earlier, to get the house ready in time for the happy invasion, whilst I returned with the children. Oddly, in both cases our planes had to over fly Kano and land at Lagos. In Toni's case this was because of a violent tropical storm over Kano and in mine because the runway had been closed temporarily 'due to an incident on the ground'.

Toni landed in Lagos at 2.00 a.m. After waiting two hours in the transit lounge, she and her fellow Kano-bound passengers were allowed back onto *Mungo Park*, as the new British Caledonian crew had received permission to fly back to London via Kano instead of directly, as scheduled. When we flew out, the children and I arrived in Lagos just before 7.00 p.m. and were not so fortunate because the return flight to London was fully booked. We spent four hours in the transit lounge which, although relatively clean and air-conditioned, was devoid of anywhere one could buy even so much as a drink of water.

At 11.00 p.m. our flight was called – British Caledonian having chartered a Boeing 737 of Kabo Air to fly us up to Kano. Kabo Air, an internal Nigerian-run airline, had opened up the flight to other passengers and the aircraft was full as we lumbered down the runway and soared upwards towards a threatening sky. Within minutes we flew into an electrical storm. I do not know if the aircraft was struck by lightning, but suddenly there was a loud crack and the cabin lights went out. The aircraft was thrown about the sky and seemed to lose momentum and fall backwards for a moment. Then the engine revs increased, the lights came back on and we regained our equilibrium as suddenly as we had just lost it.

Immediately after Easter and barely four weeks after my operation, I returned to work at Jaji. It was 1 April 1986 and I found the Command and Staff College a rather sombre place. None of my former Nigerian colleagues were there and the current staff course was being kept going largely by the remaining three British and two Ghanaian directing staff. This was the week when the main Command Post exercise took place at Jaji. Lasting some 60 hours and simulating the activities in a main headquarters during operations, it was designed to test the students' abilities in Command and Control of a fast moving battlefield scenario.

I was the exercise sponsor but, luckily, had completed all the preparation required before going into hospital and now had two days to tie up any loose ends before 'battle commenced'. The exercise proved a great success, lifting morale amongst the directing staff and students alike. Together, we were certainly going to ensure that the course would be completed successfully.

For the next term, a number of students from the police joined the course. Due to the shortage of directing staff, I was again one of the teaching staff. This was a very interesting term and there was ample opportunity for the military and civilian students to discuss matters such as riot control and managing hostage situations. One particular subject that is etched into my memory concerned the principle of 'minimum force'.

Throughout our time in Nigeria, the armed hijacking of cars on the road was commonplace. The advice given to expatriates when we first arrived was, if confronted with such a situation, act calmly and simply hand over your car keys without any further ado and walk away. The reason for this was that the hijackers were usually high on drugs and, with their adrenaline going into overdrive, they were likely to shoot at the slightest (or perceived) provocation.

Then, in an attempt to reduce the incidence of hijacking, the government introduced the death penalty for anyone convicted of armed car theft. Soon after, two Europeans in Lagos were stopped by armed hijackers. They duly handed over their car keys, but were then both shot dead. As armed hijacking was now a capital offence, the hijackers were almost certainly going to eliminate any witnesses.

Our advice was then altered to getting out of the car, throwing the keys as far away as possible and running for your life in the opposite direction. Luckily, we never had to put this advice into practice.

At the appropriate time on the course we discussed the current approach to tackling the problem of armed car hijacking. I initiated a debate, based on the principle of minimum force, whereby capital punishment would only apply in instances where the hijackers killed their victim or victims. Although this gained the approval of my students, the law remained unchanged, certainly for the rest of our time in Nigeria.

Within a fortnight of the term ending, the consequences of failing to apply the principle of minimum force were tragically exposed. My diary entry at the time, gleaned from media reports, to reassure our parents at home (we wrote in less detail to our children) reads as follows:

> *1 June 1986 – Addendum*
>
> *You may have heard something in the news about student riots in Nigeria, so I want to put you in the picture. Last Friday, some students at Ahmadu Bello University (ABU) in Zaria were sent down for 'misconduct' – I believe they were parading in memory of another student who had been killed in a riot some years ago. Apparently, the police were called in and at some stage opened fire, killing between 8-20 students and injuring several others.*
> *It is ironic that I was instructing the police Staff College (students) only two weeks ago on riot control drills and, in particular, the use of necessary minimum force in crowd dispersal. I do not know the circumstances, but it would appear that the police over-reacted. The result was a series of riots at universities and polytechnics all over Nigeria. A police station and police barracks here in Kaduna were attacked on Wednesday (the barracks was burned down) and another two students lost their lives. About 15 universities and schools of higher education have been closed to allow tempers to cool and all seems quiet now.*
> *Rest assured, we are in no way involved, no curbs have been put on our movements and our safety is not threatened in the very least. So now you have the facts as we know them.*

The students from the Police College having left, we entered into the Low Intensity Operations term. Again, I was on the teaching staff. One of the main features of this term was the number of outside experts who came to share their experiences with the students. Having been born in India, I was asked to look after Major General Gill of the Indian Army, who came to lecture the students on desert warfare. In the same week, the Australian directing staff from Camberley, Lieutenant Colonel Peter Cosgrove MC came out to lecture the College on his experiences in Vietnam. My diary entry that evening read:

> *He was really very interesting to listen to and, like all true heroes, he was very modest about the part he played and yet he won the MC and an American gallantry award (he never mentioned this in his talk).*

I really enjoyed being in charge of a syndicate during that particular term, as I was able to speak from personal experience about operating and surviving in both jungle and desert environments, having served in Borneo and the Middle East.

For the final term of the course, the students from all three services came together in mixed syndicates to consider joint service operations. I was the only British officer on the teaching staff. Unlike Britain, where the Royal Navy is the Senior Service, the army takes precedence in Nigeria and much of the discussion focused upon the support that the other two services should provide for the army during operations.

There was also a political element to this final term and one guest lecturer will always stick in my mind. He was the First Secretary of the East German Embassy in Lagos, who delivered a lecture on the German Democratic Republic (GDR). An astute diplomat, he was serious and unsmiling in his demeanour, economical with his words, and clipped and didactic in his delivery.

Only the students were allowed to ask questions, but they did not pull their punches. Asked if he wanted to see the reunification of Germany, he replied emphatically, "No!" His reason was that the country had only been unified for 70 years of its long history, so unification was not 'normal', was not what the German people were used to, nor what they wanted. Asked why the Berlin Wall had been erected, he replied that it was to keep West Germans out of East Germany. When pressed, he added that it was also to stop the West from 'stealing' East German engineers and scientists. He was a sincere man and utterly loyal to his country and the Warsaw Pact. He clearly believed in what he was saying and I had to respect him for that. I have often wondered since how he, and no doubt countless others like him, coped when the Cold War ended, the Berlin Wall was demolished and Germany was, indeed, reunified. It cannot have been easy.

The five-week term flew by and before we knew it we were getting ready for the graduation festivities, all of which took place at the Command and Staff College, Jaji. Events got underway with a formal dinner for the students and the directing staff, presided over by the Commandant. The following evening we were back at Jaji with our wives to attend the Graduation Ball. This was a wonderfully colourful affair with everyone dressed up in their own particular tribal finery. Not to be outdone, I wore my kilt, whilst Toni was dressed in the colours of Saint George. As I had been teaching for the past three terms, I knew most of the students well and thus we chose to sit with them instead of our BAT colleagues.

In Nigeria, you could never rule out the unexpected and this night was no exception. The ball ended at midnight and we all then clambered aboard our bus for the drive back to Kaduna. Our first concern was that our driver for the evening (not Sergeant Alidue) had clearly drunk too much, but we had no choice but to put our lives in his hands. Somehow, we weaved our way back to Kaduna without mishap, but then, just as we reached the outskirts of the town, we were stopped at a police roadblock. Our immediate thought was that they might arrest the driver, but no, the situation was a little more awkward; we were informed that a snap curfew had been imposed on the town and we would have to remain where we were until daybreak – over five hours away. Not only was this highly inconvenient, but it also threatened to prevent the men's return to Jaji next morning in their best bib and tucker for the Graduation Ceremony, at which the guest of honour was none other than President Babangida himself.

The situation took a turn for the worse when a Nigerian officer tried to pull rank and started shouting at the police, demanding that we be allowed to proceed. I believe that purely because I was wearing my kilt, the British contingent on the bus elected me and an equally colourfully attired Nigerian colleague to approach the police and try to defuse the situation. After some very diplomatic negotiations by my Nigerian colleague, we were eventually allowed on our way.

We had already been informed that there would be no bus to take us back to Jaji next morning for the Graduation Ceremony and that we would all have to make our own arrangements. Although we were not required to be seated in the main hall, known as the Danjuma Hall, until 11.00 a.m, we had to make an early start, as the road was due to be closed an hour and a half beforehand to ensure that the Presidential convoy had a clear run.

We were making good progress when, some ten miles short of our destination, we caught sight of two policemen on motorbikes racing up behind us. These people had a habit of kicking the side of your car with their hobnailed boots as they passed to get you off the road. Anticipating this, our driver, Paddy Dunseath, timed his swerve to a tee, almost causing the nearest policeman to lose his balance as he lashed out at us. We were ordered to pull over, but the two policemen were clearly quite taken aback to find the car occupied by three British officers in their best uniforms.

When we explained that we were on our way to attend a ceremony headed by President Babangida, they saluted and asked us to follow them. We completed the journey with the police acting as our outriders.

But that was not all. Showing true African exuberance, they treated us to a display worthy of any motorcycle display team, standing up and facing us, sitting on their handlebars, and so on. At one stage, one of them lay back along his bike and, after performing a series of 'star bursts' with his arms and legs, stretched out with his feet over the handlebars and his head bent over the back wheel, whereupon he gave us a beaming upside down smile and salute before curling back up to a sitting position in the saddle – quite amazing, albeit a little dangerous on the public highway and with our car only a few yards behind.

The Danjuma Hall was a riot of colour and pageantry. There were Emirs and their courtiers in splendid robes, Ambassadors from various countries, and senior officers from all three services wearing their Number 2 Dress uniforms. Then came the students, also similarly dressed, together with their wives decked out in their best finery; the whole scene coalesced into a magnificent kaleidoscope of colour.

President Babangida presented all the students with their graduation certificates. This qualification entitled them to include the letters *psc* (Passed Staff College) after their names in military records and opened up numerous career opportunities for them all. In his speech, President Babangida thanked Britain for having established and run the Command and Staff College for the past ten years and reminded everyone that he had been a student on the second course. He then thanked the current British officers for having handed their responsibilities over so efficiently despite 'facing some difficulties'. Finally, in a very nice touch, he presented a special award to 'our' bus driver, Sergeant Alidue, who had driven the bus taking the British team to and from work throughout their time in Nigeria.

That should have marked the end of my tour in Nigeria, but the cull amongst the Nigerian officers resulting from the coup and attempted coup had necessitated a change of plan. In my case, my tour had been extended by another seven months, meaning that I was now entitled to a mid-tour leave. This had to be taken during the summer recess, so we were soon winging our way back to Britain on *Mungo Park,* making the return trip to Nigeria with the children in early August during their summer holidays.

Whilst we had been busy keeping the show running at Jaji, life was clearly very different, indeed very hard, for those people directly affected by the crackdown following the thwarted coup against President Babangida's government. This was brought into sharp focus for us when, on 24 June 1986, Toni was taken by a missionary friend, Ruth Foxhall, to visit Edna, Mike Iyorshe's widow, and her family. Her diary entry paints a poignant picture:

Edna has a company house now – obviously the firm she works for has come to her rescue. It's quite a nice little bungalow. We met Edna's mother, her mentally-handicapped sister, her student brother and Edna's four children, plus a nephew who lives with them. Then we went outside and met Mike's mother, who lives in the dowager hut in the garden. She is still dressed in black for mourning – four months after Mike's execution. She had the three-year-old granddaughter on her back as she had been crying. In the true African manner she had tied the little girl to her back with a cloth and walked around until she had fallen asleep. It was far too much for the old lady, who was bent double under her burden. We begged her to sit. She could speak no English, but fortunately Ruth,

having lived in Nigeria with a missionary husband for 25 years, speaks Hausa.
Mama was still grieving that she hadn't been allowed to say goodbye to her son. Indeed, none of the families ever saw their husbands/sons/fathers again from the moment they were arrested in December last year until they were executed in March, despite the intervention of Amnesty International (I understand they were buried immediately afterwards without the families' involvement).
Everyone in the house now depended on Edna. Life can be so hard sometimes.

Almost as soon as we returned from leave, our neighbours in 7A, the Wards, completed their tour in Nigeria. They departed for Britain on Peter's fortieth birthday and so we decorated the bus with balloons and streamers. We were very sad to see them go; they had been great neighbours and friends, and their girls and ours were about the same age and had got on really well together. Much later, their daughter Claire was Head Girl at the Royal School, Bath when our youngest, Zoë, entered the school as a sixth former – quite a coincidence.

When the next staff course got under way in late August 1986, Paddy Dunseath and I were only meant to be used in a supporting role. Responsibility for all the teaching was now firmly in Nigerian hands. However, my diary notes indicate that, whilst we were not employed in a teaching role, we were involved in preparing course work and delivering presentations until the end of the year.

Nevertheless, within a week or two I was given a new assignment. Whilst the Nigerians wanted to assume total responsibility for running the Command and Staff College course, they wished to retain a British presence at Jaji in the short term to provide support for the Nigerians now responsible for the training. It was decided that the best way to achieve this without causing the Nigerians to lose face was to establish a small Tri-Service British team and task it to design and run a Higher Division Joint Services Staff course at Jaji. The new British team was to comprise no more than seven officers, drawn from all three Services, and was to be called the Joint Warfare Advisory Team (JWAT).

Working with Colonel Graham, I was required to help write a proposal justifying this plan to the Ministry of Defence. Once this was approved in London, we then had to find accommodation within Jaji for the new team, whilst at the same time making a start on producing its *modus operandi* – all rather unexciting, but essential work. However, I was also asked to write one of the major exercises for the new course, and this got me out into the bush for many a day. We were so short of numbers by now that I had to undertake these trips alone. I travelled in uniform and ensured that I had plenty of water, some food and spare fuel. In accordance with our procedures, I carried no money. This was generally known, so there was little point in trying to rob us. Of course, the threat from vehicle hijackers remained, but this was unlikely out in the bush far away from the main roads, or, indeed, any roads.

I really enjoyed this task, but almost came unstuck on one occasion. On 25 September 1986, Toni's birthday, I set off for the exercise area as usual in the 'Red Lozenge' – our own safari Land Rover (by now I had sold our Mercedes). It had rained heavily during the night and the bush tracks were awash with the rich red mud of Africa. This presented no problems for the Land Rover, however, provided I remained focused. I had almost completed the task I had set myself that day when my attention was taken by a brilliant flash of colour flitting in front of me. I took my eyes off the track momentarily to see what it was – a foolish mistake! In the second or two it took me to identify a Bearded Barbet, I had driven the Land Rover into an enormous hole in the track and was now trapped in mud up to the axles. To make matters worse, it had just started to rain again. Cursing my stupidity, I got out to examine the problem, the mud coming up over my boots. I was clearly not going to get myself out of this mess on my own, and I was an awfully long way from home.

Although seemingly in the middle of nowhere, within a few minutes I became aware that I was being watched. Looking round I saw a group of men standing on a low rise about 30 yards away. They did not look threatening, merely curious, but I thought it best to wave and smile just to ease any possible tension. At this, one of them walked down to me. He spoke quite good English and asked me if I needed help. When I said that I did, he asked me how much 'dash' (money) I had, to which I replied that I was carrying none. He went back to his friends on the rise and after a short discussion returned to me and declared, "Then we will not help you."

I said that I quite understood and thanked him for having come to see me. He seemed quite taken aback by my response, and perhaps he thought that I was bluffing. A hint of a smile played on his lips; the smile of a man who knows he has the upper hand.

"If we don't help you, how will you get out?" he asked. Still trying to stay calm and in all innocence, I replied: "Don't worry, Allah will help me. Soon He will stop the rain from falling and bring out the sun. Then the mud will dry up and my vehicle will rise out of the hole and I will be able to get in and drive away." At this, the man hurried towards his friends shouting, I imagine, in Hausa. They all ran back towards me and my Land Rover was very soon back on firm ground. Then the spokesman approached and said, "Please don't tell the army we asked for 'dash'." With those parting words, they all waved, flashed broad smiles at me and disappeared back into the bush as suddenly as they had appeared.

At the end of September 1986, just under five months before we were due to leave Nigeria, the country's currency, the Naira, was devalued, without any apparent warning, to a third of its former value. This was possibly precipitated by the crash in oil prices and threw the economy into chaos.

The government then introduced a two-tier foreign exchange monetary system in a brave attempt to revitalise the economy. Unfortunately, this measure had a damaging effect on foreign companies, particularly the airlines. For a time, British Caledonian and KLM curtailed or cancelled their flights to and from Nigeria. This meant that our lifeline with the UK – the correspondence with our parents and children – was interrupted. Even when flights did resume, it was difficult to purchase tickets, and when one could, the cost had gone through the roof.

The cost of living rose markedly, whilst imported goods in supermarkets, including Leventus, our supermarket in Kaduna, either disappeared from the shelves or were too expensive to buy. I recall seeing an ordinary medium-sized saucepan in Leventus priced at the equivalent of £55, instead of around the £10 that it had cost before devaluation. Luckily, we were paid in Sterling, but many expatriates living on the local economy decided to leave the country.

Just before Colonel Graham and the Commander of the Royal Navy Team, Captain Peter Broadbent, were due to depart Nigeria, the Commandant of the Command and Staff College invited the remnants of the British team serving at Jaji to a reception in Kaduna 'in honour of the British Advisory Teams 1976-1986' – a very nice gesture.

During the evening, the Commandant gave a flattering address thanking the British Armed Forces for their valuable contribution to Nigeria, to which Colonel Graham responded on behalf of all three Services. Then the Commandant made presentations to all of us, the various gifts equating to our rank and status. In my case these amounted to a Command and Staff College wall plaque, pewter tankard, tie and a statuette of an African Eagle, Nigeria's equivalent to the Staff College, Camberley's owl.

Colonel Graham and his family left in November, leaving Paddy and me as the only Army members of the original team at Jaji. Colonel Graham's replacement was Colonel Adrian Naughten, who launched into his new roles of Senior British Officer (SBO) and the (first) Commander Joint Warfare Advisory Team (JWAT) with great enthusiasm.

As the Team reduced in number, so did the requirement for our married quarters at the Nigerian Defence Academy (NDA). The plan was for the personnel remaining with the Nigerian Army School of Infantry (NASI) and the new JWAT to be accommodated in the bungalows in the vicinity of the Central Facility (our administrative office). All other accommodation was to be handed back to the Nigerians as they were vacated by their British occupants. So it was that 7B was the only occupied quarter in our road for the last month of our tour.

Astonishingly, as soon as these quarters were handed over, they were stripped of their soft furnishings, as well as kitchen appliances and utensils, ceiling fans, air conditioners and even switches. The road looked quite derelict afterwards, with huge holes in the walls where air conditioning units were once fitted. The reason for this was that all these items belonged to the Quartermaster at the Command and Staff College, Jaji, but the quarters were being handed back to his opposite number at NDA in what seemed a very wasteful bureaucratic exercise. However, I dare say we would have done the same!

The dereliction surrounding us only served to emphasise the fact that we were on our way out. On 15 February 1987, we attended Mass at NDA for the last time. At the end of the service we presented the church with six benches, one named after each member of the family. Then we were called to the altar for a farewell blessing. We had been part of that community for about two years and were sad to be leaving.

The following Saturday evening, *Mungo Park* rose into the skies above Kano with us on board. We had enjoyed quite an experience! I had been afflicted with malaria and had then had to fly home to hospital to have a, thankfully benign, tumour removed. We had been mock charged by elephants on three occasions, attacked by an angry lion and a number of baboons. We had survived the hazards of the notorious Kaduna-Kano road, as well as a coup and the ruthless crackdown of a planned coup, that tragically had resulted in the execution, imprisonment and/or dismissal of many of our Nigerian military friends.

Finally, we had experienced the rugged rural countryside of central and northern Nigeria and had enjoyed the warmth of friendship shown by the people living there. Apart from the tragic consequences of the planned coup, we had enjoyed our time in the country. We all agreed that our glass was certainly half full at the very least and were glad that we had said 'yes' when asked to go to Nigeria.

1. Lisa, our maid, was a real treasure

2. John, our very reliable house boy, preparing yams for a Nigerian party

3. Toni's class at Aisha Mohammed International Primary School

4. My 'purple' syndicate at the Command and Staff College, Jaji (Crown copyright)

5. Lt Col Paddy Dunseath facilitating his single Service (Army) syndicate on the river crossing TEWT at Bukuru, near Kaduna (Crown copyright)

6. A local at Bukuru using a novel way to cross the Turbo River

7. A breakfast picnic in the bush near Kaduna

8. A syndicate party in our house – these were always great fun (Crown copyright)

9. Artemis Naughten and me, with the Ludo inselberg in the background (note our 'snake sticks')

10. Rorie and Alex prepare breakfast after a night out on top of Bugai inselberg

11. One of our swimming holes at Bernin Gwari

12. The Caledonian Ball was a major event on the expatriates' calendar in Nigeria. It was held in the Fowley Hall, Jos, the town having been home to some 2,000 Scottish tin miners during the 1950-60s.

13. Kurra Falls, one of our favourite camping venues near Jos

14. Alex's photograph of an elephant barring our way in Yankari game reserve

15. This very aggressive lion in Yankari was guarding its mate, who was up the tree in the background. It held us up for some time and charged our Land Rover when we eventually drove by

16. Zoë at the base of Gurara Falls near Abuja

17. Taken in 1986, this photograph shows the inselberg, Aso Rock, dominating the tiny village of Abuja, now the capital of Nigeria

18. A warrior at a durbar in Kano

19. Warriors charging up to salute the Emir at a durbar in Kano

20. and 21. Wasa end of year celebrations at the National Defence Academy (NDA)

22. Two tribesmen seen smoking unusual pipes in the village of Bugai

23. An old man sits in the doorway of his rondavel in a village in the Shere Hills

24. A woman of the Fulani tribe, who are nomadic cattle herders

1

2

3

4

5

6

7

8

9

10

11

12

13

14

15

16

17

18

19

20

21

22

23

24

OMAN

Khasab
Musandam Peninsula
Madha (Oman)
Gulf of Oman
The Gulf
Sohar
Al Khaburah
As Seeb
Muscat
Jebal Akhdar
UNITED ARAB EMIRATES
Mascat Airport
Qurayyat
'Ibri
Saiq
Nizwa
Izki
Ibra'
Sur
Ras Al Hadd
Fahud
Jibal
Al Kamil
As Suwayh
Wahiba Sands
SAUDI ARABIA
Al-Ghaba
Salt Flat
Dawwah
Hajmah
OMAN
Arabian Sea
Danka
Marmul
Sharbatat
N
YEMEN
Thamarit
Mudhay
Salalah
Sadh
Raysut
Mirbat
Sarfait
OMAN - 1987

OMAN

About four months before I was due to complete my tour in Nigeria, my postings branch in the Ministry of Defence (MoD) contacted me concerning my next appointment. I was given a choice of either Saudi Arabia or Oman. Clearly, my career path now seemed to be along the 'funnies' postings route, which didn't disappoint me at all.

I knew Saudi Arabia would be a challenge for Toni and the girls. For instance, Toni would not be allowed to drive and she and the girls would have to be veiled and completely covered by wearing the all-enveloping *abaya* when moving outside our compound.

Oman, on the other hand, was far more tolerant and, moreover, had a strong connection with the British Armed Forces, going back for more than 200 years. Indeed, the cliffs guarding the entrance to Muscat harbour bore testimony to the many British sailors, including a young Horatio Nelson, who had carved their names into the rocks. The wildness of the country and its fascinating people had also captured my imagination during my short 'hearts and minds' patrol in 1969. So, Oman it was.

Before taking up my post, I was required to brush up my Arabic on a ten-week residential refresher course at the Defence School of Languages, Beaconsfield. Although I hadn't spoken Arabic for five years, it was surprising how quickly it all came back to me. I was not an expert by any stretch of the imagination, but just able to get by in the colloquial Gulf form of the language.

Meanwhile, the Army housed Toni and the children in a married quarters area, or 'patch' as they were known, in the home of the Royal and Electrical and Mechanical Engineers (REME), in Arborfield Garrison. I joined them at weekends and on the completion of my course. Luckily, our belongings from Nigeria arrived just in time for us to sort them out and get geared up to move to Oman before my departure in June 1987.

I went out ahead of the family to take over my new appointment, which was to be the Staff Officer responsible for training throughout the Sultan of Oman's Land Forces (SOLF) as the Omani Army was then known. My office was located in the very smart Sultan's Armed Forces Headquarters (SAF HQ) in a large barracks called Muasker al Murtafa'a, (meaning 'the Camp on the Heights'). Known as MAM for short, it was located just outside the fishing village of Seeb, some 20 miles west of Muscat.

Apart from the headquarters building itself, it contained other ancillary units, several messes, single and married accommodation for all ranks working at MAM, a hospital and extensive playing fields. Each of the messes had its own excellent dining facilities, a weekly film night, swimming pool and tennis courts. Depending on where you worked, you joined a particular mess, ours being the Headquarters Mess. However, you could book a table in another mess for an evening out, or to see a film. Just outside the gates there was a cluster of shops, including a 'super market', a tailor and a photographer. All in all, we were a fully self-sufficient community.

Seeb also boasted the international airport. I was quite taken aback when I saw it on my arrival. Modern, spacious and air-conditioned, it was a far cry from the tiny airfield at Bait al Falaj that I remembered from my previous visit to the country in 1969. One thing that hadn't changed was the searing summer heat. Although I had arrived at midnight, the furnace-like blast that hit me on leaving the aircraft was quite a shock to the system.

Lieutenant Colonel Tony Redwood-Davis, the person who I was replacing, met me and guided me through the process of obtaining a visa and collecting my baggage. He then drove me to the camp, a journey of barely five minutes.

Our quarter, AAC8, was right on the edge of the camp perimeter and backed straight onto the desert. It was a compact, very well-appointed air conditioned bungalow with three bedrooms, two bathrooms, one of which was en-suite, a kitchen and a single large living-cum-dining room. At the back of the bungalow there was a small, loosely paved patio area, shaded by a straw canopy, and, to one side, another small bungalow to accommodate the house staff.

We got to bed about 2.00 a.m. Before retiring, Tony told me that he would be up at about 5.00 a.m for his morning run, but I was to have a lie-in. Good, I thought, but was quickly brought back to reality when he told me that he would wake me at 6.15 a.m. in time to take a driving test at 7.00 a.m.! Driving test! 7.00 a.m.! He left me with a chart of local road signs for bedside reading.

I duly arrived at the Motor Transport Office just before the appointed time, barely half awake and very apprehensive. I was greeted by my Omani examiner who led me over to a Land Rover. Thankfully, I remembered what the three levers were for and how to drive on sand. After driving on and off road and reversing into a small space marked out with oil drums, I was quizzed on the Omani road signs. Luckily, these were largely similar to the ones found in Britain, apart from minor differences, such as a camel replacing our leaping deer. An hour later, I was qualified to drive military and civilian vehicles in Oman. Just as well, as one of the perks of the job was a Toyota Corona for our use both on and off duty.

Tony was an excellent officer – but he didn't seem to eat! That first day I survived on a few cups of coffee, a slice of bread and a piece of fruit, and when there was no breakfast or lunch on the following day I began to get quite worried. I took a quick look at our larder and fridge and found them both to be virtually bare, so I went to the little store just outside the camp gates and bought a packet of cereal, some bread and other odds and ends and brought them home. Next morning I heard Tony asking Abraham, our cook, to explain where all this 'rubbish' had come from. Poor Abraham was pleading ignorance as I rushed in to declare myself to be the culprit.

Tony was a powerfully-built infantry officer in the Duke of Wellington's Regiment, affectionately known in army circles as 'The Duke of Boots'. A former Army rugby player, he was extremely fit and went for an early morning run before work every morning. Yet he seemed to survive on coffee and thin air. Imagine my delight when he told me one evening that he would be dining at the Jebel Mess and asked if I would like to join him. I tried not to sound too desperately enthusiastic and only hoped I would have the energy to get there. It was about the fourth day of our handover and it was the first square meal I had eaten.

I was based in the Operations and Training Department in the Army Headquarters. My appointment was Staff Officer 1 (SO1) Training responsible for running the Training Department. I answered to two bosses, the first being a British Army Gunner (RA), Colonel Tom Bremridge, who was the senior British Loan Service Officer and filled the appointment of Principal Staff Officer (PSO) in the Headquarters. My other boss, also a gunner, was Aqeed (Colonel) Saud Sulieman Al Habsi, who was Colonel Operations and Training. From an Omani viewpoint, he was my immediate superior. Thanks to Colonel Tom's deft man management, the arrangement worked very well. By coincidence, the Staff Officer 2 Operations (G2 Ops), Raa'id (Major) Mohammed Saleem, who worked just a couple of doors from me, had been one of the cadets in my company at Sandhurst in 1979/80.

As the officer responsible for training standards throughout the army, I was also required to attend all sports competitions, which were usually held during the late afternoon. In addition, I had to observe or participate in a number of outdoor training exercises.

As it happens, Tony and I spent hardly any time in our office over the two weeks that we worked together. Instead, we travelled the length and breadth of Oman in Land Rovers, helicopters and a light aircraft known as a Defender, visiting some of the units for which I had a training responsibility. The terrain was striking in both variety and beauty, ranging as it did from the rugged mountains of the Jebel Akhdar (Arabic for 'green mountain') in the north, which soared to 10,000 feet, through every variation of desert to the Wahiba Sands, a sand sea roughly the size of Wales in the east of the country. The *jebels* in the south were dry and forbidding during most of the year, but became almost tropical during the southwest monsoon – a season known as the *khareef* (Arabic for 'autumn') in Oman.

The soldiers, too, were equally fascinating and varied. In the north they were all Omanis, drawn from the gravel plains, the *jebels* and the sand desert, whilst in the south the vast majority were Baluchis from Baluchistan, apart from the Firqat, an irregular force of local Omanis, many of whom had fought on the other side during the Dhofar war. The soldiers' bearing, professionalism and innate field craft skills within their own particular environments were impressive and made me realise that I would really have to be on my mettle during this tour. This was my idea of true soldiering and I just couldn't believe my luck. It was almost too good to be true. And so it almost was!

On the third day of my handover, I was asked to telephone the MoD. Fearing that something must have happened to my family, I anxiously rang the number. It was my postings branch, and I was asked if I would like to be posted to Kuwait – with immediate effect! The officer knew that I was only a day or two into my tour in Oman, but explained that the job in Kuwait meant promotion to the next rank and that opportunities for promotion were rather limited in the career path "you have chosen to pursue."

I said that I couldn't possibly go at a moment's notice. For a start, all our worldly goods were now on the high seas en-route to Oman and it would be months before they would catch up with us in Kuwait, if at all. I also argued that the Omanis might feel let down if the post I was meant to fill was left vacant for the weeks or months it might take to select a replacement and get him through the Arabic course, etc. Finally, I said that I usually discussed these postings with my family before committing them to what was often a challenging environment.

The officer fully understood my predicament, but he, too, had a problem. There was no shortage of volunteers for Oman and my post was usually filled by an infantryman, but volunteers for the Kuwaiti vacancy were a rarity and had to come from the Armoured Corps. Eventually, as a compromise, I said that I would be willing to move to Kuwait in a year if absolutely necessary, although my preference was to serve my two years in Oman. The officer at the other end thanked me and said he would see if our current man in Kuwait would agree to extend for a year.

I telephoned Toni early that evening to let her know what might happen. Like the true army wife that she was, she took the news in her stride, saying that it would give us an opportunity to see another part of the Gulf.

The fact that I could telephone Toni from MAM was an absolute bonus after our experiences both in Sudan and Nigeria. In MAM, every quarter was supplied with a telephone which we could use to make calls to anywhere in Oman. Whilst we could not make international calls from this telephone, we could receive them. However, to ring home ourselves was fairly painless. All we needed to do was purchase a phone card from our own mess, and use its international telephone facility. A two-minute call cost 6 rials, which was roughly £10; admittedly a little expensive, but there was no hassle and the system was reliable.

Two weeks after my arrival, Tony Redwood-Davis left. I was now on my own, heading up a team of three other officers, plus a clerical staff of several contracted senior ranks who had formerly served in either the Indian or Pakistani armies. One of these senior ranks impressed and worried me in equal measure. Called Younis, he was responsible for coordinating all the overseas training courses for the Omani Army, including bookings, travel arrangements and course fees. This was a big commitment and demanded minute attention to detail. Younis was absolutely on top of his job and during the year we worked together he never made a single mistake. Yet, amazingly, he never wrote anything down; it was all in his head. When I challenged him about this he was very evasive. It occurred to me that he may have wanted to make himself indispensable so as to safeguard his job. I could see his point if this was, indeed, the case, but could not risk the consequences of some disaster befalling him. We had to have a written record. Younis accepted this, albeit reluctantly.

I must confess that my overriding memories of that time, however, have nothing to do with work but of feasting like a king. Each bungalow came supported by a cook and a steward or housemaid. Our cook, Abraham, was an absolute gem. An Indian, he had been trained in the Taj Mahal Hotel in Bombay (Mumbai), one of India's most luxurious hotels. I had had the privilege of staying there with my parents as a child whilst transiting through Bombay to join the ship for the voyage back to Britain on my father's home leave, and to catch the train south on the return journey.

The salads Abraham produced for me at lunch were like exhibits for some major culinary competition – exquisitely carved vegetables, beautifully presented. Indeed, I photographed some of them, much to his embarrassed delight. My evening meals were of a similar standard. My table groaned with his gastronomic creations and yet I never seemed to be served with 'leftovers'. After a few days, I asked Abraham what happened to the leftovers and he told me that they were all thrown away as he could not possibly serve them to 'Sahib'. I explained that I couldn't afford to live in such luxury; this wasn't the Taj and we had to economise. After that we settled into a far more sensible regime, but he told me how happy he had been to be given a free hand for a while. I must confess I had rather enjoyed it too.

Our second staff member (both these staff members were provided free by the Omani Army) was a steward or housemaid. At the outset, a very efficient young Indian called Anthony was our steward. His job was to keep the house spick and span, as well as to serve at table. Anthony was really a mess cook and so was misemployed with us. Within a month or so, a cook's vacancy became available in one of the messes and Anthony left to fill this post. We were then provided with Lal, who was also misemployed and left as soon as an appropriate vacancy became available. We finally ended up with a housemaid called Winnie. She was a beautiful, young Sri Lankan and very shy. She looked after the house very well, but we felt it unfair to expect her to wait at table, as she had no experience of this. Abraham was very good to her and acted like a father figure. All this talk about house staff might seem odd in this day and age, but this was the norm in all our seconded postings and gave people employment that they may not otherwise have found.

Within days of Tony Redwood-Davis's departure, I was informed that our bungalow was due for refurbishment and redecoration. This would take about two months and in the meantime I was to be housed in another bungalow across the road.

At about the same time, I received confirmation from the MoD that I was to be posted to Kuwait in July 1988, my posting to Oman having been cut to exactly one year. My compromise had been accepted to the letter but at least we were going to have a year in this fascinating country. We resolved to make the most of the opportunity.

Toni and the children, except Alex, flew out to join me in our temporary home at the start of the children's school summer holidays. The evening before they arrived, a very anxious Abraham asked if he could see me. I agreed, fearing that there had been some calamity or other in the kitchen. After reminding me of his qualifications, he said, "Please tell Madam that the kitchen is my place," adding that he hoped Toni would not even consider entering the kitchen, let alone cook, except on his day off. I assured him that he would get on very well with 'Madam'. And so he did, despite her entering his kitchen.

Two days after her arrival in Oman, it was Toni's turn to take her military driving test. Like me, she needed a military driving licence to drive our military registered car, plus the normal civilian equivalent. Luckily, she was able to take the test in the car itself, rather than a strange Land Rover, as she was not being tested to go 'off road'. She emerged triumphant an hour later with both licences.

Alex joined us ten days later, having successfully achieved his Duke of Edinburgh Gold Award. He had to hit Oman running, as the day after his arrival we celebrated the most important feast in the Muslim calendar, Eid al-Adha. This marks the start of the Haj celebrations in Mecca and, as mentioned in the chapter on Nigeria, commemorates both Ibrahim's willingness to sacrifice his son Ishmael as an act of obedience to Allah, and Allah's compassion in letting Ibrahim know that his very willingness to submit to His will was sacrifice enough, and so providing him with a ram to sacrifice instead. The Old Testament includes the same story.

As the Eid al-Adha celebrations extended into our weekend (Friday), we all enjoyed a five-day holiday. To make the most of this break, I had organised a trip around much of Northern Oman for the family. This had only been possible for two reasons: first, the nature of my job, which gave me access to almost anywhere in Oman, and, second and even more importantly, the Omani Army's amazing generosity towards my family. Whenever I was required to spend time away from Seeb, my family was always welcome to accompany me.

The trip took us up and around the Jebel Akhdar, with half our time based at the tiny Battle Training Camp at Saiq at an elevation of about 6,500 feet. To get there we needed a 4x4 vehicle. My boss, Colonel Tom Bremridge, very kindly came to the rescue, lending me his army Toyota Land Cruiser.

Visit to Saiq, 4-7 August 1987

We arrived at the old fort of Birkat Al Mauz, which lies at the foot of the Jebel Akhdar, and ate our picnic lunch in the shade of a nearby date palm grove. Our road was now nothing more than a dusty track making directly for the mountain. Ominous clouds darkened the sky and the wind was gathering strength. Rounding a corner, we arrived at the military checkpoint which controlled access to the mountain. In addition to the military camp at Saiq, there are a number of tiny villages dotted about the jebel. *Sultan Qaboos bin Sa'id Al Sa'id, the ruler of Oman* [who had been in the same company as me – Marne Company – whilst we were cadets at Sandhurst], *was determined to protect these villages from any unwanted influences from outside. Nobody could enter the area without a military pass and obtaining one of these was well-nigh impossible without good reason. Luckily, I had a good reason: the Battle Training Camp at Saiq.*

At the barrier, the guards told us that it was too dangerous to proceed at present as a storm was raging on the mountain. We were, therefore, asked to wait until it had passed. Meantime, we all looked in some trepidation at the alarming incline of the unsurfaced track ahead as it commenced its ascent towards Saiq. No wonder only 4x4s were permitted to use the road. I had already flown up to Saiq, but this was my first experience of the road.

After about an hour we were allowed to resume our journey. We climbed steeply and steadily for about 6,000 feet, the track often a running torrent of rainwater. There was always a sheer drop on one side and sometimes both sides, where the road snaked along mountain ridges. The final climb up onto the plateau, on which Saiq and several other little villages nestled, was a daunting series of very steep and sharp hairpin bends.

Whilst we were negotiating these zigzags we met an army Land Rover coming in the opposite direction. It had been despatched from the camp to check if we were alright. They were concerned because we were overdue. The storm had knocked out their communications with the barrier and so they were unaware that we had been delayed.

At the camp we were greeted by Warrant Officer Woods, the only British seconded person living on the mountain, and the Egyptian doctor, Wagdhy. The unit was operating on a skeleton staff, most of the personnel having gone home for the Eid.

Next morning, 5 August, we were invited to celebrate the Eid with the soldiers in the cookhouse. We sat in groups on the blanket-covered floor around large circular trays piled high with fresh dates – the first time that Toni and the children had eaten them. This was followed by Omani coffee, served by soldiers using Thermos jugs rather than the elegant Arab coffee pots – progress!

The coffee was poured into tiny handle-less cups and the soldier serving you waited until you had drained it. If you wanted another mouthful – for that is all the cup held – you held the cup out again. When you had had sufficient you waggled the cup with a wrist movement, and it was then taken from you for someone else to use. If you don't waggle your cup it keeps being filled up! There are no words spoken at all. (It is polite to waggle it after two servings.)

The Jebel Akhdar Battle Training Camp boasts its own Donkey Platoon – we imagine it must be one of the very few such units still in existence. It has a complement of 14 donkeys, each with its own handler and army number. They are used to support those outlying villages which cannot be reached by road, or by helicopter in bad weather. They are also used to support soldiers operating on the jebel. *As the animals have to be exercised every day, we took full advantage of the opportunity to get about the* jebel *after breakfast. We re-joined the soldiers in the cookhouse for lunch. This time the circular trays were heaped with boiled rice on top of which lay roast meat, plus a large liver. A sound working knowledge of geometry is essential on these occasions, as everyone has to work out the exact limits of their share of the dish. There were, of course, no 'eating irons'. You eat with your right hand. Being left-handed, I always sit on my left hand to avoid committing the heinous crime of dipping it into the food on the tray. If food is 'defiled' in this way it all has to be discarded!*

Once the main course was finished, servers came round bearing a bowl, a jug of water and tissues so that we could rinse and dry our hands. Then trays laden with dates, oranges and figs were set before us. This was followed by more hand washing and coffee. We felt hugely honoured to have shared this meal with the soldiers. Expatriates call such events 'fuddles', a corruption of the Arabic term 'tafaDDal', *meaning 'come in and help yourself'.*

After a short siesta, we went out in the Land Cruiser to explore a small village, called Al Ain, which we had spotted earlier on, clinging to the southern edge of the plateau. Rounding a bend on the very steep track down to the village we came across three young girls in colourful costumes tending a herd of goats. The oldest girl, probably in her early teens, called out to us to follow her. We weren't sure what to do, as it was unusual for an Omani woman to address strangers like this. But this was the Eid and she was quite insistent. Toni and the girls got out of the vehicle, whilst the boys and I remained seated, but, no, we were to go along too. So I parked at the end of the track, just above the roofs of the houses.

We were in flip-flops (the Omanis were barefoot) and found it quite difficult to negotiate the very steep path down to the village. We passed through narrow passages and by doors opening into windowless rooms, in some of which fires were burning; we went into darkened 'tunnels' and caught glimpses of little children playing on makeshift rope swings.

At last we were through the village and standing in a narrow, beautifully tended vegetable garden looking out on a magnificent view across a deep gorge or wadi. *The vegetable patch was only about 3-4 yards wide and along its near side ran a* falaj. *This is a small, centuries-old channel with an imperceptible incline down which cool, fresh water runs for literally tens of miles; the life-blood of every community it serves. The unprotected far side of the vegetable patch fell vertically for hundreds of feet to the floor of the* wadi.

We were taken to a newly-built house perched on the very edge of the cliff and invited to sit on the floor. The man of the house was a charming young Omani in the Sultan of Oman's Navy (SON). Currently undergoing training at Dartmouth, he had returned home for the summer holidays. He recognised Alex and told us they had both been on the same flight out from London – a small world. We were surprised that a Jebali *('mountain man') should swap his magnificent eyrie up in the mountains for a life on the ocean waves. We were made to feel most welcome and invited to feast on dishes groaning with fruit, followed by coffee. Then the girls led us back to our vehicle.*

The next day, 6 August, after having exercised the donkeys in the morning, we set off in the Land Cruiser, with Wagdhy, the doctor, as our guide, to explore a little further afield on the jebel. *First we negotiated the 'thin road', a very narrow, steep and rough track hewn out of the sheer mountainside which led to the tiny settlement of Qashar at the bottom of a very deep* wadi. *Most of the villagers were toiling in the fields and we were free to wander about, drinking in the scenery and taking pictures.*

The ascent out of the village was even more nerve wracking than the descent. To make matters worse, we met a Toyota pick-up making its way down. I had to reverse until I found a slightly deeper cut into the mountainside, into which I tucked our vehicle. The pick-up then inched its way passed us, its outer wheels on the very edge of the abyss. Amazingly, the driver stopped level with us. Far from being perturbed by his perilous situation, he pleaded for us to return with him to the village for lunch! It was impossible to turn round and too hazardous to reverse back down. Wagdhy somehow made a convincing apology, but promised that we would return later if we had time.

Our next stop was at the village of Heil Yemen, sheltering in a shallow bowl and surrounded by orchards – pears, pomegranates, figs, dates – plus grape vines growing in abundance. Wagdhy was well known here and, having been asked to sit under a tree in the orchard, a mountain of fruit was set before us to taste.

Next we called upon Wagdhy's orderly in the village of Manarkin, situated up another daunting mountain track. Here we were ushered into a communal hall, where we sat on the carpeted floor to feast on more fruit and coffee. Every so often we had to stand up as the village's men folk came to welcome us. After the coffee ritual, Wagdhy's orderly insisted that we go to his house for lunch. He had been expecting us all day and had even been shadowing us all morning to see where we were going next!

The orderly's home was typical of the area, with one main room, the floor of which was covered by matting. This served as sitting room, dining room and bedroom. It contained no furniture of any kind. Tiny palliasses rested on wooden prongs protruding from the wall near the ceiling and all his worldly goods hung in bags from hooks around the walls. The place was spotlessly clean, neat and tidy.

Humble though his dwelling was, the feast he set before us was anything but – a fatted lamb no less and Omani bread, which was a very dry and thin, wafer-like pancake, just the right accompaniment for the lamb.

After washing our hands and drinking coffee we were allowed to take pictures of some of the colourfully dressed girls, who were shyly looking on from around the doors. It is very difficult to take pictures of people, especially women, in Oman and so we welcomed this opportunity, the more so as they were wearing their Eid clothes. Some of the women perched on the roofs to watch us, but did not want their pictures taken, which we respected. We promised to return in due course with copies of the photographs of those people we had been allowed to photograph.

Despite being full to bursting, Wagdhy told us that we had to return to the village at the bottom of the 'thin road' as he had promised we would. We wished he had given us prior warning! He pointed out that he had to live amongst these people and did not want to offend any of them. So off we went. Once there we were served with fruit and coffee in the communal hall before repairing to our invitee's home for another sumptuous meal of roast meat and rice. Somehow we all managed to please our host!

It was quite late in the afternoon when we eventually returned to camp, only to find that the staff had laid on a barbecue for us that evening!

At last to bed after a quite remarkable day, full of wonderful experiences and staggeringly generous hospitality.

After breakfast next morning, 7 August, we said goodbye to our friends at the camp, especially those at the donkey platoon, and then dropped in on our midshipman's family in Al Ain, as we had promised. Over yet more fruit and coffee we commented upon the hospitality strangers enjoyed in Oman in comparison to what they might expect in Britain. He was the consummate diplomat, stating that the weather in Britain was cold so that people kept their doors shut, whereas in Oman it was hot so that the people kept their doors open. Having said farewell, we set off down the road to Birkat Al Mauz. About three-quarters of the way down this tortuous road our brakes failed, so we inched our way towards the barrier using the gearbox to control our descent, and at the barrier used the handbrake to bring the vehicle to a halt. On reaching level ground at the fort in Birkat al Mauz, we stopped again for me to check the brake fluid level. All seemed fine, so we decided to allow the vehicle to cool down as we stretched our legs in the shade of the date palm grove. When we resumed our journey half an hour later, the brakes were working normally again.

Once down on the desert floor, we headed northwest for the army fort at Buraimi on the border with Abu Dhabi. On the way we stopped at Nizwa to see its impressive old fort – a massive circular tower – and the livestock souk (market) under a tree beneath its walls. As it was Friday and as people were still celebrating the Eid, the fort was closed and the souk was dead. Nevertheless, the sight of the mud dwellings clustered around the imposing fort made the stop well worthwhile.

Our next stop was at Jabreen, a beautiful fortified palace rather than a military fort. Our route took us through Bahla, the black top road running right under the walls of the decaying old fort. Bahla was now a bustling little desert town and bore no resemblance to the mystical oasis outside which I had spent two days with a blown engine during the Omex patrol in 1969. How Oman had changed in the intervening 18 years.

Jabreen was actually a little out of our way, but well worth the detour, despite it also being closed. The magnificent looking Omani guard, sporting a gleaming silver *kunja* (Omani dagger) on a belt around his waist, was glad to talk to us and have his photograph taken. He also allowed us inside the palace walls to get a better view of the building.

Just before we reached Buraimi our route looped through the city of Al Ain in Abu Dhabi, United Arab Emirates. This was another surprise. What I remembered as a remote oasis with little more than a detachment of the Trucial Oman Scouts in permanent residence, was now the second city in Abu Dhabi. Fort Jahli, the 'Beau Geste-like' fort which was the headquarters of the Trucial Oman Scouts' detachment in those days, was now the centrepiece in a children's play park! It had completely lost its romantic aura, which saddened me. However, I am sure the inhabitants of modern Al Ain appreciated their more comfortable lifestyle.

Opposite Al Ain, on the Omani side of the border, an impressive modern fort stood on the gravel plain where, in 1969, military aircraft used to land when supporting us in the vicinity. Buraimi fort was home to the

Oman Coast Regiment, the unit responsible for the security of this part of Oman, and we were their privileged guests for the night. Actually to be accommodated in a real fort, albeit fleetingly, was a thrilling experience, especially for the children.

Next morning we headed east through the Wadi Jizzi towards Sohar on the Batinah coast of Oman. In 1969, travelling in the opposite direction, it had taken us two days to find a route through the Wadi Jizzi. I can remember an incident when one of our Saladin armoured cars was in danger of tipping over as it edged up the side of a steep slope. We evacuated the crew and then secured the stricken vehicle to the mountainside with tow ropes until the REME could recover it. Now the same journey was completed without the slightest difficulty in around two hours on an excellent black top road.

On reaching the coast we stopped at the fort in Sohar. Set right on the sea front, it is rumoured to be the site from where Sinbad the Sailor set forth on his epic voyage. The glare from its dazzling white walls made it almost too painful to admire. The heat coupled with the humidity that day was frankly unbearable, so we didn't dally. Instead, we were soon on our way home, with the promise of air conditioning, a refreshing swim and a sumptuous meal prepared by Abraham to spur us on; a fitting end to a memorable Eid al-Adha holiday.

Just over a week after our return, I managed to get Toni and the children seats on a Sultan of Oman's Air Force (SOAF) helicopter taking supplies up to the camp at Saiq. The only downside to this venture was the need to get up at 4.30 a.m. After a very early breakfast, I dropped them at the military side of Seeb airport, where they were ushered into a bus and driven out to the helicopter.

Flying up to Saiq is always an exhilarating adventure, especially in a helicopter. The route took them over our house and on towards the *jebel*. One seems to edge up the sheer wall of rock, rather like an eagle soaring on a thermal, before entering a *wadi* and flying right into the heart of the mountain. Here, the wind seems to come from all angles, buffeting the aircraft like a leaf caught in a gale. The engine screams, everything shakes and rattles, whilst all around there is nothing but sheer, unforgiving jagged mountains. Try as you might you cannot see the sky, but then, quite suddenly, the ground levels out – you have reached the plateau and soon you can see the welcome sight of the camp alongside the airstrip at Saiq.

Wagdhy was on hand to meet Toni and the children and take them to the medical centre for a cup of sweet, milky tea spiced with cinnamon – quite an acquired taste. Whilst there, they saw a SOAF Skyvan coming in to land on the tiny airstrip. These small aircraft brought up supplies for onward distribution to the more remote villages on the *jebel*.

Depending on the direction of the wind, aircraft taking off from Saiq headed straight for a *jebel*, necessitating a sharp bank to port immediately after getting airborne, which was always quite exciting. On the desert floor on the southern side of the Jebel Akhdar there was an airstrip at Firq, where aircraft would also fly straight for the *jebel* on takeoff, demanding a similar banking manoeuvre to that at Saiq. In the 1960s, you joined an elite club if you made the flight from Firq to Saiq four times! Unfortunately, I never had the opportunity to qualify in 1969 and, by 1987, the airstrip at Firq was no longer in use.

After an enjoyable couple of hours exercising the donkeys, followed by a slap-up breakfast in the mess, it was time for Toni and the children to return to the airstrip for the journey home. The helicopter soon hove into view and, once it had been refuelled from oil drums at the edge of the airstrip, they were given the signal to board. Soon it was skimming across the plateau and plummeting down the mountainside towards Seeb, where it landed in the late morning.

Very early the next morning we were all down at the military airport again! This time the family was accompanying me on a visit to Salalah in the south of Oman, where I was to spend the next four days visiting units in the area. The SOAF flight took us over Birkat Al Mauz and we could clearly see the start of the tortuous route leading up the *jebel* to Saiq. Then we were over the barren desert of the Empty Quarter. The sun blazed down from a cloudless sky and the desert below shimmered in the blisteringly hot heat haze. Just over an hour into the flight, the whole scene was transformed in a split second. As we descended into Salalah, we entered a dense bank of wet cloud. As I mentioned earlier, this phenomenon is known as the *khareef* and is the consequence of the moisture-laden winds of the southwest monsoon striking the *jebels* of southern Oman. From June to September, a blanket of cloud hangs over Salalah, and the coastal *jebels* are shrouded in a dripping wet mist, transforming the whole area into lush verdant pastures for a few precious weeks every year.

When over-flying Salalah during the *khareef* you can clearly see the cloud blotting out the coastal plain and the *jebels*, but not encroaching so much as 100 yards into the desert to the north. The effect is even more striking when flying over this area a week or two after the *khareef*, when the sun blazes down on the whole area once again from a clear blue sky. The scene below is now divided into three distinct strips: the sparkling blue sea fringed by the white foam of the breakers striking the shore, the rich green blanket of the coastal plain and the *jebels*, and then the barren desert beyond – the line between the green and the sandy brown as abrupt as if it had been drawn using a ruler. Within a few weeks, the entire landscape takes on its uniform brown hue once more, as the vegetation withers and dies under the merciless glare of the sun.

On arrival in Salalah, we were met by an Omani army officer, plus two cars with drivers, and were whisked off to a military apartment block in town, in which we were given a sizeable flat for the duration of our stay. I had travelled down in uniform and so within minutes I was on my way to a unit up in the *jebel*. I soon found myself travelling through dense fog. The barracks itself had not seen the sun for several weeks and would not do so for some weeks to come. Everywhere was soaking wet and oil skins seemed to be the order on days like this.

Even indoors everything was damp and the smell of mould hung in the air. It reminded me of my childhood days in India during the monsoon, when we had to seize every opportunity during breaks in the rain to air our clothes and shoes outside. If anything, this was worse as we never had to live in the gloom of permanent cloud in India. I marvelled at the resilience of the officers and soldiers here, as living in this cool, wet twilight world week after week could not have been easy. Yet respite was only a maddening two miles or so north, where the wall of cloud ended and the arid ground baked in the sun.

I arrived back at our flat in time for a late lunch. Toni and the children had been exploring Salalah and buying in a few provisions for our stay. After a siesta, we decided that, despite the dull weather, we would go down to the beach. We had not brought swimwear with us as we had been warned not to swim, the currents on this coast being notoriously treacherous, particularly during the *khareef*. The angry sea bore witness to this. Nevertheless, the children could not resist splashing in the surf and soon Toni resembled a living clothes line, trying to dry clothes on her outstretched arms in the stiff onshore breeze.

Unsurprisingly, we were the only people on the beach, but we were not alone; half a dozen camels were promenading along the sands with us. They looked quite incongruous against the backdrop of the sea as we had only ever seen them previously in the heart of the desert. Numerous crabs scurried around the sand at the edge of the surf. Some of these were the size of a man's fist. Aptly referred to as ghost crabs, they were a white, opaque colour with sandy yellow legs and were almost invisible when still.

Friday, our 'weekend', fell midway through our stay. We took the opportunity to visit Mirbat, some 30 miles along the coast east of Salalah, the scene of the battle in 1972 when a large *adoo* (enemy) force launched a surprise attack against a Special Air Service (SAS) BAT team of only nine men. The SAS, eventually helped by SOAF and other SAS reinforcements, won the day, displaying courage of epic proportions even by their own peerless standards.

That same afternoon, Major Tony Usher, the Second-in-Command of Al Kateeba Al Janoubia (the Southern Regiment) (KJ for short), took us to a beautiful hanging valley half way up the *jebel* a few miles down the road from the barracks. We turned inland at a little inlet called Khor Rhori (pronounced Rorie, much to the delight of our Rorie). At times, during the *khareef*, this is the site of one of the few waterfalls in Oman, as water spills over the edge of the hanging valley and falls in a silvery curtain to the desert floor below.

After a short climb we turned off the main road and made our way along a track towards an opening in the bastions of rock that towered either side of us. As we breasted the gap, a magnificent and quite unexpected vista greeted our eyes. Below us a clear stream cut a path through lush green pastures, trees, shrubs and wild flowers. Birds flitted about the scene and the air was filled with their music. Camels and domestic cattle grazed at the waterside and Omani families picnicked in the fine 'Scotch mist'. This was Wadi Darbat, a scene of utter tranquillity. Yet this had not always been the case. During the Dhofar War, which had ended barely ten years before, this *wadi* had been a haven for the *adoo*. One could easily see why; the jagged *jebels* that surrounded it were riddled with near inaccessible caves that made excellent hideouts. There were stories of leopards living in this *wadi* before the war, but we could see no evidence of them now.

We descended into the valley and made our way towards its head. The track finally gave out at a beautiful lake, complete with reeds, lily pads and waterfowl. The temperature was almost chilly and it was hard to believe that this was Oman. We could not help but get out and walk. The grass was knee high and drenched by the 'Scotch mist', whilst the light was almost too gloomy for photography. Nevertheless, the thrill of being in such fantastic countryside more than compensated for these minor inconveniences.

Undoubtedly, the best time to visit this Omani jewel is immediately after the *khareef*, when the valley is still lush and the skies above are an uninterrupted blue canopy. But one has to be quick! Within a matter of a few days most of the vegetation withers and dies, the stream runs dry and the lake shrinks to a mere pond, all thanks to the searing gaze of the sun.

Either side of our 'weekend break', whilst I was visiting the various units in the area, Lieutenant Colonel Bill Logdon, the British contract officer commanding KJ, very kindly took Toni and the children under his wing. He also invited all of us to be his guests at a Regimental dinner night on our last evening. All the officers were in mess kit, the table was adorned with Regimental silver including candlesticks, whilst smartly dressed waiters provided an efficient silver service. This was a unique experience, not to mention a privilege, especially for the children. Alex, aged 16, and Rorie, aged 15, greatly enjoyed talking to the young Omani officers, who were splendid hosts, whilst Hannah, aged 13, and Zoë, aged 11, said afterwards that they had been made to feel like princesses.

On our last morning, Colonel Bill took Toni and the children to his house where four sets of Omani army fatigues were neatly laid out on a bed in the spare room. After the children had donned their uniforms, he took them out into the desert in two of his army 6x6 Pinzgauer vehicles. These marvellous vehicles were made in Austria and named after an Austrian breed of horse. The Pinzgauer has a remarkable cross-country capability and was ideal for use in Oman as a troop carrier.

Once Colonel Bill had taken his party far into the desert away from any living creature, he let the children have a go at driving, under the watchful eye of an (on board) Omani instructor. This experience capped the pomp and ceremony of the dinner night and became the highlight of their visit to the south.

Sunday saw me back at work in the Headquarters in Seeb and the next day the Commander Sultan of Oman's Land Forces (CSOLF) and I left early to visit the armoured Regiment at their barracks deep in the desert, a journey of some two and a half hours. This was quite a nostalgic experience for me as, although I was in the Royal Tank Regiment, I had not served on tanks for quite some time; my last tour of duty with my Regiment had ended in 1977 – ten years earlier – and my only opportunity since had been my two years in Sudan, where I worked on Russian and Chinese tanks.

Whilst I was at work, Toni took the children to the Sultan's Armed Forces (SAF) beach club, near Muscat. This was a wonderful facility and included a restaurant that served excellent, yet inexpensive meals, the Aqua Mega Breakfast being a particular attraction. Here, you could swim, snorkel, dive, water-ski and sail in beautiful, clear waters with small patches of coral teeming with brightly coloured fish. We spent very many happy hours here as a family.

By coincidence, when we reached Muscat in 1969, our squadron leagued on the headland that now served as the club's (unsurfaced) car park and we used the same cove in which to swim. Then, I remember having to go up in the helicopter to keep an eye out for sharks whilst the squadron was in the water. Worryingly, we saw quite a number of them lying about 40 yards or so off shore, but luckily they showed no interest in our soldiers. The threat in the 1980s, however, came not from sharks, but from the box jellyfish that occasionally found their way into the cove from, we believe, a small mangrove swamp nearby.

These jellyfish look like transparent plastic bags and are almost impossible to see in the water. They have long trailing tentacles that possess literally thousands of very poisonous stinging cells. The venom, which attacks the heart and nervous system, can be fatal to humans. A supply of vinegar was kept in the club to administer immediate first aid and relief before taking victims to hospital.

The club was managed by Major Bill Foxton, a contract officer with SAF. A fascinating man, he had formerly served with the French Foreign Legion and the Royal Green Jackets before joining SAF. He lost a lower arm in the Dhofar war and sported an impressive 'Captain Hook' prosthetic arm. Every inch a soldier, he was someone you could rely on in an emergency.

During our time in Oman, a group of British soldiers, visiting the country to carry out an exercise reconnaissance, had gone down to the SAF beach club during a rest day. Running into the sea, one of the soldiers performed a racing dive into the surf and struck his head on a sandbar. I was told later that Bill Foxton's intervention probably saved him from ending up in a wheelchair. First, he helped to get the injured man out of the surf. Then, sensing that his neck might be broken, he got a towel, twisted it to increase its firmness and carefully wrapped it round the casualty's neck, thereby giving it support and keeping it as stable as possible until medical help arrived.

Next day, I visited the patient in the impressive SAF hospital in Seeb. To my amazement he was quite literally attached to the wall behind his bed! A bolt had been screwed into the top of his skull and cemented into the wall. He was also strapped to the bed so that he was totally immobilised. He had, indeed, broken his neck, but his spinal cord was intact, thanks, in part, to Bill Foxton's quick thinking. He was going to have to remain like this for some weeks, but was expected to make a full recovery. I left Oman whilst he was still bolted to the wall.

Sadly, whilst I was drafting this chapter on Oman, I read of Bill's tragic death on 12 February 2009. Apparently he had lost his life savings in the Madoff ponzi scam that came to light in December 2008 and had taken his own life. May he rest in peace.

The Muslim New Year fell at the end of our first week back from Salalah. We joined up with the Bremridge family to explore the coast southeast of Muscat. Our intended goals were Wadi Shab and the village of Tiwi, a distance of about 100 miles from Muscat. Alix and Tom Bremridge's two sons, Henry and Will, were just a little younger than our four, so we made a good team. By now I had bought a second-hand Nissan Patrol, as we had realised that to make the most of Oman we needed to get off the black top roads and into the wilds. This was the vehicle's first test – and what a test – but it did not let us down. The following extracts from our diaries give a flavour of the trip:

> *About a mile from the Shell garage in Qurayyat (where we filled up with petrol and drinking water), we turned off the black top and made our way cross-country towards a graded track marked on our map. This was not easy as we were driving along a* wadi *strewn with large pebbles. We stopped in the shade of some gnarled trees for our picnic lunch. For the next hour or so the vehicles were well and truly put to the test as we made slow progress across some really inhospitable country. A few stunted trees were the only relief on this 'moonscape' of razor-sharp flints and small rocks. The graded track that we were now on ran over larger boulders that lay hidden in the dust. It also twisted and turned acutely, and climbed and plunged at amazing gradients. Bouncing along inside our Nissan, we were grateful for its specially heightened roofline, which saved us from banging our heads. However, the carefully stowed luggage at the back soon became a jumbled heap. To make matters worse, as we drew nearer to the sea the weather grew steadily more humid and*

hotter, making life fairly uncomfortable.

On reaching the coast, we stopped to look for shells on a shingle beach that was marked 'Shell Beach' on our map. The shells in Oman are really beautiful and we all enjoy looking for them. However, today the freak weather, with a heat haze, searing wind and humidity such as we had never experienced before, made life most uncomfortable. Even paddling in the sea failed to refresh us, so we were soon on our way again.

The next checkpoint on our route was an enormous blow-hole some way inland. Here, the sea had forced its way along a horizontal fault line in the rock until it had found a weaker vertical fault line. Over millennia, the water being forced up this vertical fault had formed a huge subterranean cave. Eventually, the roof of the cave had collapsed leaving a hole some 20 feet deep to become a circular seawater pool with a diameter roughly the width of a tennis court.

Darkness was rapidly approaching so we hurried to find a suitable campsite behind some dunes just back from the shoreline. Here we unpacked, set up the camp beds and made a fire to heat up the bolognaise sauce that Toni had prepared and to cook some spaghetti.

After supper, the children went down to the shore and they soon came running back in great excitement to tell us the sea was lit up. We all went to investigate. As each wave broke on the shore, millions of fluorescent 'lights' were left on the tide line, like countless little stars. If you touched these particles they remained where they were, but also transferred some of their 'light' to your finger. We were soon all painting our faces and hands and generally playing the fool in the pitch darkness. We imagined that this phenomenon must have been caused by minute sea creatures – plankton perhaps? [On reading this account in our diaries, my mother reminded me that we sometimes used to see phosphorescence in the wake of the ship during sea voyages between India and Britain when I was a boy.]

The night was an experience; we were bothered neither by mosquitoes nor midges, but the heat and humidity were so oppressive that the slightest movement generated a river of perspiration that soaked us. Only two weeks previously, people camping near here had required two jumpers at night!

Next morning we washed in the sea, our fresh water being too precious to waste on mere ablutions. We then treated ourselves to a full cooked breakfast, spoilt only somewhat by some rather fearsome looking hornets, one of which stung poor Toni.

We set off after breakfast and reached Wadi Shab a little before midday. We approached down a steep incline to a tiny settlement beneath the cliffs, where a sand bar separated the sea from a lagoon. Small fishing boats lined the seashore, and beyond the sand bar the majestic Wadi Shab, its sides rising vertically like two gigantic walls, cut its way deep into the jebel. *Beyond the lagoon, the floor of the* wadi *was carpeted in lush grass, upon which donkeys and goats grazed peacefully.*

We elected to walk down the wadi, *following a well-worn path along the base of the southern bastion. We soon came across a large expanse of fresh water. A little further on, the water came right up to the base of the cliffs and our path ended. However, on the shore was a galvanised metal water tank attached to a rope system running across to the other side. An elderly man was in charge of operations and told us what to do. Being flat-bottomed, the water tank was extremely unstable and water rushed in through the holes that secured the rope as we pulled ourselves across, helped by some eager young lads on the other side. It took three journeys to get all ten of us across – great fun. At the end of each crossing, the old man pulled the 'ferry' back to the near bank.*

> *Once across the water we walked up the* wadi, *the* jebels *either side towering above us and coming ever closer together. We were now walking beside a clear and cool stream running through rich pastures interspersed with date palms, bananas and pawpaw trees. Our path criss-crossed the stream many times as the* wadi *grew steadily narrower.*
>
> *We made a quick dash to Tiwi, the very dusty, higgledy-piggledy village at the end of our track. There was another inviting verdant* wadi *running inland here, but we had to make for home. A hard drive saw us back at Qurayyat just before sunset, where we refuelled and quenched our thirst on chilled soft drinks. We were back in the capital area before the darkening skies extinguished the glow on the western horizon and arrived home in time for a take-away supper purchased at the HQ Mess.*

Re-reading our diary notes now, almost 30 years after the event, it sounds as if this trip was a real struggle, especially the first 24 hours. Yet we remember it with great affection and it made a lasting impression on us. Indeed, we undertook many similar trips into the wilds of Oman during the year we were there, discovering new *wadis*, visiting forts or just camping in the desert. We spent virtually every other weekend and most religious/national holidays exploring Oman, hardly ever retracing our steps in the process, as there was so much to see.

It was unwise to venture off the beaten track on your own, so on most occasions we teamed up with the Bremridges for these so-called '*wadi* bashes'. These trips were always challenging. The driving was demanding and, as often as not, one or other of us needed a tow. But they were all real adventures. The magnificent scenery, forts and, especially, the people we encountered, coupled with the excitement and sense of achievement the harsh conditions generated, were hugely rewarding. We really lived every minute in Oman.

We were never as alone in the desert as we might have imagined. This environment, after all, was home to the *Bedu* and they would often surprise us by making an appearance seemingly out of nowhere. A case in point was when we and the Bremridges were en-route to Ibri, a desert village renowned for its atmospheric souk, where traders selling brilliantly coloured bolts of material, spices, ancient firearms and livestock vied with each other to attract business from the milling crowd. The resultant cacophony, the kaleidoscope of colours, the rich aromas and the seeming chaos made for a thrilling experience.

We had opted for the scenic route and taken a detour into the surrounding desert. As the light began to fade on our first day's journey, we made camp amongst some shallow dunes. After supper, we enjoyed a chat and story-telling session around the camp fire before turning in to spend a peaceful night under the stars.

Next morning we were up with the sun and busy preparing breakfast when we suddenly caught sight of a woman striding purposefully across the sands towards us. She was completely enveloped in her black *abaya* and, as she drew nearer, we could see that her face was covered by a most unusual mask or *burka*. This, too, was black and made of leather and had an extraordinary protrusion, or vane, extending for two to three inches out from her face and running between her eyes from the top to the bottom of the mask. It resembled a medieval visor and gave her quite a sinister appearance.

Speaking in a very deep voice, and having exchanged greetings, she told us that she had seen our lights in the night and had come to see if we were all right. Did we need water? Did we need food? Would we like to visit her tent for refreshments? This willingness to help was so typical of the *Bedu* in Oman. They are proud people and at one with their hostile environment; never once can I remember being asked for anything, but they were always most generous to us. What was remarkable in this instance, however, was that we had been approached by a woman. Maybe all the men folk were away looking for grazing for their animals and she had felt compelled to come herself to see if we needed help. Seeing that the women and children in our party outnumbered the men must have helped her reach her decision.

There was still one more adventure in the children's action-packed summer holiday. A SOAF C-130 Hercules aircraft was flying up to Khasab, the main town in the northern 'island' of Oman – the Musandam, the peninsula which forms the southern flank of the Hormuz Straits. This region was highly restricted and even Omanis from other parts of the country found it difficult to visit the area. It was also the one region I had not been able to visit. Yet here I was being offered a free trip for the family, on the strict understanding that this was a round trip just to experience the flight and we would not be permitted to venture further than the tiny airport building. As this was really only a 'jolly' with no military value, my work in the Headquarters had to come first, unfortunately. However, I was delighted that Toni and the children could seize the opportunity. Toni's diary entry reads as follows:

> *Once we were called through to the departure lounge at Seeb military airport, the girls and I were requested to sit in the 'Purdah Area' screened by wooden panels, much to the amusement of the boys. However, we were allowed to re-join them on the VIP bus that took us out to the aircraft, where it stopped to let us board via the flight crew's steps instead of the loading ramp at the rear. We sat sideways on red webbing along the insides of the aircraft with the cargo fastened to the floor in the middle. As we taxied to the runway, the British loadmaster undid the boys' straps and took them into the cockpit, where they remained for the whole journey – takeoff,*

flight and the exciting landing approach through the jebels *into Khasab. What an experience! The girls and I were very envious, but military law forbids females on the flight deck.*

Anyway, given this wonderful opportunity, we were content to contort our necks to peer through one of the few portholes behind us. The scenery in the north is magnificent and reminiscent of Norway, with jagged mountains plunging vertically into the sea to form spectacular fjords.

We disembarked at Khasab, but the loadmaster told us to remain very close by, as the aircraft was on a rapid turnaround. We made our way to the arrivals lounge, essentially to escape the burning sun, and caused some confusion when we headed straight for the departure area. The officer on duty could not understand why we were not staying. By the time this was sorted out we received the call to re-board the aircraft. We arrived home well in time for lunch after yet another memorable experience.

Two days later the children flew back to school in England after what had been their most adventurous summer holiday ever. We watched with heavy hearts as they boarded their Gulf Air flight, Rorie's red jumper and Zoë's green top making the 'clan' easy to spot. We could only imagine how they, too, felt. It was strangely quiet when we returned home. Neither we nor the children ever really got used to these partings. I can remember how my own parents dreaded the similar occasions when we went to school in England from our home in India, knowing, in our case, that it would be almost three years before we returned home. At least we didn't have to wait so long to be reunited.

We were not given the opportunity to mope. Later that day we were asked to start preparing to move out of our temporary home and back into our original bungalow, AAC8, across the road. The task took the best part of a week, as it had to be fitted around our work. I say 'our work', because Toni had started work as a teacher at the Royal Flight School at the beginning of the new school year. Located just outside our camp, this school catered essentially for the children of parents working in the Royal Flight, but included some children whose parents worked in other capacities for the Sultan. So it was that Toni had the son of the Egyptian royal head gardener in her class. As a result, our house was often filled with the most magnificent blooms from the Palace gardens.

I was kept busy, both in the office and on a number of outdoor exercises. In fact, our diaries indicate that I spent two to three days a week in the field throughout my year in Oman, wearing what our steward, Anthony, called my 'painted suit', my disruptive pattern combat kit, and a similarly patterned *shemagh*, the Omani headdress.

The emphasis of the training was on basic infantry tactics and individual skills, such as field craft, fire and manoeuvre and skill at arms. As the topography of Oman varies widely, the soldiers had to learn to be equal to the demands of operating in the *jebels* or the desert, and in searing heat or freezing cold weather. Perhaps their strongest card was their marksmanship. Indeed, to capitalise on this asset, my department included an instructor seconded from the British Army's Small Arms School Corps. He was responsible for maintaining the high standard of shooting throughout the army, and, as importantly, training the shooting team to represent the Omani Army at prestigious events, such as the British Army Small Arms Championships held annually at Bisley, in which Oman had an enviable record.

Arguably, the most prestigious event in SOLF's annual training calendar was the Skill at Arms Meeting (SOLFSAM). This was run on Bisley lines at the Sultan's Armed Forces Training Regiment's (SAFTR) barracks in

Ghala over a four-day period in December. My department was responsible for planning and running the event. Whilst it was the army's meeting, all the other uniformed services in Oman were invited to participate. This increased the pressure on SOLF and, indeed, my training department, as it was important that SOLF won all the major prizes, especially the Sultan's Medal (Champion Shot) and the Falling Plate competition. If this did not happen, the training branch and the army would have been deemed to have failed, and the meeting regarded as a total flop by all the army's top brass! So, no pressure then! We duly met their expectations.

If SOLFSAM was the most prestigious military competition in Oman, then the Northern Oman Brigade March and Shoot Competition was arguably the most arduous. Every major unit in the Brigade had to enter two teams, each of 30 men, whilst each minor unit was required to enter a single team of the same size. The event took place annually in February, towards the end of the cooler winter weather. The teams set off at timed intervals to undertake a daunting ascent of Jebel Akhdar from a start point at Birkat Al Mauz at the base of the mountain along awe-inspiring mountain tracks up the Wadi Muaydin to the training camp at Saiq. They arrive exhausted, their chests heaving as they try to gulp in air in the more rarefied atmosphere at over 6,500 feet. However, there is no respite; they must now race to the rifle range and complete a falling plate practice. A complex mathematical formula is used to combine the time taken to reach Saiq and the score achieved on the range practice to determine the winners.

The high priority given to training, combined with the quality of the Omani soldiers, means that the army can hold its own on the world stage. In 1987, the Omani Shooting Team came second at Bisley, whilst 'our' Parachute Team won the Rhine Army Championships. To mark these achievements, CSOLF laid on a joint *hafla* (party) for both teams, which was attended by all the competitors, most of the army's top brass, plus myself and the seconded instructors who had coached the men. We gathered in a large hall where we were split up into groups and invited to sit in circles on the floor. I have never before, nor since, attended such a feast.

> *First came all manner of fruits, including the finest Omani dates and local grapes. Then we were served with enormous mountains of rice upon which was more roast meat than I have ever seen at one sitting: a whole sheep lay across the top of each mound of rice, whilst four chickens were positioned round the base, a grand total of six sheep and 24 chickens to be shared amongst just 44 of us! Although the soldiers did their best, we weren't expected to devour the lot. Arab hospitality is legendary and this was just CSOLF's way of thanking his men.*
>
> *I was thoroughly enjoying the experience of tearing away meat with my right hand and eating greedily, until an enthusiastic soldier sitting beside me grabbed a sheep's head, wrenched off its lower jawbone and then used this to gouge out the animal's brains for me to eat! I had eaten brains as a child – not my favourite dish – but never served up as graphically as this. I survived!*

Some people might be offended at the apparent waste resulting from such feasts, so let me say a word about Arab hospitality. In my experience, Arabs always seem to cater for anything up to ten times the number of invited guests. In this way, the host not only honours his guests, but also ensures that there is plenty of food left over to feed the army of people responsible for preparing and serving the banquet and even their families. This is particularly so concerning religious feasts such as Eid al-Adha, where, I was told, a third of the food is for the family, a third for guests who drop by (invited or otherwise), with the remaining third going to the poor. This benevolence is not just practised amongst the better off in society; the poorest *Bedu* in the desert will share his last cup of water with a complete stranger.

When we were both at home during the week we played a lot of tennis in the evenings using the splendid facilities available in MAM. In addition to 'social tennis', there were regular tennis tournaments, both for the adults and the children, if one wanted to be a bit more competitive. Whilst there were some really good tennis players on camp, nobody took themselves too seriously, so entering the odd tournament was quite good fun. My doubles partner in the men's events was Sergeant Gary Corkish of the RAF Regiment. He was a parachute instructor and lived out in the sticks at Rostaq. A far superior tennis player to me, he was on an unaccompanied 18-month tour. We had the pleasure of meeting his wife, Yvonne, when she came out for a short holiday. They took us on at doubles one evening and won handsomely.

We also enjoyed being able to walk straight onto the *jebels* from our patio for a stroll in the cool of the evening. Desert foxes were a common sight in this area and it was fun watching them on our patio at night. Sometimes, when the children were home, we would take our Nissan Patrol out onto the *jebel* behind the house at night to spot foxes in the headlights.

When we were not '*wadi* bashing' at the weekend, we spent our time down at the SAF beach club, swimming, skiing or snorkelling. Another popular early morning attraction was to visit the souk on Seeb's beach, just a few minutes' drive from MAM, to watch the fishing boats returning from their night's work. Getting up before dawn, we would arrive in time to see the boats all racing for the shore to unload their catches – large numbers of sharks, tuna and other sizeable fish that we couldn't identify. Amazingly, all these fish were caught on hand lines. As the souk was right on the beach, the fish were sold within minutes of being landed – they could not have been fresher.

Omani colleagues also invited us to visit them in their villages on Fridays, occasions that really enriched our lives and cemented our love of the country and its people. A number of these visits were to Muqaddam (Lieutenant Colonel) Hilal's family in the village of Rawdah, deep in the gravel plain south of Jebel Akhdar. Hilal was the commanding officer of the Battle Training Camp at Saiq – an unaccompanied posting. Therefore, he went home at weekends as often as possible. It was very kind of him to share some of those precious weekends with us, bearing in mind that he would only arrive home late on Thursday afternoon and would have to set off for Saiq again on Friday afternoon – not much of a break.

Rawdah turned out to be a little oasis amidst the gravel plain, with date palms giving shade to the cluster of houses. When we reached his house we were ushered into the main room, leaving our shoes outside (we soon learnt to wear flip-flops or sandals on these occasions as they were easy to slip on and off). Hilal had bowed to Western culture and there were a number of easy chairs to sit on rather than the floor. On our first visit, we were joined by Hilal's dignified old father, Bader and his brother, Saud. Inquisitive faces peered around the door – Hilal's six children and Saud's only child, a son named Sultan. Both the men's wives came forward to be introduced to us, but then slipped away.

Hilal was keen to show us Rawdah and its surrounds. Jumping into the driving seat of our car – it was a military car after all – he invited me to sit beside him, whilst Toni and Saud got in the back. This was indeed a peaceful place, a haven of cool palm groves, watered by *falajes* that criss-crossed the ground beneath the trees. Birdsong filled the air. Outside the village were a number of apparently deserted '*barusties*' – shacks made from palm fronds – which Hilal told us were occasionally used by the *Bedu* as they wandered the gravel plain.

We arrived home in time for a sumptuous lunch, after which Hilal's 14-year-old son, Ahmed, took us for a walk amongst the palms. We noticed an old man and a woman approaching one of the trees, and he carried a basket, a length of cloth and rope, plus a large knife. Ahmed told us to stop and watch them. On reaching the tree, the old man placed the cloth around his waist and, looping it around the trunk of the tree, tied the ends together to make a sling. Then, carrying the knife and the basket, he lent back in the sling and placed his bare feet on the tree trunk. Once in position he straightened his legs and, in a flowing movement, leaned forward to loosen the sling and move it quickly further up the trunk, before falling back to tighten the sling again. He repeated this process several times until he was at the top of the tree ready to harvest the dates.

Relying solely on the sling to hold him, he used both hands to cut away bunches of dates and place them in his basket. When the basket was full he used the rope to lower it to the woman on the ground. Once she had unloaded the dates, he pulled the basket back up again to continue gathering the harvest. When the job was done he descended the tree, using the same method he employed on his ascent.

We enjoyed one or two high profile national and social events during November and December. The first of these was the parade to celebrate Oman's National Day and the Sultan's Birthday. This event took place in the Police Stadium in Muscat on 18 November, in the presence of the Sultan. Although very much a civilian event, the military was expected to attend. At the stadium we were rather surprised to find that the men and women had to sit in different areas of the stadium. The men were under cover and out of the sun, whilst our poor wives sat opposite us in the open and at the sun's mercy. Luckily, Toni had a bottle of water and another wife had brought along some apple juice which saved the day.

Once the Sultan was in position, hundreds of men, representing every aspect of life in Oman, paraded past to honour their ruler. Artisans, representing miners, metal workers, carpenters, welders, etc., were uniformly dressed in colour-specific working clothes complete, where applicable, with their appropriate protective headwear. These were followed by wave upon wave of other workers, such as fishermen, farmers and traders, wearing Omani national dress. Next came the musicians – mostly drummers – who raised the tempo several notches as they entered the stadium. Bringing up the rear were other groups brandishing camel sticks and swords.

Once everyone had entered the arena, the Sultan made a short speech and then presented medals to those nominated in this Birthday Honours. A spectacular fireworks display, culminating in an explosive finale in the Omani colours of red, green and white brought the evening to a close.

Next morning, we got up before dawn to go out into the desert to watch the National Day Camel Race Meeting. This was voluntary, but something we wanted to see. It is fair to say that it wasn't as slickly run as its equestrian equivalents, but was great fun nonetheless. The jockeys were mainly very young boys and the camels seemed to set off whenever they wanted. Many chose to leap the rope barrier marking the edge of the track and scatter the spectators or career off into the desert. Yet, the best camels won and everyone was happy.

Armed Forces Day on 11 December was marked by a dinner in the beautiful grounds of the Sultan's mother's palace on the seafront outside Muscat. It was quite a chilly evening and by the time the Sultan arrived we were all feeling rather cold. The band signalled his arrival by striking up the National Anthem, after which we sat down to a sumptuous meal served by numerous Chinese and Filipino waiters in blue Omani-style dishdashas. This event, too, culminated in an impressive fireworks display out over the sea, the colourful reflections on the water adding to the spectacle.

Sandwiched between these two events was the Caledonian Ball, arguably the main event of the year for most of the expatriates. In 1987, the Ball Committee played an absolute blinder, securing the Bustan Palace hotel as the venue. At the time, the Bustan Palace was reputed to be amongst the top ten hotels in the world. It was sumptuous beyond measure and we had only been there once, for a brunch to celebrate Toni's birthday. Dinner would have been way beyond our means. Yet, not only was the ball to be held here, but we were offered rooms for the night, plus breakfast next morning, for the equivalent of around £20!

The evening lived up to expectations and was memorable in so many ways, especially so for the display put on by SOLF's pipes and drums, resplendent in their uniforms. British trained, they could more than hold their own in any setting. Indeed, we had seen them performing at the Edinburgh Tattoo some years earlier.

As Catholics, we could fulfil our Sunday obligation by going to Mass on Friday and Saturday evenings as well as on Sunday. This was to accommodate the different weekends taken by people depending on where they worked. Initially, we went to the tiny original church in the middle of Ruwi in the heart of the Capital Area. The Sultan was keen to absorb the prime land on which the church stood into the development of the area, so, whilst we were in Oman, he sanctioned the building of new Catholic and Anglican churches side by side in a new development in Ghala, much closer to MAM.

However, there was a Christian cemetery on the site of the Ruwi church. Indeed, it was the final resting place of a friend of mine, Captain Mike Offord, who sadly died during the Dhofar War. He and I had been in the same intake at Sandhurst and had both been commissioned into the Royal Tank Regiment (RTR). As soon as the Sultan heard about the cemetery, he decreed that the site remain as it was, but allowed work to continue on the new, larger churches. So we ended up with two churches, although the one at Ghala was only just completed before we left the country.

Whichever Mass we attended, the church was always full, the vast majority of the congregation being expatriates from Kerala, South India. Over the centuries, Oman had enjoyed strong trading links with the Malabar Coast of India and was now providing mutually beneficial employment opportunities for thousands of people from the subcontinent.

Although my tour in Oman had been reduced to a year, I was entitled to four weeks' leave. Due to the large number of South Indians working in Oman, Gulf Air flights to and from India were very attractively priced. We therefore decided to spend a fortnight in India with the children during the Christmas holidays in 1987. Amazingly, our cook Abraham's sister worked as a travel agent in Trivandrum, the capital of Kerala, so he volunteered to make all the necessary arrangements for us. Some cook! All we did was to give him our intended itinerary. Maybe we took a chance, but we trusted Abraham and that trust was richly rewarded.

We flew to Bombay (Mumbai) on 19 December and, after an overnight stop, caught the Indian Airways flight down to Trivandrum. Here we were met by Abraham's sister, Mrs Kunien, who briefed us on the arrangements she had made for our visit and handed over all the documentation and tickets. A most efficient person, she had met every single one of our requests.

A minibus and driver took us to Kovalam, the beach near Trivandrum where I saw the sea for the first time in 1942. The spot where my father used to park the car under some coconut palms at the edge of the sandy beach was now occupied by a cluster of tasteful, single storey cottages. Hidden amongst the palms with an uninterrupted view of the sea, these cottages were part of the Kovalam Ashok Beach Hotel. The main hotel building had been built on the slopes of the headland to the south of the beach. Following the contours of the hill and never going above the height of the coconut palms, the building was hardly noticeable from the beach. (In the old days there was just a small, open-sided shelter up on the headland, where we used to eat our picnic lunch.)

Life on the beach was very much as I remembered it as a child. Fishing boats bobbed up and down in the water just beyond the surf, whilst others lay idle on the sand above the high water mark. Men hauled on nets or sat quietly checking their catch or repairing damaged nets. The boats were still the same as I remembered them. Some were long, pointed at both ends and wide enough at the beam for two men to sit side by side. They were quite deep and stable in the water. Black in colour, they were made using rough planks of wood that were stitched together with coir string, rather than using nails. Propelled by men with paddles, these boats went far out to sea and often stayed out all night.

Other boats were nothing more than narrow, elongated rafts called catamarans. These comprised three or four coconut palm tree trunks tied together with coir rope. The craft could carry two men who used long poles to punt themselves through the surf and out into the shallows. A second team stayed ashore holding the end of a long rope attached to the net, which was aboard the catamaran. The craft would then be punted in a wide semi-circle back to shore further along the beach as the net was being played out. Once back on land, the two teams would haul the net back in. This was really hard work for what were usually meagre rewards.

This timeless scene took me straight back to the carefree days of my childhood in the 1940s, when I was blissfully unaware of the threat to our safety posed by the Japanese and the war being waged by the Allies in Burma to halt their advance into India.

My old *ayah* (nanny), Cecily Daniel, now in her 80s, lived in Trivandrum and we had arranged to meet her in Kovalam. It was an absolute joy to see her again, especially as she looked so fit and well. She was much shorter than I remembered – barely four feet tall. We all had breakfast together, whilst she regaled the children with hugely embellished stories of all the dreadful things 'Bruce Master' and 'Hedley Master' did to her as children, such as hiding her false teeth and trying to set fire to her hair when she was asleep!

After a really happy reunion we took Ayahmo, as we used to call her, back into Trivandrum. She didn't want us to see her 'jungly house', and we feared it must have been a slum dwelling. It was with very heavy hearts that we said goodbye, as we all knew that this was probably our final parting. As she walked away, we watched and waved until she was swallowed up by the sea of people.

Having said farewell to Ayahmo, we made our way to the bank to change our Omani banker's draft into rupees. The bank was quite Dickensian and in sharp contrast to the computerised system employed in Oman – clerks pored over books and ledgers in dingy offices, peons ran hither and thither with messages, there were old black telephones with the finger dialling system and, dominating the room, a large clock ticked noisily away on the wall. Yet the antiquated appearance belied the bank's efficiency and we were soon on our way with our rupees.

After a pleasant stay in Kovalam we set off across the plains for the Periyar Wildlife Sanctuary in the hills of Peermade. The reserve is set around a massive artificial lake, which was formed in 1895 by damming the Periyar River to provide water for Tamil Nadu State (formerly Madras State). The drive took us through rural India, our route lined with fields of corn and rice paddies, where once there had been nothing but scrub jungle. Working elephants competed with pedestrians and normal traffic for space on the road. Farmers took advantage of the traffic, laying their cut corn on the road for the vehicles to run over and thresh. Any lull in the traffic saw them running out to sweep up their grain for winnowing.

In one village we saw two men in the shade of a tree directing an enormous set of bellows at a small charcoal fire, by which a third man fashioned metal into farming implements. A barber plied his trade under another tree. The clamour and the thronging crowds were evidence of the India's burgeoning population.

Eventually, we left the plains and started to climb the Peermade *ghat* up into the tea-growing area. Once we started climbing it became obvious that our driver had never driven in hilly country before. He struggled with his gear selections, especially when negotiating steep, tight corners. The engine laboured and I became every driver's worst nightmare of a back seat driver. Eventually, the engine died. The driver got out to investigate and the concerned look on his face didn't bode well. "Engine too much hot, sahib," was his diagnosis.

This took me back almost 40 years to an occasion when my mother was driving us back to school across the hills in our Hillman. It had been raining and the jungle section was particularly challenging. She had got us nearly to the top and was negotiating one of the final hairpin bends when the engine died. Our kitchen 'matey' (helper) who was with us got out to investigate and came back to declare, "Engine melting, Madam!" Now, as then, we decided to let the engine cool down and then topped up the radiator when it was safe to do so. After about an hour we were on our way again and reached Periyar just before dusk. Our hotel had seen better days (or perhaps not!) but this was all part of the experience of venturing off the beaten track in India.

Driving on from Periyar we descended back down onto the plains and headed north for Kodaikanal (Kodai for short), a beautiful hill station at about 7,000 feet, where I first went to school. We planned to spend Christmas here. The Kodai *ghat* brought back many memories for me.

The road was still narrow, but there was now a low protective wall on the open side almost the entire way up. It had been raining heavily and the road was wet and slippery (Kodai just catches the northeast monsoon, which blows between December and March). As we climbed higher, the temperature began to drop rapidly and for the last hour of the journey we were enveloped in a thick mist. Thankfully, our driver was now getting the knack of driving amongst the hills and so we reached the top of the *ghat* without incident.

Amazingly, despite having been away for 33 years, I remembered the way to our school, the Presentation Convent, Kodaikanal (PCK). It stood on the crest of a hill we called Calvary, about a mile or so out of town. The nuns gave us a very warm welcome when we arrived. Theirs was a small community, about a dozen in total, all of whom were Indians, apart from two nuns from Ireland. (In my school days, all but one of the nuns came from Ireland.) Most wore attractive orange/fawn coloured saris, apart from one or two older nuns who wore simple white blouses, blue or black skirts and matching veils. The school was closed for the holidays and we were given free rein to wander around as we pleased. The family was particularly interested in my old dormitory, in which I was even able to show them where I slept. I'm sure it was the self-same metal bed! Everything in the school was as I had remembered it, albeit much smaller than the picture in my mind's eye.

The nuns accommodated us in a small cottage that had once been home to an English teacher at the school. Set in the midst of firs and eucalyptus trees, it was perfect for our needs. Martin, one of the cooks when I was at school, came out of retirement to cook for us. He remembered me and took delight in telling the children that I was "very small, eating too much and somewhat trouble-making!" It was wonderful to see him again and we certainly needed him, because the kitchen stove was a museum piece which only he knew how to operate. It was, in fact, a Spencer's Torpedo No.

1 wood burning stove, just like the one we had at home when I was a boy.

Our poor driver was now shivering with cold. As mentioned earlier, he had never ventured into the hills and had no warm clothing. At Periyar we had been at a relatively low elevation, but now we were above 7,000 feet and it was cold, wet and windy. So we dashed down to the town and bought him a warm blanket to wrap himself in.

We had arranged to meet the driver at 9.30 a.m. the following morning – Christmas Eve – but he didn't appear. Eventually, he arrived on foot and told us that the Chief Minister of Tamil Nadu had died during the night. As a mark of respect, no vehicles were allowed to move and all shops, restaurants, and cinemas were to remain closed until 4.00 p.m. We therefore decided to explore the school and its grounds in the morning and then went for a walk around the lake in the afternoon, a walk I had undertaken many times as a schoolboy. Set in a shallow bowl above the town, this is a very picturesque expanse of water. Smart houses hide amongst the wooded hills that surround it, and here and there at the water's edge are elaborate boathouses in which elegant wooden rowing boats are moored; boats that would not have looked out of place on the Thames at Goring or Henley in the 1950s.

The bazaar was near the lake, so when it opened we paid a visit to do our Christmas shopping, ending up in Khutais Curio Palace, where prices seemed ridiculously cheap after Oman. We had told Martin our plans and when the driver arrived with the car he sent him to the bazaar to look for us. We were very grateful, as none of us fancied the long walk back to school up Calvary, laden as we were with our 'goodies'. That evening after supper everyone hid in various nooks and crannies, the only noise being the rustle of wrapping paper.

We attended midnight Mass in the convent chapel, followed by coffee and cakes in the convent, where we met an American surgeon. It transpired that he had been a pupil at High Clere, the large American school in Kodai, at the same time as I was at PCK. After leaving school, he had qualified as a surgeon in the United States and had then returned to Kodai, where he worked in the General Hospital.

We also met an English former Jesuit priest. He had been in Libya when the Libyans were expelled from Britain following the shooting of PC Yvonne Fletcher in 1984 outside the Libyan Embassy in London. Life had been made very difficult for him. He had since left the priesthood and was now married to a lovely Indian lady. She had lived in Jos, Nigeria, but returned to India when her Nigerian husband was killed in a car crash on his way to Kano – a road we had travelled many times.

Christmas morning dawned cold and wet, but nothing dampened our spirits. Father Christmas had visited us in the night and filled the children's stockings and ours as well. We had much fun undoing the various packages all attractively wrapped up in newspaper and loo paper! There were presents as well for Martin, the driver and the nuns.

After breakfast, despite the weather, we set off for one of my old haunts, Bear Shola. A quiet, wooded valley with a beautiful waterfall, this had been one of the favourite spots for a school picnic during my school days. The little track leading up the valley was now a road lined with houses, but the area around the falls remained largely unspoilt, albeit quite popular with people living in the area. However, when we scrambled up the side to the top of the falls we were entirely on our own amidst the most beautiful and restful scenery, the only sounds being the babbling stream and the birds chirping in the trees overhead.

Martin had asked us to be sure to return for lunch and so we did, and we were not disappointed. He had made us a meal of roast chicken, stuffing and roast potatoes. This was followed by Christmas pudding and a Christmas cake provided by Abraham, via his sister in Trivandrum. What a wonderfully thoughtful gesture and what forward planning and organisation!

After lunch we set off again, this time for Pillar Rocks. These two enormous monoliths stand out from the sheer cliffs at the top of the mountains, which sweep down to the plains thousands of feet below from this point. They looked eerie indeed as we glimpsed them through breaks in the swirling mist and rain.

Our next port of call that wet afternoon was Berijam Lake, 15 miles or so from Kodai. In good weather, this is a shimmering blue jewel set in a *shola* (stunted forest) out on the grasslands, but today it looked rather dour and menacing. It lies along the route running across the tops of the hills, mentioned earlier, between Kodai and the High Range, the idyllic tea-planting district in which I grew up. This unsurfaced track is only 60 miles long, whereas the route via the plains is some 170 miles; hence its name, the Kodai Shortcut.

This road was often impassable beyond Berijam Lake, particularly during the southwest monsoon, but when it was open it was certainly an exciting way to go to and from school. The most demanding bit was the 'jungle section' at the High Range end, where the road climbed up the mountainside in a series of 20 or more acute hairpin bends. We didn't have the luxury of a four-wheel drive vehicle when my parents used the route in the 1940s and 1950s, but had to make do with a 1947 Hillman Minx and, later, a 1952 Morris Oxford. We always travelled with a 'momerty' (the Indian equivalent of a spade with the blade at right angles to the shaft) and sacking for when we got stuck. When we used this route we would always stop for a long break at a remote stream called the Pilchar, where there was excellent trout fishing. During the Michaelmas holidays in September, the grassland around the Pilchar was covered with large white arum lilies, which the non-fishers used to pick. The only drawback to both of these activities was that these grasslands were also home to the deadly Russell's Viper, so we all had to 'gang warily', as the Scots would say. (Unfortunately, when we returned to India in 2008 and wanted to travel this route in a 4x4 vehicle we found it had been closed at the High Range end by the Forestry Department.)

We returned to Kodai via Fairy Falls, which, as the name suggests, had a delicate, captivating beauty, making them seem almost unreal. This was another favourite picnic spot during my school days. Being much further away than Bear Shola you had to be aged at least ten-years-old before you could visit here – we had to walk to and from all these picnic outings. As we arrived back at Kodai lake, the clouds lifted and I was able to point out the extinct volcano, Perumal, which rose majestically on the horizon. We also made a quick dash to a viewpoint at Coaker's Walk. This pathway skirts along the edge of the mountains and, on a fine day, gives walkers an uninterrupted view of the plains far below. Today, however, it looked as if we were looking out of a window in an aircraft, as there was nothing but cloud below us.

We spent Christmas evening in the convent with the nuns, who laid on a buffet supper for us. Afterwards, two of the younger nuns, including the headmistress, Sister Rose, performed some traditional Indian dances for us. We responded with The Dashing White Sergeant, which they all found hilarious. We ended up around the piano, initially with Alex playing dance music, and then rounded off a really happy evening with a good rendering of Christmas carols.

Next morning, after 'photo-calls' with the nuns and Martin, we bade a fond farewell to PCK and set off from Kodai as we had arrived, in thick mist. Luckily, this cleared just enough for me to point out another magical waterfall, Silver Cascades, just by the roadside a little way down the *ghat*.

We were soon down the *ghat* and back onto the hot, dusty, crowded plains, competing with other traffic, plus cyclists, pedestrians, cattle and stray dogs on the road. Our destination was the High Range, but first we made a detour to visit the city of Madurai. Reputed to be the oldest continually inhabited city in Peninsula India, Madurai is famous for its

Hindu Temple, which covers an area of about half a square mile.

Indeed, the temple is the very heart of the city, which seems to have been built up in concentric rectangles around it. The temple's intricately carved pyramidal towers dominate the skyline for miles around, but are so hemmed in by the surrounding buildings that it is difficult to capture them close up on film. Unfortunately, a lack of time prevented us from touring the temple complex; we were still a long way from the High Range. We did, however, have time to experience an interesting way of collecting money for its upkeep. No willing volunteers rattling collecting tins here, but a temple elephant instead. Ridden by a *mahout*, it would stop the traffic and use its trunk to collect the money, carefully handing the offerings up to the *mahout*. Having an elephant's trunk poking through your car window is quite persuasive! And it wouldn't move until it got a result.

We were soon back on the busy plains road, heading for a distant range of hills on the horizon. After about three hours' driving, we reached the town of Bodinayakkanur (known as Bodi) at the foot of the *ghat*. When I was a child this *ghat* was just a track passable only by pack animals, but it had now been widened (only slightly) and tarred. The narrowness of the road, the incredible, largely unprotected drops, and the 17 hairpin bends that were too acute for our vehicle to negotiate in one move, made this one of the most frightening journeys we had ever experienced.

Looking out of the windows on some stretches of the road you could have been forgiven for thinking you were in a plane; you were so close to the edge that you could not see the road, only the cavernous drop to the valley below. Rorie was sitting at the back on the near side and his involuntary interjections of "Ooh...eerh" each time the vehicle appeared about to go over the edge didn't help our poor driver who was clearly very nervous himself. As mentioned earlier, he had never ventured into the hills before, let alone experienced a road as challenging as this one.

Luckily we reached Top Station, the end of the *ghat*, before nightfall.

Top Station is so called because in earlier times there was a ropeway from here down to Bodi (also known then as Bottom Station), which was used to transport goods to and from the High Range.

We were now driving through the tea fields in my beloved High Range, making for the town of Munnar and the High Range Club. We arrived just in time for supper and were soon tucked up in bed in one of the club's annexes.

Next morning we awoke to the lovely sound of a 'Whistling Schoolboy', India's Whistling or Malabar Thrush, just outside our bedroom window. An iridescent dark blue bird, it has the wonderful ability to mimic the melodies it hears and incorporate these into its joyous birdsong, lifting the spirits of all who hear it. If it is alarmed, however, it emits a very unmelodious shriek as it makes good its escape.

To me, our visit to the High Range was like entering a time warp and being taken back to my childhood days. The club building was exactly as I remembered it. The Men's Bar was still the dark and rather dingy room furnished with the same brown leather armchairs and sofas I can remember glimpsing as a child, and it was still strictly reserved for men only. The heads of various unfortunate animals glared down from the walls, trophies of a bygone age, and the photograph of Wally Mackay and his massive Mahseer, caught at the Kurram Gugan, still graced the mantelpiece.

Adorning the wall behind the bar was perhaps the greatest relic of the past, the hats of all the planters who had served for 30 years or more in the district, all of whom were Europeans. These included my father's battered old trilby, emblazoned with his initials R.I.M.D and bearing the dates 1926-60. My mother's name, too, lived on in the library, where a board on the wall recorded the winners down the years of the Blanche Duncan Ladies Table Tennis Cup. The only thing that had changed was that the rugby pitch had disappeared, the area being incorporated into the nine-hole golf course.

Our vehicle was playing up, which was no surprise after the demands that had been made of it. We therefore chose to venture into Munnar on foot. Nothing much had changed in the little town itself, but the road leading to this hub of the district was now lined with slum dwellings, more evidence of India's growing population. I took the family to Marikar's, the only shop which sold toys when I was a child, and introduced them to Mr and Mrs Marikar. It was marvellous seeing them again and reminiscing about the old days. We also visited the Catholic church, set on a hill overlooking the bazaar. There we met Father Pinheiro, who remembered me and my parents and asked that we give them his salaams.

The name Munnar means 'three rivers'. The town is at the confluence of these rivers and is surrounded by the walls of the valleys through which they run. The Catholic church stands on one of the three most prominent hilltops, with the Hindu temple and the Mosque occupying the other two. Throughout my childhood, the town enjoyed total religious harmony, with everyone celebrating all the various feast days, and that happy state of affairs seems to have endured to the present day. The High Range was, and remains, a place as close to Utopia as I'm ever likely to find.

At supper that evening, Mr Murthy, the Acting General Manger of the district, came to the club to meet us. After listening to what we hoped to achieve over the next four days, he kindly volunteered to make all the necessary arrangements. He also provided us with a company car and driver for the duration of our stay, whilst our vehicle was being repaired. So it was that over the next few days we toured the entire district, visiting the estates and bungalows I knew as a child: Kadalaar, where I was born, and Aravikard, Grahamsland, Pullivasal and Chokanad, where I grew up. We were kindly allowed into the bungalows at Pullivasal, where I had spent most of my young life, and Chokanad, the last bungalow in which I had lived. Clearly, the district was thriving. Everywhere, the tea looked absolutely pristine, resembling a beautifully manicured lawn hugging the contours of the hills. This effect can only be achieved by skilful pluckers, who use long bamboo canes which they lay on top of the bushes they are working on to ensure that they pluck evenly from bush to bush.

I also took the family to visit my old fishing haunts: the picturesque jungle streams of Pettimudi and Rajamally, the dams at Kundale and Madupatty and the exquisite little lake tucked away in a valley at Davicolum. We also attempted to climb Anamudi, using a local Mudavan tracker as our guide. At 8,842 feet, this is the highest mountain in the Indian subcontinent south of the Himalayas and dominates the Munnar skyline. Its name refers to its shape, which resembles an elephant's head. Perhaps due to the altitude, first Zoë and then I completely ran out of steam and became giddy and disorientated. As it was dangerous to be left alone in such wild country – we were unarmed and in a big game reserve – Toni stayed with Zoë and Rorie kindly stayed with me, whilst Hannah and Alex pressed on to the summit. As we all eventually made it home in one piece, we considered the expedition to be a qualified success.

One afternoon we were given a conducted tour round my father's former factory on Pullivasal, where a new process of manufacture had been introduced. In my father's day, tea brought in from the fields was first placed in withering sheds for two or so days. Once this process was complete, the leaf was then taken into the factory, where it was broken down gently in huge rollers, before being allowed to ferment in heaps on the factory floor, again for a day or two. Finally, it was fired in the furnaces and then sifted into its various grades, before being packed in tea chests for transportation out of the district.

This had now been replaced by a swifter, more efficient, albeit aggressive, new process, called CTC (cut, twist, curl). The green leaf was now withered in enormous trays inside the factory, using hot air blown from fans to complete the process in a matter of hours rather than days. The withered leaf is then shredded in a cutting machine – and then twisted and curled in a series of grinders, each finer than the last, from which it emerges as a mush, for want of a better word. It is then fermented in drums, the process taking about an hour and a half, as opposed to days, before being fired and sifted into its various grades. Finally, it is put into hessian sacks for transportation.

The fine tea produced by this process meets today's demand for tea bags. In 1987, some loose leaf tea was still being produced in Pullivasal factory by the old process for the specialist market. Needless to say, this was extremely expensive to buy. Mr Murthy said this was the tea that my parents would remember and kindly gave us two kilos of it to take home with us. This caused quite a stir at Heathrow when the children returned to school at the end of the holiday. Rorie, complete with guitar and red bandana, was stopped and searched at Customs. The young official was not convinced that the 'strange substance' in his suitcase was tea destined for my parents! Eventually, however, he was allowed through with his precious cargo.

Our most important visit whilst in the High Range was to look up my parents' old butler/*shikari* (hunter), Anthony, who was now living on Kundale Estate. We went to see him on 30 December, Alex's 17th birthday. It was really touching to see his home, the walls of which were covered in photographs of my parents and us children at every stage of our lives. It was like looking through our own family albums. Anthony had been a great *shikari* and, competing with the photographs on his walls, was his prize trophy – the extraordinary head of a sambar with four horns, a true rarity. He was an old man now, but the person who taught me to fish and to track game still exuded a sense of noble dignity. At the end of our visit, we all had to endure another painful final parting. Anthony lived for a number of years after our visit and my brother, Hedley, was the last of our family to see him when he visited the High Range a year or so later. We both still keep in touch with Anthony's son, Peter, and his family, who live on Davicolum Estate, where Toni and I last visited him in 2008.

On our last day, New Year's Eve, Mr Murthy invited us to a true Indian curry lunch with his wife and family at their home, Munnar bungalow. During the meal he talked about the old days and said how he would never forget the kindness my parents showed him in 1960 when he was a young, very lonely engineer. At the time he was staying at the High Range Club whilst working on an engineering assignment, and knew none of the (mostly British) planters who dropped in. Apparently, my parents had taken him under their wing. He was now delighted to have been given the opportunity to repay their kindness.

Indeed, everywhere we went it was truly heart-warming to be greeted by so many people with fond memories of my father. He was much liked by the estate workers and was still known as the 'Tungan Dorray', a play on his name Duncan Dorray, but significantly meaning Golden Master. I'm proud to say this did not refer to the colour of his hair, which was jet black, but to the esteem in which he was held.

On New Year's Day, having listened to our 'Whistling Schoolboy' for the last time and having said goodbye to the club's staff, we made our way down the Cochin *ghat* in our now repaired minibus. This is quite a gentle *ghat*, but a very busy one and we had all aged appreciably by the time we arrived at Cochin airport, where we bade farewell to our driver.

From Cochin we flew to Delhi via Goa with Indian Airlines. At Delhi we were met, quite unexpectedly, by one Mr Matthew Vergese and his Ambassador taxi. It transpired that he was one of Abraham's cousins! For those who don't know, the Ambassador was built by the Hindustan Motors company and is modelled on the 1950s Morris Oxford. Somehow, Matthew fitted all six of us plus himself and our luggage into and on top of the vehicle.

Our hotel, the Ashok Yatri Niwas, was quite an experience. According to the blurb in our room, it was designed to cater for the 'low-budget tourist who demanded a high standard'. In keeping with the 'high standard', there on a table were two cakes. They had been ordered by Abraham, one for New Year and the other for Alex's birthday. The floor of our room was bare concrete, painted brick red. There were no beds, but where you would expect to find one the concrete floor had simply been raised by about 18 inches to form a platform upon which there was a mattress – simple. The only slight worry was an enormous plate glass window, starting less than a foot from the floor and devoid of any form of protective rail – we were five floors up! However, we weren't staying long and the main purpose of coming here was to visit the Taj Mahal in Agra.

We were up and away by dawn next morning to catch the Taj Express, an impressive, modern train that transported us the 150 miles to Agra in considerable comfort. As always, the visit to the Taj Mahal was an experience that will live with us forever. Mere words can never do justice to this exquisite monument. This was my second visit and yet I was as awe-struck by its beauty as the rest of the family, who were seeing it for the first time.

Surprisingly, my parents never visited this wonder of the world, despite their 24 years of married life in India (my father spent 34 years there). However, one has to appreciate that for most of that time air travel wasn't an option. Planters were initially granted six months' home leave every ten years. Sometime between the two World Wars, this interval was halved to five years and halved again in the mid-1950s to two and a half years. The journey from the High Range to Britain took the best part of a month, meaning a round trip of two months. Families were reluctant, therefore, to reduce their time at 'home' any further. The planters were also granted a fortnight's furlough in-country every year. My parents chose to reserve four days of this to visit us at school in Kodai, and spent the remainder roughing it on *shikar* (hunting) trips in the scrub jungles of the plains, my father being a keen *shikari*. My mother nobly acceded to his wishes, especially as we children loved the jungle. So the opportunity sadly passed them by.

The only real hiccup of our Indian adventure occurred on the trip back to Delhi at the end of our day in Agra. I thought it odd when 'our seats' on the Taj Express appeared to be taken, but rather than make a fuss we agreed to settle down in the corridor. It was only when the conductor came to check our tickets that we found we had been issued (and paid for) only a single ticket to Agra. As everything was written in Hindi, I had no way of knowing. Initially, the conductor wanted to arrest me, but finally accepted that there had been a genuine mistake and accepted my suggestion that I pay the standard fare. The next problem, however, was that he could accept nothing but cash. We had more than enough money in travellers cheques to meet the bill, but insufficient rupees. Luckily, some kind English tourists came to our rescue and the problem was solved. On arrival in Delhi we settled up with our 'rescuers' and were safely in bed back at our 'budget' hotel by midnight.

Barely three and a half hours later it was time to get up and make our way to the airport. On 3 January 1988 we were back in Oman, where we were met by two of my office colleagues and driven home to a warm welcome from Abraham and Winnie. As we noted in our diary:

> *So ended a holiday of a lifetime; its success due in no small measure to Abraham.*

Almost before we knew it we were all back into our familiar routines. The children had flown back to school and Toni and I were back at work. For several weeks before our trip to India I had been involved in designing and writing a major exercise deep into the desert some three hours' drive from MAM. The aim was to conduct a study period for most of the Lieutenant

Colonels and Majors in SOLF to examine all aspects of aggressive mobile defence in desert terrain. The most ambitious Tactical Exercise Without Troops (TEWT) to be held in Oman up to that point, it had five stands and was scheduled to last three days.

First I had to select a suitable piece of ground and then set the various problems for discussion. Once this was done I took my Omani boss, Colonel Saud, out to the area to walk him through my plan, staying out overnight so that we could see the position at both first and last light. It was quite an experience living in the desert with Saud. He was very much at home in this environment and we travelled light. Camp was quite simply a patch of sand with a warming fire. He did the cooking and after a chat by the dying embers of the fire we simply curled up in our sleeping bags on the sand and drifted off under the stars.

Once Saud was happy, we had to gather a team of experts from the various arms that form a battlegroup to discuss the various problems in detail, write the scenarios and the directing staff solutions to the problems posed. We also had to look at other possible solutions that might be proffered and be prepared to evaluate these as well. Saud and I then walked Colonel Tom, our joint boss, through the whole exercise in one, long day.

All that remained was to gain CSOLF's approval, as it was he who had initiated this project. On the appointed day, Saud and I left MAM early to go by road to the area. I warned Toni that I was unlikely to be home until dusk. CSOLF flew out to the area at a much more civilised hour. He was quite a difficult man to please and we were all a little apprehensive. Saud was now in charge of talking him through the plan. To our relief he declared himself delighted with the whole package. So satisfied was he that he invited both Saud and me to fly back to MAM with him in his helicopter. I was thus able to surprise Toni by getting home for a late lunch. Our poor driver, of course, had to bring the vehicle home.

The study period itself was held in mid-January, when the desert is comfortable by day, but really cold at night. My task had been confined solely to the tactical aspects of this venture and nothing else. Taking as much warm clothing as I could muster, I set off for the location. On arrival, I was surprised to see that a veritable tented village had been erected in the administrative area, complete with electric lighting and running water! The officers' mess was two marquees laced together to make an enormous covered space containing a full complement of furniture and carpets. An orderly escorted me to my tent, a 160-pounder containing a proper bed with crisp white sheets and blankets, carpet and, of all things, a telephone! I tested it by ringing Toni to let her know just how rough life was out here! If I thought that I had had a tough assignment it was nothing compared to this massive logistical undertaking.

The whole affair ran very smoothly, the problems were tackled with gusto and generated a healthy level of discussion. The DS solutions were not taken as 'gospel', but were debated and evaluated against other solutions, just as we had hoped.

The final evening saw us all sit down to a Bedouin-style feast in the mess. Gone were the tables and chairs, and we sat on the carpets in four long lines using our right hands to dig into the huge trays of rice and roast meat. Morale was very high, despite the fact that we still had the Counter Attack Battle Stand to consider at first light next morning. The exercise came to an end just before noon the following day. CSOLF and all the senior officers who had come to observe the proceedings were well pleased with the outcome, as were all the participants. This had been a great achievement both tactically and, especially, administratively.

As a 'thank you' to the training branch, Toni and I arranged a branch outing on a quiet beach outside Muscat on a work day, rather than a Friday. On arrival, we tucked in to an Omani-style breakfast of chapattis, fruit and hot sweet tea. We then introduced people to the game of boules and ran a knockout competition, which turned out to be quite competitive as Omanis,

Asians and Britons vied with one another to become the champion. Our Skill at Arms expert, Major Roger Williams, had brought along a putter, golf balls and a bucket and we all had a go at putting. We then explored a nearby *wadi* and enjoyed lunch in the shade of an acacia tree, following which we all went our separate ways. Meeting each other, especially the clerical staff, in a relaxed, non-work-related setting on a working day had been a very rewarding experience.

In mid-March 1988, I was invited to accompany the Commander of Northern Oman Brigade, Ameed Yussef, and his team on an operational reconnaissance to Musandam, the peninsula bordering the Hormuz Straits. This is one of the most strategically important waterways in the world and the task of protecting it from an Omani viewpoint was part of Brigadier Yussef's remit. The Iran/Iraq war was still raging and Oman was just a few miles from Iran at this crucial bottleneck. Iran had also been quite active in the waters of the Gulf in recent months.

I flew to Khasab in a SOAF C-130 Hercules with Aqeed (Colonel) Mehdi, an Indian doctor serving in MAM, who was also part of the reconnaissance party. Our flight took us over the huge tanker fleet anchored off Fujairah waiting to be escorted through the straits – ample evidence of the strategic importance of this area and the vital need to ensure its defence.

The exciting approach into Khasab got our pulses racing, but we were soon safely down on the ground and taken to the Peninsula Security Headquarters (PenSec HQ) Mess. It was just before midday and we were advised that the reconnaissance would commence at 2.00 p.m. Mehdi suggested that we should seize the opportunity to visit the town as I was most unlikely to get a second chance, so off we went in one of PenSec's white Toyota Land Cruisers.

We had just visited the souk and were heading towards the little fort on the beach, when a vehicle tore past us at breakneck speed, then performed a handbrake turn in the middle of the road and raced back towards us. I was in the middle of decrying the fact that there were joy-riders even up here, when the vehicle stopped in front of us and a man in a white coat leapt out yelling, "Is anyone here 'O' Positive?" Like most people, I'm not very fond of needles, but I am 'O' Positive and owned up to the fact. "Quickly," he said, "please follow my car. I need your blood!" Clearly, we had to help.

Apparently, a woman was haemorrhaging. Giving blood was something few people in this remote part of the world would have heard of, so volunteers were virtually non-existent. This was why the medic had stopped our car – we were in uniform and he knew that soldiers would help if they could. I had a similar experience to this when serving in Brunei. On that occasion the State General Hospital telephoned our Medical Officer with an urgent request for blood donors to save a patient who was haemorrhaging. Twenty-two of us, the vast majority being Brunei Malays, responded.

The little hospital was only two or three minutes down the road and I was lying on an examination couch with a needle in my arm in next to no time. I warned them that I had been in Nigeria and had had malaria. However, they had no other option and, indeed, asked if they could take more blood than usual, to which Mehdi gave me a nod and I agreed.

As soon as they finished taking my blood, we had to make our way back to PenSec as quickly as possible. Mehdi told me not to worry as he would be on the reconnaissance with me. In the event, we spent most of the time in our vehicles rather than on foot, traversing some of the harshest country I have ever seen: razor-sharp barren *jebels* and seemingly bottomless dry *wadis*. We hadn't seen a tree or blade of grass all afternoon until we topped a crest and there, far below us, was a tiny rectangular patch of green, a defiant speck of life amongst the tortured rocky landscape. This was the settlement of As Sayh, but was also known, unofficially, as Twickenham, named, no doubt, by a nostalgic British soldier at some point in the past.

We spent the second day in two helicopters traversing from point to point across these awesome *jebels*. Whilst the scenery was stunning, it wouldn't have done to suffer an engine failure up here. Quite simply, there was a dearth of safe places to land in an emergency. There was, however, one enormous bowl amongst the *jebels*, where we did land. Resembling a gigantic natural amphitheatre, it was a flat expanse of gravel plain large enough to accommodate a short landing strip, albeit one surrounded by soaring *jebels*. This was the Rawdah Bowl.

Whilst we were discussing matters here, a group of very wild looking tribesmen approached us. These were men of the Shihuh, the masters of this inhospitable region. They had come to greet us as 'fellow warriors'. After exchanging niceties, the leader of the group handed Ameed Yussef his Shihuh axe. This weapon is unique to the Musandam. It comprises a slender shaft about 35 inches long, at the end of which is a tiny, very sharp metal axe head. To my amazement and delight, Yussef suggested that the axe be presented to me so that I could take it back to show people in my country. So it was that I came to own one of these special weapons. That spontaneous act also speaks volumes about the innate man management abilities of Ameed Yussef; he was tough and demanding, whilst being compassionate, selfless and utterly fair.

On the morning of our final day we were due to travel to the very tip of the peninsula by sea, but the weather was against us so we flew by helicopter instead. The view below us as we followed the fragmented coastline was breathtakingly beautiful, yet hostile and menacing. Rugged *jebels* penetrated by deep fjords plunged into an angry aquamarine sea topped with white horses, the spray streaming from their crests sparkling in the sunlight.

Our destination was Goat Island. This is little more than a barren rock just off the western coast of the peninsula and immediately around the apex of the Hormuz Straits. Its strategic importance in modern times is obvious, but it was also a vital telegraph relay point on the trade route to India and the Far East when ships like the *Cutty Sark* were sailing the high seas. There was precious little to occupy people in their spare time out here, and in the days before air conditioning and electricity life must have been unbearably tough. Indeed, I was told that the origin of the saying 'going round the bend' might relate to the time when British sailors had to man the telegraph relay on Goat Island. Going round the bend (of the Hormuz Straits) for any appreciable time might well have driven people to distraction. There are other explanations for the saying, of course, but I rather like this one.

Our business completed here, we flew back to Khasab, where a SOAF C-130 Hercules was waiting to take us back to Seeb. I was home in time for tea.

Within a week I was down in Salalah again, visiting, amongst other places, our outpost at Sarfait on Oman's south western border with the Yemen. Situated on the edge of the *jebel*, which fell in a series of vertical steps 4,500 feet to the sea, some of the defensive positions could only be reached by using steel ladders and ropes secured to the cliff face. Our Yemeni counterparts were in yelling distance just across the *wadi* to our west, which helped to keep our soldiers focused. An airstrip suitable for small aircraft, like the Skyvan, had been constructed above our position by shaving off the top of a *jebel*. It didn't allow much room for error, as the ground fell away sharply on all sides. A crashed aircraft beside the runway didn't do much for my morale!

On returning to my office in MAM following this visit to Salalah, I received a totally unexpected, but welcome piece of news. Apparently, the powers that be in Musandam had heard that I had donated blood whilst in Khasab and, by way of thanking me, had invited me to visit the region *with my family* during the children's Easter holidays.

For various reasons, the children flew out at the start of holidays on three separate flights. Three of them had arrived safely, but when we went to the airport to meet Rorie's plane he was not on it. Panic! We knew that his British Airways flight had been cancelled, but the carrier had arranged for him to fly with Cathay Pacific to Bahrain, where he had been due to connect with the Gulf Air flight we had just met. Nobody could give us any answers, so we had no option but to leave a message with the British Airways Office in Muscat and return home.

The British Airways Duty Officer rang us at 9.00 a.m. to say that he had received our message and was on the case. However, it wasn't until midday that we received an answer. The Cathay Pacific flight had been delayed and so Rorie had missed his connection in Bahrain. He had been booked on another flight and was due to arrive at Seeb in just over an hour.

Rorie had been blissfully unaware of our concern, having asked for a message to be sent to Muscat to let us know he had missed his connection, and that he would be arriving the following day. He had spent the night in the VIP Lounge in Bahrain airport and had quite enjoyed his adventure, not knowing that his message had not been passed on to anyone in Oman.

Easter was not a recognised holiday in Oman, so I was back at work on Holy Saturday and, of course, Easter Sunday. The local schools, however, were on holiday, so Toni was at home for the children. Moreover, the 'Easter Bunny' visited Oman and various presents were hidden about the house and garden. The best present, of course, was the unexpected visit to Musandam, the most remote and restricted region of Oman.

We flew up to Khasab on the scheduled SOAF C-130 Hercules afternoon flight on 6 April, Rorie and Alex taking it in turns to travel in the cockpit. We were met on arrival by Bill McDonald, the Pay Master at PenSec HQ, who took us to our accommodation in the barracks. Toni and the girls were in the grandly named 'PenSec Hotel', which was a portable building with two bedrooms, a bathroom and a sitting room with a fridge and tea-making facilities. The boys and I were in single bedrooms with our own bathroom just across the compound. Arrangements had been made for us to take all our meals in the mess and, to cap it all, two self-drive Toyota Land Cruisers had been placed at our disposal!

After a snack lunch we went to the souk in Khasab, where we bought a Shihuh axe and visited the fort before driving on to the nearby coastal villages of Khasat and Quadah. We went a little way inland from Quadah to see some ancient rock paintings of camels.

Until very recently, both Khasat and Quadah, and many more villages besides, could only be reached by helicopter or boat, but now a black top road, hugging the coastline, has quite literally been blasted out of the sheer cliffs. It was quite an experience driving on it, with a short drop to the sea on one side and a solid wall of rock towering hundreds of feet above on the other. It reminded me of my schooldays at PCK in India, where we boys carved a network of 'roads' into the vertical side of a clay bank bordering the playground, along which we pushed our Dinky toys for hours on end.

Next day we set off to explore the *wadi* used as the approach for aircraft landing at Khasab. It was a delightfully quiet place (when planes were not flying down it!) and ended in a bowl covered in a rich green carpet of vegetation, comprising mainly a yellow flowering shrub (later identified as *Zygophyllum simplex*), coarse grass and acacia trees. Goats grazed peacefully and countless butterflies of various hues flitted about. We also came across numerous colourful caterpillars and chrysalises.

Having taken in the scene we made our way up a steep, narrow dirt track to a saddle in the *jebels* and then made our way down the other side to a beautiful fjord-like inlet called Khor Najd. The still, clean aquamarine waters looked so inviting that we decided to have a swim, or rather Toni did, as the rest of us paddled at the water's edge. Suddenly I spotted a sinister black triangular fin not 20 yards from Toni, so we all left the water rather quickly. I was told later that there is so much food up here that sharks rarely trouble people. Still, we weren't taking any chances.

During the next day and a half we explored the western side of Musandam towards the border with the Emirate of Ras al Khaimah. Hugging the coast on the road blasted out of the cliffs, we travelled north until we reached a delightful little fishing village in a sheltered cove. To Hannah's delight, it was called Hanah! This is a boy's name in the Arab world, the girl's equivalent being Hannan. From here our road climbed up and over the towering *jebels* in a series of very steep, tortuous turns and then descended down to the western coastline in an equally alarming manner. The scenery was awe-inspiring and spectacular and, at the same time, daunting in the extreme. Whilst driving I, at least, had to keep my eyes glued to the road – in reality all of us did – so we stopped frequently to drink in the view.

Once down by the sea again, we made our way to Bukha, complete with its defiant little fort with the Omani flag fluttering proudly from its turret. Bukha was a few miles short of the border with Ras Al Khaimah. Here, we dropped in to the Musandam Security Force camp to see Alex Brodie – the Training Officer and sole Briton for miles around. Life for him could get quite lonely, so we invited him to join us on our picnic, as it was Friday – his weekend. He readily accepted and took us to a secluded little inlet where it was safe to swim. The water was lovely but, unfortunately, the shingle beach was covered in globules of oil from an oil tanker that had recently been attacked and damaged. Refusing to be put off, we found driftwood to sit on to reduce the risk of getting covered in oil.

We were up at dawn next morning to try walking up Wadi Hanah in the cool of our final morning in Musandam. This proved quite a challenge as the *wadi* floor was a mass of enormous boulders and polished rocks, the result of flash flooding. Seeing the size of the boulders, one can only wonder at the force with which the water sweeps down these *wadis* during a flash flood. Indeed, whilst we were in Oman, a police Land Rover that had gone to warn a village of an imminent flash flood at the base of Jebel Akhdar was swept away when it was struck by the rushing wall of water.

Alex had almost reached the top of Wadi Hanah, but time was against us. We got back to camp for a late breakfast and then had to make our way to the airport for the flight back to Seeb. The visit had been a unique experience and one we would never forget. However, the following excerpt from our diary indicates we had probably sated our thirst for adventure here, at least for the time being:

> *We travelled through some really spectacular mountain scenery; too beautiful, dramatic, savage and rugged to fully comprehend. We found ourselves snaking down sheer cliffs, traversing along the tops of ridges with yawning drops on either side of the vehicle and looking down on the aquamarine waters of spectacular fjords. In fact, some of the views and hill climbs are so awe-inspiring that after a while one simply can't take in any more.*

Our original plan for the children's Easter holidays had been to take a week's holiday to trek across the Wahiba Sands by camel and spend a night on a beach in the vicinity of Ras al Hadd to watch turtles coming ashore to lay their eggs. Toni and I had visited the turtle beaches with Alix and Tom Bremridge, and we were keen for the children to enjoy this experience. My Omani boss, Colonel Saud, was also keen for us all to visit his home, which was roughly halfway between MAM and the turtle beaches.

Before I received the invitation to visit Musandam, I had contacted the Coastal Security Force (CSF) in Sur, the unit responsible for patrolling the Wahiba Sands and the adjoining coastline, and asked if they could give me some advice on where to hire a guide and some camels. Quite rightly, my contact in CSF was reluctant to let us venture into the Wahiba alone. In any event, our focus then suddenly switched to Musandam.

However, CSF hadn't forgotten my request. The unit proposed that I accompany one of their routine patrols into the Wahiba to assess their professional ability at first hand. Moreover, as these patrols were essentially 'hearts and minds' operations, my family was welcome to come with me, provided they were willing to 'rough it'. I still had some leave available and this was partly job-related. So it was that, after a very long day clearing my desk in MAM following our return from Musandam, we were on our way to Sur. Meanwhile, Toni and the girls had *shalwa kameez* outfits run up by the tailor to wear on the adventure so as not to cause offence.

When we reached Sur, we had sufficient time to show the children the boatyard, where craftsmen (mostly Indians) were busy making dhows. Several dhows in various stages of construction were being worked on where they lay along the shore of a shallow creek, whilst others rode at anchor. No modern equipment was being used, so the only sounds were the gentle chipping of a paring axe against wood or the dull thud of a hammer on wooden pegs.

We arrived at CSF's camp after the afternoon siesta, where we were welcomed by the Officer Commanding (OC), Raa'id (Major) Hilal, and the Training Officer, Captain Greg Bruce, a contract officer from New Zealand. The mess had kindly laid on a barbecue supper in our honour, during which we were briefed on our next adventure. The patrol would depart next morning commanded by Raqeeb (Sergeant) Mohammed.

Well before 8.00 a.m. next morning, four, fully stowed 1960s-vintage Toyota Land Cruisers and their crews were lined up on the square for

Raqeeb Mohammed's inspection. Three of the Toyotas were stripped down, with no canopy, doors or windscreen. These were the operational vehicles and were painted in a disruptive camouflage pattern. The other Toyota was the same model of vehicle, but was not stripped down and was painted a uniform sand colour. This was an administrative vehicle. There was a strict rule in SOLF that you had to be dressed in uniform to travel in an operational vehicle. Anyone in civilian dress, be they soldiers or civilians, could only travel in an administrative vehicle.

The purpose of the patrol was to visit all the settlements and Bedouin encampments in a particular sector of the Wahiba, a routine task undertaken by CSF so that everyone in the sands was visited at least once a year. In effect, the unit 'policed' this area, settling minor disputes and generally checking on people's welfare and whereabouts. This approach was well received by the local population, as almost all CSF's soldiers came from the Wahiba.

To avoid any confusion, we had all been asked to wear civilian clothes – Toni and the girls in their *shalwa kameez* outfits and myself and the boys in shirts and long trousers. So the sand-coloured Toyota was for us, although it was driven by a member of the patrol. We had all been told to bring *shemaghs* (Arab headdress) to protect our heads and faces from the sand and were also issued with sand goggles.

The next two days travelling over this vast sand sea was a most thrilling and memorable experience. We visited numerous Bedouin encampments and were privileged to share in their lives, albeit only fleetingly. Some of the sand dunes we encountered stretched across our front from horizon to horizon and rose to heights of 200 feet or more. Here and there, little clumps of palm trees defied the encroaching desert, their soft green colour a welcome contrast to the glare of the shimmering sands.

The following extracts from our diaries give an insight to life with the Bedouin:

We stopped at a tiny temporary Bedu *settlement. The soldiers, Bruce and the boys joined the men for a 'fuddle' (coffee and dates), whilst the girls and I were taken to see a tiny 'woollen' camel that had been separated from its mother. The animals had been tethered about ten feet apart and the baby was calling plaintively – very sad!*
We journeyed on to a larger settlement where Raqeeb Mohammed's sister lived with her family. Mohammed took Hannah, Zoë and myself [Toni] into his sister's barusti *dwelling. This was a fenced in area made of brushwood, with corrugated iron sheeting and palm fronds acting as partitions to divide the enclosed space into separate 'open' rooms. The floor was just sand and goat droppings. Hooks along the makeshift walls were used to hang up cooking utensils and clothes. A few old and battered suitcases lay along the walls – storage bins perhaps?*
Mohammed's sister was beautiful. She unveiled her face for us and when Mohammed brought in some kohl in a little box, together with a stick with which to apply it, she outlined our eyes for us. Then frankincense was added to some hot embers in an incense burner and we were invited to use it. This involves allowing the smoke to billow up inside your clothes. A liberal spraying of perfume completed the ritual.
Meanwhile, Bruce and the boys were with the men outside the barusti *enjoying a 'fuddle' (more dates, oranges and coffee), but now the trays were passed over the* barusti *fence for us. At this point Mohammed's mother appeared. (He never knows when or where he is likely to meet her in the sands, because she leads a very nomadic life.) She also unveiled her face once inside the* barusti.
Mohammed's sister's two little children were in the barusti *– one about four and very frightened of these three large, white strangers – and a baby girl about a year old. The little one could stand and was*

tethered to a wall by a long piece of cloth attached to her dress to prevent her from wandering. Mohammed's sister suckled her quite openly.

The women ensured they were veiled before leaving the barusti *to bid us goodbye, Mohammed's mother leaving only one eye uncovered.*

We stopped at the next settlement for lunch. This was the home of Salim, one of the soldiers in our party. Bruce drove our vehicle to some shade a little way away from the rest of the patrol to give the soldiers some privacy as they prayed. After prayers, carpets were brought out and laid on the sand. We were then invited to re-join the soldiers for lunch, which was provided by the Bedouin, probably Salim's father.

Then the fun started! We had initially wanted to ride camels in the Wahiba, and so that's what we were going to do! Two camels were produced and we took it in turns to ride them. Some young Bedouin lads then started to show off their tricks; riding whilst facing the rear and standing up and challenging us to do the same – which we did! The sand was quite soft to land on when we fell off!

Our final settlement that day was the most remote and basic example of habitation we had ever seen. This was the shanty barusti *settlement of Juhaid. It comprised a few flimsy* barustis *in a sand sea with rusty oil drums scattered about, which were used as work surfaces. We were near the coast here and the sea was clearly visible beyond the sands. The* Bedu *come here to fish and that was what all the men folk must have been doing when we arrived, as there were only women and children at home. The women were tiny and completely covered in black* abayas *and the strange* burkas *with a vane that we had encountered near Ibri. They were extremely friendly and willing to be photographed. They were keen, however, for Hannah and Zoë to be veiled but, though they let Toni try on a* burka, *they said it wasn't necessary as she had four children and wouldn't attract much interest from men. What a cheek!*

After a very enjoyable interlude, we retraced our steps through some impressive dunes to Salim's father's settlement for the night.

Before supper, which I believe was again provided by Salim's father, the girls and I were joined by some of the women for hot tea and dates, whilst Bruce and the boys joined the men. Then the women melted into the darkness and the soldiers gathered on one carpet and gestured for us to do likewise on another nearby (it would not have been acceptable for them to sit with women in the dark).

A huge tray of rice and roast meat was laid before us. Rorie was the first to spy teeth and it soon dawned on us that we had been served the goat's head – apparently an honour! Mohammed then joined us, sitting between Bruce and Alex, and started sharing out the 'goodies'; an ear for Rorie, a piece of tongue for Hannah, throat for Bruce, brains for myself and Zoë, and, as the eldest son, Alex was honoured with an eye! He ate it too! He's always been an adventurous eater. His job done, Mohammed re-joined his colleagues as we picked at more recognisable bits of meat around the cheeks of the animal.

When Bruce walked over to the soldiers after supper, he heard them discussing how many camels and goats the girls were worth, but he had to disappoint them by saying they were not for sale!

A number of the soldiers had brought along their musical instruments, including an oud, a stringed instrument which was probably the inspiration for the Western lute. So after supper we were treated to a really enjoyable impromptu concert of Arab music and song. Sitting out on the sands under the myriad stars of an Omani night sky listening to this haunting music was the perfect end to a memorable day.

Before we all settled down for the night, Bruce drove our vehicle a little way off to give both us and the soldiers a little privacy.
We were up with the sun next morning and Bruce lit a fire and brewed us all a cup of tea. We then packed up the vehicle and re-joined the soldiers and the locals for dates and coffee.

Raqeeb Mohammed spent the first half of the morning honing the patrol's sand driving skills on some steep dunes in a surprisingly wooded area nearby. The soldiers practised crossing dunes and reversing safely back off those which the vehicles could not surmount. The vehicles assumed some alarming angles at times and had to be kept in line with the direction of movement or risk tipping over and rolling to the bottom. This is not easy! They were, of course, fitted with roll bars. The soldiers were also required deliberately to get the vehicles well and truly stuck in the sand in order to practise their recovery drills. We watched in admiration as they revelled in the challenge.

Then it was time to move on. Crossing a genuine sand sea feels almost like being in a boat on the sea proper; the vehicle pitches up and down and rolls as it rides small dunes and also veers from side to side as the tyres fight for traction. It is really exhilarating.

We were now making our way to the coast at a point where there was a wrecked cargo ship on the beach. It was quite eerie seeing the Indian Ocean breakers crashing around it. From here, we drove north along the beautiful and utterly deserted sandy beach to reach the village of Al Ashkharah (we had been here with the Bremridges on our trip to Tiwi). Whilst the soldiers rested and cooked lunch, Mohammed took us into the village and its harbour. Numerous dhows were riding at anchor and Mohammed asked if we would like to go aboard one, which, of course, we did. Mohammed was well known in these parts and within no time we found ourselves in a Boston whaler powered by a 25 horsepower outboard motor making our way to one of the larger dhows. We clambered aboard to be greeted by a crew member, who had been busy repairing one of the nets.

The scene on board was fascinating. Numerous nets were carefully arranged on deck, as were large shark hooks and buoys; everything in its place. There was also an enormous ice box in which to keep the catch. At the stern was a tiny gas ring enclosed in a protective metal 'cupboard' and some cooking utensils. Showing typical Omani hospitality, the crewman immediately dropped what he was doing and brewed us an excellent cup of sweet tea, which we sipped as we watched him back at work repairing his net.

After our visit to the dhow we returned to the patrol and a wonderful lunch of roast chicken and rice. We then headed north up the coast towards Ras al Junayz, a remote headland just south of Ras al Hadd. We had arranged to meet with our Nissan Patrol en-route and the link up went without a hitch. It had been driven down from Sur by Areef (Corporal) Rashid of CSF. However, we had all become quite attached to 'our' Toyota and nobody wanted to leave what the children now called their Sand Cat. So I accompanied Rashid as we drove on to our destination.

We reached Ras al Junayz just before sunset. The beach was pristine and utterly unspoilt. At the headland itself (*ras* means 'head' in Arabic), the sands backed onto a crumbling sandy cliff, but to either side of this were low sand dunes topped with tufts of grass that whispered gently in the breeze. We made camp in the lee of the cliffs, again a little apart from the soldiers, but we all came together for supper. Although it wasn't the height of the turtle laying season, 'tank tracks' on the sands and turtle sightings out to sea gave us cause to be optimistic. Our optimism increased when night fell and it became really dark, there being no moon.

After supper, we went for a stroll along the beach in the pitch darkness to look for signs of activity. Sadly, there were none and we returned to camp a little disappointed. Hannah and I went on another 'recce' at 11.00

p.m. and had almost given up hope when we came across a massive turtle, over three feet long, busy laying her eggs. I remained to mark the spot, whilst Hannah ran back to fetch the others. We watched quietly as the turtle continued to lay, her occasional sighs an indication that this was no easy task. Alex and I took photographs, but because we had to use the flash, we restricted ourselves to just two or three pictures each.

As we were unlikely to experience such an event again, we remained close behind the turtle throughout; keeping still and silent so as not to disturb or worry her. We were suddenly showered with sand – she had finished laying and was now covering the burrow, which was about four feet in diameter and three feet deep. As she covered her eggs, she moved slowly forward. By the time she had completed the task she had advanced by about three feet. The sand over the actual spot where she had laid her eggs was now level with, if not a little higher than the rest of the beach, whilst the point at which she had completed the task now looked like a burrow about four feet across and two feet deep. We wondered whether this was nature's way of safeguarding the eggs, by hiding their true location from foxes, many of which lurked in the dunes just a few yards away.

Having completed her task, our huge turtle heaved herself laboriously out of the dummy burrow and made her way slowly and painfully back to the sea, gasping every time she lurched herself forward. Falling into another burrow en-route, she took over half an hour to cover just 20 yards. Our diary states that, at 1.06 a.m., she was finally back in her own environment once more, her task duly accomplished.

My alarm went off just before 5.00 a.m. – turtle patrol! It was still pitch dark, but the eastern sky hinted at the approaching dawn. We soon came across two more turtles, late arrivals that were just completing the task of covering their burrows. The first made it back to the sea just before sunrise, followed closely by the other in the first rays of the new day. These two creatures had had a narrow escape, less than an hour later and they might well have suffered 'heat stroke' and died before reaching the safety of the sea.

By now we had been joined by some of the soldiers. A fox had spotted baby turtles erupting from under the sand. We chased it off and then (conservationists forgive us) decided to give this little clutch a helping hand. The soldiers cleared away the sand with their hands, whilst the children carried as many of the little hatchlings as they could, their tiny flippers working nineteen to the dozen, down to the sea. Other hatchlings seemed literally to 'swim' across the sand to the water's edge. Yet these, too, were rather late in making their bid for the sea. Most 'home runs' are timed, how I know not, to take place at night. In daylight, hatchlings, too, run the risk of being 'fried' by the sun and are also easily picked off by the foxes and numerous gulls that crowd the beaches to take advantage of just such an opportunity.

We hadn't really taken much account of the sea until the children, in their excitement, started to go further into the breakers to prevent the hatchlings being washed back ashore. In his enthusiasm, Rorie entered waist deep into the water. It was then that we learnt just how treacherous the sea can be here. The undertow was so strong that he could not get back to shore and was being lifted off his feet. A massive wave was building behind him and as it did so it sucked all the water from around him until he was actually standing on dry land, but with a wall of water about 12 feet high curling above him. We all screamed for him to run and as he did so the wave crashed just behind him and swept him unceremoniously up the beach, shaken, but unhurt.

We left Ras al Junayz and made for a tiny settlement called Bani Abu Ali, where Rashid lived. After dates and coffee at his home, we set off once more, heading for the village of Karmil, where we joined the black top road. At this point we bade a fond and rather sad farewell to our CSF colleagues. They had been tremendous companions and had given us a truly memorable experience. Whilst they headed northeast for Sur, we drove northwest, our destination being the village of Zahib, near Mudaybi, where we had a lunch appointment with my boss, Aqeed Saud, and his family.

Our interlude at Bani Abu Ali had put us a little behind schedule and, to make matters worse, our carburettor jammed at full throttle just as we reached the village of Mudayrib. It was past noon, siesta time, and the start of the weekend. Everywhere was closed. I spotted the local roadside garage – nothing more than a dilapidated tin shack – with a small group of Indians sitting in the shade of a nearby tree. I went over to them and explained my problem, but they told me the workshop was closed and would not be open again until Saturday. I decided to play my 'Indian card' and asked them where they were from. They replied "South India", to which I responded by asking which part of South India. The spokesman replied, "You will not be knowing," and I came back with, "Try and see." When he said "Kovalam" and I told him that I was born in Kerala and knew Kovalam well – indeed, I had visited there with my family only a few months earlier – the whole situation changed. "My God, you are a cousin brother!" he exclaimed. "Bring your car now!" In next to no time, the problem was fixed for a mere pittance.

We were now running seriously late and so decided to cut across the gravel plain to Mudaybi on a compass bearing instead of using the road. This direct route would be about 45 miles, more than halving the distance by road. So we informed our Indian friends of our plan in case of mishap and set off into the desert (we had ample supplies of water, food and fuel).

We reached Aqeed Saud's house in Zahib, near Mudaybi, almost two hours late, but he put us at our ease and was just delighted that we had come. His wife, too, appeared totally unruffled. How she had kept the feast she had prepared for us so piping hot, yet perfectly cooked, we'll never know.

After lunch, Saud took us for a walk round this cool and peaceful village. As we walked along a *falaj* system we were protected from the sun by the date palms, whose fronds rustled overhead in the gentle breeze.

This large date palm grove was divided into definite sections, each belonging to someone in the village and each connected to the main *falaj* system. We noticed that only one or two of these subsidiary *falajes* had water running down them. Saud took us to his section of the grove, which he called his farm. We arrived just as the water from the main *falaj* was being diverted to water his area. With water being such a precious commodity, the system of distribution was very carefully worked out and controlled. Saud told us that he had five watering slots per week, each lasting two hours. Each villager has to bid annually and pay a fee for the number of watering slots they want, whilst the elders ensure that a rich person cannot monopolise the supply to the detriment of others.

The devices used to control the allotted times are rudimentary in the extreme. By day, a sundial in the centre of the village is used. This comprises a stake standing upright in the sand with lines drawn in the sand in front of it, each line representing half an hour. Further marks against these lines identify the days and the recipients. When the sun's shadow falls on a particular line, the *falaj* to that plot is opened and it is closed again when it reaches the end of that person's allotted time. The subsidiary *falajes* are opened and closed simply by using mud and debris. By night, a more complex system, based on the stars, is used to control the distribution of water.

We left Saud's home and started to head back towards Muscat. We didn't intend to go straight home – we were very tired after a virtually sleepless night on the turtle beaches and also wanted to visit Jabreen and Nizwa forts next day. I had obtained the necessary permits this time. In any case, we were strongly discouraged from driving in the interior at night due to the hazard presented by camels. These animals roam free in the desert and at night tend to gravitate to the black top roads as they retain their heat for longer. If they are sitting on the road they are usually easy to spot, but if they are standing up, your dipped headlights do not pick out their bodies and it is all too easy to fail see their long slender legs.

We drove for barely an hour and found a secluded spot in a 'finger *wadi*' off the Wadi Andam in which to spend the night. Our camp was sorted and the cooking fire lit in time for us to sit and admire a beautiful sunset, as our supper gently bubbled in the pot. It was strange being alone and we all agreed that we missed the company of the soldiers and their music.

We were up with the sun next morning, as always happens when you sleep under the stars – we never used a tent whilst camping in Africa or the Middle East – but took some time to get moving as we were all still a bit weary. I got the fire and a brew going, and then Alex cooked us a superb breakfast as we struck camp and stowed the vehicle. We were then on our way to Nizwa with Alex driving (I had started giving the boys driving lessons on a suitable piece of desert near MAM). However, as soon as we approached the black top road I took over.

When we reached Nizwa, the souk was a hive of activity, a truly marvellous sight. The biggest crowd was at the livestock area, set in the shade of an enormous tree in the lee of the fort. Here, sheep, goats and cattle were being auctioned. Elsewhere, there were people selling magnificent *kunjas* (Omani daggers), *saifs* (swords) and ancient firearms. In 1969, I had bought a handsome Omani *jezail* (tribal gun) and a beautiful *kunja* here, but prices were a lot higher now.

The fort wasn't open, so we made a detour to Jabreen, the fortified palace beyond Bahla. This had now been beautifully restored and the elaborately painted ceilings in most of the rooms were a special attraction. In one of the main rooms an Omani caretaker pointed out some concealed trap doors in the floor under the windows. These led to a secret hiding place under the floor. The children had great fun going down to have a look.

Whilst we were at Jabreen a coach arrived and out poured a group of about 20 Japanese tourists with cameras slung round their necks, together with two Omani guides. Up until now, Oman had been closed to tourists. We had heard, however, that the country was considering entering the tourist market. This group, apparently, was the pilot designed to assess Oman's potential in the industry, together with the resultant impact on the country. They seemed quite oblivious of us, as they jostled to take photographs. On seeing this, 'our' friendly Omani caretaker opened another trap door and led us along another secret passage to a quieter part of the fort.

We returned to Nizwa in the afternoon and were at last able to enter the fort. This is arguably the most famous fort in Oman after the forts of Jalali and Mirani, which guard the entrance to Muscat harbour and the Royal Palace. Built by Sultan Ibn Saif over 300 years ago, Nizwa fort took 12 years to complete. Throughout Oman's turbulent history, it has been attacked many times, but has never once been taken.

Its main feature is its huge round tower. To gain access to the fighting area at the top of the tower, attackers had to climb endless stairs and break through seven defensive doors. Above each door is a slit which is open to the sky, enabling defenders on the roof to fire at, or pour boiling oil on, attackers trying to break down the doors. The roof of the tower is surrounded by a wall about ten feet thick and some 30 feet high. Cannons were positioned at intervals right around the base of the wall. Stone steps, devoid of a protective banister, enabled defenders to reach a narrow ledge that runs right round the tower about six feet from the top of the castellated wall. From here, defenders were able to fire on attackers through the gaps between the castellations without endangering themselves unnecessarily.

Amazingly, there was a well opening on the roof that went right through the tower to a water source deep in the ground. Thus defenders always had access to water. The fort also had dungeons and, on the roof, two or three pits, sealed by metal grilles. These were called *oubliettes*, because the prisoners in them were largely forgotten and left to die.

Right next to the fort there was a magnificent new mosque. Its modern design, gleaming white walls and bright blue and gold dome and minaret were in stark contrast to the old battle-worn stone masonry of the fort.

Over the next few days the children left Oman for the last time and returned to school in England at the end of another quite exceptional holiday. Alex summed up what they all felt in his first letter home, stating that he never thought it possible for someone to fall so much in love with a country and its people in such a short space of time.

A matter of weeks before my premature departure from Oman, we all received a sharp reminder of our *raison d'être*. A hot-headed young Yemeni officer, apparently acting on his own initiative, launched an attack across our south western border, capturing one of our outposts. Our soldiers were hopelessly out-gunned and after, sadly, taking casualties had no option but to withdraw from the area. Eventually, SOAF was called in to drive the Yemenis back across the border and the situation was restored. The incident gave SAF and SOLF, in particular, the opportunity to review their command and control systems and procedures.

I was sent down to the border area once the situation had been restored to see if there were any training lessons to be learned. Our border posts were lightly manned by infantrymen, an overt presence indicating the limit of Oman's territory in the largely featureless desert of the Empty Quarter. Whilst the soldiers were capable of patrolling the border to deter would-be smugglers, none of the posts was mutually supporting, nor were they equipped to withstand a deliberate attack by a superior force.

Clearly, we needed to bolster the firepower of these outposts and tighten procedures for the prompt availability of effective backup, such as air support, in an emergency. I left Oman before any action could be taken on our recommendations.

Our hectic pace of life, both at work and play, continued until the final day of our tour, and so the last few weeks flashed by in a blur. The nearer the end came, the more we regretted the fact that our time in this wonderful country had been reduced to just one year. The soldiering had been almost 'boys own' in nature; rugged terrain, hair-raising drives up the roughest of mountain tracks, traversing sand seas and exhilarating flights in all manner of aircraft. Recreationally, too, the opportunities had been legion, especially as the Omanis had been so accommodating towards my family. I almost resented handing over to my successor, John Williams, and told him he was the luckiest officer in the army. It was with very heavy hearts that we boarded the Gulf Air flight at Seeb on 16 June 1988.

1. Eid al-Fitr *Hafla* (party) at the Jebel Akhdar Battle Training Camp, Saiq. Toni and the children, plus WO2 Woods flanked by the Egyptian doctor, Waghdy (wearing glasses), and an Omani soldier, ready to tuck into the feast before us.

2. With Captain Mohammed Mohenna, a member of my team in Training Branch, and one of his children astride a *falaj* on Jebel Akhdar

3. Members of Captain Mohammed Mohenna's extended family dressed in their colourful Eid clothes

4. The town of Bahla and its fort (1987). With the exception of the fort, Bahla was unrecognisable from the isolated oasis I had visited in 1969

5. Nizwa fort

6. Nizwa livestock souk just outside the fort

7. A typical shop in Nizwa's covered souk

8. Wadi Darbat, Salalah, during the *khareef* (southwest monsoon)

9. Toni's photograph of me, Will and Henry Bremridge, and Alex crossing Wadi Shab in a tin water tank

10. The dawn fish market on the beach at Seeb

11. Kovalam beach, South India (1987); a scene unchanged from my earliest memories in 1944/45

12. Reunion with my *ayah*, Cicily Daniel ('Ayahmo')

13. Pullivasal manager's bungalow, Munnar, High Range; my main childhood home

14. Reunion with Anthony Gomez, my parents' butler cum shikari (hunter), who taught me to fish

1

2

3

4

5

6

7

8

9

10

11

12

13

14

15

16

17

18

19

20

21

22

23

24

15 The newly-built coastal road from Khasab to Bukha, Musandam, Oman, 1988

16. Bukha fort, Musandam, Oman

17. CSF soldiers relaxing in a *Bedu* settlement. Most, if not all, the soldiers in CSF came from the Wahiba Sands region

18. In the Wahiba Sands on patrol with the Coastal Security Force (CSF). The Arabian Sea is just visible in the background

19. Toni, rather rashly accepting a challenge from a young *Bedu*!

20. Zoë being fitted with a burka by Bedouin woman on arrival at the remote settlement of Juhaid in the Sands. Hannah also had to wear a burka here. With four children, Toni was exempt!

21. Alex's photograph of a turtle laying eggs

22. The CSF patrol and us on the beach at Ras al-Junayz

23. and 24. Examples of the fascinating men of Oman

KUWAIT

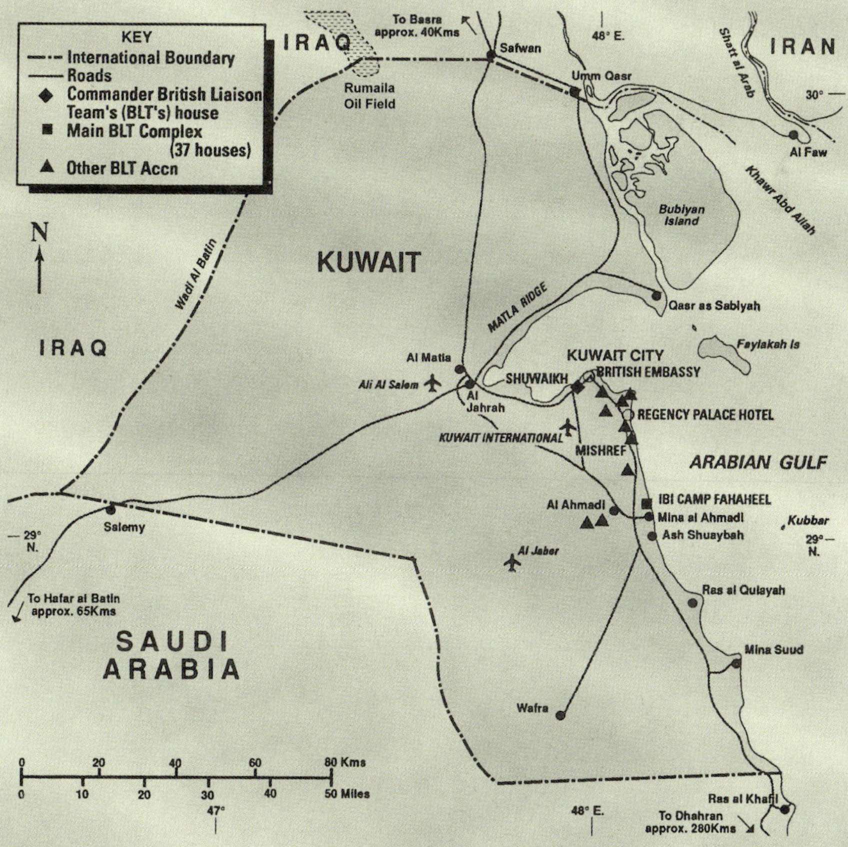
KEY
International Boundary
Roads
Commander British Liaison Team's (BLT's) house
Main BLT Complex (37 houses)
Other BLT Accn
N
IRAQ
Rumaila Oil Field
To Basra approx. 40Kms
Safwan
48° E.
Umm Qasr
Shatt al Arab
IRAN
30°
Al Faw
Khawr Abd Allah
Bubiyan Island
KUWAIT
Wadi Al Batin
MATLA RIDGE
Qasr as Sabiyah
Faylakah Is
IRAQ
Al Matla
KUWAIT CITY
BRITISH EMBASSY
Ali Al Salem
Al Jahrah
SHUWAIKH
REGENCY PALACE HOTEL
KUWAIT INTERNATIONAL
MISHREF
ARABIAN GULF
Al Ahmadi
IBI CAMP FAHAHEEL
Mina al Ahmadi
Ash Shuaybah
Kubbar
29° N.
Salemy
Al Jaber
Ras al Qulayah
To Hafar al Batin approx. 65Kms
SAUDI ARABIA
Mina Suud
Wafra
0 20 40 60 80 Kms
0 10 20 30 40 50 Miles
47°
48° E.
Ras al Khafji
To Dhahran approx. 280Kms

KUWAIT

DEDICATED TO ALL THE SERVICEMEN AND FAMILIES OF THE BRITISH LIAISON TEAM, KUWAIT, BOTH IN AND OUT OF STATION, AT THE TIME OF THE IRAQI INVASION AND OCCUPATION OF THE EMIRATE – 2 AUGUST 1990

On our return to England we were, once again, allocated a temporary home in the REME barracks in Arborfield. The timing of our short sojourn in England could not have been better, enabling us to attend Toni's sister, Anni's, marriage to Keith Gallon – a joyous occasion – as well as squeezing in an invigorating short break in Dartmouth as guests of our Regimental friend, Chris Dick, who we had last visited before our posting to the Sudan in 1980.

Barely a month after leaving Oman, I found myself heading back to the Middle East to command a joint Army/RAF team of over 70 officers and senior ranks, accompanied by their families.

On my arrival in Kuwait, I was met by Colonel Patrick Keightley of The Blues and Royals, the officer who had kindly agreed to extend his tour for another year to enable me to serve in Oman, and whom I had now come to replace. The airport stood in the midst of a featureless, barren desert a few miles from the ultra modern concrete jungle of Kuwait City.

Our new home was about half a mile west of the city. An old, single storey Arab dwelling, it stood in the sand some 200 yards back from the sea and the entrance to the main Port of Shuwaikh. Built around a small central courtyard, it was painted white and blue; the colours of the old

Kuwait Oil Company. Indeed, it had been the transit building for employees of the company in the days when the flying boats used to come in and out of Kuwait from the calm waters in front of the house. The ceilings were fascinating, being made of date palm matting supported by dark stained wooden poles.

Due to its previous status, the property boasted a tennis court, although this had been allowed to fall into disrepair during the many years since the company had dispensed with the building.

My Deputy Commander was an RAF Wing Commander, Andy Jones. He and the team's five other officers lived in modern apartments in Kuwait City, whilst my warrant officers and sergeants, the main body of the team, lived in several separate locations up to 40 minutes' drive south of the city. The vast majority lived in the old International Bechtel Inc. (IBI) construction camp, dating from around the 1950s, when the adjacent oil refinery was being constructed. The accommodation here comprised prefabricated bungalows and boasted a Warrant Officers' and Sergeants' mess complete with a tennis court and swimming pool. Its location on the beach seemed ideal, but the total absence of black top roads within the camp made it a very dusty place, whilst the air was always heavy with the fumes from the oil refinery on the other side of the perimeter fence. Nevertheless, it lent itself to a relaxed, beach-barbecue style of living, perhaps too relaxed at times, as the excellent young Regimental Sergeant Major (RSM) Haynes of the Prince of Wales's Own Regiment of Yorkshire strived to maintain proper military standards in the mess!

The Team's *raison d'être* was to provide hands on technical support and advice and limited training assistance to the Kuwait Army and Air Force. Accordingly, the men were all highly experienced specialists in their own fields, the vast majority being aircraft or electrical and mechanical technicians. We were strictly non-operational and unarmed.

Toni remained in England until the start of the school holidays and then she and the children flew out to join me. By the time she arrived I had acquired a very friendly house guest called Libby; a ragbag of a long-haired terrier with a constantly wagging tail. She had originally been bought from Harrods by a sheikh and the feeding instructions included in the bill of sale listed salmon and lightly-cooked chicken! The sheikh had since died and a long-term resident English family, the Austins, had taken on Libby. They lived in another former Kuwait Oil Company house similar to ours, just a hundred yards or so across the sand. Apparently, when they went on leave Libby spent her holidays with whoever lived in our house.

Within a day or two of their arrival, the children also acquired a black kitten. It was a very scared little creature and gave a fine impression of a hedgehog – all spikes – on first meeting Libby. She soon discovered that Libby was a 'push over' and made herself at home. However, 'Blackie' was feral and eventually decided to join the hundreds of semi-wild cats that wandered the streets around our house. Later, we acquired lovely female kittens, Dotty and Maud.

Our predecessors had employed a Goan maid called Rita, who lived in the purpose-built servants' wing of our quadrant. She was very keen to stay and we were delighted to take her on. Although she did not cook, she was a real treasure, keeping the house as clean and tidy as possible. This was no mean feat, given that we were surrounded by fine sand that filled the air whenever there was the slightest hint of a breeze, not to mention the frequent sandstorms that occurred during the hot summer months. When we were on the periphery of such storms, a dense pall of dust would hang in the air like an abrasive fog. The more violent storms would turn the sun and sky blood red and cause people to run for cover. Indeed, the sand was so dense that, on one occasion, the day was quite literally turned into night as the storm, accompanied by thunder and lightening, engulfed the city, closing the two seaports and the airport.

The house was served by two separate sources of water. Fresh water (known as sweet) was pumped from the mains into a large storage tank on the flat roof, whilst brackish water could be accessed from taps outside the house for watering the garden and generally keeping down the dust. During the winter months, hot water was provided by a small immersion heater inside the house. However, during the summer, the water in the tank on the roof became piping hot, meaning that hot water was now running from the 'cold' taps, whilst we drew cooler, as opposed to cold, water from the 'hot' taps by switching off the immersion heater. It was all rather confusing, but added to the spice of life!

Our electrical supply was equally quaint, with several uncovered fuse boxes, crammed full with a bewildering tangle of wires. This was probably the original wiring. Within a few weeks of our arrival, we lost power to part of the house. The electrician who came to rectify the problem declared our electrics to be a serious hazard, but as this was an old property, the Kuwaiti authorities only sanctioned the rewiring of the affected area.

The job wasn't done properly until the electricity failed completely some 15 months later, burning out our fridge freezer, microwave, washing machine, TV and video recorder in the process! The subsequent rewiring of the whole house took almost three months, meaning we were without power during the early summer of 1990, which was the hottest since records began thirty years before. One false dawn was when the job was initially declared complete after about six weeks; we plugged in our newly purchased appliances (we had been compensated for the losses we had sustained) but quickly realised all was far from well when Toni went to use the washing machine and got an electric shock. It turned out that nothing was earthed. New contractors eventually completed the work.

The local Western expatriate community lived in relative luxury in modern houses and apartments in Kuwait City. The vast majority comprised business or commercial professionals, unlike the expatriates we had met in our previous postings, who were mainly aid workers or missionaries. Again, unlike our previous experiences, we found that there was very little, if any, integration between the Kuwaitis and expatriates. Indeed, although I wore Kuwaiti Army uniform, I felt very much as though I worked for, as opposed to with, my Kuwaiti colleagues. This was a new and disappointing experience.

The vast majority of expatriates were Catholics from South India and the Philippines. Unlike Saudi Arabia, Kuwait permitted Christian worship. There was an enormous Catholic cathedral in Kuwait City, which included a Coptic Christian church in its grounds, and a Catholic church in the Kuwait Oil Company's complex at Al Ahmadi in the South. So huge and diverse was the Catholic community that 'Sunday' Mass in the cathedral was celebrated in several different languages from Thursday evening through to Sunday evening, with every Mass filling the cathedral to capacity. To their credit, many of the Kuwaitis would drive their domestic staff to the cathedral for these services. Indeed, for many of these expatriates, the time spent at Mass and, for the lucky ones, the few minutes chatting to friends in the cathedral's grounds afterwards, was the only free time they enjoyed during the week.

Our Team was known as the Kuwait Liaison Team (KLT) but later was re-named the British Liaison Team (BLT) Kuwait. Unlike other equivalent teams, the American team, for example, we did not enjoy any diplomatic protection whatsoever. Whilst, as service families, we reluctantly accepted this limitation, it was to have serious consequences later on. It also posed immediate challenges for our dependants; for example, if I had been implicated in a serious offence, such as the possession of alcohol, I would have been deported, but Toni would potentially have faced a prison sentence in Kuwait.

Indeed, we came close to experiencing a horror like this when a Kuwaiti woman drove into the back of our car when we were stationary at a T-junction. Toni was driving at the time. Both we and the Kuwaiti were required to go to the police station. Whilst we waited in the reception area, the Kuwaiti went into one of the offices. After some time she came out and, smiling smugly at us, left the building. I smelt trouble and demanded to speak to my contact in the Armed Forces Headquarters. It transpired that Toni had been accused of reversing into the Kuwaiti woman's car. We would have had a hard job to prove otherwise. Thankfully, the intervention of the military authorities resulted in the charge being dropped.

Although we men were spared the ignominy of medical and criminal screening on entering the country, the lack of any diplomatic cover meant that our dependants were not so lucky. Toni and our children, along with all the team's other dependants, had to undergo an AIDS test and a visual skin examination, the latter requiring them to parade around a room in their underwear. Surprisingly, our Embassy friends, who were spared this humiliation, showed us little sympathy.

Managing a team made up entirely of 'Chiefs' and no 'Indians' would be difficult enough with only one Service involved, but striking the right balance in a joint Army/RAF team proved to be one of my greatest challenges, and especially so when tempers were frayed by constant frustrations, such as those outlined above, together with the searing summer heat and the cultural differences, which were unfamiliar to most members of the team. Moreover, we hardly ever got together during the working day, as we were employed as individuals or 'sub-teams' in the Emirate's various barracks, workshops and airbases.

To keep our fingers on the pulse, my RAF deputy and I paid regular visits to team members at their places of work and I also held monthly out-of-hours meetings in our house for key post personnel. In addition, we staged several 'all ranks' social and sporting activities to include the families and foster a true spirit of togetherness. Toni, too, played an important part in fostering unity by running a 'Wives' Club'. She frequently had to deal diplomatically with the fallout from petty inter-service rivalries that had been blown out of all proportion. This was disappointing, but almost inevitable given the frustrations of the claustrophobic bubble in which we were all living.

Quite my biggest challenge, however, was trying to ensure that the Team was properly managed by our Kuwaiti hosts in their various places of work. By way of illustration, Kuwaitis are very conscious of rank and status. Thus, on a certain airbase, only officers were allowed to park their cars inside the camp, whilst other ranks had to park in the desert outside the camp perimeter. This meant that the most junior Kuwaiti second lieutenant was allowed to drive into camp, whilst the senior, highly qualified and experienced BLT advisor supporting him was required to park outside and walk half a mile or more in the searing heat, carrying his heavy testing equipment to his place of work.

I worked at the Team's administrative offices, which were located in the Kuwait Armed Forces Headquarters in Kuwait City. My office was just a stone's throw from that of my interface with the Kuwaiti Armed Forces, the Kuwaiti Liaison Officer, a Major, by the name of Shameri, if memory serves me right. An affable man, he came from a Bedouin tribe and his father still lived as a traditional Bedouin, wandering the deserts between Kuwait, Iraq and Iran.

Major Shameri was very easy to get along with and we soon struck up a good working rapport. On one occasion, when he heard I was planning to take a break with my family in Iraq, he told me he was going to be on holiday in Iraq at the same time and invited us to join him in searching for his father. This sounded a marvellous opportunity until I asked him where he was planning to go and discovered that it was possibly on the Iraq/Iran border. I did not want us to end up in a jail in Baghdad or Tehran, so I declined his kind offer with all the grace I could muster. Weeks later, he told me that he had found his father well inside Iraq and that, therefore, we could have accompanied him after all.

Pleasant and helpful as he was, Major Shameri did not wield much power. I, therefore, had to win the trust and respect of His Excellency, Mr Faisal Doud, Under Secretary of State for Defence. To his great credit, he had reached this powerful position despite not being a First Class Kuwaiti. Kuwait society was built on a bewildering class hierarchy, ranging from First Class to something like Nineteenth Class, the latter being Bedouin without Kuwaiti papers. These people were known as the *Bedoon*, meaning 'without' in Arabic. In our diary, I attempted to define the main classes in Kuwaiti society as follows:

First Class: The true Kuwaitis who were living in Kuwait prior to 1920. These people enjoy full rights.

Second Class: Kuwaitis who settled in Kuwait between 1920 and 1961, when Kuwait gained independence. These people have lesser privileges.

Fifth Class: Non-Kuwaitis married to Kuwaitis who take out Kuwait nationality. These people can never own property and can never improve their class, even for their offspring.

Seventh Class: All offspring of Fifth Class Kuwaitis. The offspring of Second and Seventh class Kuwaitis are accorded First Class status.

I never asked to which class Faisal Doud belonged, but suffice it to say that he held the purse strings within the Ministry of Defence. Without his approval no money was forthcoming to improve our Team's conditions of service. Thankfully, we enjoyed a really strong professional relationship and his was the only Kuwaiti family we got to know socially. Mrs Doud was equally friendly, as were their children, and we were privileged to be entertained not only in their palatial house in Kuwait City, but we were also invited to join them at their holiday villa on the coast in the south of the country. My diary entry, covering a banquet hosted by Faisal Doud at his home in Kuwait City for a visiting delegation from the Royal College of Defence Studies (RCDS), sheds some light on the lifestyle of prosperous Kuwaitis. I should add that we, as a family, were treated to the same lavish hospitality whenever we were invited to dinner:

> *Faisal Doud lives in a true palace of a house. The floors are of pink marble and adorned with beautiful silk Persian rugs. The furniture is French and the chairs and settees are finished in gold leaf! A spiral staircase leads downstairs (underground) to a magnificent through-room, in which the 'windows' are actually mirrors. Here there was a veritable banquet laid out for us. One could hardly see the table for all the food upon it: two enormous roast fish, six roast chickens on mounds of yellow rice, two cuts of beef, two cuts of lamb and numerous bowls of vegetables and salad. No less than six different desserts and a huge bowl of fruit followed! When we all rose, replete, at the end of dinner, we had made very little impression on the mountain of food that had been set before us.*
>
> *Faisal Doud then led us off to another part of this underground haven, which contained a 20-yard swimming pool, changing rooms, a mini gym and a bar, including a microwave (in case one felt peckish and wanted a snack), built-in stereo, video and cinema screen. What luxury! Here Faisal Doud showed us a video of old Kuwait, dating back to the beginning of the century – fascinating. I wonder if the people in those days would recognise Kuwait today; it is so utterly different.*

After eight months or so of hard negotiating with Faisal Doud, I paved the way (no pun intended) to getting the roads within IBI Camp properly surfaced, thereby greatly enhancing the quality of life for those living there. I also managed to get the tennis court at our house resurfaced as a Team facility, especially for those of us living in and around Kuwait City.

Kuwait did not permit embassies to appoint military attachés to their staff. I, therefore, attended the British Embassy's weekly meetings as a quasi military attaché. I enjoyed an excellent working relationship with my first Ambassador, Peter Hinchcliffe. Being a former soldier himself, he could see things from my viewpoint and was generally very supportive of the Team. He allowed me and Andy Jones, together with our families, to use the Embassy swimming pool, as we were the only members of the Team without access to one where we lived. The Team was also permitted to use the Embassy tennis court, although Embassy personnel understandably took priority. Indeed, Peter and I organised a number of tennis matches between the Embassy and the KLT/BLT, which were fiercely contested. When I organised an 'American Tennis Tournament', the Embassy was delighted to participate.

During Peter's time, the Embassy's recreational facilities were upgraded to include a new outdoor bar and swimming pool complex next to the tennis court. Peter and his wife, Archie, soon became good friends of ours and due to the rapport between us these facilities were made available to all BLT families when they were in the vicinity. It was a sad day when they were posted to Zambia in March 1990.

The new Ambassador, Michael Weston, arrived a fortnight later and, as one would expect, set about putting his own stamp on the way the Embassy was run. I was somewhat taken aback when, at one of his first weekly meetings, he ruled that, henceforth, the Embassy's recreational facilities were not be used by my Team, apart from the bar on Fridays, our day off, due to overcrowding and the resultant noise, especially during school holidays. He added that this ruling didn't apply to me or my family, because of my link with the Embassy. I thanked him for his gesture, but explained I could hardly let another BLT family watch me or my family cooling off in the swimming pool whilst they sweltered at the bar by the poolside; either we continued with the existing arrangements, or the privilege (for that's what it was) should be withdrawn from all BLT personnel. To their credit, my family gave me their full support. In any case, within days of surrendering our use of the Embassy's facilities, the manager of the Kuwait International Hotel, a German called Hermann Simon, gave us six months' family membership of his hotel's Executive Fitness Club, with its superb swimming pool and air-conditioned gym. Had he got wind of our plight, or was this pure coincidence? We never did find out, but we were extremely grateful.

I also had more contact with my masters in the Ministry of Defence, London than in any of my previous loan service appointments. Much of this was by phone, and because our 'weekend' was Friday I would often be telephoned at home. I can remember one Friday afternoon when I was on the roof of our house trying to fix a problem with the water tank, when Toni called up to me saying the MoD was on the line. When I picked up the phone the caller apologised for ringing on my day off and, with breathtaking honesty and not the slightest hint of irony, declared that, "I just wanted to clear my desk before the weekend."

On another occasion, the Civil Service team that travelled the world setting the rates of Local Overseas Allowance (LOA) rang to tell me that they had had to revise their inspection programme and, apologising for the short notice, gave me their new dates for conducting our pricing review. Realising that these coincided with the important Muslim feast of Eid al-Adha, I explained that Kuwait would virtually close down over these dates and that none of the supermarkets or shops that they would need to visit to check on prices would be open. Moreover, during such times many of the Team took the opportunity to visit other areas of the Gulf, as

Kuwait offered very little by way of recreation. Indeed, I had planned to take my family to visit the Marshes in southern Iraq during the Eid. By way of making my point, I asked him how he would feel if I insisted on coming to see him in London on a Bank Holiday weekend.

He was unmoved; they were coming as planned and would conduct the review with or without our assistance – it was up to us. I should explain that all loan service personnel are paid and taxed as if they were serving in the UK. However, they also receive LOA at specific levels to offset the wide-ranging variations in the cost of living/degree of hardship in loan service postings across the world. This is an important allowance and it was, therefore, essential that I and other key BLT members (and our wives) were present when such an inspection was undertaken. The LOA team knew this.

I had to cancel a number of people's leave plans at short notice to prepare for the visit, asking the Administrative Officer and his wife, for example, to conduct a survey of a typical weekly shopping basket for food and household essentials and then go around the supermarkets to cost these items.

The LOA Team duly arrived a day or two before the start of the Eid and we managed to complete all the necessary groundwork, briefings, interviews, costings, etc. before the start of the holiday. The LOA team then retired to their hotel to work on their findings through the three days of celebrations.

I was not best pleased when the phone by my bed sprang into life at 6.00 a.m. on Friday, in the middle of the Eid, and even less amused when I heard the voice of the LOA Team Leader on the other end. However, I quickly realised that he sounded harassed and anxious. He told me that he and his colleagues had been arrested by the military authorities and that they were being held in the Armed Forces Headquarters. He was speaking from the office of the Deputy Commander of the Armed Forces, General

Sheikh Jaber Khalid al Sabah, a member of the ruling family. He had been called in to handle the situation. The General ordered me to come to his office immediately to vouch for the men and explain why they had entered the highly restricted military area bordering the Shatt al Arab the previous afternoon, where they had been arrested whilst photographing a strategic bridge.

After eating copious slices of humble pie and undertaking to ensure that there would be no further breaches of security, I was able to obtain their release without charge. I can take no credit for this; the decision was entirely due to the General's commonsense. He could see that this had been an entirely innocent, albeit silly mistake. We were all very lucky.

It transpired that the team had picked up a 'flyer' in the hotel that talked about an impressive and beautiful bridge in the Shatt al Arab area, implying that it was well worth a visit, but omitting to mention that this area was strictly out of bounds.

Not all our official visitors caused us problems. Most were connected with Defence Sales, which, from my point of view, were easy to manage and enjoyable, although the salesmen often returned home empty handed – the Kuwaitis drove a hard bargain.

The most memorable visit was that by Their Royal Highnesses, Prince Charles and Princess Diana, in March 1989, in which Toni and I were privileged to be involved. Our diary entries at the time give an insight into this wonderful experience:

Saturday 11 March

Yesterday's severe thunder and sand storm apparently closed both seaports and the airport. Today, a major clean-up is in operation and the city's streets are being bedecked with Kuwaiti and Union Jack flags in readiness for the Royal visit starting tomorrow. It's lovely to see the Union Jacks – quite nostalgic – but, alas, at least 40% of them are upside down! As there are over 2,000 of them the official line from the Embassy is 'ma' lesh*! (it doesn't matter).*

Sunday 12 March

The Town Crier of London turned up today at The English School (where Toni works) adorned in all his regalia. An amazing 76-year-old called Alfie, he has proclaimed all Royal announcements outside Buckingham Palace for 42 years (except the birth of Prince Harry; the baby was a week early and Alfie happened to be abroad at the time, so proclaimed the event outside his hotel!).
Alfie is here to promote British Week during the Royal visit. He is the fifth generation of his family to be the official Town Crier of London. His coat/waistcoat has been embroidered with badges/coats of arms by himself – he went to embroidery classes for three years to learn how to do this.
Their Royal Highnesses arrived this evening! Toni was one of a select group of wives who entertained Lady Anne Blunden to dinner. She is the wife of the Deputy Governor of the Bank of England and is part of the Royal visit/British Week.

Monday 13 March

A dull overcast day. The rain held off until moments before the Embassy reception in honour of Their Royal Highnesses, the wet weather programme having to be adopted with just minutes to spare. We were all presented to the Royal couple indoors at the top of the Embassy stairs. Both looked relaxed and immaculate – how do they maintain such a presence in their busy lives. Princess Diana looked stunning. As she was going on to a Royal state banquet, she was wearing a ball gown, a simple classic line in lilac with a beautifully embroidered bodice and long sleeves. And she is every bit as beautiful as in her pictures. I must quickly add that Toni, too, looked stunning in her vibrant new evening dress!

Having been presented to the Royal couple we walked straight through the Embassy, down the back stairs and were then taken in Embassy cars on to the Sha'ab Palace, the residence of Kuwait's Crown Prince and Prime Minister. His Highness, the Crown Prince and his wife, Sheikha Latifeh, met us at the entrance to the magnificent reception room and made us feel very important. We were, indeed, most honoured, being amongst the 18 British people to be invited.

The palace was exquisite in every detail: superb Arabic/Oriental decor, enormous cut glass chandeliers and a beautiful covered inner courtyard with lovely mosaic surrounds and cooling Moroccan fountains.

Just before dinner, we were, once again, presented to the Royal couple. The banquet was absolutely first class. We ate off heavily gold-plated crockery set on solid silver salvers. The tablecloth and napkins were of white linen with a very tasteful, fine solid gold thread design. The food was superb and served in just the right proportions; five courses comprising seafood hors d'oeuvre, an excellent consommé, fish, a meat course, including quails – an Arab speciality. The dinner was rounded off with a superb fruit salad, which was served in trays that were lit internally, making the fruit salad sparkle. Sitting on top of each tray was a model of an Arab dhow, sailing, as it were, on the sparkling 'sea'.

After the banquet, we returned to the original reception room for tea and coffee (both Arabic style) and then were ushered into a lovely

> diwaniya, *or sitting room, off the inner courtyard, where a male group entertained us to Kuwaiti traditional songs and dances to the accompaniment of incessant vibrant drumming. Prince Charles delighted his hosts when he was persuaded to join in towards the end.*

The visit that caused me the greatest difficulty, and had the potential to threaten my career, was when a visitor I was hosting was presented with a gold-plated Colt 4.5 Magnum hand gun. I gulped as I knew what was coming; he could not possibly get the weapon out of the country! Sure enough, he later handed it to me and smilingly told me to use my initiative. Well, the Kuwaitis were unwilling to help and, quite rightly, the British Embassy said there was no way they would abuse privilege by using the diplomatic bag; this was my problem and would have to be resolved accordingly.

My guardian angel came to my rescue. About a week later, we were notified that the Royal Navy, for the first time in almost 20 years, was due to make a goodwill visit to Kuwait in about six weeks' time. I was tasked to make the necessary arrangements. The ship, *HMS Beaver*, a Type 22 Broadsword Class frigate, duly arrived at Shuaiba Port in the south of the country on 30 October 1989. During the course of the visit, I told the Captain of my dilemma and asked if he could help me. He kindly agreed to allow the weapon to be held in the ship's armoury, provided I was able to get it aboard. I was very grateful to him.

However, this was no easy task. All vehicles entering and leaving the port were liable to be searched by a very efficient, if rather naive, Bedouin guard force. For example, the (Kuwaiti) Port Commander had once been refused entry in his private car, as the guard on the barrier objected to his car aerial. When the Port Commander told him not to be so stupid, the guard simply showed him the orders he, himself, had issued, stating that no radios were allowed in the port! He did not accept the argument that this referred to walkie-talkie radios; a radio was a radio and that was that! Even the Executive Officer and some of the crew of *HMS Beaver* had difficulty re-entering the port one evening after a function in Kuwait City, as the guard was unhappy about their documentation.

I waited and waited for an opportunity, but none was forthcoming. The day that *HMS Beaver* was due to leave port, I told Toni that I was going to risk taking the weapon to the port and that I could be arrested. With that I left for work at the Armed Forces Headquarters with the pistol in my briefcase. I had not been in my office more than half an hour when the phone rang and I was summoned to the Chief of the Defence Staff's (CDS) office. My heart sank. Had somebody discovered that I had brought the weapon into the Headquarters? Fearing the worst, I entered CDS's office but was immediately put at ease – my guardian angel was looking after me again. CDS wanted me to deliver two huge sealed polystyrene boxes of Kuwaiti prawns to the captain of *HMS Beaver*! I asked for a letter of authority to show the port guards and gave the registration number of my car. I also asked if his staff could contact the port to let them know when I would be arriving. What luck!

I set off feeling much more confident, but as I approached the barrier at the entrance to the port, I noticed that it was down and about a dozen guards on motorcycles were barring my way. My heart skipped a beat, but then the guard commander gave me a snappy salute and with six motorcycles on either side of my car and sirens blowing I was escorted like royalty to the ship. The ship's company was highly impressed! I was piped aboard, handed over the prawns and the 'golden gun', thanked the captain, said my farewells and, having been piped ashore, was escorted back to the port gate. Job done!

As had been our experience in all our previous loan service postings, Toni was contacted by several schools almost as soon as she arrived and agreed to be interviewed for teaching posts after the children had returned to school in England. She was delighted to be accepted by the school of her choice, Surra, and loved her time working there.

Shopping in Kuwait offered a wide variety of experiences. At the top end, were the modern shopping complexes, such as the Sultan Centre, typical of any wealthy nation's capital city, whilst at the other end of the scale were the local markets, where vibrant colours, enticing aromas, the hubbub, hustle and bustle of hundreds of people provided an authentic taste of 'old Kuwait'.

One of our particular favourites was the *Bedu* market at Fahaheel, where the atmosphere conjured up scenes that I feel would not have been out of place in biblical times. In one patch of sand, weather-beaten men in flowing robes bought and sold sheep and goats. The dust kicked up by the animals' hooves filled the air with a fine haze, lending an almost dreamlike effect to the spectacle, especially when lit up by the glowing embers of the setting sun. In another area, veiled women and their children were spinning yarn, constructing makeshift looms on the desert floor and weaving traditional 'Sadu' rugs, saddle bags and cushion covers in vividly coloured geometric patterns – a photographer's paradise. On one occasion, a weaver invited Toni into her tent to meet her daughter, Amina. Toni's diary entry states:

> *Amina was dabbing a small carpet with liquid from a soaked bit of material bound round a stick. On closer inspection I saw that she was using bleach to carefully clean areas of the white pattern which had been spoilt by the slight weeping of adjacent coloured dyes. What a painstaking task and no wonder poor Amina's eyes were stinging.*

Another equally compelling venue was the camel market/farm in the desert some 15 or so miles north of Kuwait City, where literally hundreds, perhaps thousands, of camels were held in ramshackle corrals made out of corrugated iron sheeting and scrap metal – functional but uneasy on the eye.

On our first visit, a camel herder 'kindly' offered us some camel's milk to drink. It was freshly drawn, warm and frothy, with bits of straw and other debris floating on its surface. To drink camel's milk like this can give the uninitiated severe tummy trouble and diarrhoea, but to refuse would have been hugely insulting, so we all had a tiny sip and got away very lightly. Many of the female camels had young and on another occasion we arrived within minutes of a foal being born. We watched as the camel herder first milked the mother to give her baby the scent and then helped it to its feet to suckle for the first time.

Quite the most stunning shopping experience was to be found in the centre of town – the gold souk. Here, the shops were literally dripping with gold, the merchandise ranging from the highly elaborate and ornate designs favoured by the Bedouin to the chic, sophisticated simple designs more suited to Western tastes. I well remember the occasion when I visited one of these shops to buy a Christmas present for Toni. As I browsed, I calculated that the gold on a single shelf was worth as much as a top-of-the-range Rolls-Royce, and this was but one of very many such shelves! As I contemplated this thought, the owner came up and told me he had to go and pray. Far from inviting me to leave, he asked if I would mind the shop for him in the meantime, and let any prospective customers know that he would be back shortly. What trust! Was I glad when he returned! In the end we were both winners; I bought Toni's present and he gave me a 'special price'.

Entertainment in Kuwait was largely of an urban nature; smart restaurants, well-appointed hotel clubs and, for the children, a permanent fair ground at Fun City. A favourite haunt of ours was the Mövenpick ice cream parlour – licking the delicious ice cream as fast as it melted in the scorching sun was challenging and enjoyable at the same time. We treated ourselves to a night out once or twice every school holiday, usually at Le Meridien hotel, where the food was excellent and accompanied by live music ranging from classical piano pieces to swing and traditional jazz numbers. Here we met a talented Goan musician called Remy de Melo, who sang and played the trumpet (amongst many other instruments) just like Louis Armstrong. He was a charming man, who inspired Rorie to write and perform his own music, and even visited us at home once or twice to offer Rorie encouragement and advice. Sadly for us, he and his family moved to Canada shortly after we met him.

Being a strategically important and very wealthy State, Kuwait also attracted a lot of 'goodwill' interest from outside. We were therefore privileged to enjoy some unique experiences here, such as a sublime concert given by the Vienna Boys' Choir, and an equally uplifting, but far from tranquil concert given by the Red Army Choir. Their stirring melodies and rich harmonies were interspersed with some amazing Cossack dancing – thrilling stuff! As the West and the Soviet Union were still entrenched in the Cold War, I found it paradoxical to be in the audience to marvel at this spectacle.

Japanese Week was another cultural experience made all the more memorable by a thrilling drumming display, as noted in our diary:

> *There on a stage constructed in the middle of the beach a troupe of very muscular Japanese men hailed the arrival of the Japanese Ambassador, a very dignified-looking man, who then announced the opening of Japanese Week. This was the signal for the men on the stage, all professional drummers from Japan, to give us a quite thrilling, almost alarming, display of Japanese drumming. The largest drum was bigger than any we had ever seen and stood on a*

stand about five feet above the ground. Two drummers using small clubs rather than drum sticks took it in turns to draw out its vibrant, thunderous roar. The whole spectacle was more like an awesome martial arts display rather than a musical one, and sent a chill down our spines – thrilling!

From a photographic point of view it was well worth being in Kuwait on 25 February – Kuwait's National Day, which celebrates the creation of the nation in 1961. At this time, all the major buildings in town are decked out in lights in Kuwait's national colours of red, white, green and black, the latter colour represented either by very dark blue lights or unlit areas. In many cases, the lights are arranged to form the nation's flag. The people themselves dress up in these colours and come out to celebrate, and we were always encouraged to join their festivities.

Urban entertainment is all very well, but for us the main attraction of living in the Middle East was the lure of the desert and the people who called it home. In this respect, Kuwait offered very little by comparison to the other places in which we had served. The desert was generally flat and uninteresting and, in any case, was largely out of bounds, either for military reasons or because it belonged to the oil industry. But one must always make the most of what's available. The only feature of note was the Mutla Ridge, a low ridge, some 300 feet high, that straddled the main highway running north about 50 miles short of the Iraqi border. We joined a group of expatriates here on Christmas Eve for an impromptu carol sing-along round a fire, followed by mulled wine and soup as we watched the sunset. The Mutla Ridge was also a good spot for a barbecue during the cooler months.

In a funny sort of way, the Kuwaitis, too, were still drawn to the desert and their Bedouin roots. Every winter, tents of all descriptions, from lavish marquees to traditional Bedouin examples, sprang up all over the desert surrounding the city, even directly under electricity pylons, as many of the inhabitants vacated their luxurious homes to experience the life of their forefathers for a couple of weeks or so. Indeed, Kuwaitis still held firm to the Bedouin tradition of never passing by on the other side when a person needed help in the desert, even if that person was an 'infidel'. If anyone ever broke down on the highway, the first Kuwaiti on the scene, young or old, would always stop to lend a hand.

Women were not permitted to wear swimming costumes on any of the beaches in the vicinity of the city, except the private beaches owned by some of the hotels. There were, however, numerous places on the deserted coastline in the far south of the country where we could enjoy a day out as a family, the only drawbacks being the searing heat and total absence of shade. There was also a resort in the early stages of development at Khiran, on the coast near the Saudi border. Here you could rent a self-catering chalet and also hire twin quad pedal bikes, which our children found great fun.

At the beginning of our tour we visited Failaka Island, where we had heard you could hire holiday chalets. Failaka is nothing more than a sandbank in the sea, about 30 minutes by hovercraft from Kuwait City. Flat and largely treeless as well as very hot and humid, it didn't offer much to the expatriate community; men and women could not use the swimming pool together, nor could women be seen on the beach in swimwear. There were Stone Age remains on the island, but these were not accessible to the public. The only attraction, therefore, seemed to be the journey to and fro by hovercraft.

Midway through our tour, I acquired a part share in an old, rather temperamental speed boat. We spent many an enjoyable afternoon out in Kuwait Bay water-skiing and fishing, and almost as many frustrating afternoons trying to breathe new life into the rather tired outboard motor. Although we knew of no shark attacks in Kuwaiti waters, we always felt a little uneasy when we fell off whilst skiing – after all we used to catch sharks when fishing in this very area!

We were, of course, operating in the vicinity of the shipping channel, so decided not to ski for a week or so after the arrival of a sheep ship. These vessels, which emitted the most pungent smell, looked like floating blocks of flats, each deck laden with hundreds of live sheep from, I believe, Australia or New Zealand, ready for the halal butcher. This was a fearful journey for the poor animals and many didn't survive the ordeal. Because the dead animals were thrown overboard, sheep ships attracted a lot of sharks.

In Spring, parts of the southern desert would turn green and there would even be splashes of colour here and there as flowers bloomed for a few weeks in defiance of the burning sun. On one Eid holiday we went into the southern desert looking for irises and, having spotted some through our binoculars, started to drive towards them. Coming out of a shallow depression we suddenly noticed a small fort over to our left, its flag resting motionless against the flagstaff in the still air. As I looked through the binoculars, the flag momentarily unfurled as it was caught by a gentle breeze and, to my horror, it showed the fort to be a Saudi border post. I could now make out a group of men in uniform, sitting on the ground in a circle, tucking into their Eid feast. Carefully reversing our Nissan Patrol back into the depression, we beat a hasty retreat.

It wouldn't have done to be caught on the Saudi border with a camera and telephoto lens! Stories about irises wouldn't have got us out of jail and, quite possibly, a very embarrassing mention in the newspapers back home!

We spent most Eid breaks visiting other parts of the Gulf. On one visit to the United Arab Emirates (UAE), I took the family back to Sharjah, where I had been posted for nine months in 1969 to 'think' about my impending marriage to Toni. Sharjah was now another concrete jungle and I couldn't find a trace of our living accommodation or our vehicle park.

Yet, extraordinarily, the RAF runway, complete with its control tower, was still there in the heart of the city, the runway being used as a road.

Adjacent to the runway I found remnants of the RAF/Army stores, including the old pattern water bottles insulated with RAF blue and khaki blanket material. I even found the site of our outdoor cinema, including the framework for the screen and the terraced scaffolding which once held the seats. Part of the old souk down by the creek (the Sharjah I knew) – including 'Robin Bastard's' shop – had been preserved as a monument to bygone days, but I found it hard to conjure up the atmosphere, the smells, the noise, the bustle, the sheer vibrancy of old; it was just like an empty tomb.

On another occasion we visited Abu Dhabi, where we hired a Daihatsu Rocky and ventured a little into the desolate wastes of the Liwa Sands on the edge of the Empty Quarter. The Rocky was so light that it seemed to float atop the sand and soon we were surrounded by the most impressive sand dunes. There wasn't a sign of human habitation in any direction right out to the horizon. The ground appeared to be in constant motion, the fine sand being driven along at ankle height by a constant warm breeze.

We stopped on a dune to take in the spectacle and Alex decided to run down the steep slope, setting off an 'avalanche'. To our amazement this caused the sand to 'sing' with a sound that reminded us of a didgeridoo. We then had great fun 'playing' our new musical instrument until a yellow scorpion emerged from the sand between Alex's toes. Luckily it didn't sting him, but we were more respectful of our surroundings after that. Although we sat on the sand and ate our supper as the sky reddened under a beautiful sunset, we abandoned our plans to sleep on the ground that night – we didn't have any bedding with us. Instead we spent a rather cold and uncomfortable night in, or on top of, our Rocky. It was well worth it; the clear night sky in the desert, unpolluted by any hint of artificial light, is a sight to behold.

Our favourite escape from the concrete jungle of Kuwait, however, was northwards into Iraq and, especially, the marshlands west of Qurnah at the confluence of the Euphrates and the Tigris. This was the home of the Marsh Arabs, made famous by Wilfred Thesiger, author of the book by that name, and Gavin Maxwell, who was introduced to the area by Thesiger in 1956 and wrote *A Reed Shaken by the Wind* to record his adventure. Our base for these trips was the Sheraton hotel in Basra.

The Iran/Iraq war had ended on 20 August 1988, barely a month after my arrival in Kuwait. It had started eight years earlier, on 22 September 1980, when Iraq invaded Iran with the purpose of establishing itself as the dominant power in the Arabian Gulf. In this, arguably the most violent conflict since World War Two, Iraq was supported by the West, which made it easier for us to obtain visas to visit the country.

Our diary entries give a feel for what we experienced:

Monday 3 April 1989

Basra, only 30 miles from the Kuwaiti border, showed all the signs of a war-torn city. Many roads were impassable, many buildings were damaged or destroyed by air or artillery bombardment, whilst those left standing, including the Sheraton hotel, were splattered with shrapnel and bullet holes. Gangs of workmen were everywhere, clearing rubble and rebuilding. Apparently work goes on 24 hours a day, every day.

The Sheraton hotel is situated on the Corniche bordering the Shatt al Arab, the disputed waterway between Iraq and Iran. Two sunken ships blocked the channel in front of the hotel and a military pontoon bridge spanned the waters beside the destroyed bridge.

When we ventured out for a stroll along the Corniche, men in a variety of military uniforms seemed to be everywhere we went. All the once beautiful buildings along the Corniche were derelict, destroyed or riddled with bullet holes, as were many of the trees that lined the road. It must have been lovely once; the Sheraton with its relative luxury and splendour was in marked contrast to the ruins around it.

Tuesday 4 April

We took ages finding our way out of Basra due to the destruction of many roads and the lack of road signs. However, we managed to reach Qurnah by midday. En-route we had noticed the marked contrast in the traffic compared to Kuwait; far less congested, but slow-moving. The vast majority of vehicles were very old and comprised mainly lorries, taxis and buses; there were very few private cars, a sign of an impoverished nation.

Qurnah is at the confluence of the Euphrates and the Tigris. Once a beautiful hotel had graced the confluence, but now it was totally derelict with sandbagged gun emplacements in the abandoned gardens and on the roof. Paradoxically, this very area is reputed to be the site of the Garden of Eden; indeed, there is a very rundown symbolic 'Garden of Eden' adjacent to the hotel with its very own (apparently dead) apple tree, that it is claimed, is a direct descendant of the famous tree mentioned in Genesis. It is also claimed that Abraham prayed at this site circa 2,000 BC.

From Qunah we headed west and soon entered a fascinating – if wet – new world of marshes, reed huts, wooden boats, beautiful birds and friendly people – utter tranquillity. But for the fact that the area was also teeming with soldiers, either patrolling or manning numerous road blocks, this could easily have been a modern Garden of Eden. However, I must say the soldiers appeared to be friendly and gave us no trouble.

We made our way to the village of Chibaish in the midst of the marshes, stopping regularly to take photographs, but never failing to ask permission of the nearest soldiers before doing so. Surprisingly, not only were they generally agreeable, but some even asked me to photograph them. We then retraced our steps, stopping at a little cluster of dwellings that had caught our attention earlier. Here, we succeeded in getting a ride on one of the narrow black canoes that are the main form of transport in this area. These vessels are made of wood and are coated with a 'skin' of bitumen, that literally oozes from the ground in this area, to make them watertight (we watched this being done in another village – the craftsmen employing the same skills as their ancestors must have done in Abraham's time). The generic name given to these craft is *mashoof*, with the larger ones called *tarada*.

The boatman took us over to his home. Like the others, it was set on its own tiny island that measured no more than 20 yards by 10 yards. Three generations of the same family lived here in a stone-built house of three rooms and an outside clay oven for making bread. There were also two reed shelters, in one of which were two cows and a day-old calf. Much of the island was artificially constructed out of compressed reeds and the ground everywhere moved underfoot.

The family was very friendly and invited us indoors, where we were served orange juice. The boatman's name was Rousaan. He took us on a tour of his village, punting his *mashoof* in the shallows and changing to a paddle when in the deeper waters of the main stream, where the water is crystal clear and you can clearly see the bed of rushes a few feet below the surface. The waters teem with fish, which the locals catch in nets or with fearsome five-pronged barbed spears.

The *mashoof* is a really unsteady craft and you have to be skilful to handle it. But for Rousaan's ability, we would have capsized our boat within seconds, for the slightest movement threatened our stability.

We took photographs of Rousaan and his family and paid them one or two further visits over the months that followed. In trying to make small talk, we quickly realised that we must not mention politics, ask why there were so many soldiers in the area or even talk about food supplies or the cost of living. I also noticed that a large picture of Saddam Hussein was prominently displayed on a wall in the main room. One day, when we were alone in the *mashoof* with Rousaan, I asked him about the guarded nature of our conversations, assuring him that I was not a spy.

To my amazement and deep sadness, he said he knew that I wasn't a spy, but he couldn't be sure if any one of his family was. Nor, he added, could they be sure he wasn't a spy. He said that he couldn't blame anyone for being a spy, as the regime could make life unbearable if you refused to cooperate, so the family had agreed to talk only about inconsequential matters. In that case, I asked, why did he have a picture of Saddam on the wall of his home? "To stay alive," he replied. By way of explanation, he told me of a little girl who asked her teacher who the man was in the picture in the classroom. The teacher asked her if there was a similar picture in her house, to which the little girl replied, "No." Within days the family was murdered. Of course I cannot verify this story, but in Saddam's Iraq it does not seem too far-fetched.

We visited Nasiriyah, a town on the Euphrates, a couple of times in an attempt to see the famous Ziggurat of Ur, but, although we saw it from a distance, it was in a restricted military area and tourists were not welcome. On the first occasion, we were told that a dusk to dawn curfew was in operation outside Nasiriyah, so we had no option but to find a bed for the night.

This was a rather sinister, scruffy town. It was swarming with soldiers – there were numerous military camps in and around the place – and a complete absence of women and girls. The main hotel had been commandeered by the Iraqi Army. After some time, we found a very run down hotel for the night and left soon as we could next morning.

Whenever we visited Iraq we had to ensure that our stay did not exceed 72 hours, after which point we would have to undergo an AIDS test before being allowed back into Kuwait. Once we cut things rather fine, arriving at the border post with only a few hours to spare. It was the last day of an Eid and the place was teeming with Kuwaitis returning home. After an hour or more, I noticed that many people who had arrived long after us had had their passports stamped and been allowed to continue their journey. I approached the desk and asked the official, very politely, if he could kindly process our passports, as we had been waiting rather a long time. He asked me to identify them from amongst the mountain of passports heaped upon his desk. Once I had done this, he simply placed them all at the very bottom of the pile and waved me away dismissively. Rarely have I felt so angry and so impotent. It was another hour or so before he deigned to stamp our passports and allow us through.

Enjoying both enormous wealth and huge strategic importance, Kuwait attracted a lot of visitors from both the political and commercial walks of life. These visitors and, indeed, their Kuwaiti contacts expected to be entertained in a manner befitting of such an opulent place. However, Kuwait was a dry state and, although the main hotels served the finest international cuisine in their restaurants, alcohol was not on the menu. Thus much of the entertainment was carried out in private homes, like ours.

Despite the Kuwaiti ban, we were expected to serve alcohol on such occasions. Thus we were expected to include beer and wine-making kits in our luggage (although we had to take responsibility if caught) and some of the supermarkets even sold items to make gin – juniper berries and ethanol – usually side by side on the same shelf. The ethanol was labelled as 'computer cleaning fluid'! One could also buy bottles with kilner-type sealed tops in which to store beer.

When we first arrived, embassies were unofficially allowed to import alcohol under diplomatic privilege for consumption on Embassy premises – I heard a lovely story of an Embassy being rung up by Customs and asked to come and collect their 'piano' as the crate was leaking! I did not enjoy the chore of making beer and wine and would have preferred to do without, but this was very much part of life in Kuwait.

Although we could serve our guests alcohol, our culinary skills were no match for the fare on offer in the hotels. The practice, therefore, was for a hotel to produce the meal of your choice and provide the waiters to serve it in your home.

On these occasions, we had to keep a very close check on the alcohol, counting every bottle out at the start and accounting for every bottle at the end, including empties. The numbers had to tally exactly before the hotel staff could leave. The reason for this is that the police would always be aware of your party. Whilst they would not enter your house, they often stopped and searched people on the way out, especially the hotel staff, who were almost exclusively Asian. For some of these poor people, your alcohol was more attractive than a modest tip.

In 1990, we heralded in the New Year by attending a fancy dress party, the theme of which was, 'What were you doing when the ship went down?' In hindsight, this seemed like an omen, a warning of what was to befall us as the year unfolded, as was Toni's diary entry on New Year's Day: *'I wonder what this decade will bring.'*

The year started promisingly enough. My mother spent a very happy four weeks with us from mid-January to Valentine's Day. We took her into the desert, visited the various traditional markets, and travelled to the mud flats in Shuwaikh Bay, north of the city, to see the flamingos. Kuwait boasts a small resident population of Greater Flamingos on these mud flats, which is increased by several hundreds of migrant 'cousins' during the winter months.

As a finale, we took my mother to dinner at the SAS Hotel's floating restaurant, Al Boom. *Boom* is the Arabic word for a large traditional Arabian Gulf dhow. This particular vessel was built in 1979, on the Malabar Coast of South India at a place called Calicut. Thus it was a particularly apt venue, Ma 'D', as she was known, having spent much of her life in this part of India. The cuisine on offer was arguably the best available in Kuwait, with prices to match – a very special treat! We made our way home through the centre of the city to let Ma 'D' see some of the illuminations that had already been installed in readiness for National Day.

During her stay with us, we were also actively involved with a visit by the Chief of the Defence Staff (CDS), Marshal of the Royal Air Force, Sir David Craig GCB OBE and his wife, Lady Craig. I was part of the welcoming party at the airport, where the CDS and Lady Craig were greeted by the entire hierarchy of Kuwait's Armed Forces. We were then whisked off to the British Embassy in a very ostentatious convoy – bullet-proof Mercedes, outriders, flashing lights and blaring sirens – quite an experience!

Such a high-powered visit could have been very daunting, but Sir David and Lady Craig were so approachable, so undemanding that we really enjoyed the privilege of our time with them.

As the Spring gave way to early Summer, storm clouds began to gather on the political horizon. Iraq had been financially crippled by its war with Iran, and Saddam Hussein felt that the Gulf Arab countries should help Iraq to rebuild its economy, arguing that Iraq had protected them from Iran. Moreover, he accused Kuwait and the UAE of having brought down oil prices, and thereby adversely impacting Iraq's economy, by vastly exceeding their OPEC oil production quotas. Finally, he accused Kuwait of stealing Iraqi oil from the shared Rumaila oilfield that straddled the Iraq/

Kuwait border in the north, and demanded $27 billion in compensation. In June 1990, negotiating teams from both countries held talks in Kuwait to try to resolve this dispute, but failed to reach an agreement.

Meanwhile, our life in Kuwait continued as normal. Our diaries make no mention of the slightest hint of trouble. This, in itself, is understandable; the purpose of these diaries was to keep our four children and both sets of parents fully up to date with the positive aspects of our life in Kuwait. We certainly didn't want to worry them in any way. However, the fact that all the Team's boarding schoolchildren were flown out for the summer holidays in July, and new team members were posted in just days before the invasion, confirms the relaxed attitude to the crisis being taken by our masters in the UK. This, too, was confirmed by the stance adopted by the British Embassy. I even approached my opposite number in the American Embassy on several occasions during the second half of July and he confirmed that his Embassy did not believe that Iraq would invade.

At a meeting on 25 July 1990, the US Ambassador to Iraq, April Glaspie, apparently told Saddam Hussein that the United States had no opinion on disputes between Arab nations. Why, one wonders? This was a case of mixed messages if ever there was one. Certainly it must have seemed to the Iraqis that they need not fear the United States (and, therefore, the world) if they did choose to invade Kuwait.

Not only were all our children now in Kuwait, but Zoë had invited a school friend, Vanessa Nickerson, to stay with us as well. I was now concerned for her safety and I did not want the responsibility of someone else's child if things turned nasty. Equally, I felt that her parents would expect me, quite rightly, to send her home if there was the slightest risk to her safety. Although she was due to fly home in the first week of August, I decided to go to the airport to see if there was a possibility of bringing her flight forward, but to no avail.

Someone must have reported my inquiry to the Embassy, as I had not been home long before I received a phone call from the Ambassador, who gave me a not so gentle slap on the wrist, pointing out that my actions could cause panic amongst the British expatriate community. Given my status as the BLT Commander, I could see he had a point, but this was someone else's child, not mine, and I was not making a song and dance about getting her out, but quietly enquiring about the possibility of so doing.

More talks between the two countries took place in Jeddah on 31 July, but broke up in disarray. On the news that night we were told that Saddam Hussein had said that more talks would be held in Baghdad the following week.

Next morning, I saw the Kuwaiti Chief of Staff's Principal Staff Officer (PSO), an Air Force brigadier, and asked him how he viewed the situation. I cannot remember his exact words, but he told me that this was the end of the twentieth century and that Arab countries no longer went to war with each other. Moreover, both Iraq and Kuwait were members of the Arab League and so there would eventually be a negotiated settlement to the dispute; after all, Saddam had said there would be more talks in Baghdad the following week. Moreover, Saddam had also assured President Hosni Mubarak of Egypt that he would not use force against Kuwait, prompting Mubarak to describe the tense situation between Iraq and Kuwait to be nothing more than 'a passing cloud'.

That afternoon, the Ambassador called a meeting of all the key post personnel amongst the British expatriate community to brief them on the crisis and allay their fears. He stage-managed his entrance to the proceedings by breaking off from a game of tennis to come and address us, lending a sense of *sangfroid* to the occasion. In essence, he urged us all to remain calm, arguing that a mass exodus might, indeed, encourage Saddam Hussein to invade, something he did not appear to be contemplating at present.

If talks failed, he believed that Saddam Hussein's most likely response would be to seize the Rumaila oilfield. As the army man, I was invited to give my thoughts as well. I supported the Ambassador's view, adding that I had been told that intelligence assessments of air photographs indicated that the forces massed on the border lacked the command and logistical backup to support a full-scale invasion. At worst, this pointed to a limited incursion, just as the Ambassador had suggested. Of course, I had not seen these air photographs. With the benefit of hindsight, I now know that the information I had been given was incorrect. Was this down to human error? I do hope so. We were a little apprehensive as we went to bed that night, but certainly did not anticipate the fate that was about to befall us.

In the early hours of 2 August, the phone by my bed rang. It was Group Captain Brian Wright, my boss's deputy in the MoD. He was calm but sombre: "Bad news, Bruce. Iraqi forces have crossed the border into Kuwait." I asked him whether he knew if they were advancing along the main highway into Kuwait City, or had they crossed the border on a broad front, suggesting that they were intent on seizing the Rumaila oilfield. He said that they appeared to have crossed on a broad front, but this was uncertain.

I then tried to contact my deputy, but his phone was on the 'answer phone'. Next, I rang the Embassy to warn them. The Ambassador answered the phone. Clearly annoyed at being disturbed at this critical time, he told me that he was well aware of the situation and he and his staff were busy destroying classified documents. It crossed my mind that, as he seemed to have known about the situation for some time, why had the Embassy not warned me? Our house was on the extreme edge of Kuwait City, adjacent to Shuwaikh port. It would be the first house the Iraqis would reach if making for the city. However, this was not the time to pick a quarrel; I apologised and hung up.

Before I had time to gather my thoughts, the sound of battle was all around us; the Iraqis were attacking the port. I was not too worried about the gunfire from the tanks, as I felt this would be quite accurate and unlikely to target an insignificant house like ours. I found the small arms fire much more unnerving. This seemed to be coming from all directions. Toni and I quickly got the children out of their bedrooms and into the corridor that bordered the inner courtyard. This at least would protect all of us from stray, or aimed, small arms fire coming through the windows. At one stage an Iraqi jet screamed very low over the house. It must have released a missile or bomb, which exploded in the sand about 50 yards away. Its intended target was, perhaps, a palace used by royal visitors about 200 yards further on.

I should reiterate at this point that the BLT was an unarmed group of technicians and advisors and that our Memorandum of Understanding strictly forbade us to take up arms, unless ordered to do so by the British Government. In the event of hostilities, the Commander was to seek permission to withdraw the Team. I therefore contacted the Embassy to request permission to withdraw my Team. The Ambassador told me he would seek direction from London.

Later, he rang to tell me that my instructions were to lend all possible assistance to the Kuwaitis, but without endangering my men. I told him this was an impossible order; we were all unarmed and in our homes, far from our places of work. Even attempting to reach our bases would endanger my men. I said that I should either be ordered to fight alongside the Kuwaitis, or to withdraw the Team. My family and I, in any case, were now trapped, with Iraqi soldiers taking up positions all around our house.

The Ambassador accepted my reasoning and said he would seek clarification. By the time he rang to order me to withdraw the Team, Iraqi troops were swarming all over Kuwait. All we could do now was to sit tight and take stock, like the rest of the population. None of us was able to go anywhere.

Whilst the problem over our future was being decided, we were astonished to hear reports on the BBC World Service that a British Airways flight, BA149, had landed at Kuwait International airport long after the Iraqis had launched their invasion. As a result, some 350 passengers and crew had fallen into Iraqi hands and become 'guests' of Saddam Hussein. That this could have been allowed to happen has since been the subject of many a conspiracy theory. I have been implicated in some of these, due to the reassuring statement I made in the Embassy the previous afternoon. Indeed, almost 17 years after this curious event, I was interviewed about the incident by an investigative journalist during the making of a documentary, which was broadcast on BBC 2 in March 2007. It was clear from the outset that I could shed no light on why the aircraft had landed and, thankfully, I did not feature in the documentary.

Minutes after the Ambassador authorised me to withdraw the Team, the Iraqis disconnected all the international phone lines and also the local landlines into the Embassy. We did not have a radio link with the Embassy, so now the only way I could communicate with the staff there was to telephone an Embassy house and ask the family to relay my message to the Embassy by radio.

I rang all the Team locations, advising everyone to remain indoors and to stay calm. After all, we were not being directly targeted by the Iraqis; things would settle down in a couple or so days and then our situation would be resolved. I arranged to call each location briefly every morning and evening, but said that anyone should call me at any time, day or night, if they had any concerns.

From our house, I was able to see a lot of Iraqi military activity around the port and along the seafront, including the movement of tanks, infantry and multiple rocket launchers. I reported these activities to the Embassy and was quite flattered when my first report was broadcast almost word for word by the BBC World Service. However, when this happened a second time I realised that if Iraqi intelligence was listening to the BBC it would become clear that they had a 'mole' in their defensive position around the port. I therefore decided to be less specific in my reports.

One of the most incongruous sights we witnessed was a team of Asian expatriate municipal workers, dressed in their orange overalls, going about their daily task of sweeping the roads as Iraqi tanks rolled by.

Meanwhile, isolated in the middle of an Iraqi defensive position, we faced an uncertain future if discovered. We therefore had to give the impression that our house was deserted and hope that none of the Iraqi soldiers surrounding us tried to break in. This meant keeping out of sight, not using the air conditioners and keeping as quiet as possible. Try cooking without the usual clatter of pots and pans! Living in almost complete silence in the narrow confines of the inner corridor, sitting or sleeping on mattresses, not being able to peer out of windows to see what was going on outside, for fear of being seen, was all very disconcerting. There was a sense of tension, even fear, in the air, that was exacerbated by the fact that we were all living on top of one another – there was no 'private space' for people to escape into. The greatest challenge was arguably at night when we had to live in the dark – quite unnerving.

Next day we received very disturbing news; the Iraqis had entered IBI Camp, where most of the Team was stationed, and had taken away all the men 'for their own safety', leaving the wives and children completely at the mercy of the Iraqi soldiers who now occupied the camp. We were now the victims of our government's decision not to afford us the slightest degree of diplomatic immunity, unlike our American counterparts. Ironically, during my time in Kuwait I had submitted a proposal for us to be granted Administrative and Technical (A&T) diplomatic status, but without success. The powers that be must have had their reasons, but now we were living with the consequences.

The Iraqi soldiers were thoroughly ill-disciplined, racing and crashing the Team's cars around camp like so many dodgems at a fairground, breaking into houses, stealing, and even assaulting some of the wives at gunpoint in front of their terrified children. I was asked to help, but, surrounded by Iraqi soldiers myself, could do nothing personally.

Initially, the Ambassador was reluctant for the Embassy to assist; British nationals were being targeted and diplomatic immunity isn't body armour, it doesn't stop bullets fired by ill-disciplined, trigger-happy soldiers. The Canadian Chargé d'Affaires, Bill Bowden (and either the Danish or Dutch Embassy, if memory serves me right), offered to help, but when I advised the Ambassador of this, he said, quite rightly, that this was a British problem. So, accompanied by Donald Macauley, one of his diplomatic staff, he then visited IBI and also spoke to the Iraqi General commanding the troops in that area. Donald Macauley volunteered to remain in the camp until the wives and children could be moved into a hotel in Kuwait City, where they could be better protected.

The capture of our team members at IBI was broadcast on the BBC World Service. Not only did the bulletin identify the men as belonging to the British Armed Forces (information the Iraqis probably already had) but went on to say: "This leaves 30 members of the Team still in hiding..." Unbelievable! I contacted the Embassy immediately and asked them to stop the BBC repeating that broadcast; we did not want the BBC doing the Iraqis' work for them.

Initially, Saddam claimed that he had invaded Kuwait at the request of its oppressed people, but there was nobody cheering his troops on the streets. When he came to elect a puppet government, there were no Kuwaitis wanting to oblige. Eventually, he declared he was acting on behalf of the Palestinians, annexing the State and declaring it to be the 19th Province of Iraq.

Hundreds of Palestinians were then bussed down from Iraq and let loose in Kuwait. The ever helpful Bill Bowden warned us that an unruly Palestinian mob was advancing towards our area and he was concerned for our safety. He tried to come to rescue us, but was unable to get through, as the Iraqis had sealed off the area around the port. I dread to think what would have happened to us had the mob overrun our house but, luckily, it too was diverted around us by the Iraqis protecting the port. So our would-be captors became our unwitting protectors.

On Sunday, 5 August, three days into the invasion, we gathered as a family to read the Sunday Mass. The Entrance Antiphon – the Opening Prayer – was uncannily apt: *God, come to my help. Lord, quickly give me assistance. You are the one who helps me and sets me free: Lord, do not be long in coming.*

Almost miraculously, having finished reading the Mass, we looked out of our window to see columns of tanks and busloads of soldiers streaming out of Kuwait City past our house along the coast road. The Iraqis were leaving Kuwait – or so we thought!

In fact, these were the elite Republican Guard troops that had spearheaded the invasion. Their job done, they were now returning to Iraq, having handed over to a much larger occupying force comprising poorly trained, poorly equipped and poorly fed conscripts. If anything, these soldiers were likely to be more dangerous, being nervous, even more ill-disciplined and disillusioned. Many had been told that they were invading Israel, not their Arab neighbour. We felt it was only a matter of time before these wretched soldiers broke into our house to find food and water. How they might react when they found us, particularly Toni and the girls, did not bear contemplating.

On 7 August, we had just finished lunch when we heard a knock at the front door. Was this the moment we had been dreading? I told everyone to remain calm and keep out of sight and then went to peep through a spy hole we had created. To my amazement and relief, it was the Ambassador and Larry Banks, the Consul. They had come to our rescue and it was great to see them. But this was no time for a chat; we had to leave there and then.

We had already packed our essentials into our two vehicles – an old Range Rover and the boys' even older Mitsubishi Pajero – ready for just such an eventuality. We each had just one suitcase and, for some reason, Alex decided to fill his with our photograph albums rather than his own things; a very touching gesture that became all the more poignant later on.

Luckily, both cars started and we set off in convoy, the Ambassador leading with the Union Jack flying, and Larry bringing up the rear. We had barely covered 100 yards before we were stopped and arrested. With armed soldiers for company, we were now ordered to drive to Shuwaikh Port, a stone's throw from our house, which was now the headquarters of the Iraqi troops in the area. Years later, Zoë told me that this was the first time she had experienced real fear – she could taste and smell it. This was when she learnt what it was like to have a cold sweat.

The sergeant in my vehicle apologised for his actions. It was he who told me that he thought they were attacking Israel. He spoke perfect English and said he was an air conditioning technician by profession. When I asked him not to point his rifle at my daughters, he unloaded it and offered to give it to me! I told him that that might not be a good idea, as he could find himself in front of a firing squad. He was clearly as much a victim of this awful situation as we were.

On arrival at the port, we were taken to a room in the Port Authority building and held for about two hours whilst an Iraqi Lieutenant Colonel discussed our situation with the Ambassador. Michael Weston remained calm and repeatedly reminded the officer of the dire consequences he and his country would face if they continued to violate the international code of diplomatic immunity. The Colonel could see that the Ambassador and Larry were diplomats, but the rest of us had no such stamp in our passports. Even worse, I had a Kuwait MoD stamp in mine. I heard him ask the Ambassador if I was the military attaché, to which the Ambassador responded by reminding him that Kuwait did not permit embassies to appoint military attachés. Eventually, our inquisitor went to seek his superior's advice and moments later a full colonel arrived and, with handshakes all round, he sent us on our way.

Our route back to the Embassy was strewn with wrecked and abandoned vehicles on streets bordered by bullet-riddled buildings. The saddest sight was the carnage around the walls of the Dasman Palace, where the Emir lived; burnt out armoured cars and other military vehicles and equipment bore testimony to the bravery of the Kuwaiti defenders, who may not have known that the Emir had made good his escape during the night.

Once inside the relative security of the Embassy grounds, we were filled with a tremendous sense of relief. After six tense days cooped up in our house, where the slightest noise or the accidental switching on of a light could have resulted in our capture, it was just wonderful to be able to stroll in the garden and, even better, to go for a swim.

However, we were soon jolted back into the real world. Toni and the children were taken to an Embassy house in the still unoccupied suburb of Mishref, whilst I was required to remain at the Embassy to help man the radio, etc. The Mishref house was home to an Embassy staff member, whose family was on holiday in England. He had now moved into the Embassy, where we shared a room.

I was unable to keep in direct contact with my Team from the Embassy, so Toni undertook this task. Either she or one of the children relayed messages to and from me by radio. We had to observe strict radio procedure and there were no 'personal touches' which, under the circumstances, was quite hard for the children, as a comment in Toni's diary note shows:

> *Alex was on radio watch when the Bahraini Ambassador was trying to contact the diplomat who was now in the Embassy building. Alex contacted the Embassy and thinks it was Bruce answering – all in strict radio procedure, no wastage of time or even a quick "Hello".*

After spending three nights in the Embassy, I was allowed to rejoin my family, mainly to reduce demands on the diminishing food supplies in the Embassy. However, I was still required to work at the Embassy daily, which entailed a rather risky two-way journey through Iraqi roadblocks and patrols. I packed an overnight bag of essentials in case of capture and, driving a car with diplomatic plates, tried to look confident as I passed through the roadblocks.

I was also able to visit all the Team locations on one occasion to try to boost morale and, indeed, had my own morale lifted by the tremendous spirit displayed by everyone. They were, of course, frustrated, even annoyed, that 'nobody had seen this coming' and were naturally concerned about the future. However, they were unbowed. Indeed, in one complex the wives had organised a 'school' to keep the children occupied – true British grit!

As I drove through Kuwait, I was amazed to see convoys of trucks stacked to the gunwales with looted furniture and white goods – mainly fridges, freezers and air conditioning units – heading for Iraq. Kuwait was being sacked. The most gruesome sight I saw was the body of a man hanging from the extended jib of a mobile crane.

I almost came unstuck one morning when an Iraqi soldier at a roadblock tried to stop me on my way into the Embassy. I gave him a friendly wave and drove on in the hopes that he would see my Corps Diplomatique (CD) plates and realise his 'mistake'. I reported the incident when I arrived at the Embassy and the Ambassador said that I should not have been driving a CD-plated car; I was not a diplomat and, therefore, did not possess a diplomatic ID card. Given my true identity, an embarrassing diplomatic incident would erupt if I were caught masquerading as a diplomat.

From then on, I had to travel as a passenger in a CD-plated car driven by a diplomat. If we were ever stopped, I would, of course, have been arrested and taken hostage, but at least now I could not be accused of impersonating a diplomat.

During this time, two seemingly quite innocuous incidents highlighted the difference between the position of a diplomat and my own situation. First, whilst returning home one day, my colleague noticed that his car was low on fuel and wanted to stop at the next garage to fill up. I objected, explaining that Iraqi soldiers were stationed at every garage to check on people and I would be taken hostage. On another occasion, as we approached my house I noticed an Iraqi patrol moving down the street towards us. I urged him not to stop but to drive on past, otherwise not only I but also my family would be endangered. In neither case did he seem aware of what it meant to be a non-diplomat in this hostile environment. I got the impression that he felt I was being over cautious – perhaps even cowardly.

However, on another occasion, when the Ambassador had required us to stay quite late at the Embassy, Larry Banks, the Consul, and I had to risk returning home in the dark during the night curfew. This was quite unnerving, especially as we had to make our way past some Iraqi soldiers guarding the burned out wreck of a tank transporter that had been attacked by the Kuwaiti resistance. In the dark, would inexperienced, trigger-happy soldiers wait to see our CD plates before opening fire? Larry Banks reported the incident to the Ambassador when we returned next morning and he ruled that nobody should travel during curfew again.

For the first few days, life in Mishref was really quite relaxed. There seemed to be no Iraqi presence in the area and we were able to walk relatively safely across a stretch of open sand to visit friends, including other members of the Team. This enabled us to break up the day and, more importantly, to redistribute food supplies. Each area also boasted a Co-op and, initially, we were able to buy essentials at the Mishref store. However, our financial resources were limited to the cash in our possession at the start of the invasion; the banks remained closed and there were no other means of obtaining more money.

In the end, a lack of money was immaterial as, to prevent the movement of people within Kuwait, the Iraqis ordered Co-ops only to serve people from their area. Our ID cards showed that we lived in Shuwaikh and so now we found it impossible to purchase items at the Mishref store, and even risked being reported to the Iraqis by the increasingly more frightened manager. Our garden, however, boasted two date palms and the fruit was ripe for picking in August. We were therefore able to augment our rations quite substantially at the cost of a few beads of sweat.

Our relatively carefree existence in Mishref was short-lived. As the Iraqi Army's numbers swelled, its soldiers spread out across the city and its suburbs. The first hint of things to come was when an Indian saw our boys walking back across the sandy wasteland to our house and warned them that he had seen Iraqi soldiers "looking for white faces" in the area. Next, the Iraqis set up checkpoints at key facilities, such as Co-ops and fuel stations. On 14 August, they gave notice that, as Kuwait was now part of Iraq, all embassies were to close by 24 August, after which date diplomats in Kuwait would lose their diplomatic status.

Meanwhile, a number of people, mainly Kuwaitis, had taken fate by the horns and tried to escape across the desert into Saudi Arabia. This was a dangerous gamble as not only had escapees to evade the Iraqis, but they also had to contend with the searing heat of the Kuwaiti summer, when midday temperatures could exceed 50°C.

In the days immediately following the invasion, the advice from Western governments was for all Western nationals to stay put. As far as the BLT was concerned, the Ambassador made it clear that this was an order and not an option, lest we gave Saddam Hussein a propaganda coup if a serviceman were to be captured on the Saudi border. However, as Iraq's grip on Kuwait began to tighten, Saddam's policy of taking hostages, coupled with the threat of Embassy closures, caused this order to be withdrawn and it now became a matter of personal choice. But by this stage the border with Saudi Arabia, which had been reasonably permeable in the early days, was more closely guarded. In addition, Saddam had warned that anyone trying to escape risked being shot. Staying put was now the safer option.

We knew the southern desert quite well and had two 4x4 vehicles at our disposal. While escape was still a realistic proposition, my family had their opportunities. But, as Toni commented in her diary:

> Bedu *are helping, but in no way can we do that* [escape] *and leave the Team behind.'*

On 14 August, friends of ours, well-versed with the desert, planned to escape and asked if Alex and Rorie would like to join them. Again, Toni's diary note highlights our dilemma:

> *We would love to tell the boys to take their chance, but what about the morale of our people?*

As this was the school holidays, almost all members of our Team were accompanied by their children, and very few families had a 4x4 vehicle. Later, once we were 'permitted' to escape, Toni wrote:

> *Friends of ours are making a dash for the Saudi border; we've talked about it, too, but Bruce is still responsible for over 100 people,*

including a very pregnant wife, small children and even babies. We hope our friends make it.

With Iraq's threat of stripping diplomats in Kuwait of their diplomatic immunity after 24 August, the Ambassador arranged for all Embassy dependants and non-essential staff to leave Kuwait for Baghdad by road early on the morning of 16 August. The BLT families, who had been evacuated from IBI Camp and housed in the Kuwait International Hotel, were included in the party; they numbered 73 wives and children. The plan was to drive in convoy with an Embassy vehicle equipped with radio at the head and tail to maintain control. With a total of 29 vehicles in the convoy, this was a truly daunting undertaking, albeit the Iraqis had guaranteed to escort and protect the convoy, which, I was assured later, they did as best they could.

Dale Millar, a young REME captain, and I went to the Embassy, driving a CD-plated car, to try to reassure our travelling families and bid them farewell. I also briefed the convoy commander – an Embassy official – and some of the drivers on the basics of convoy procedure, such as flashing headlights in the event of a breakdown and stopping at regular intervals to allow the convoy to close up. Of course, this all takes practice and they were facing the real thing, not a training exercise.

It was also distressing for our wives to see the Embassy vehicles loaded to the gunwales with personal belongings, sleeping bags and cool boxes, whilst all they had were the clothes they were wearing, plus a meagre packed lunch and one or two bottles of water donated by the Kuwait International Hotel.

When the convoy was lining up ready to depart, I noticed that all vehicles belonging to our IBI wives and their families were positioned behind the Embassy's vehicles. I therefore asked the convoy commander, who had a radio, to place the Embassy's only other radio vehicle at the rear so that it could communicate with him at the head of the convoy, thus giving him some measure of control. This he did, but as the convoy set off, this rear vehicle promptly started to overtake our wives' cars. I asked the radio operator beside me to tell the driver to get back to his station, but he refused, saying he was part of the Embassy and was going to the rear of the Embassy vehicles. I ordered the convoy commander to sort things out, but lost radio contact before discovering whether he had been able to do so.

Late next day we received the welcome news of the convoy's safe arrival in Baghdad. The journey had taken 26 gruelling hours – a truly horrendous experience. We heard later that chivalry had deserted the Embassy personnel when the convoy halted in a car park for about three hours during the night for the drivers to get some rest. The Embassy families wrapped themselves up in warm clothing, ignoring the plight of our poor families, who were left to shiver in the sweat-soaked lightweight clothes they were wearing. Understandably, they were not impressed.

When the convoy finally reached Baghdad, the Embassy personnel were directed to the British Embassy, whilst our families were taken to the Mansour Melia Hotel, where they were now effectively hostages. This was another morale-sapping blow; rightly or wrongly, they had assumed that they would be re-united with their husbands. The whole experience was yet another example of the manner in which we were disadvantaged by not having the minimum level of diplomatic protection.

Just before the night curfew on 16 August, the day the Embassy convoy departed, the Iraqis ordered all foreign nationals still in Kuwait to report to named hotels. British nationals were to report to the Regency Palace Hotel. The advice from the Embassy was to ignore the order, unless or until the Embassy was forced to close. Toni's diary note next morning sums up our situation:

> *With the sinister news that they* [the Iraqis] *are still trying to round up US and British nationals, we've now been advised to lie low.*

In effect, we were now confined to the house, apart from the times I was called into the Embassy, when I was a passenger in a CD-plated car.

In an effort to protect the true identity of the Team members still in hiding, the Embassy agreed to issue us with emergency passports which, crucially, did not bear a Kuwait MoD stamp. These were distributed, at some personal risk, on 18 August by Dale Millar, who was driven to the various locations by an Embassy official in a CD-plated car.

The British government, along with a number of other countries including the United States and France, decided to defy the Iraqi order to close their embassies. Larry Banks volunteered to remain in the building with the Ambassador. The rest of the British staff left for Baghdad in a second road convoy, which departed on 22 August.

At one point it was thought that the BLT members and their families still in hiding in Kuwait might be permitted to join this convoy, but the Iraqis made it clear that only diplomatic personnel would be allowed to travel. We took the opportunity to write letters home for Embassy friends to post either in Baghdad, or when safely back in the UK, to give family some reassurance that we were safe and well.

The day before the convoy set off, a group of Palestinians, headed by the Embassy's 'Mr Fix It', Mussalim, arrived unannounced to pack up the house we were living in. It was Embassy property, even the TV and video, our only sources of entertainment. We were left with the furniture and virtually nothing else. Once the boxes had been packed and stowed in the sitting room, the packers left. We managed to break into the maid's room (she had left before the invasion and was obviously not coming back) where we found some plates and cooking utensils.

Toni wrote in her diary:

It's hard to see a house being packed up – all the little luxuries taken away – when we know we've lost all of ours. Larry Banks did go back to our house but the whole place had been ransacked – an unbelievable mess. I felt sick and tearful for a few minutes – and then realised I was just as materialistic as the next person. It's not so much the expensive equipment, but things like school projects that so much work went into. We knew this could happen, but now it's a reality.

At 9.00 p.m. that evening we were given the fright of our lives when the door bell rang rather insistently. We thought our time had come, but it was the packers back to collect the boxes! I wanted to give them a piece of my mind, but had to bite my tongue; if we upset them, any one of them could have let the Iraqis know where we were. Any of them, that is, except Mussalim, who was utterly loyal. Clearly, if you are able to live and move around relatively freely, like these packers, it must be very difficult to put yourself in the position of people living like hunted animals; the slightest unusual noise made our hearts skip a beat, let alone a ring at the door during curfew.

By this time the telephone line into the Embassy had been reconnected. We imagined that the only reason for this was to enable the Iraqis to listen in and trace callers. On 24 August they cut off the Embassy's water and electricity supplies. Life must have been very tough in the months that followed, but the Ambassador and Larry rose to the challenge. Larry, in particular, was very resourceful, even digging in the garden to find a source of water. He richly deserved the recognition he received when appointed OBE in the Gulf War Honours List.

We were all now isolated in our various hiding places scattered around Kuwait, unable to forage for food and other essentials. But then a magnificent thing happened, which highlighted all that is so marvellous about Islam. The Kuwaitis, whom it is fair to say we had not warmed to during our time in their country, came to our rescue. In our case, we were helped by two families – complete strangers – in our street. Apparently, during Friday prayers at the mosque on 16 August, the Imam had told the congregation that they were responsible for protecting Westerners in their area, because they were being treated outrageously by people of their faith. The locals had voted 100 Kuwaiti Dinars (approximately £200) per week of their own money to supply people in their area with the essentials.

Our Area Committee was headed by Abu Saad (not his real name). He was responsible for such things as security, refuse disposal, food re-supply to the Co-op and to locals in hiding, and also the distribution of water to houses without a mains supply. The man specifically tasked with helping us was Abu Loay (again, not his real name). He told me that the Mishref committee included a fundamentalist, who could have vetoed any decision to help 'infidels', but he had chosen to vote in support of the proposal. Abu Loay was an oil industry executive by profession. A middle-aged man, he had a large family and eight of his children were still living at home. By assisting us, both he and Abu Saad, together with their families, were risking their lives.

In another demonstration of kindness, the Danish and Dutch Embassies each donated a TV and video recorder to a BLT group hiding nearby, to replace those taken by our Embassy. Dale Millar, at considerable risk to himself, brought the second TV and video recorder round to us. So we could now watch videos and, more importantly, the Iraqi news.

We survived quite well through the rest of August and into September, although we all lost a lot of weight as we eked out our food supplies. We were, however, unable to go outside and lived indoors with the shutters closed on all the windows. During the day, we were able to use a single light in the sitting room, which was in the middle of the house – I had checked that the strength of the sun masked any light escaping from within the building. However, as evening approached, the light had to be switched off.

The house had internal stairs up to its flat roof, which was bordered by a low wall. Thus we were able to crawl out and lie on the roof for a few minutes during the day to get some fresh air and sun. In the early days, we also went out onto the roof after dark to watch the night sky being lit up by tracer bullets and flares. There was a special show of defiance on the night of 2 September, exactly one month after the invasion, when thousands of people shouted defiantly from the roof tops, whilst others fired their weapons into the night sky.

To keep fit, we all had our own daily exercise routines; the boys would do press-ups and lift weights (anything that came to hand) whilst Toni and I used to walk briskly around the house and up and down the stairs for about 30 minutes.

On 29 August, the Iraqis entered the building containing the largest concentration of BLT members and their families still in hiding – 31 people altogether, including the wife who was now over eight months pregnant. She and her husband must have been worried stiff throughout their time in hiding and, especially, at the moment of capture. Nevertheless, they remained positive and cheerful. In the event, she was treated well by the Iraqis and gave birth to a son on 12 September; what an amazing start to a new life!

At the beginning of September, Saddam took everyone by surprise by announcing the release of all women and children trapped in Kuwait. In response, on 3 September, the British Embassy in Baghdad made arrangements for a convoy of buses to evacuate the British nationals from the Emirate. The plan was to move them to Baghdad, from where they would be flown back to the UK, via Jordan. The buses were to depart from the Sultan Centre, Kuwait's main shopping mall, early on 4 September. All those wanting to travel would have to reach the meeting point by 5.00 a.m. This meant travelling during the curfew. We had but a few hours to make our plans.

Alex was duty cook on Sunday, 2 September, the day of Saddam's announcement. Anticipating that the family might soon be separated, he wanted a special meal. It so happened that our Kuwaiti neighbours had kindly brought us a welcome resupply of food that day – a couple of chickens, bread, apples, oranges and potatoes. Instead of eating in the kitchen, Alex laid the dining room table, complete with a white tablecloth (a bed sheet) and a couple of candles. Toni found a packet of stuffing in the larder and the girls made bread sauce by crumbling bread with their fingers – we had no kitchen utensils apart from a knife, a wooden spoon and a couple of pans. Nevertheless, we dined on roast chicken and roast potatoes, followed by jelly topped with instant whipped cream, all washed down with a bottle of the Diplomat's wine.

We called the event 'Our Last Supper'. Little did we know at the time just how chillingly apt this title was to be.

As far as Saddam's amnesty was concerned, our prime consideration was for the safety of Alex and Rorie, who were aged 19 and 18 respectively. Would the Iraqis regard them as children, or as adult males? If they were judged to be the latter, they would be taken as hostages. I consulted Abu Loay and Abu Saad, who both felt that the boys were in danger of being taken hostage. We discussed the situation as a family. I knew Toni would fight to protect our sons, but when you are all effectively prisoners, there is only so much you can do. We had settled into quite a steady routine in Mishref, and this seemed to be an unnecessary risk. Both the boys were old enough to vote and so deserved their own say. In the event, they elected to remain behind with me. As a result of what happened later, I will always regret not having been more forceful. Sometimes hindsight can be merciless in its clarity.

The next immediate problem was how to get Toni and the girls to the rendezvous which was several miles from our hideout. We decided that she should drive out with the girls in our car in the hope that the Iraqis, who we assumed would know of their release, would either allow them to pass or escort them to the agreed meeting point. However, John Stirling, one of another group of Team members hiding out nearby, managed to acquire a bus to take our families from Mishref to the Sultan Centre. This seemed a much better solution. I felt, however, that the Iraqis might be watching the bus and learn where everyone was hiding. I therefore arranged for us to meet the bus at a rendezvous away from our house.

Next door to us was a deserted, partly-built house, which bordered the waste ground at the end of our street. Just after 4.00 a.m. next morning, 4 September, we made our way to this house, where we hid until we saw the lights of the bus. Then we said our farewells to Toni, Hannah, Zoë and her friend Vanessa, before they went out into the open to hail the bus. To the bus driver, they appeared to be on their own and could have come from anywhere in the area. When the bus departed the boys and I remained hidden until we were sure that the coast was clear. We then returned home, still under cover of darkness. Mission accomplished! It felt very strange and lonely without Toni and the girls, but we were very relieved that they were being freed. I was especially relieved about Vanessa; after all, she was someone else's daughter. Her family must have been beside themselves with worry.

The British Vice Consul was a very dignified Indian called Mr Rajagopalan. Because of his nationality he was able to move fairly freely around Kuwait City. Both he and his wife went to the Sultan Centre and visited every bus to record the names of all the British 'refugees' and then forwarded this information to the British Embassy in Baghdad.

Mussalim, the Palestinian 'Mr Fix It', not only travelled up on the convoy to Baghdad to make sure everyone got there safely, he scoured Kuwait City beforehand to buy as much bread as he could to help feed them.

The girls' journey to Baghdad was not as arduous as that undertaken by the families on 16 August, but it was no picnic either, as the following extracts from Toni's diary confirm:

> *On the bus at 4.30 a.m. and off into the night. Stopped at a road block and asked to get out for the vehicle to be searched. I tried to explain in my basic Arabic that we were on our way to join a British convoy at the Sultan Centre. The soldiers were in complete ignorance of the fact that the convoy had been arranged with Iraqi approval. Reached the RV (Sultan Centre) at 5.10 a.m. No buses! At 7.30 a.m. a big lorry turned up for the luggage! What luggage? Buses, nine in all, arrived later...*
> *We didn't start moving until 10.30 a.m. How sad to drive through Kuwait – a dead city, shops shuttered, very few cars, wrecks of others strewn everywhere. Anything of value is being transported to Baghdad – evidence all the way along the route – convoys of lorries and pick-up trucks loaded with ACs, fridges, etc. Rubbish everywhere – Kuwait will soon become just like Iraq – dirty, squalid and unkempt.*
> *Our bus nearly didn't make it up the Mutla Ridge – luckily it's the only hill on the entire journey! Long wait at Safwan* [Kuwait border post] *but straight through at Abdali* [Iraq border post].
> *The other buses peeled off for Baghdad, but ours went shooting on towards Basra on its own. We were rather worried, especially when we turned into a military site, but were told that we needed petrol. We caught up with the other buses just before reaching Nasiriyah, where we stopped at a roadside café. Cans of drink cost 1.5 KD each (about £3)! We managed to get some water. The loos were predictably awful and swimming in filthy water, but we had no other option. We reached Baghdad about 10.30 p.m., but then another night-*

mare started – we went round and round Baghdad visiting hotels, but there were no rooms available for us (had our first glimpse of reporters at the Sheraton). Eventually, someone from the Embassy appeared and told us we were to go to the Palestine Hotel (we had already been turned away from there). We arrived at the hotel to be 'greeted' by the Press. Allocated rooms straightaway, but the three girls only had two beds between them. Too late for dinner, but got something to eat about an hour later. Two Englishmen – complete strangers – thrust bundles of notes into our hands! Quite overwhelming!

One of the half-British boys on our bus has asked to return to Kuwait to celebrate his ninth birthday – how sad. He and his brother are travelling unaccompanied; they were put on the bus in Kuwait by their Lebanese father and their mother lives in Scotland. We managed to get a cake for him and the young made him a card. Someone also had some Smarties and we all sang 'Happy Birthday' to him!

Knowing that Toni and the girls had now departed, Kuwaiti women in our street – complete strangers – brought delicious, cooked meals to our house. What kindness. They must have sensed that the boys and I were not very adept in the culinary department. This lasted only a couple of days, as the security situation worsened, but it bought us valuable time to read through the hurried recipe notes left by Toni. As food was so short, we could not afford to make mistakes – we simply *had* to eat what we cooked.

For Toni and the girls, the psychological impact of leaving Kuwait whilst the boys and I remained there in hiding was far greater than the physical ordeal of their horrendous bus journey to Baghdad. When the time came for them to leave Baghdad, on 6 September, this sense of 'desertion' intensified tenfold, as Toni's diary note explains:

> *None of us wanted to leave Kuwait; we had seen it through together, and now we're not ready to leave Baghdad – the girls are quite tearful about leaving – the last tenuous thread with 'D'* [Bruce] *and the boys gone.*

They flew in a dilapidated Iraqi jet from Baghdad to Queen Alia International Airport, Amman, Jordan, where a British Airways jumbo jet, with a volunteer crew, was waiting to fly our loved ones home. Throughout this emotional flight they were treated with the utmost sensitivity and kindness by the cabin crew. At 4.00 a.m. on 7 September they touched down at Gatwick and fell into the loving arms of waiting friends and relatives.

They found it strange to be truly free again and it took time for them all to adjust – the slightest sudden or unusual sound caused them to jump. Although the new academic year had already started, the girls remained with Toni for a week before returning to school.

Meanwhile, in Kuwait, the boys and I quickly settled back into our routine. However, it was not long before we were given a sharp reminder about the seriousness of our situation. On 10 September, six days after the departure of Toni and the girls, my worst fears about the bus were realised. Hearing a commotion outside, I looked through the shutters to see Iraqi soldiers swarming all over the unfinished house next door. A truck then drove into our street and a number of soldiers got out. To my dismay, I saw that John Stirling and Dale Millar were with them. They had been arrested. Dale was clearly being asked if he knew where we were, but he bravely shook his head, opened his arms and pointed to the waste ground beyond. The person I assumed to be the bus driver nodded in agreement. After what seemed an age, the truck departed, with John and Dale aboard. Once again, I was left feeling utterly impotent.

Next day, when I started my morning calls by telephoning my Deputy

Commander, Andy Jones, he opened the conversation by telling me he had 'visitors' and advised me to ring off – he and his son, Ian had been found and arrested. There were now just nine Team members and two dependants, Alex and Rorie, left in hiding.

The Iraqis, no doubt surprised at the number of foreign women and children who had come out of hiding, intensified the search for their men folk. Abu Saad and Abu Loay kept us informed of the worsening situation. Patrols and snap roadblocks were now more frequent and helicopter activity over the city had also increased – the net was tightening. Search teams were about 20-strong, comprising a mix of uniformed soldiers, armed with AK-47s, machine guns and RPG-7 anti-tank rocket launchers, plus a few 'soldiers' from the Popular People's Army of Free Kuwait (PPA) who wore civilian Arab dress – the dishdasha – and carried AK-47s. The PPA was made up of Arabs living in Kuwait who chose to side with Iraq. They were drawn almost entirely from the Palestinian community.

Soon we were advised to stop crawling out onto the roof due to the number of helicopters flying overhead. Next, we were advised to make as little noise as possible. We moved the phone into the kitchen, which was at the back of the house, to reduce the chance of anyone in the street hearing it ringing. We talked in whispers and had to take particular care not to clatter pots, cooking utensils and cutlery. When washing up, we took one item at a time and then gently laid it on a towel to deaden the inevitable sound. We kept flushing the loo to a minimum and always checked the street and garden from behind the shuttered windows before pulling the chain.

The front of the house was, in effect, a large sun room with the three outside walls, including the one incorporating the front door, comprised almost entirely of wall-to-ceiling tinted glass windows. Occupants in the room had no difficulty looking out, but were given some privacy from people looking in from the street. However, it was still possible to detect movement and, peering in with hands cupped against the glass, the scene inside was absolutely clear. Therefore, not only did we decide not to enter this room, but we put the chairs up on the table and stacked a lot of boxes on the floor to give the impression that the house had been packed up and vacated by the occupants.

One potential 'give away', however, melted our hearts. A beautiful cat had turned up at the kitchen door a day or two after we had moved in. Obviously its owner had left and, quite unable to fend for itself like the numerous feral cats, it was now starving. The children had started feeding it before I rejoined them after my stay in the Embassy and it now depended on us for its survival. After Toni and the girls departed, I considered leaving the cat to its own devices, as I predicted that the Iraqis would intensify their search for those of us in hiding. However, Rorie said that he had promised Zoë that he would look after this defenceless animal. I argued that if the Iraqis saw a well fed cat in our garden they might be tempted to investigate. This cut no ice; a promise was a promise and that was that. I relented – there was enough tension in the house as it was. Perhaps I gave the Iraqis more credit than they deserved as, although we shared our food with the cat, it never attracted unwanted attention.

The Iraqis then changed their search tactics, sealing off an area and systematically breaking into each house, one by one, in search of foreigners or Kuwaiti resistance fighters. Clearly, this spelt the beginning of the end for all of us. But then Lady Luck intervened. On 14 September, during a systematic search in the area adjacent to ours, the Iraqis broke into a French Embassy residence and seized the four senior French diplomats living there.

Like many foreign governments, the French had defied the ban to close their Embassy in Kuwait. Moreover, France was looked upon more favourably by Iraq than most other countries, as its government was taking a more moderate line on how best to resolve the crisis. After this outrage, however, President Mitterrand committed France fully to the international community's efforts to force Iraq out of Kuwait, even to the extent of providing additional troops to join the Coalition, and calling upon the United Nations to strengthen its international sanctions regime against Iraq by including an air embargo.

Apparently, as a direct consequence of this blunder, Iraqi forces no longer broke into properties unless they were absolutely sure about the identity of the occupants. Just occasionally, soldiers would come into our garden and rattle the front door and the ground floor windows, but we kept quiet and out of sight and eventually they would leave.

They also introduced another tactic which, initially, proved successful. Knowing that we were keeping in touch with one another by telephone, they would ring numbers at random to see if a foreigner answered, whereupon a search team would descend upon the unfortunate occupants. We and our civilian contacts, including Abu Loay and Abu Saad, introduced a 'telephone call code' devised by John Stirling. When making a call, we would dial the number and allow it to ring three times and then replace the receiver before lifting it again and redialling immediately. When answering a call, we would pause to allow the caller to speak first. This worked well and may well have saved us – I once received several suspicious calls in a single day, all of which I ignored, thanks to the ring code.

With the Kuwaiti resistance active after dark, the urgent crackle of small arms fire and the thunder of occasional explosions filled the night air. Whilst this made sleep difficult, it prevented the Iraqis from conducting search operations. Therefore, as soon as the mosque sounded the evening call for prayer, we were able to relax a little until first light next morning, when we had to be fully alert again. Thus, we lived from day to day, or hour to hour, even less when soldiers searching our area entered our garden.

Abu Loay and Abu Saad still supported us, but it was getting ever more difficult and dangerous for them to do so. On one occasion, a search party entered our garden only minutes after a food delivery from them.

Abu Loay had already told us of a number of atrocities; two young lads in our area shot in front of their parents and siblings for distributing anti-Saddam posters, and two Co-op managers shot in front of their stores for refusing to remove pictures of the Emir and the Crown Prince from their offices.

On 3 October, 17 Kuwaitis in our area, Mishref, were rounded up and shot in front of their families, on suspicion of being connected with the resistance. Three of these men were doctors, including a friend of Abu Loay, whose only 'crime' was to have treated injured Kuwaitis. It now seemed inevitable that sooner or later the same fate would befall Abu Loay and Abu Saad, as well as their families, if they continued to help us.

Ali Hassan al-Majid, dubbed Chemical Ali by the Kurds for ordering the gassing of 7,000 Kurdish citizens in Halabja in 1988, was now the Governor of Iraq's 19th Province – Kuwait. His remit was to crush the resistance. He made little attempt to find actual resistance fighters, but would simply select and execute a number of men at random wherever an attack had occurred. Now, with Chemical Ali in charge, the frequency and severity of reprisals for anyone acting against Iraqi interests intensified disproportionately. For example, Abu Loay told us that the resistance had detonated a bomb at the Kuwait International Hotel, which resulted in several prominent Iraqis being killed or injured. The Iraqis responded by rounding up between 100-120 men and youths from all over Kuwait, and shot them in twos and threes in front of every Co-op in the Emirate. This act was so barbaric that it prompted Kuwait's Minister of Planning, Sulaiman Al-Mutawa, who had fled the Emirate, to go on the radio to urge the resistance to cease their activities, as they were endangering the lives of innocent Kuwaitis. Ali Hassan al-Majid was close to achieving his aim, but the resistance remained active, albeit at a less intense level.

With the pressure mounting, Abu Loay clearly wanted to be relieved of this awful burden, but was reluctant to abandon what he considered to be his religious duty of care. I reassured him that, thanks to him and Abu Saad, we had enough food to last out for several weeks. They had done more than enough to help us, but should now look after themselves and their families. It was then that he said that the Imam had told them to treat us as family. I persuaded him that he and his family had exceeded their obligations in this regard, especially given the risks they were now running. Protecting us from being taken hostage simply did not justify them risking their lives. He seemed truly grateful. We hugged and said our farewells.

From then on we had to tighten up our food rationing to eke out our supplies for as long as possible. A typical daily intake was a cup of tea and a few dates for breakfast, a meagre meal at lunch of, for example, a tomato, a small piece of cucumber and a two-egg omelette shared between us. To conserve our stock of powdered milk, we had to use more and more water in the omelette mix. Eventually, this prevented the omelettes from forming properly and, due to their unappetising appearance, we christened them 'vomlettes'. We enjoyed another snack of tea, reusing old teabags, and dates at 5.00 p.m. Supper was our main meal and typically comprised a teacup-full of rice between us and a small amount of meat. For example, a scrawny Kuwaiti chicken – about the size of a bantam – had to last for two or three meals. We would then boil up the bones to make soup for a further two meals. Although we all lost weight, we remained remarkably fit and healthy.

The meals were just part of a strict daily routine. Other activities included set times for the twice-daily telephone calls to check on our contacts, discussion periods designed to take stock and ease concerns, TV and radio news bulletins, rest periods and, importantly, daily gentle physical exercise sessions.

After we had relieved Abu Loay of his burden of supporting us, we had the occasional telephone call, but very soon we had no further contact with our two Kuwaiti 'guardian angels'. They had been outstanding in their efforts to assist us and we shall be forever in their debt.

Towards the end of September, flocks of European Bee-eaters arrived, as usual, in Kuwait en-route to their wintering grounds in sub-Saharan Africa. Their brilliant flashes of colour and constant cheerful chattering seemed to bring a sense of normality to our chaotic situation.

By this stage, the BBC World Service had introduced a 15-minute slot called Gulf Link, broadcasting recorded messages from loved ones at home to boost the morale of people in hiding in Kuwait. The programme was transmitted every evening at 7.30 p.m. and repeated the following morning at 7.30 a.m. Dependants with loved ones trapped in Kuwait were allowed 30 seconds of air time to pass on messages. This initiative proved so popular that the programme was increased, first to 30 minutes and then 45 minutes. Like most people, we listened to both transmissions every day. This was the only contact we had with our families but, of course, it was only 'one-way'; we had no way of letting them know how we were faring. We knew from the news that our loved ones were safely back home, but on Toni's birthday, 25 September, we heard her own voice on the airways – a wonderfully uplifting experience.

Access to this facility had to be shared, but we heard quite regularly from Toni over the coming weeks. She and the girls even went up to Bush House in London to record a message that was broadcast on 18 October, our 21st wedding anniversary. It was so wonderful to hear their voices. By now Toni had joined a helpline, set up in the MoD by members of the Team and their wives who had been on leave at the time of the invasion.

Days passed with no apparent Iraqi activity and then, without warning, the area would swarm with Iraqi and PPA soldiers. We could never, therefore, allow our guard to slip for a moment. Then, on 21 October, when I went to make my routine morning phone calls, I found the line was dead. Hoping that this was just a temporary fault, I tried again later, but the line was still dead. Later that morning we heard noises outside. Peering through the slats in the shutters we saw that the street was crawling with soldiers.

A group entered our garden and rattled our windows and doors, shouting to be let in. The situation reminded me of the way beaters try to flush out game ahead of the waiting guns; the wise bird, or animal, stays put. We did likewise, but I advised everyone not to run if the soldiers broke into the house and found us, as in their agitated, excitable mood they were likely to shoot first and ask questions later. We just hoped that the order not to break into properties still applied and that if they peered into the front room they would assume the house had been packed up and deserted by its occupants. After what seemed an age, the soldiers moved on. We endured this experience several more times on this and the next day.

I occasionally checked the phone, but the line remained dead until the evening of 22 October when, to my relief, I found we had been reconnected. I immediately contacted the Embassy to let the Ambassador know we were safe and to explain why we had been out of contact for the past 48 hours. He was delighted to hear from me because he had been trying to contact me since the previous afternoon to tell me that Saddam Hussein had agreed to allow Alex and Rorie to leave Kuwait and travel back to the UK.

Alex was an undergraduate at Balliol College, Oxford, and when the Master of Balliol, Dr Baruch Blumberg, heard that Edward Heath, a graduate of the College, was about to go to Baghdad to try to negotiate the release of certain hostages, he contacted Toni to check if he could ask for Alex's name to be included. Thinking both as an Army wife as well as a mother, Toni told him that Alex had a brother, Rorie, who had also been accepted for a place at Oxford (St Edmund Hall). Whilst she would be delighted if her sons could be set free, Toni stressed that Dr Blumberg should first contact the MoD to seek approval, as the presence of British military personnel and their dependants in hiding in Kuwait was something that had to be kept secret. In the event, the MoD gave its approval and Edward Heath successfully secured the boys' release. However, they had to get to Baghdad before Edward Heath's plane left on the evening of 23 October – less than 24 hours away.

It was arranged for Mr Rajagopolin, the Vice Consul, to break the curfew and come into our street in an hour's time. He would take the boys to the Regency Palace Hotel, where the Iraqis were to assume responsibility for getting the boys to Baghdad.

The boys had nothing but their washing kit to pack – Alex gave me the book he was reading at the time, as he said I would enjoy it and he could get another copy back home. As the pick-up time approached, we all crept out of the back door and made our way to the front gate. There we crouched until we heard a car coming up the street. It stopped, as planned, by the unfinished house and I peered out to check that it was a single saloon car and that there were no soldiers about. Seeing the coast was clear, I bid the boys a fond farewell and watched them get safely into the car and head off into the night.

About an hour later, Alex rang quickly to say they had arrived safely and were being well looked after. They were to leave for Baghdad next morning. He said he had to be brief and rang off. I understood why – unwelcome ears were probably listening in and also trying to locate my position.

Alex telephoned again next morning to say they had had a good night and an even better breakfast! They were just about to leave for the airport. I wished them God's speed. He rang again just after midday to say he and Rorie were now safely at the airport after a long delay leaving the hotel.

I had just finished supper and I was about to make my evening calls when the phone rang. I was expecting the good news that the boys had arrived safely in Baghdad, especially when it was the Ambassador calling. However, he opened with the words, "Bruce, what is the worst thing you can imagine happening to you?" My heart sank. "We have been tricked and the boys have been taken hostage," I replied.

"Worse than that," came the response. I paused to take stock and then, almost unable to voice the words, I asked: "Has the plane crashed?"

"No," he replied, "but their car crashed on the way to the airport and I'm sorry to tell you that Alex is dead and Rorie is very badly injured."

Clutching at straws and not wanting to believe this horror story, I responded: "That's not possible! I spoke to Alex at the airport just after midday. He said they had arrived safely."

This confused the Ambassador. He didn't understand how Alex could have telephoned from the airport, but he was absolutely certain that his dreadful news was accurate. Mr Rajagopolin had been to the hospital, where the casualties had been taken.

I felt as if I had been hit by a wrecking ball. Completely and utterly numb, I started to wash up. My hands were working, but my mind was blank. I had been elated when the boys had been granted their freedom and my spirits had been lifted even higher when I received Alex's call from the airport. Now that the boys were there, I had thought, they would be fine and soon they would be winging their way back to England. Now, I had been thrown into the depths of despair.

Then I remembered an exercise during my basic training. We were drawing to the end of a forced march and were exhausted, wet and hungry. Breasting the brow of a hill, we saw the trucks waiting to take us back to camp. Our spirits lifted and there was a spring in our step as we strode the last few hundred yards. We weren't going to show our instructors that we were running on empty. Just before we reached the vehicles, they moved off and, in the blink of an eye, our morale was at rock bottom. Somehow we managed to rally and tap into hitherto unknown reserves. We found the trucks parked up and waiting for us just around the corner. We had passed the test and had learnt a valuable lesson. That's what I had to do now, albeit this was no exercise. There would be no happy ending.

About an hour later the Ambassador rang again. He told me that he was unable to do anything to help the boys as he was trapped in the

Embassy. Moreover, the Embassy in Baghdad could not assist either, at least not immediately. Therefore it had been decided that I was to come out of hiding. Mr Rajagopolin would meet me at the spot where he had collected the boys and take me to the hospital where they were.

All my instincts shrieked at me to go to the aid of my sons, especially Rorie, who was still alive. But where did my duty lie? My loyalties hopelessly torn now, I explained that I couldn't desert my post and leave my fellow Team members in the lurch unless authorised by the MoD. To my relief, the Ambassador assured me that the plan to come out of hiding had been approved by none other than the UK Secretary of State for Defence, Tom King.

I had only a few minutes before Mr Rajagopolin would arrive. My dilemma eliminated, I telephoned the one officer remaining in hiding, Major Ben Tyler, told him what had happened, and said I was now having to hand over command to him. He confirmed that he had all the contact numbers, expressed his sympathies and bade me farewell.

I have always cursed picking up the phone to speak to the Ambassador on that fateful evening of 22 October. Had the phone remained out of action until the next day, it would have been too late to release the boys to catch Edward Heath's plane. Fate is always coupled with 'if onlys'.

A sad and shaken Mr Rajagopolin met me. Alex had taken a summer job in the Embassy and had been working under Mr Rajagopolin in the Consulate section until just before the invasion.

Almost as soon as we had set off, we were stopped at a roadblock. We were both ordered out of the car by some very excitable soldiers. Mr Rajagopolin showed them his Indian passport and was released, but I had an emergency British passport. With the barrel of a rifle pressed against my left kidney, I was marched over to their patrol base and unceremoniously pushed into the back of a pick-up with a couple of guards for company. I was then driven to their headquarters. I remember being amazed at how close it was to our hideout – barely a three-minute walk away. On arrival, I was bundled out of the vehicle and marched into the building, again at gunpoint.

I must have painted a wretched picture. Thin and pale, in need of a haircut and scruffy – I was wearing a tee-shirt, crumpled cotton trousers and sandals. My only possession, my washing kit, was in a plastic Co-op carrier bag. Certainly, I looked nothing like a military figure, which was clearly to my advantage. But then I saw their headquarters; my Regimental sergeant major would have had a fit and my poor turnout didn't look too out of place here.

Having been processed, I was taken to the Regency Palace Hotel. The reception hall was full of Iraqi soldiers and armed people in white dishdashas, who I took to be *Mukhabarat* (secret police). I was led across to an officer seated behind a desk. He was a Lieutenant Colonel. A dignified man with a pleasant manner, he appeared genuinely upset by what had happened. He told me how courteous and correct the boys had been and how sad he was about the accident. Both were now in the Al Sabah hospital. Bearing the Emir's name, this was one of the main hospitals in Kuwait. In fairness, I did not have to fight to be taken there; he fully understood my need and readily agreed. Then, eyeing the room and choosing his moment, he said that, once I had seen my sons, I could go back into hiding and he would not come looking for me. I thanked him. He was probably not a professional soldier and I felt that, in happier times, we could perhaps have been friends.

Rumours that the Iraqis had ransacked Kuwait's hospitals were confirmed when I arrived at the Al Sabah. It had been stripped virtually bare. I was informed later that there was only one doctor and no anaesthetist on duty when Rorie and the other casualties were brought in. Rorie, who had fractured a number of vertebrae in his back and was initially paralysed, had been taken to x-ray by a Bangladeshi tea boy on his tea trolley.

Apparently, Alex had been taken to another hospital, but had not survived the accident. I was assured that arrangements would soon be made for me to see his body. Meanwhile, I was taken to see Rorie. It was now around midnight on 23 October – a date that will live forever in our family's memory. He was in one of a series of eight-bed bays in a large ward. Apart from his serious back injury, he looked remarkably unscathed, although his face was a picture of pain. The Iraqi driver, an army Lieutenant, who had escaped serious injury, was in the same bay, diagonally opposite Rorie. Although his reckless driving had devastated my family, I found it hard to hate him. Was he under orders to drive as he did, or was the car he was driving – a Mercedes looted from the Crown Prince's palace – simply too powerful for him?

Rorie told me that when Mr Rajagopolin handed Alex and him over to the Iraqis at the Regency Palace Hotel the previous evening, he had asked for permission to drive them to the airport himself. Although his request was refused, he returned to the hotel early the next morning, asked again and also volunteered to help them complete the necessary documentation. He was told brusquely that the boys were in Iraqi hands and his help was neither needed nor appreciated. Nevertheless, he remained at the hotel until the boys departed.

In reality, the Iraqis at the hotel didn't appear to know what to do with the boys and were so inefficient they missed their intended flight on the morning shuttle to Baghdad and were in danger of missing the afternoon shuttle by the time they set off for the airport.

When Alex and Rorie got into the back of the car they were unable to see out of the side or back windows, as the blinds had been drawn. When Alex moved to open his blind, he was warned sharply to leave it alone. Rorie went on to say that they had been taken on a circuitous route to Kuwait International Airport, probably to prevent them seeing the worst of the damage Iraq had wreaked on Kuwait. They were also travelling at breakneck speed and had several very near misses en-route to the airport. Terrified, the boys had looked to fasten their seatbelts, but none were fitted.

On arrival, Alex had been allowed to phone me. He had sounded calm and made no mention of their hair-raising journey. Within minutes of that call, however, they were told that they were at the wrong airport; the Iraqis were using the Ali Al Salem military airbase, some 25 miles away. This is what had led to the confusion when the Ambassador had told me that the boys had been involved in a fatal car accident *on the way to the airport.* Although they were now far too late to catch the second and last shuttle flight of the day, rather than returning to the hotel their panic-stricken Iraqi minders opted to attempt the impossible. Not knowing the way, they grabbed a Kuwaiti airport official and, once everyone was back in the car, they raced off. Less than five minutes later, and travelling at well over 100 miles per hour, they slammed into a vehicle joining the Ring Road. In addition to Alex, the Iraqi escort and the unfortunate Kuwaiti guide were killed. Only Rorie and the driver survived. Alex had been killed just a few minutes after making his phone call to me. His last words to me: "Don't worry about us 'D', we're fine. Good luck, 'D' – bye."

After being x-rayed, Rorie had been taken down to the ward on the bare metal tea trolley and left without any medical treatment or pain killers for about six hours. He was in terrible pain and paralysed, he thought permanently, from the waist down. He had been told that Alex was injured and had been taken to another hospital (all the injured had been taken to hospital in civilian cars whose drivers had stopped to help).

Once in the ward, an Iraqi dressed as a nurse, but clearly with no idea of nursing, had come and removed the rings off Rorie's fingers, including a gold signet ring bearing our family crest. He then took Rorie's cigarettes, lit one in front of him, but denied him one and refused his requests for painkillers. He and another Iraqi in plain clothes then proceeded to question Rorie: "Where were you hiding?" "Who has been protecting you?"

"Where is your father hiding?" "We can't treat you without your father's permission."

Rorie noticed that both men had pistols tucked into the waist bands of their trousers and assumed they were *Mukhabarat*. Despite his pain, terror and utter anxiety, he told them nothing. Instead he kept asking to contact the Embassy. His questioners took great pleasure in telling him that, "There is no British Embassy in Kuwait." He was left in no doubt that he was now on his own and needed to cooperate; nobody knew what had happened to him! But he didn't cooperate. Had he done so, Abu Loay and Abu Saad, together with their families, would almost certainly have lost their lives. For an 18-year-old lad straight out of school, in great pain and desperately needing help, this was nothing short of torture. The courage he displayed was amazing and left me feeling very humbled and proud.

After about six hours, a Filipino nurse had seized his moment whilst the two men were out of the room and given Rorie a dose of morphine. By the time this was wearing off, I had arrived on the scene.

Clearly, this tragic incident had been a hugely embarrassing one for the Iraqis. After all, Edward Heath was waiting for the boys to arrive in Baghdad in time to join him on Richard Branson's mercy flight home to the UK. Mr Heath and the British Embassy in Baghdad had initially been told there was a delay in the boys' arrival, then that there had been a slight accident, but that the boys had suffered only minor injuries. On hearing this, the mercy flight was fuelled and made ready to fly down to Kuwait to pick up the boys, but was refused clearance for the flight. It was only after Edward Heath had left Baghdad that the Iraqis came clean and informed the British Embassy about the full horror of what had occurred some eight hours earlier.

Meanwhile, back in England, it was half-term. Toni and the girls were staying with Toni's sister, Pip, and her family in the village of Cropredy, near Banbury. The BBC News at 6.00 p.m. on 23 October included an interview with Edward Heath, who talked about the 33 hostages he had been allowed to repatriate from Baghdad and of two others, "who have not yet arrived from Kuwait." Toni knew at once that these two people were Alex and Rorie. She telephoned the MoD, which confirmed her suspicions, but had no further information at that stage.

As the news began to filter in, so the MoD kept Toni informed. First, she was told that there had been a slight accident, but that the boys were fine and had been taken back to the hotel; later that one boy was in hospital with slight bruising; then, at 10.30 p.m., that the accident had been more serious and that the driver had been killed. It was only when the phone rang at 6.30 a.m. next morning that Toni received the numbing news that Alex was dead and Rorie seriously injured.

Breaking the news to Hannah and Zoë was dreadful. The children were all very close and there were only five years between them. Alex was the eldest and regarded as their 'leader', and Rorie was equally loved. Telling our two recently widowed mothers was almost as traumatic. Both had played such a full part in looking after the children on half-terms and exeats whilst we were abroad. Indeed, my poor mother suffered a stroke three days after receiving this awful news.

During the early hours of 4 September, the day Toni and the girls left Kuwait, Alex had written a letter to his school friend, Stefan Reynolds, for Toni to post on her arrival in the UK. Alex had spent a lot of time with the Reynolds whilst we were abroad and was regarded very much as part of their family. Their elder daughter, Olivia, was also a close friend. On hearing the tragic news of his death, the family was so moved that Mr Reynolds wrote to *The Times* newspaper, enclosing extracts from the letter Alex had written to Stefan. I believe his letter displays a sense of honour not always associated with young university undergraduates and I am proud to include extracts from it here:

4 September 1990

Dear Stephan [Stefan],

With luck my mother and sisters will have made it to England and you will be reading this...

My mother woke me at 6.00 a.m. on the second of last month. Since that extraordinary moment, our lives have been most unusual. Our house being near Kuwait's main port, we found ourselves in the midst of very heavy fighting for the first week.

After six days of living in what must have been the only inhabited house in the area, we were evacuated to a much quieter part of town, where we have been hiding ever since.

I never liked living in Kuwait. Life for the foreigner was fraught with difficulty, frustration and inconvenience. The Kuwaitis appeared aloof, superior and arrogant. My views have changed with Kuwait's demise. Annoying the Kuwaitis may have been, but what everyone took for granted was that they were above all peaceful.

They have responded admirably to their country's invasion. Brave and doomed resistance fighters daily announce their patriotism by attacking Iraqi army targets. The Kuwaitis have shown overwhelming generosity and hospitality at the risk of losing their lives. In the crisis their deep-rooted Arab traditions have come in force to the surface...

And so to the present. It is 1.30 a.m. At 4.00 a.m. my mother and sisters will rise, bid us farewell and make their way to a rendezvous where nine coaches will – God willing – be waiting to evacuate British women and children. They will be driven the hundreds of miles to Baghdad and then, if fortune is kind, will be taken out of this mess, probably by road via Jordan.

Rorie and I spent many hours this evening debating whether to try and go with them; the risk that, both being over 18, someone might object to us being 'children'. We would then have been incarcerated with other Western men at some interesting military installation in Iraq. We decided to stay.

Our reason, you may have guessed, was not the one expounded above. Although commonsense told us to take our chance and go (many 18+ male dependants are), our place and loyalty is here with our father. Our childhood is over and we will take the consequences of its sad departure.

I have no idea when we will get out of here, situations under which this would be a possibility seem very improbable.

Back in Kuwait, there was no way I could leave Rorie – I was his only protection. In any case, wherever I went I was under armed guard. I did manage to find a doctor, who apologised for the state of the hospital and for being an Iraqi, stressing he was not part of the invasion force, but had worked in the hospital for several years. He confirmed that Alex was dead and that his body would shortly be transferred to the Al Sabah hospital's mortuary. I told him that I was unhappy with the manner in which Rorie had been treated and demanded that he be given proper attention. He accepted the criticism, but said that staff shortages and the number of casualties with life-threatening injuries meant that they had to prioritise treatment and care. I also spoke to a Sudanese doctor and, thanks to him, recovered Rorie's rings from the thieving Iraqi 'nurse' – a minor victory.

The events of 24 October are something of a blur in my memory. At some stage we were visited by the Roman Catholic Vicar Apostolic in Kuwait, a Maltese, Monsignor Francis Micallef, who was accompanied by another priest. They came with me when I was escorted to the mortuary to identify Alex – an experience for which I was quite ill-prepared, despite steeling myself beforehand.

Alex looked peaceful and unmarked, as though he was merely asleep. Up until this point I had been so numb and angry that there had been no room for tears, but on seeing him lying there I broke down and swore at my *Mukhabarat* 'minders' to leave the room and give me some privacy. Of course they didn't comply and, in fairness, I suppose they couldn't.

The two priests were equally moved by the cruel turn of fortune that had brought about this tragedy and the Bishop had difficulty reciting the prayers for the dead. Afterwards, he gave me the maroon-coloured prayer book which he had used; a simple, but very touching gesture. I still have it.

I had kept the awful truth of Alex's death from Rorie up until this point, because of his own poor condition. However, arrangements were now being made to transfer us to Baghdad and Rorie was getting more and more agitated about Alex and was adamant that he was not leaving without him. So, on returning to the ward, I told the doctor that I would have to tell him the sad news. Reaching his bed, I took his hand and said: "Rorie, I'm afraid Alex didn't make it." We both broke down and the Iraqi driver, who may not have known Alex was dead either, also burst into tears.

Next morning, 25 October, we were told that we were being transferred to Baghdad. News that we were departing prompted a young Iraqi soldier to approach me and ask if I would contact his parents when we reached Baghdad. I had noticed him on the ward, along with a rather overweight and slovenly looking Iraqi major. I thought, correctly, that the soldier was the officer's batman. When I remarked that surely his officer would allow him to contact home or send messages on his behalf, he said, dismissively, that the officer only gave him orders and treated him very badly. On seeing my minders approaching he slipped a piece of paper into my hand and departed. I never saw him again, but hope he survived the conflict; he was probably younger than Alex and Rorie.

Rorie told me of another very young Iraqi 'soldier' he had heard of in the Regency Palace Hotel. Apparently, the young lad was close to tears and asked an Indian waiter for a cigarette. In conversation, he told the waiter that his father and brothers had lost their lives during the Iraq/Iran war. He, being the youngest son, had not been old enough to be called up, but had been required to work in a munitions factory towards the end of the war. Prior to the invasion of Kuwait, recruiters had visited his home, but he told them that he could not join up as he was now the only male in his household and was responsible for looking after his mother and his sisters. The recruiters appeared to accept this argument and departed.

However, the next day another party visited the house, shot his mother and sisters and told him that he now had no excuse not to enrol in the army. No wonder the poor lad was so miserable. Of course, this story cannot be verified, but it seems unlikely that this youngster would have made it up and, unfortunately, such atrocities appeared quite credible in Saddam's Iraq.

When it was time for us to go, the doctor asked my Iraqi minder how long the journey would take, and was told it would be about one hour. So he prepared a dose of morphine sufficient to give relief for about two hours, which he planned to administer to Rorie at the last possible moment. Meanwhile, the Iraqi 'nurse' ordered Rorie to get out of bed and walk to the ambulance, which was several hundred yards away. I explained that Rorie couldn't walk, as he was paralysed from the waist down. At this, the 'nurse' went off and came back with a pair of crutches. He was on the point of manhandling Rorie out of bed, and I had stepped between him and Rorie to prevent him doing this when, luckily, the doctor appeared to administer the morphine. He was furious with the 'nurse' and insisted that Rorie be moved on a stretcher.

A bare metal transit stretcher was produced and Rorie was placed on this, lying on his back, without any padding whatsoever. We were then taken to the ambulance, which had been stripped of all its medical and life-support equipment. The Lebanese ambulance driver apologised for the state of his vehicle, which was now little more than a cargo van. Alex's body was placed in another, similarly ravaged ambulance and we set off in convoy for Ali Al Salem airbase.

On arrival, we were ushered into an empty room and Rorie, still lying on his stretcher, was placed on a large table. The room was guarded by uniformed soldiers, and a civilian, who spoke good English, was also assigned to keep an eye on us. After about an hour, I was called to have lunch with the Iraqi officers. I refused and asked when would my son be given something to eat and drink and when would our plane be departing? There was a bit of a stand-off and the atmosphere became a little tense. The officer who had come to collect me left with the civilian. Eventually, the civilian returned and warned me that life could be made 'very difficult' for me and, especially, Rorie if I refused to do what I was told. We were well out of the public gaze here and he feared for our safety.

I was duly marched off to the Mess and seated beside an officer who I took to be the commander of the base. As soon as lunch was over, I asked when we would be leaving; one plane had already come and gone without us and we had now been kept waiting for well over two hours. I was told that we would be leaving 'soon', but when yet another plane came and went, I began to get very anxious. The effects of the morphine had long since worn off, leaving Rorie in agony on his stretcher. Moreover, Alex's body was still inside the empty shell of an ambulance baking in the blazing sun. When I protested I was told that we were waiting for a special ambulance plane.

Finally, some four hours after our arrival at the airbase, a third aircraft arrived and we were taken out to it. It was certainly not an ambulance plane and, initially, the captain refused to take a stretcher case. A heated exchange ensued between him and our Iraqi minders, after which we were told to board. Rorie's stretcher was laid across a row of three seats at the rear of the cabin, without any form of restraint. The aircraft filled up rapidly with some passengers complaining that Rorie was taking up too much space. Nobody seemed to be concerned for us and we were disgusted by their callous behaviour.

On arrival in Baghdad, there was nobody to meet us and no way of disembarking Rorie from the plane. Night had fallen, the passengers and crew had long since departed and the cabin lights had been turned off, whilst we still remained on board! A team of cleaners arrived and started cleaning the cabin, hoovering the floor around us as if we weren't there. It was quite bizarre! All my requests for help met with verbal abuse. Nobody knew what to do.

Finally, an official from the British Embassy arrived and, after more than two hours on the tarmac, Rorie was eventually disembarked, using the lift on a catering wagon. We were then taken in a proper ambulance to the Ibn Al-Bitar hospital in the centre of Baghdad.

This was a marvellous, caring facility, run by an Irish charity. The concern, warmth and compassion with which we were received by the Irish doctors and nurses were in sharp contrast to the callous manner with which we had been treated by the Iraqis.

The doctors were horrified that Rorie had been strapped to a transit stretcher for over nine hours as it was only meant to be used to move a patient from one bed to another or onto an operating table. Rorie's condition had deteriorated considerably as a result of this inhumane treatment.

He was given a thorough medical examination and was found to have several broken vertebrae and severe internal bruising, which had been exacerbated by his time on the stretcher. He now had great difficulty in eating and digesting his food. He had also suffered severe mental trauma and, in his own words, had lost the will to live. The combination of these factors prompted him to go on hunger strike, accepting only water. He had already lost about two stone in weight due to our meagre diet when in hiding, so it wasn't long before the doctors became anxious about this development.

I shared a room with Rorie and tried every way I knew to encourage him to regain a proper sense of proportion. After five days, in utter desperation, I told him that I, too, was going on hunger strike, and would not eat another thing until he started eating again. This did the trick. Rorie always thought of others before himself. In his present, disturbed mindset, he was quite prepared to starve himself to death, but he couldn't bear to see me suffering, especially when he could prevent this happening. Within hours, we were both eating again; he painfully and I ravenously! Rorie had turned a corner on the long journey towards as full a recovery as we could reasonably expect.

I, too, was checked over on arrival and found to have very high blood pressure due to severe stress. This gave the doctors the excuse to hospitalise me, thus enabling me to help in Rorie's recovery. I later discovered that the Iraqis had wanted to use me immediately as a human shield at a strategic site, just like all the other hostages, which was understandable.

The day after we arrived, I telephoned the young Iraqi soldier's parents. His mother answered and, speaking in Arabic, I said I had met her son whilst I was in hospital. At the Arabic word for hospital, *mustashfa*, she became hysterical. I could hear her calling out to her husband in Arabic, telling him that their son was in hospital. Her husband then came on the phone. He sounded calm and spoke excellent English, and I assured him that his son was fine. He was in the hospital acting as a batman to an Iraqi officer, and he had asked me to let them know that he was fit and well and in no danger.

The father was extremely grateful, as they had had no news of their son. He and his family had only recently returned from America, where he had worked for several years as a university professor. He asked who I was and when I told him he expressed amazement that I should help an Iraqi family. I assured him I had no quarrel with the ordinary Iraqi people, just their regime. Wisely, he made no comment and we ended the call.

An important Iraqi – possibly one of Saddam's relatives – was being treated in the room next door to ours. Guards were posted outside and, in effect, these became our guards as well. Although we were no longer in hiding, we were still subconsciously very much in that mindset. We had been in the hospital for three days when one of the nurses pointed out that we no longer had to live in the dark behind drawn curtains. We simply hadn't realised we were behaving in this way.

During our time at the Ibn Al-Bitar hospital, apart from the excellent care and attention we received from the doctors and nurses, we enjoyed enormous support from many other people. Foremost among these was the British Ambassador, HE Mr Harold Walker, who visited us every day and made us feel that our welfare was his only priority in life when, in truth, he couldn't have been busier. When not visiting us, he also found the time to work tirelessly for our release.

Donald Macauley, formerly of the Embassy in Kuwait, was another regular visitor. My American opposite number in Kuwait, Colonel John Mooneyham, a giant of a man in every sense, also visited us, bringing us some fresh clothes when he saw us dressed in paper pyjamas supplied by the hospital. On another occasion, he and one of his sergeants scoured Baghdad to find a guitar for Rorie to help his recovery. This gesture, undertaken at considerable personal risk despite their diplomatic status, really touched Rorie. The Iraqis wanted to get 'Big John', as John Mooneyham was affectionately known, and thereafter he had to remain in the Embassy.

The Canadian Chargé d'Affaires, Bill Bowden, who during the early days of the invasion had tried to rescue us from our house in Kuwait, was also now in Baghdad and came to visit us. It was nice to put a face to the very helpful voice at the other end of the phone.

We were also visited regularly by two Catholic priests. The first of these was a charming, very old Irishman who had come to try to secure the release of a young man. He had a lovely way with words and the patience of a saint. He would turn up daily at the appropriate office in, I believe, the Ministry of Foreign Affairs (MFA) and simply sit and wait all day. The authorities told him that it would take a long time to negotiate the release of his man, but he smiled serenely at them and said he had all the time in the world. In the end they quit stalling and the old priest went back to Ireland with his man.

The other priest was Bishop Michael Kenny, Bishop of Juneau, Alaska, who was also in Baghdad to secure the release of a number of hostages. He was positive, energetic and brimming with enthusiasm, but was also an excellent listener, who helped to lift our spirits. He would say Mass around Rorie's bed, using a teacup for the wine and a bread roll. Both Rorie and I also had a teacup and a piece of bread roll. Thus, if an Iraqi came in unannounced it would appear that we were just chatting over a cup of tea.

I 'celebrated' my 50th birthday at Ibn Al-Bitar hospital, my present being a phone call from Toni. To her enormous credit, she had continued to work as a volunteer on the BLT Helpline after Alex's death, and she always sounded so positive and up-beat to us.

Once the trauma caused by his severe internal bruising had eased, Rorie slowly regained the use of his legs. After about ten days he was able to shuffle around our room using a Zimmer frame. By now, he had lost three stone since 2 August and looked a shadow of his former self. But, at least, he was up and getting mobile. His motivation now was to be able to walk unaided at his brother's funeral; that's what was driving him.

Exactly two weeks after arriving at the Ibn Al-Bitar hospital, the Ambassador secured our release from Iraqi custody. Rorie was still on medication to alleviate the acute pain he was experiencing, as well as to stabilise his mental trauma. As yet, he could not walk unaided, so had to be pushed in a wheelchair.

Leaving Baghdad whilst most of my Team were either hostages in Iraq or still in hiding in Kuwait was a very traumatic experience for me. I could see that Rorie desperately needed me, but my military duty was to my Team. I resolved to return to Iraq just as soon as Rorie was back safely with Toni.

We said goodbye to the wonderful doctors and nurses at the hospital and were driven to the airport accompanied by the Ambassador in his official car. He remained with us throughout all the check-in and passport control procedures and stayed with us in the departure lounge until we boarded our Iraqi flight to Jordan. This was just as well, because shortly before we were due to board, an announcement over the loud-speakers requested, "Mr Bruce Duncan to report to the information desk." The Ambassador told me to stay where I was and went to investigate. When he returned, he told me that an Iraqi official had wanted me to go outside and move my car, which was 'parked in the wrong place'. He had replied: "Do you mean the car flying the Union Jack?" They apologised and said there must have been some mistake. I heard later that a news report had disclosed my identity whilst I was still at the airport. Whether or not this was so, Rorie and I were still not out of the woods because we were being flown to Amman by Iraqi Airways. Either way it was a close call.

The aircraft was very crowded and nobody took any notice of seat allocations. Rorie was pushed around horribly, and he and I were made to sit several rows from each other by very unfriendly cabin staff. The flight to Amman was unpleasant, hostile, but thankfully short. On arrival, we were met by the British Defence Attaché, Colonel Phillip Goddard and taken back to his home for the night.

With great sensitivity, the Goddards had prepared two rooms for us, unsure whether we would want to be together or sleep apart. Without hesitation we opted to share. The next evening, we boarded the British Airways flight back to Heathrow. We were given VIP treatment, yet we were acutely aware that our dear Alex was also on the plane.

Toni, Hannah and Zoë were watching the TV news when they saw a clip of Rorie and me at Queen Alia International Airport. Whilst Rorie was in a wheelchair, he was not visibly disfigured in any way, which was an enormous relief to them. Although we had assured them on the phone that he didn't look too battered about, seeing was believing.

On arrival in Heathrow, we were driven straight to a VIP lounge at the back of the airport, where we were, at last, reunited with Toni, Hannah and Zoë. (An airport official took our passports away to be stamped and we had no luggage so clearance through Customs was waived.) Brigadier Peter Little, my boss in the MoD, was also in the lounge to welcome us home. I remember telling him of my intention to return to Iraq once Rorie was safely home with Toni. He was non-committal and said we could talk about that later.

Once our passports had been stamped and returned to us, we were driven in two cars out of the back of the airport to avoid the press. However, one photographer was covering this exit road and struck lucky. Next morning, the *Sunday Express* featured his photographs of us above a rather over-the-top article on its front page despite, I was informed, a 'D-Notice' having been issued.

Toni had been allocated an army quarter in The Keep, Kingston, and this would be our home for the next 18 months or so. It became quickly apparent that I was not going to be allowed to return to Iraq/Kuwait. This added to my sense of guilt for having deserted my Team. Likewise, Rorie was consumed by guilt at having survived the accident.

Within a couple of days, Rorie and I were sent to the Queen Elizabeth Military Hospital (QEMH) at Woolwich for medical check-ups. We were both found to be suffering from severe stress. In addition, Rorie's back injury meant he had to wear a tight-fitting corset. Whilst this was obviously essential, it exacerbated the effects of his internal bruising, leaving him in constant pain from indigestion and stomach cramps.

As part of our treatment, we were each assigned to a psychiatrist, an experience we both found traumatic. After the first session, we seemed to be full of anger and almost incapable of being civil to each other, or anyone else. Therefore, before starting the next session, I discussed the purpose of the therapy with my psychiatrist. He told me that they first had to, "get all the anger out of you and then build you up again."

I felt neither of us was ready for such a 'head on' approach. I still had over four years left to serve in the army and three children to put through school and university. I was fearful that if I were to 'crack' I would be invalided out of the army. In such an eventuality, I would be unable to fulfil my family commitments – and I wasn't prepared to let Saddam do that to us.

Rorie, too, had fears about what might become of him, and he was just on the threshold of adult life. So, with his agreement, I asked for us to be taken off the programme. My psychiatrist warned me that it would take us far longer to recover if we declined treatment. No doubt he was right, but at least we felt more in control of events.

However, we would occasionally get flashbacks to life hiding in Kuwait and suffer inexplicable panic attacks. I can remember one evening when I was sitting in the dark in our quarter and spotted a light on in another room. Back in hiding mode, I dashed out to switch it off and to berate Toni for being so careless, only to realise that there was now no need for such action.

Initially, as a family we experienced a troubling sense of 'distance', especially between Rorie and me on the one hand and Toni, Hannah and Zoë on the other. We had all suffered horribly. Toni and the girls' journey to Baghdad must have been a nightmare, not to mention the anxiety they had endured once back in England, which turned to utter misery after the road accident. Rorie and I didn't share these experiences, but had a whole horror story of our own, Rorie's version being immeasurably worse than mine – I wasn't in that horrendous car crash. We all had to realise that each of us had a different 'take' on this tragedy and that we all had to deal with it in different ways. In his official statement submitted to the MoD, Rorie talked about this very movingly: "Within the family the very separate experiences of my sisters and mother in England and my father and myself in Kuwait and Baghdad created a tangible, though un-talked-of divide between us that hurt me greatly. The fact that we had been separated for two and a half weeks following the death of Alex helped to propagate this strange and very distressing lack of understanding between the remaining family members."

Alex's funeral took place at Worth Abbey, his old school, on 19 November. Although the saddest of occasions, it was also up-lifting and, to an extent, brought a sense of closure to this awful chapter in our lives. The Abbey church was filled with friends, family and members of the public touched by this tragedy. Even Edward Heath paid us the great honour of attending – the security sweep of the area prior to his arrival gave the monks something to talk about! Witnessing this enormous congregation reminded me that Alex had once commented when we were in hiding in Kuwait that we all had to die one day and that meeting one's end in Kuwait would be part of an historic event. He certainly received a warrior's send off.

He was laid to rest in the monk's own cemetery, a tranquil spot overlooking the South Downs. The following morning dawned beautifully crisp and clear and, before returning to Kingston, we all visited Alex's grave. As we walked down to the cemetery we saw a handsome young stag in the adjoining field. It stood and looked at us for a moment, before moving off unhurriedly into the cover of the nearby wood. This strangely symbolic sight has stayed with us ever since, and although we have visited the grave many times, we have never seen another deer in the vicinity.

At the time of Alex's funeral, Rorie wrote a poem to him. It is deeply poignant and betrays Rorie's despair at the loss of his brother, his best friend, his soul mate, and the burning guilt eating away at him for having survived the accident.

In Memory of Alex Duncan

To die in sight of freedom
After so long in the shadows
Where death was whispered in single shots
And left as if to echo ever...

To spring the trap that fate had laid
And faith was made to answer
Broken body in a broken city
Dust to dust among the ashes.

And now this real world is far from me
A fiction played out nightly, and sanitised on ITV
Whilst your spirit stalks the city's shell
And mine is idle, fat and free.

No, I have never left your side.
I left my ghost in sight of freedom,
To wait with yours
Until we come that close again.

Until then we stalk that hell of hollowed husks –
Two ghosts in a ghost-town's dust.
The ruins raped and rank we roam,
As near as two smashed ghosts can get to home.

Rorie Duncan – November 1990

I still cannot read this poem without my eyes welling up with tears, and I hope I never will be able to; our love for Alex and Rorie must never die.

Some years later, thanks to the (late) Baroness Strange, Alex's name was engraved on a plaque in the crypt of St Paul's Cathedral in London, dedicated to people who lost their lives, either training for Desert Storm or, in Alex's case, during Iraq's occupation of Kuwait. Thus, he really has left his mark on history.

In December, Saddam Hussein agreed to release all the hostages and those foreigners still hiding in Kuwait. Toni and I went to Heathrow to meet every single flight with BLT members aboard. Of course, we were little more than 'onlookers' now, but we felt we had to be there. Toni's record of these events sums up our feelings:

> *It was a very stressful time watching the jubilant reunions of families after our sad ordeal. The hardest to bear was when 'The Kuwait Eight' returned – the eight members of the team who had evaded capture. We knew in our heart of hearts that that plane was the one that he* [Bruce], *Alex and Rorie should have been on.*

To add to that sense of loss, I heard later that, after the intensive search on 21 and 22 October, our area was left alone by the Iraqis. If only the phone had remained dead for just one more day – if only, if only.

With the Team now safely back home, I turned my attention to getting official recognition for them. Given the unprecedented circumstances of our experience, I thought this was only right. It is one thing for service personnel to go to do their duty in another land as part of a well-organised force, with all the necessary command and support elements in place.

It is quite another for an isolated team of unarmed servicemen to find themselves *and their families* caught up in someone else's war.

Every one of our dependants came face to face with hostile Iraqi soldiers at some point; some were even threatened and physically assaulted. The young boy seen on television, cringing as Saddam Hussein patted him on the head, was a BLT child. My MoD boss, Brigadier Peter Little, agreed in principle to my quest for recognition, but said I would have to clear my recommendations with the Ambassador.

A week or so after his return to the UK, the Ambassador arranged to meet Peter Little in the MoD. I asked if I could also see him, either alone or, preferably, together. I was told that I could come and wait in the outer office and see if the Ambassador would have time to see me following his official meeting. Clearly, I no longer enjoyed the status I had when commanding the Team. I was now the commander of nobody and got the impression that I was regarded as something of a nuisance. Nevertheless, I was hopeful that the Ambassador would see me.

When the official meeting broke up, the Ambassador seemed to be unaware that I wanted to see him. He was also in a hurry. Our discussion couldn't have lasted more than three minutes. The Ambassador was curt: he wasn't recommending many people for an award himself and he would accept one nomination from me – and absolutely no dependants. I had listed several people (a single figure total) in order of priority, whom I believed to be worthy of consideration, including dependants (no one in my family – their merits would have to be considered by others).

I told the Ambassador that I had dependants on my list who, I felt, deserved recognition, including a civilian unconnected with the Team. He asked who that person was and, when I told him, confirmed he also had listed him, thereby, in my view, contradicting his earlier assertion that he wasn't recommending any dependants for an award. Ending the discussion, his parting words as he left the room were that he would support one military nomination, provided it had the approval of the MoD. That was the last time we met or spoke to one another.

I was disappointed that my boss hadn't lent me any support. Perhaps they had already discussed the topic during their meeting. Alternatively, he may have considered it better to broach the subject privately with the Ambassador at a later date.

When the Gulf Honours List was published, the number of civilians in Kuwait it featured, including members of the Embassy, was in stark contrast to the single award for the 66 members of the BLT and their families trapped in Kuwait; the richly deserved MBE awarded to Captain Dale Millar. I felt badly let down and, in turn, felt that I had let down my family and the Team. For the first and only time in my career, I asked to see my superior and vented my anger at how, in my view, we had been short-changed.

Apart from the people on my list, rightly or wrongly I felt that my omission indicated that I had failed to measure up to the daunting challenge with which I had been presented. After all, I had put military considerations ahead of my own family's safety on a number of occasions, with tragic consequences. Whilst no amount of official recognition could have possibly compensated for the loss of our beloved son, to my grieving mind the total lack of any recognition whatsoever seemed to suggest that the MoD considered Alex's death to be of no consequence. This hurt. To me, Toni also deserved some form of recognition. She had assumed the responsibility of the Commander's wife during her time in occupied Kuwait, helping to maintain morale, maintaining the links between the Team and operating the radio link to the Embassy when I was stationed there, and, most importantly, she had supported me on decisions I had to make, including those affecting our own family. Furthermore, she had joined the helpline on her return to the UK and had continued to carry out her duties even after the tragedy that befell our family.

What hurt me most, however, was that Rorie's bravery following the fatal accident had been totally ignored. For an injured and terrified 18-year-old to resist interrogation at the expense of being denied medical treatment, whilst not knowing if anyone was even aware of his plight, was commendable. His courage almost certainly saved the lives of our Kuwaiti guardians. Yet he never received so much as a letter of thanks. In his utterly depressed and pitiful state, an official 'pat on the back' would have helped him enormously and in my view was richly deserved. As it was, he was left feeling worthless, unappreciated and forgotten.

In retrospect, I was wrong to challenge my own omission from the list and regret that I did so. After all, I only did what I was paid to do, albeit in difficult circumstances. On the other hand, Toni and Rorie's actions exceeded expected norms. Clearly, I was unable to recommend them for consideration, but had hoped others would do so. As for other members of my Team, Brigadier Little was gracious enough to hear me out and agreed to support a recommendation for one further MBE and three Commendations but, alas, nothing for any of the Team's dependants.

Unwilling to accept defeat, I submitted a case for all the dependants caught in Kuwait to receive some tangible official token of recognition – be it a commemorative medal or a brooch. After all, with the exception of the fall of Hong Kong and Singapore during the Second World War, when have British Armed Forces families been taken hostage by hostile invading troops? A gesture of recognition on the lines proposed would have cost so little, but would have meant so much to those concerned. I was saddened, but not surprised when nothing came of this proposal. One of the wives put the whole question of honours into perspective when she remarked to Toni: "So what if we didn't get a medal. We all know what we did." Nevertheless, I would have liked others to have known.

When the Gulf War campaign medal was struck, the MoD did award it, with a unique clasp inscribed '2 August 1990' – the date of the Iraqi invasion – to all 66 Team members trapped in Kuwait. I am sure I am not alone amongst my former colleagues when I say that I wear mine knowing that my entire family earned it.

Toni also delivered an inspiring presentation at the Federation of Army Wives' (FAW) Ninth Annual Conference in the presence of the Under Secretary of State for the Armed Forces, Lord Arran, the Adjutant General and the Quartermaster General, highlighting the ordeal faced by the Army and RAF wives and children during the invasion and occupation of Kuwait. The transcript was published in the *FAW* magazine and in the Royal Tank Regiment's magazine, *Tank*. The Army's magazine, *Soldier*, also published extracts from her presentation. In this way our dependants' plight did get some much deserved exposure.

Brigadier Peter Little did work tirelessly to ensure that we were financially compensated for our material losses in Kuwait – insurance companies exclude liability for acts of war from their policies. This was undoubtedly an enormous help. Anybody who has played Kim's Game, where you have to memorise a number of items on a tray and record them when the tray is removed, will appreciate how difficult it was to recall every item in every drawer and cupboard in every room, and on every floor and wall – and this after a period of months rather than minutes. Years later, we would look for an item and then realise that we had lost it in Kuwait.

The MoD, however, dragged its heels over Rorie's criminal injuries claim. This was only settled in 2003 – 13 years after the event – and only because Zoë, by then an MoD civil servant, intervened directly with the desk officer responsible. This was shameful.

The only person directly connected on the ground with the conflict who really seemed to understand the ordeal we had experienced, and empathised with us in our struggle to get back on track, was General Sir Peter de la Billière, Commander of the British Forces in Desert Storm, the 1991 Gulf War to drive Iraq out of Kuwait.

On his return home, he made a point of contacting us and inviting us to join him for lunch at his London club. The meeting was inspirational: he was an excellent listener who showed a genuine interest in, and concern about, what we had been through. He also found time to write a very supportive article in the *Army Quarterly & Defence Journal.* For the Army's most high profile General at that time to show such support for an ordinary army family speaks volumes. We left that lunch meeting feeling much better about ourselves and have kept in touch ever since.

Tom and Alix Bremridge, with whom we had enjoyed such a happy year in Oman, were also very sensitive and supportive, especially in the raw, early days as we tried to get to grips with our demons. Inviting us to spend a few days with them, they let us 'do our own thing', but were always there when we needed them.

Both Rorie and I spent much of the first nine months or so after our release, in and out of hospital, myself in QEMH and Rorie at Headley Court and the John Radcliffe in Oxford.

When not in hospital, I spent the next few weeks in DMAO's (Loan Service) department in the MoD, winding up the Team's affairs. During this time I can remember being asked one day to make a series of simple telephone calls. To my horror, I found it almost impossible to undertake this task, so traumatised was I after that fateful call from the Ambassador on 23 October, informing me of the disaster that had befallen our sons. I realised then that I would have to get a grip of myself, or my days in the army were at an end. Apart from my family, the MoD doctor in Central London at the time, Dr Jean Peacey, and our wonderful priest in Kingston, Father John Lavery, both helped me tremendously in this regard.

Rorie's condition was much more serious than mine and he ended up having a quite miserable time, both mentally and physically, in what was meant to be his gap year. By now three stone below his correct weight, he was always famished yet, due to his severe internal bruising, he found eating both difficult and painful. Dr Jebb, our GP in Kingston, worked tirelessly on his behalf, but it was more than three months before he was well enough to go to the rehabilitation unit at Headley Court to be treated for his back injury.

To his credit, Rorie did take up his place at St Edmund (Teddy) Hall, Oxford in September 1991, but only after changing his subject from English to Arabic. He was determined to get back into the Arab world – and specifically Kuwait, which, to his mind, he had never left.

A capable rugby scrum-half, who had represented Sussex at Under 16 and Under 18 level and had aspirations of playing for Scotland one day, he was given a trial for the Hounds, Oxford University's feeder team for the Blues. He hadn't mentioned anything about his recent past, as he wanted to be accepted for who he was, not for what he had experienced. Tackled at the first breakdown in play, he ended up in hospital – his severely damaged back just couldn't cope with the rigours of rugby any more.

Undaunted, once recovered, and with medical approval, he joined the University Boxing Club and won a Blue in his first year. Channelling all his aggression and pain into his sport, he defeated the Cambridge captain during the Varsity Match, watched by his proud father. Unwilling to give himself any quarter, he even won another contest on points, despite suffering a fractured jaw during the bout. He captained the Oxford University team in his last two years and was also the British Universities Sports Federation welterweight champion in 1993.

The girls, too, were suffering and their schooling was inevitably disrupted. At the time, Hannah was in her final GCSE year. Yet she and Zoë were determined that Saddam Hussein was not going to ruin their lives and they did both themselves and us proud.

Toni was undoubtedly the strongest amongst us. Her unshakeable Faith, plus her ability to talk openly about her experiences (the rest of us bottled up our feelings), enabled her to cope much better than the rest of the family. In many ways, she became the 'glue' that held us all together.

The Royal Tank Regiment also lived up to the best, close-knit family traditions of the British Army. The day after Toni and the girls returned to the UK, they were visited by the Regimental Colonel, Colonel John 'Woody' Woodward, to sort out their immediate needs and to offer the Regiment's full support. Days later, Toni had to get all our belongings out of store (on loan service postings most of our belongings had to be put into store in the UK at government expense). The gods were certainly not smiling on us during the autumn of 1990. When the first container was opened, the contents were literally moving with Woolly Bear (carpet beetle larvae). All our clothes, all my British Army uniforms and our soft furnishings, such as treasured oriental rugs, had been destroyed. Indeed, Toni had to call in a pest control unit to fumigate our quarter and all the salvageable items amongst our possessions. Woolly Bear was classified as vermin and not covered by insurance. When hearing that I had lost all my uniforms, Brigadier Greg Reid, a former Commanding Officer and friend who had just retired, told Toni that when I returned I could have all his. This gesture saved us literally hundreds of pounds.

Chief of the Defence Staff (CDS), Marshal of the Royal Air Force, Sir David Craig GCB OBE, and his wife, Lady Craig, who had visited us in Kuwait at the start of the year, were also very supportive. CDS had sent the Team a message of support soon after the invasion that lifted our morale – here was the Head of the Armed Forces acknowledging the plight of a small Army/RAF team and their dependants.

When Toni arrived back in the UK, Lady Craig was amongst the first to contact her and when she heard of the 'Woolly Bear disaster', she gave Toni an overcoat to ease her financial burden – she and the girls had nothing but the clothes they were wearing on their return and there was now an autumn chill in the air. On my return from Kuwait, I, too, was invited with Toni to a relaxed, informal lunch by Sir David and Lady Craig at their flat in London.

This sorry episode in our lives wouldn't be complete without mention of the extraordinarily generous gesture by American Tours International Inc. In a spirit of compassion and solidarity, in September 1991 this American tour company put together an all-expenses-paid fortnight's holiday in the United States for all British families who had been bereaved during the Gulf War. Our family was included, as Alex had been killed during Iraq's occupation of Kuwait.

Unfortunately, none of our children could accompany us, as the holiday took place during term time, but they all urged us to go. The highlights of a very wide-ranging itinerary included New York and Washington, where we toured the White House before being hosted by President George and Mrs Barbara Bush to tea in the Oval Office. The climax of the holiday was four days in the 50th State in the Union – the magical archipelago of Hawaii – where we celebrated Toni's 48th birthday.

Thus ended the most traumatic period of my army career for me and my family, and one that changed our lives for ever. But, of course, we weren't alone in having our lives changed as a result of Iraq's invasion of Kuwait. Everyone in the Team suffered, not to mention the thousands of expatriates and Kuwaitis who had been caught up in this barbarous show of aggression. Poor Mr Rajagopolin suffered more than most. As an Indian working in the British Embassy, he was relatively free to move about Kuwait (Indian nationals weren't on the Iraqis' wanted list.) Consequently, it fell to him to assist British nationals in Kuwait, especially after 24 August 1990, when Iraq ceased to recognise the embassies in the Emirate. A true, peace-loving man, he found this whole experience very stressful, and we were greatly saddened to hear that he had died shortly after the liberation of Kuwait.

1. Our house in the sand at Shuwaikh, Kuwait City

2. Our fuse box with its bewildering tangle of wires!

3. Toni and I relaxing in our inner courtyard with Blackie, the cat

4. A 'key post' meeting in our house (Crown copyright)

5. Being presented to Their Royal Highnesses, Prince Charles and Princess Diana on 13 March 1989. Unfortunately, Toni cannot be seen behind the British Embassy official in the foreground (official Embassy photograph and included by kind permission of Kensington Palace)

6. The invitation to the banquet hosted by the Crown Prince and Prime Minister, Sheikh Saad and Sheikha Latifeh at Al Shaab Palace

7. and 8. Scenes at the *Bedu* souk, Fahaheel

9. This baby camel at the camel market was barely an hour old and suckling for the first time

10. Japanese martial drummers performing during Japanese Week

11. Kuwait City lit up in celebration of the Emirate's 29th National Day Anniversary, 25 February 1990, just over five months before the Iraqi invasion

12. Christmas Eve celebrations on the Mutla Ridge, north of Kuwait City, 1988

13. Many city dwellers in Kuwait would go back to their Bedouin roots and camp in the desert for a few weeks during the winter

14. Sand dunes as far as the eye can see; the Liwa Sands on the edge of the Empty Quarter, Abu Dhabi

15. This falconer with his Arabian falcon sat across the aisle from me on a Gulf Air internal flight!

1

2

3

4

5

على شرف
صاحب السمو الملكي
الأمير تشارلز ولي عهد المملكة المتحدة
وقرينته الأميرة ديانا
مأدبة عشاء يقيمها
سمو الشيخ سعد العبدالله السالم الصباح
ولي العهد ورئيس مجلس الوزراء
وقرينته الشيخة لطيفة الفهد السالم الصباح

قصر الشعب
الاثنين ١٣ مارس ١٩٨٩م

DINNER BANQUET

IN HONOUR OF

THEIR ROYAL HIGHNESSES
THE PRINCE AND PRINCESS OF WALES

HOSTED BY

H.H. SHEIKH SAAD AL ABDULLAH AL SALEM AL SABA
THE CROWN PRINCE & PRIME MINISTER
AND
SHEIKHA LATIFEH FAHAD AL SALEM AL SABAH

AL SHAAB PALACE
Monday 13th March, 1989

6

7

8

9

10

11

12

13

14

15

16

17

18

19

20

21

22

23

24

Map of Kuwait

The map of Kuwait, modified to include the Rumaila oilfield, is included by kind permission of Taylor & Francis Ltd. It is taken from an article I wrote for the *Army Quarterly & Defence Journal*, Volume 121, No. 2, Gulf War Issue, 1991

JORDAN

SYRIA
IRAQ
Irbid
Mahattat al Jufur
Al Mafraq
Mahattat al Hafif
ISRAEL
Az Zarqa'
As Salt
'Amman
Queen Alia International Airport
Dead Sea
Qasr Tuba
Al Mazra'ah
Al Karak
As Safi
JORDAN
At Tafilah
Ba'ir
Ash Shawbak
Al-Jafr
Petra
Ma'an
N
Ras an Naqb
Wadi Rum
SAUDI ARABIA
Al 'Aqabah
Al Mudawwarah
JORDAN - 1993

JORDAN

Once I was on my feet again, I requested to be posted back to the Middle East. I felt that this was the only way I was going to get over the trauma of Kuwait and Iraq. The family supported me wholeheartedly, although, understandably, we all harboured some reservations about returning to the region.

I was selected to become the Defence Attaché in Jordan, an appointment I grabbed with both hands. My uncle, Major John Duncan MC, had served under Glubb Pasha in the (Jordanian) Arab Legion, and his son, Angus, was born in the capital, Amman, so I felt I had a connection.

The general brief I received indicated, amongst other things, that we would have to possess sufficient crockery, cutlery and assorted glasses to cater for buffet suppers for up to 36 people. We would be given an interest free loan, to be paid back during the tour, to purchase these items. We were also required to purchase at least 100 suitable British manufactured gifts to present to our hosts when attending their official functions. We chose to buy various small Wedgwood pieces to meet this requirement.

The brief explained that we would receive an annual entertainment allowance during our time in Jordan. We were expected to pay up front for official functions and then submit claims for reimbursement, backed by receipts, including the cost of our gifts. If we overspent our allowance, that was our problem. Toni kept a book detailing the menus and wines for each of our parties, so as to avoid, as far as possible, serving the same fare to the same people too frequently. She also itemised the gifts we had given to our hosts for the same reason.

The Defence Attaché's appointment in Amman was for a Colonel, so I wasn't unduly concerned when I received a letter from the MoD telling me that I was in the bracket for the next tranche of Army redundancies in the Armed Forces 'Options for Change' programme and, as such, I would not be considered for further promotion. This, after all, was my final posting.

Knowing that we would be abroad until a few weeks before my retirement, we took the opportunity to look for a house whilst we were in the UK. We were keen to settle in a rural, rather than an urban, area and so concentrated on Oxfordshire, where my parents had retired and my mother still lived. The children knew the area quite well, having spent many a half-term and exeat with my parents when we were abroad. So it was that, in March 1992, we moved into a cottage in a delightful village in this largely rural county.

In October 1991, I was sent on the long Arabic course at the Defence School of Languages, Beaconsfield. This provided me with a structured, if intellectually demanding, re-introduction to full-time working. I still suffered from inexplicable panic attacks, which manifested themselves in acute chest pains, dizziness and difficulty in breathing, but I was getting better at controlling these, rather than rushing to the nearest A & E hospital department thinking I was having a heart attack.

I left the Arabic course at the midway point in order to attend the Attachés' course, before departing for Jordan in early September 1992. At least by then I had sat and passed the GCSE Arabic exam. Going back to school to sit the exam had been quite an experience!

Rorie had elected to do the second year of his Arabic degree course at the University of Alexandria, Egypt. He, therefore, flew out to the Middle

East again at much the same time as I did. Meanwhile, Toni remained at home to settle the girls back into school, the plan being to remain in England until after half-term and the second anniversary of Alex's death before flying out to join me.

I found it strange to be back in the Goddards' house in Amman, but was kept too busy to dwell unduly on the past. I learnt a valuable lesson on the second day of my handover, when I received an invitation to a reception at one of the embassies. No sooner had I accepted, than another invitation arrived. I casually remarked that I would have to decline, but Philip Goddard, the outgoing Defence Attaché, corrected me straight away; we had to accept all invitations so as not to send out 'misleading political messages'! The only exception to this rule was when the Foreign and Commonwealth Office (FCO) ordered us to decline.

Similarly, we were always required to attend these functions in uniform, unless ordered to do otherwise by the FCO. Throughout our three years we must have averaged about three or four receptions a week and at least one dinner party per fortnight, including those hosted by ourselves. Once we had to attend two formal dinners and a reception on the same evening – an unforgettable experience. I should add that one of the points made during the pre-tour briefings was that we should stick to soft drinks on these occasions, so as to remain both alert and discreet: "Remember you're on duty. By all means have a stiff whisky in the privacy of your own home afterwards."

The Jordanian landlord wanted to carry out some essential maintenance work on the Defence Attaché's house as soon as the Goddards vacated it. I was, therefore, accommodated in another building fairly close by, which I shared with the delightful Jordanian family who owned it. The only potential drawback with this property was that it was slightly isolated within the local community, whereas the permanent house was situated in the diplomatic area, thus benefitting from the security of the many guarded embassies and residences in the vicinity and, in addition, an adjacent military barracks.

I used to jog around the area in the cool of the evening before going on my round of receptions, but had the feeling I was being watched. Then one evening, I noticed an Arab apparently watching the house as I returned. I decided to run on by and, when out of sight, back-tracked, only to find him still there. In the end I had no option but to go in to get ready for the evening's functions. It was then that I saw the man get into a car bearing diplomatic plates. Just prior to my arrival in Amman, an American diplomat and his family had been forced to leave Jordan for their own safety, after being harassed, reportedly by Iraqis. I therefore reported this 'encounter' to our Deputy Head of Mission next day and, as well as other measures, my jogging excursions had to be curtailed.

In August 1992, His Majesty King Hussein had undergone treatment for cancer in the Mayo Clinic, Minnesota. News of his impending return to Jordan on 24 September visibly lifted the spirits of the entire nation, Jordanians and Palestinians alike. Indeed, the day was declared a national holiday and by noon Amman was at a standstill, as over a million people converged on the city to welcome him home.

The King's plane, a Royal Jordanian Airbus, piloted, I understand, by the King himself, was escorted by 16 fighter aircraft of the Royal Jordanian Air Force (RJAF). The aircraft made two passes over the city, whilst seemingly the whole of Jordan gathered in the streets and on the rooftops, cheering and ululating their welcome. In the traditional Arab way of celebration, a continuous crescendo of rifle fire filled the air that night – nobody was going to waste a single moment of this memorable day by going to sleep!

Selfishly, I wished I had been able to catch a few winks, as by 9.00 a.m. next morning I was on my way down to the River Jordan to meet a contingent of students from the Royal College of Defence Studies (RCDS) at the start of the Jordanian leg of their Middle Eastern tour. Talk about hitting the ground running – I had been in the chair barely a week before being involved in this high profile visit. The party had just completed their visit to Israel and were due to cross into Jordan at the King Hussein (formerly Allenby) Bridge border control point on the River Jordan. The Israeli side was bristling with guns, defence works and Israeli flags, which was in stark contrast to the single guard post and lone flag on the Jordanian side.

My Palestinian driver, Auni, was particularly excited, as his brother, whom he had not seen in years, was one of the drivers bringing the RCDS students to the bridge. The actual border was marked by a white line at the middle of the bridge. We moved on foot up to this point to greet our guests. It was then that I saw for myself the tension that existed between the Arabs and Israelis: Auni's brother tried to run to meet him on the bridge, but was quite roughly prevented from doing so by Israeli border guards, who manhandled him back off the bridge to his vehicle – the brothers never did meet, which they found deeply distressing.

The week-long RCDS visit was a prestigious annual event, and was accorded the highest priority by the Jordanians. Usually the programme included an audience with King Hussein, but as he had only just returned from surgery, the Crown Prince, Prince Hassan, fulfilled this commitment. The programme endeavoured to give the RCDS students as comprehensive an overview of Jordan as time would allow. There were political briefings by the British Ambassador and government ministers as well as a meeting with representatives of the Palestine Liberation Organization (PLO), the latter preceded by a visit to one of the UN-run Palestinian refugee camps. The various military briefings were followed by visits to a number of units from all three services. Whilst we were in Aqaba visiting the navy, we were also taken to a Jordanian watchtower on the border with Israel, where a mere strip of 'no man's land' separated the thriving tourist resort of Eilat, Israel from the Jordanian town of Aqaba.

For me this visit had been absolutely invaluable. Not only had it given me a sound understanding of the country – its politics, culture, and geography – it had also enabled me to cement my relationship with, and gain the trust of, the top echelons within the Jordanian Armed Forces. In addition, I had met the Crown Prince and had also been unexpectedly pulled out of the official programme for an hour to meet Prince Mohammed, the second eldest of the princes, at the latter's behest.

As the one rock of stability in an otherwise turbulent region, Jordan attracted an almost continuous flow of important visitors. So it was that nine days after saying farewell to the RCDS visitors I found myself at Queen Alia International Airport to greet the Chief of the Defence Staff (CDS), Field Marshal Sir Richard Vincent GBE KCB DSO and Lady Vincent, who were guests of CDS's Jordanian counterpart, Field Marshal Fathi Abu Talib. The five-day programme followed much the same lines as that afforded the RCDS, but with some finer touches to reflect the CDS's status as Britain's most senior officer: a 72-man-strong Guard of Honour outside the Jordanian Armed Forces Headquarters, a formal parade by 5th Tank Battalion in their Chieftain tanks (a nostalgic moment for me – it had been 15 years since I had last served on Chieftain), plus formal visits to the Royal Jordanian Air Force at Azraq airbase and the Royal Jordanian Naval Force (RJNF) in Aqaba.

During my time in Jordan, I was involved in two more RCDS visits, and what set these apart was the opportunity of an audience with a now fit and well King Hussein. I was privileged to meet him on a number of occasions whilst accompanying visitors. He was disarmingly courteous and, wise and empathetic, he was an excellent listener and communicator. Often when he had met with a group of senior officers, individuals would remark that they felt as if they had been the only guest in the room. Once, during an informal meeting with the Ambassador, he learned about my experience in Kuwait and immediately showed his compassionate, human side, by expressing his surprise and appreciation at my willingness to return to the Middle East.

Towards the end of my time in Jordan, I was also involved in the visit of Sir Richard Vincent's successor, Field Marshal Sir Peter Inge GCB, at the invitation of his recently-appointed Jordanian counterpart, Field Marshal Abdul Hafez Mara'i Ka'abneh. One of the highlights of this particular visit was a flight in a RJAF helicopter along the entire length of Jordan's borders. This was a unique opportunity and I was keen to take along my camera. But a standard SLR is very much an 'in your face' piece of equipment. Not wishing to cause any embarrassment – or worse – I decided to seek Field Marshal Mara'i's permission. His astonishingly frank reply to my request made me realise just how lucky I was to be in Jordan: "Of course you must take your camera, Bruce. You are the legalised spy!" I felt myself to be very much one of them here and very privileged to be so well accepted.

Unfortunately, Field Marshal Sir Peter Inge's visit had to be cut short very suddenly due to developments in Bosnia, the call coming just moments before we were due to visit Petra.

As the second anniversary of Alex's death approached, my extended responsibilities as Defence Attaché came into play for the first time. I was also the Naval Attaché, because the RJNF, being such a small force, came under the Army's wing. Second, my responsibilities included being the interface between the UK and Jordan on all matters connected with polo. Both countries regarded polo to be a prestigious vehicle for cementing relations, especially so as members of both royal families actively participated in the sport. So it was that on the afternoon of 21 October 1992 I had to meet a visiting team from the Combined Services Polo Association, who were guests of the Royal Jordanian Polo Club, before dashing off to host our Trafalgar Night Dinner in the Plaza Hotel, where we had taken over the entire Andalusia restaurant.

The hotel staff had excelled themselves; the whole place was bedecked in red, white and blue. The dining table was covered with a blue silk table cloth to represent the sea and the centrepiece was a spectacular floral arrangement in the shape of a galleon atop which flew a White Ensign – magnificent. Our menu was unapologetically British and included: Fruits from Scottish Waters (salmon!), Roast Beef and Yorkshire Pudding and Lady Hamilton's Queen's Pudding.

I had to deliver a speech to the immortal memory of Admiral Lord Nelson in the presence of our Guest of Honour, the British Ambassador, and representatives from the United States, Russia and China. To lend some credibility to my right to host this prestigious event, I pointed out that the Royal Navy played a major part in the development of the tank and, in the earliest days, tanks were referred to as His Majesty's Landships. Furthermore, the RTR still continued the naval tradition of naming our tanks; in my Regiment, 3RTR, all our tanks' names started with the letter 'C'.

That same day, Rorie started out on the not inconsiderable journey by public transport from Alexandria to join me in Amman. This entailed travelling by bus from Alexandria to Cairo and then across Sinai to Nuweiba, roughly halfway up the Gulf of Aqaba. Here he boarded a ferry to Aqaba, before catching the Jet Bus to Amman – a total distance of about 625 miles. Despite the rigours of the journey, when I met him just before dusk the next day, he looked to be in fine fettle and was full of enthusiasm about his life in Alexandria.

Although he must have been exhausted, he was immediately caught up in the social whirl of my life in Amman. Both my hosts that evening had very kindly included him in their invitations, and I had been able to borrow a suit for him to wear. Our first port of call was for drinks with the British Embassy's Commercial Secretary. Then we went off to Salt, a village on the edge of the Eastern heights overlooking the Jordan Valley, for a dinner hosted by General Nazir Rashid, the Chairman of the Royal Jordanian Polo Club, to welcome our polo playing visitors.

Luckily, Alex's anniversary, 23 October, fell on a Friday, the start of my weekend. It so happened that this was also the day when I had to move back into my official house, a task made much easier with Rorie's help. The Ambassador and his wife, Heidi, aware of the significance of this day, very kindly included us in a tennis party at the Residence, after which they insisted that Rorie and I stay on for an informal supper. Of course we didn't forget Alex, but our very full day prevented us dwelling on his death and becoming morose and depressed.

Next day, Rorie and I visited Jerash and had lunch at the splendid Lebanese House restaurant I had discovered during the RCDS tour, before heading back to Amman in time to attend the reception at the UN headquarters to celebrate UN Day. Sunday saw me back at work until early evening, when, with Rorie, I attended a lively polo match between our Combined Services Team and the Jordanians, which ended very satisfactorily in a 3-3 draw. I then attended yet another reception, this time at the Romanian Embassy, before Rorie and I were able to enjoy a farewell supper at a local Chinese restaurant. Rorie departed next morning; we had had a really enjoyable and interesting time during what might otherwise have been a rather sad and dreary few days.

I was up just before dawn next morning and set out for the polo stables in Zerka, about 15 miles from Amman, with the Ambassador and Heidi to join the visiting polo team. The Jordanian polo team had invited us all for a ride into the desert before the sun rose too high into the sky. When we reached the stables it was as if we had been transported back in time to the beginning of the century – 22 ponies had been saddled and lined up for our inspection. I was the only non-rider, having not sat upon a horse for well over 40 years! Colonel Mohammed Sama'an, who managed the stables, knew my limitations and had selected a calm, good-natured pony for me. I duly mounted my beast along with all the other riders, my Regimental motto, 'Fear Naught', ringing in my ears, and then we were off.

We had a wonderful three hours' ride in the cool, clear morning air, stopping at a well far into the desert for refreshments. I was fine at the trot and the canter, but had great difficulty staying in contact with my mount at the gallop. Still I managed to cling on, quite literally; one hand on the poor horse's mane and the other holding the reins and gripping the front of the saddle! That afternoon I attended the 'international' polo match, with the Crown Prince captaining the Jordanian team. A closely fought, spirited contest saw the Jordanians emerge as the winners, 2-1, but only just, with the Crown Prince scoring the winning goal with the final strike of the game.

My diary note states that, after the match, the Crown Prince chose to walk back to the Polo Club alone with me, just to see how I was settling in and, no doubt, to gauge my ability in the role. I felt very honoured by this gesture and only hoped he hadn't heard of my riding prowess – or lack of it.

The next day found me hard at work in my office at the Embassy, preparing to set off the following morning for the Middle East Attachés' Conference in Cyprus. This was an opportunity for all the Attachés in the region to brief our MoD masters and one another on developments in our various countries and also, most importantly, to be briefed on the 'bigger picture' by the MoD representatives. Being the 'new boy', it was good to get to know my counterparts in the region and hear what they had to say, as well as meeting some of the people to whom I reported in the MoD.

I would be dishonest if I didn't say it wasn't all work; Cyprus is a very nice place to be, even in late October/early November. But what made it all the more special for me was that I was reunited with Toni, who had flown out to join me. She had broken her journey in Cairo and had been able to visit Rorie in Alexandria.

At the end of our conference, Toni and I flew back to Amman. It was wonderful to be together once more, but our gain was our daughters' loss. With the rest of the family all back in the Middle East, Hannah and Zoë became anxious for our safety and found it difficult to settle in England. The answer was to let them join us in Jordan and complete their studies at home, a solution made possible thanks to the excellent support provided by the British Council in Amman.

To their enormous credit, neither daughter was going to allow Saddam Hussein to ruin their prospects. They both worked really hard at opposite ends of our dining table, often foregoing interesting trips with us into the desert. Their dedication paid off and they both gained university places – Hannah at the University of Kent, Canterbury, and Zoë at Jesus College, Oxford.

My main priority was to re-establish military relations between the UK and Jordan. The prime vehicle for achieving this was to organise and run a number of joint training exercises, which proved both rewarding and great fun. All but one of these exercises were single-service events involving British and Jordanian army units, but the final exercise comprised units from both armies supported by RAF and RJAF fighters. I also won agreement for Jordan to host our students on the Interpreter Level Arabic Course at the Defence School Languages, Beaconsfield for the 'Arabic Immersion' phase of their training.

Military Attachés wanting to visit HQ JAF were required to report to the Jordanian Military Liaison Office just inside the entrance barrier. However, as military cooperation between our two countries became ever stronger, I was given free access to the Headquarters and virtually shared an office with my contact in the Training Department, Colonel Yahyah, with whom I became good friends. I was also privileged to work closely on occasion with His Majesty King Abdullah, who was then an Army Brigadier. When my time in Jordan came to an end I was very touched to be presented with a Jordanian ceremonial military headdress and Armed Forces tie – a great honour and the best accolade I could have received.

Initially, our joint exercises took place deep inside the evocative and majestic wastes of Wadi Rum. Apart from operating over ground once trodden by Lawrence of Arabia, on the first exercise, in November 1992, we were treated to an unexpected bonus. An international hot air balloon rally was held in the *wadi* on 14-15 November 1992 to mark King Hussein's 57th birthday. My diary notes record the event:

14 November 1992 – King Hussein's birthday.

In celebration of King Hussein's birthday, 50 of the world's top balloonists had been invited to Jordan for a 'Champion of Champions' Competition for King Hussein's Challenge trophy. The event took place in Wadi *Rum and I was able to get permission for the exercising troops to attend. The viewing area was a massive Bedouin tent. Initially, security was very tight, but when King Hussein's helicopter landed at 1.00 p.m. the friendly crowd streamed past the soldiers and police to greet him. I was thus able to take photos (along with a million others!) from about ten feet.*
Before the first ballooning event there was a ceremonial march past by some 500 soldiers of the Badia (Bedouin) Force, riding four abreast mounted on camels. King Hussein took the salute. The soldiers looked resplendent dressed in their khaki frock tunics, distinctive red and white chequered shemaghs *(Arab headdress), red leather ammunition bandoliers and holsters, and carrying their rifles with their white dust covers at the high port. The camels, too,*

> *were decked out in richly coloured* Bedu *rugs and harnesses. As the Force moved down this famous* wadi *they kicked up a fine dust haze lending an almost mystical dimension to this feast for the eyes.*
> *As the Badia Force faded into the distance, the Royal Jordanian Airline's balloon rose up into the sky. Once it had gained height, the remaining 49 balloons were all inflated and took off en masse – another magnificent sight. After about two hours the Royal Jordanian Airline's balloon landed. This was the cue for all the other balloons to land, the winner of this particular event being the balloon that landed closest to the Royal Jordanian balloon.*

This was the first of three competitions, held over two days, to test the balloonists' skills at navigation and manoeuvring to decide the overall winner – the intervening evening being given over to 'Bedouin-style' barbecues under the stars in this magical *wadi*. I rode in the City of Bath's balloon in the second event.

Although our training in Wadi Rum was well away from the tourist sites, it soon became clear that the sound of gunfire reverberating around the *jebels* was deterring visitors to the area. We therefore had to move to another far less spectacular area of desert well away from any tourist hotspots, but one that, nevertheless, more than met our training needs.

The use of live ammunition added greatly to the realism of this training, but meant that fire control and range safety procedures had to be of the highest order. Prior to an exercise, Colonel Yahyah and I would visit the designated training area and ask any Bedouin within the range danger template to move out for the duration of the training. Only once did we encounter a problem, when a very dignified old man made it clear that he was unwilling to move. We adjusted our plans so that his encampment was outside the danger area – but only just. During the exercise a stray mortar bomb fell uncomfortably close to him and we went to see if he was alright.

He appeared completely unfazed by the experience, proclaiming that Allah clearly didn't want him to die yet. He did, however, agree to leave the area, together with his mixed flock of sheep and goats, but insisted that his wife and family stayed put! We had no option but to alter our plans again to reach a safe compromise.

Midway through the exercise the Regimental padre flew in from Cyprus to visit his troops in the field and conduct a Sunday service for them. This was his first visit to the Middle East and he appeared a little ambivalent in his attitude towards Arabs and Islam. I therefore offered to take him and some others to meet our Bedouin friend. As our two Land Rovers approached his tent I could see that he was praying on the sand outside, so we stopped and waited until he got up and went back in.

Greeting us like long lost friends, rather than the inconvenient neighbours we obviously were, he ushered us all into his home and invited us to sit down. He then ground some coffee beans, roasted them on the fire and proceeded to make us coffee, which he served with a few dates. When it was time for us to go, I thanked him on our behalf and, rather foolishly, asked how we could repay his hospitality. His eyes turned towards our Land Rovers, which were loaded to the gunwales with all manner of useful items. My heart was in my mouth; in the Arab culture if someone admires something of yours it is customary to give it to them. Yet nothing on those vehicles belonged to us, but to Her Majesty! It therefore was not ours to give.

I needn't have worried. Looking back at us, he said: "You are gifts from Allah. What need have I for anything else?" We were hugely impressed, no one more so than the padre, and I was told that he had mentioned this incident in his sermon next day.

All in all, I was involved in five joint training exercises, all of which helped to cement relations between our two countries. Whilst all the units taking part co-operated well during the tactical training phases, perhaps the unit that integrated most fully was the Royal Irish Regiment. At night, during non-tactical phases, mixed groups of Irish and Jordanian soldiers could be heard singing and playing their instruments round all the campfires, their music overcoming all language barriers.

My role as Naval Attaché gave me further opportunities to strengthen ties between the armed forces of our two countries. Naval vessels involved in enforcing the blockade of Iraq following the Gulf War often visited Jordan on goodwill visits and/or to be replenished. I was the facilitator for all such visits made by the Royal Navy. By the time I arrived in Jordan, the procedures, protocols and administrative requirements for these events had been well established. In addition, I was luckily able to observe visits from the navies of the United States, Australia and France before the arrival of the first of three visits by the Royal Navy.

I would base myself down at Aqaba about three days prior to the ship's arrival and check that all programmes, fuel and stores requirements, etc., were in order. Once the ship had docked I would then go down to the quay to introduce myself to the Captain. I always felt that there was a justified sense of disappointment – even indignation – when I, a soldier, emerged from my staff car, especially as I was flying the White Ensign. But the Royal Navy were very polite and always piped me aboard.

I accompanied the Captain on his official programme, which included courtesy calls on both the Governor of Aqaba and the Military Commander of the region, and would advise him on the plans we had made for entertaining the ship's company. Central to the 'goodwill' aspect of these visits was a reception held on board for key political and military figures and members of the Diplomatic Corps. These receptions always took place in the evening and culminated in the flag-lowering ceremony at sunset. By way of reciprocation, I was responsible for organising and hosting a reception in one of the hotels in Aqaba for a cross-section of the crew.

The last ship's visit during my tour, *HMS Montrose* in April 1995, included an added dimension in the form of a short joint exercise with the RJNF in Jordan's miniscule territorial waters. The limitations on space posed considerable problems, but the two navies practiced a number of manoeuvres and drills, including 'man over board' procedures. I was an observer on one of the three RJNF patrol boats taking part. On the successful completion of the exercise, the three RJNF naval craft escorted *HMS Montrose* to the limit of Jordan's territorial waters, where, sirens sounding, we all bade farewell to one another, a moment I found quite emotional.

The previous evening I had organised a more informal party for members of the crew – a typical Jordanian affair. After the meal, the waiters cleared the tables and then placed a lit *shishas* (hookah pipe) and scented tobacco on each of them for the sailors to try. This proved a very popular move, but nearly ended in disaster. Procedures were brought to a halt when a passing patrol from the ship's police thought we were smoking hashish, or worse! I looked anything but a Naval Attaché, dressed as I was in a Hawaiian shirt and trousers, as I leapt to the sailors' defence to explain that this was nothing more than scented tobacco and had been ordered by me. Although the police accepted this explanation they, nonetheless, felt it was time to get their sailors safely back on board.

One morning, about nine months into my tour, the Ambassador asked me to come to his office. As I had settled into my new role quite well and, in particular, had established a strong working relationship with the Jordanian Armed Forces – the first joint exercise having been a success – the last thing I expected was to be given bad news. But bad news it was; I had been selected for redundancy. I was given a year's notice and told that

I could spend my last six months in the UK to help with the transition to civilian life.

This was a real body blow. I had been struggling to get back on my feet after the horrors of Kuwait, but now I felt as if I had been kicked whilst I was still down; and not just kicked, but unceremoniously booted onto the unwanted scrap heap by a callous and dispassionate MoD.

I discussed the situation with Toni when I returned home that afternoon and she agreed with my intention to remain working in Jordan for as long as possible. Next, I wrote a rather bitter letter to my manning branch within the MoD, acknowledging the fact that I had been notified of my fate and telling them that, whilst I reluctantly accepted the decision, I considered that it rode a coach and horses through the ethos of care upon which the Army prided itself.

I received a letter back almost by return of post. Far from being terse, it was empathetic – almost apologetic. It explained that, in the interests of impartiality, the selection process for redundancy had to be made 'blind' to individuals' own personal circumstances or performance in their role. The only criteria to be considered was the age, rank and length of service of those in the bracket for redundancy, and the percentage cut required by rank in each of the myriad army establishments.

I had to accept that this was fair. If personal circumstances were taken into account, anyone who wanted to remain in the army could argue that they were a special case. I resolved to make the most of the time remaining to me in Jordan, both at work and play. To avoid damaging my credibility with the Jordanians, I was asked to keep this matter from them for the time being.

As luck would have it, just a few weeks after receiving this dispiriting news, I found myself involved in yet another high-powered visit, but this time it was the Military Secretary, Lieutenant General the Hon Sir William Rous KCB OBE, Head of Officer Manning and a member of the

Army Board. He was accompanied by Lady Rous. Toni and I both told Sir William and Lady Rous of our disappointment at having been selected for redundancy. Whilst he was careful to point out that he couldn't take sides, Sir William urged me to lodge a formal appeal as he felt that I had a cast iron case. Indeed, at the end of a very successful and enjoyable visit, his parting shot to me was: "Make sure you get that appeal in as soon as possible." I did, and to my relief it was upheld.

Lieutenant General the Hon Sir William Rous died of cancer in May 1999.

Another aspect of my role was to get to know my 'patch' really well. Jordan has an extremely varied topography. The West of Jordan is part of the Great Rift Valley, running from the Sea of Galilee, in the North, through the Dead Sea to Aqaba in the South. The Northern part, down to the Dead Sea, ranges from 650-1,300 feet below sea level. Popularly known as the Jordan Valley (or al Ghor in Arabic – not a translation), it is highly fertile, despite enjoying an arid desert climate, thanks to irrigation from the River Jordan that forms the country's Western border. The Dead Sea is land-locked with a salinity eight times more concentrated than the world's oceans and seas. It is the lowest point on the surface of the earth. The area from below the Dead Sea to Aqaba is a truly desolate sandy waste. Known as the Wadi Araba, it rises to just above sea level before gently falling back to meet the sea at Aqaba.

The Jordan Valley, Dead Sea and Wadi Araba are bordered on the East by the Eastern Heights. These vary in elevation from 5,000 feet in the North to 2,000 feet in the South. The higher levels of this region enjoy a largely Mediterranean climate, but snow can be expected in winter. Going further East, the land falls gradually down to about 2,000 feet into the

Eastern desert, which covers about 75% of Jordan. In the North, this desert comprises basalt rock, colouring the desert a sombre black. Below Amman, it is sandy and, as it approaches Aqaba, it becomes mountainous, forming such iconic sites as Wadi Rum.

In winter, it is not unusual to experience snow in Amman – we once had a fall of eight inches. At such times, it is possible to leave the snow behind and enjoy a 'swim' in the Dead Sea in temperatures in the high 30°C. Spring on the Heights, however, made the greatest impact on us. For about four-six weeks, the whole countryside is transformed by a riot of colour as anemones and other wild flowers bust into bloom. It is a truly magical time. Our 'lawn' at home was nothing more than a dusty patch of ground throughout the year until Spring, when it was transformed into the most beautiful carpet of flowers.

The Heights were also home to wild tortoises, which came out to forage in the Spring (we never saw them during the rest of the year, but perhaps they came out to forage in the cool of the night). We had a rockery in our garden that was home to about a dozen of these little creatures. One of my predecessors must have painted numbers on them, but some of the numbers were missing by the time we arrived and there were also some without numbers, new arrivals perhaps.

Getting to know Jordan without attracting unwanted attention was made all the easier, and certainly more interesting, by the plethora of natural and archaeological sites that abound in this fascinating country: the Jordan Valley, the River Jordan and the Dead Sea, Wadi Rum, Roman ruins, desert castles, Crusader castles, biblical sites and, of course, Petra.

One site, Qasr al-Tuba, presented us with quite a challenge. This Umayyad ruin, dating from around 745 AD, was located in the middle of a featureless expanse of desert some 60 miles South East of Amman. It was well off the beaten track, or, indeed, any track at all, so wasn't on any tourist itinerary. Yet in Umayyad times it was probably a *caravanserai*, the equivalent of today's motel, meaning that originally it must have been on a well-trodden trading route.

When Toni and I went looking for this ruin we were unable to interest anyone else in joining us (as a rule one didn't venture deep into the desert with a single vehicle). Undaunted, having left our route and timings with the Embassy, and equipped with a radio and carrying sufficient food and water just in case things went wrong, we set off alone. We searched all day, but to no avail. Later, I discovered that we'd been within 200-300 yards of our goal, but as it was in a shallow depression we had failed to spot it.

A few weeks later, I happened to mention my desire to visit the site when talking to a Jordanian guide at Qasr Amra, a desert 'castle' – probably a former hunting lodge – at the entrance to the panhandle in the North East of the country. He said he knew how to get to Qasr al-Tuba and arranged to take us there the following weekend. Again, no luck. We agreed to meet up once more the following weekend to resume our search.

By this stage, the Embassy had been issued with a ground positioning system (GPS). So when we next went to meet our Jordanian guide, I took this along as back-up. However, I didn't want him to lose face, so we set off as before. After scouring the desert for two hours or so, I suggested we stop and have a cup of tea. As Toni poured out the tea, I placed the GPS on the ground a few feet from the vehicle. Then, as we were packing up, I checked the readings, found our exact position on the map and set a compass bearing towards our objective. We stopped half an hour later to take a further reading and I was able to declare that Qasr al-Tuba was just over the crest in front of us.

As we set off, a beautiful desert fox appeared from nowhere and ran in front of us, up and over the crest, as if showing us the way. Sure enough, as we breasted the crest there was Qasr al-Tuba, laid out before us in its illusive shallow depression. It was a remarkably large site – about the size of three to four football fields and, unlike the other ruins we visited, was constructed largely from sun-baked mud bricks. The best preserved structure on the site was a narrow building with a barrel-vaulted roof which was lovely and cool inside.

When we returned to our guide's village he took us to see the headman, who insisted we sit down and have a cup of tea. Meanwhile, the guide slipped away, returning a few minutes later with what appeared to be a gathering of all the village elders. Then the headman told the attentive crowd how I had found Qasr al-Tuba. "This soldier stopped the Land Rover to drink tea. He put this 'magic box' [indicating to me to raise the GPS aloft] on the ground and when he had finished his tea the magic box told him where to go!" With a twinkle in his eye, he ended by saying: "We must be good citizens – the army is very clever!"

There were many impressive castles in Jordan to fire the imagination, but the one that made the greatest impression on us, perhaps, was Shoback. This was not so much due to its size or structure, but because of its position on top of a steep-sided conical mountain. A Crusader castle, it was built by King Baldwin I of Jerusalem in 1115. It lies just off the King's Highway, around 125 miles south of Amman. When we were there, it was accessed by a steep, narrow track that wound around the mountainside; in short, the very image of a castle in a child's fairy story.

Driving up this track for the first time was quite scary. It was barely wide enough for our car, the drop was unprotected and, due to the steepness of the gradient, I was unable to see the road immediately in front of me. We were the only visitors at the time and the delightful old Jordanian caretaker took great trouble to point out things of interest to us – the original Crusader remains and later additions by the Mamluks and Ottomans. He also showed us some original stone 'cannonballs' lying undisturbed amongst the ruins. Significantly, the castle had its own protected water supply, accessed by a deep well shaft within its walls.

Herod's Palace at Mukawir, overlooking the Dead Sea some 40 miles south-west of Amman, was another fascinating site. We were unable to drive up to this site, so faced quite a hard 20-30 minute slog, initially downwards which made the steep climb up to the summit even longer. Little remains of the palace, but there was a particular piece of flat ground on which, we were told, Salome danced for Herod and then asked for Saint John the Baptist's head as a reward.

Down one side of the mountain was a large opening into a cave some 60 or so feet deep. According to the caretaker, this was where Saint John the Baptist had been imprisoned before he was beheaded. A natural dungeon, it was dark, damp and sinister. Nearby was another cave, the entrance to which had been filled in with a breeze-block wall complete with a door and two windows. This was home to a Bedouin family, giving us a tangible connection between the present day and the dawn of Christianity 2,000 years ago.

Possibly the most significant biblical site was Mount Nebo, a promontory on the Eastern Heights reputed to be where Moses set eyes upon the 'Promised Land'. Indeed, the view is splendid; your eye is taken from the lush Jordan Valley bisected by the River Jordan, and the Dead Sea, to Jericho on the West Bank and up the Western Heights to Jerusalem and Bethlehem. Moses died on this mountain and in the 4th century a church in the form of a basilica was built here in honour of 'Saint Moses'. This church is now in ruins, but an 'outer shell' has been built over the site to allow worshipers to pray and to protect the ancient mosaic floor.

The site is also home to a small monastery and, at Christmas, Midnight Mass is celebrated by the monks amongst the ruins. This was a truly uplifting experience, with an international inter-denominational congregation, including some locals dressed not unlike their forefathers. Mass was said in several different languages to make us all feel at home as we gathered around the altar amongst fallen pillars and other bits of masonry. A carpet of snow covering Mount Nebo in 1992 added greatly to the atmosphere for our first Christmas Midnight Mass. As we came out of the church at the end of Mass, we saw the lights of Jerusalem and Bethlehem twinkling on the Western Heights under a star-studded sky, with the brightest star low on the horizon over Bethlehem.

As we admired this spectacle, we began talking to a Jordanian couple, Alfred and Leila Sawalha, who invited us back to their house in Madaba for a Christmas breakfast. Madaba is one of two towns in Jordan with strong Christian communities, the other being Kerak. Situated between Amman and Mount Nebo, Madaba also boasts a church, St George's, with a mosaic floor incorporating what is thought to be the oldest map of the Holy Land.

Over breakfast, we learnt that Alfred ran a freight business and, amongst other things, was responsible for packing up and shipping the personal effects of British Embassy staff at the end of their time in Jordan. He also had two nieces who were actresses in Britain. A former soldier in the Arab Legion, he got me doing rifle drill with him for the amusement of our wives!

At Easter, there was an Anglican-led midnight service at Mount Nebo attended by largely the same congregation as at Christmas, including the Sawalhas and ourselves. Once again, they invited us home for breakfast and this became a popular tradition during our time in Jordan.

Down the northern side of Mount Nebo there was a massive rock at the head of a *wadi* from which clear spring water flowed. This spot, known as Ayn Musa (Moses' Well), was said to be where God ordered Moses to strike the rock to find water and we often used to go for walks in this area when visiting Mount Nebo.

The Dead Sea was an obvious attraction for us and our visitors alike. Everyone was keen to demonstrate its buoyancy by having their photograph taken whilst floating on their backs reading a newspaper. Indeed, the water is so buoyant that you have to be quite careful when wading not to allow your feet to be lifted off the bottom, thus tipping you forward face down.

The salt is so concentrated that should any of the water get into your eyes the pain is excruciating. The remedy, we discovered, was simply to put a towel over our eyes for a moment and then gently remove it, thereby lifting off the salt crystals. We also soon learned to walk backwards into the sea to minimise the risk of getting our faces wet, and we always kept a dry towel as close as possible to the water's edge – just in case.

The RJNF was responsible for patrolling the Jordanian half of this sea, using small patrol boats specifically designed to operate in these overly buoyant waters. Due to the corrosive nature of the salt, these craft had to be hoisted out of the water after each patrol and thoroughly hosed down – no mean feat. I was once given the privilege of joining one of these patrols, including the launch and recovery phases, and was very impressed by the professionalism and dedication of the crews.

Petra was another firm fixture on any visitor's programme. I had the privilege of visiting this unique site on about two dozen occasions, albeit mostly in an official capacity. If official visits entailed an overnight stay, we were booked in to the luxury hotel at the entrance to the site. However, when visiting as a family we preferred to stay at the Al Anbart hotel in Wadi Musa. This was a small homely Jordanian hotel and gave us a much better feel for the country.

Petra itself is about a mile from the entry point to the site, the route taking one down a *wadi* to the mountain barrier. There one enters a fissure, known as the Siq. This is so narrow in places that the soaring mountain walls all but blot out the sky above. As one nears the end of the Siq there is the first glimpse of the treat in store for you – the magnificent sight of the Treasury, or, *Al Khazneh,* as it is known to the Jordanians, an elaborately carved building hewn into the mountainside.

The sandstone rock in this region is a mix of colours: various shades of red, pink, brown, saffron and white strata combine to form the most stunning patterns, especially in the gentler light of dawn and dusk

Whenever we visited Petra, fascinating as it was, our eyes were always drawn to a tiny white domed building perched upon the highest point of the mountains ringing the site. This was the mosque above Aaron's tomb and the mountain was Jebel Haroun – Aaron's mountain. Toni and I resolved to visit this site before we left Jordan.

Having gained permission to climb up to this holy site we were put in touch with a young Bedouin called Qassim. On the day of the expedition, we drove to the *Bedu* village, just outside Petra, where Qassim met us. He had two camels for us and a donkey for himself. Once we had loaded our equipment into the colourful *Bedu* camel bags, we set off. Our diary notes take up the story:

> *We started off on foot leading our camels as the first part of the journey was a steep descent into Petra and camels find it difficult to go downhill. In Petra, we were joined by Qassim's wife, Hatama, and their lively three-year-old son, Firaas. They were riding a donkey. We mounted our camels and our little convoy set off through Petra and up the Wadi Thugra. We were amazed by how our camels negotiated the steep, rocky terrain, as we had always associated them with the soft sands of the desert. We passed through Little Petra along the route with* Bedu *still living in many of the Nabataean caves (these caves were well away from the tourist sites and so the* Bedu *had been allowed to continue living here). As we neared what is known as the Snake Monument, we came to a beautiful Nabataean cave dwelling, which turned out to be the home of Qassim's mother. Of course, she invited us all in for tea. Refreshed, we set off again, often having to dismount as the route became too steep or rocky in places for the camels to carry us safely. Mohammed, the guardian of the tomb, was waiting for us with his donkey roughly half way up the mountain. After a long slog we*

reached a plateau, just a 15-minute steep climb from our goal.
As the sun dropped lower towards the horizon, Mohammed led us up on foot to the mosque. Reaching the crest we were rewarded with a fantastic panorama that took our breath away – we could see across the Wadi Araba to Israel, the whole of Petra and up Wadi Musa. We were surprised at how minute the massive edifice of the monastery appeared from up here. Mohammed unlocked the door to the mosque with an enormous key. Apparently, Greek Orthodox monks lived here until the 13th century and, after they left, Aaron's tomb was restored and placed in the building. However, Mohammed led us down by candlelight to the tomb's original site some way underground beneath the mosque.
He also showed us an underground cistern. Built by the Nabataeans, it was brimming with fresh water [rain water] *in an area where you would least expect to find any – what a feat!*
As we descended once more towards the plateau in the chilly evening air, we could see the warming glow of a fire beside Mohammed's cave dwelling. Hatama was cooking us all a Bedu *supper of chicken and 'parcels' of potatoes, onions and tomatoes, whilst Qassim prepared a salad and cut up some bread. As night fell we all sat round the fire enjoying a delicious meal and soaking in the simple pleasures of life. We then turned in for the night on flattish rocks outside Mohammed's cave.*
It wasn't a bad night – dry and not too cold – but in the early hours the wind picked up and the donkeys brayed their displeasure until morning. Surprisingly, we were up before our Bedu *friends and clambered back up the mountain to catch the dawn, but the wind had kicked up a thick dust haze, so we couldn't see much at all.*
We were back in time for a communal breakfast of bread and local cheese washed down with copious amounts of hot sweet tea. We then

> *started to make our way down the mountain again. We hadn't gone far before we met a* Bedu *family climbing up towards the summit. The mother was carrying a tiny baby in a very novel way; the baby was in a sling across her back and the sling was held in place by a carrying handle round the mother's forehead, similar to the way tea pluckers in South India carry their plucking baskets. The sling was held at an angle so that the baby's head was uppermost. We stopped to have a chat and discovered the family was on a pilgrimage to the mosque to present their newborn baby to Aaron.*

Dana was another as yet unspoilt treasure. The village, reputed to be about 500 years old, stood at the top of an amazing *wadi*, the Wadi Dana, that ran down the Eastern Heights to the Wadi Araba far below. The *wadi* appeared to have been made by a giant plunging his spade into the mountainside and turning over the soil. The result was a landscape of tortured rock formations that gave the area an alien appearance, particularly so in the hot summer months when there was virtually no vegetation to soften the contorted jumble of peaks and troughs.

In Spring, however, the ground was covered in a riot of colour from millions of wild flowers, transforming Dana into the most exquisite playground. We often camped here overnight, on a flat rock on the edge of the *wadi*, overlooking the tangle of contours – a slightly precarious campsite due to the drop, but an excellent viewpoint from where to watch the sunset. Towards the end of our time in Jordan, Dana was beginning to be developed as a tourist site; work began on building a visitors' complex and the entire area was declared a nature reserve. This was excellent news for Jordan and, in particular Dana village, as the initiative would bring in much-needed revenue and employment. However, it marked the end of wild camping.

Toni and I often dropped in on Bedouin encampments on trips into the desert and, certainly, we found the true Bedouin to be very close to God. They live a precarious, unforgiving, hand-to-mouth existence, made possible, I believe, only because of their utter faith in Allah.

On one occasion when our family was camping out in Wadi Rum, we had a distinctly 'exciting' encounter with some Bedouin. We had just finished clearing up after supper and were getting ready for bed. This was always a special time in the desert, because the night sky was covered from horizon to horizon with millions of sparkles of light. As we lay looking up at the sky, our peace was suddenly shattered by gunfire. Some of the bullets were striking the rocks uncomfortably close to us.

I didn't think we were under attack, but suspected that some Bedouin were out hunting for the pot. Telling everyone to keep lying down, I crawled to our smouldering camp fire and, feeding it with brushwood, got it roaring again. Then calling out I asked the hunters to stop firing in our direction. I heard a Land Cruiser (the modern ship of the desert) start up and move off – tranquillity reigned once more.

We were captivated by Wadi Rum and the surrounding desert. So much so that when I asked Toni what she wanted to do on her 50th birthday, it was to wake up in Wadi Rum. So that's what we did, along with our daughter, Hannah.

There were three ways of reaching this area and Aqaba beyond. The most obvious was down the main road between Amman and Aqaba – fast, uninteresting and sometimes quite dangerous, due to speeding traffic or lumbering, over-laden lorries. Another route was along the King's Highway. This was the original road between Amman and Aqaba. It was slow and twisting but, clinging as it did to the very tops of the Eastern Heights, it afforded the most spectacular views of the Jordan Valley, the Dead Sea, the Wadi Araba (the valley south of the Dead Sea) and iconic places like Jerusalem and Bethlehem on the Western Heights. In Winter, this route could become quite treacherous due to ice and driving snow. We were caught in such conditions driving to Aqaba one Christmas Eve and had to stop for a squall to pass. It was then that we noticed the ice building up on the stunted trees and bushes. The wind was so cold and strong that the ice was seemingly defying gravity, protruding horizontally from the branches for some four to five inches.

When Jordan signed a peace treaty with Israel in October 1994 a third route to Aqaba was open to us. This route descended into the Jordan Valley from Amman and ran along the Eastern shores of the Dead Sea and then through the Wadi Araba, along the border with Israel to Aqaba. This was a novelty and enabled us to visit sites which had previously been barred to us. One of these was Lot's Cave. The site had only recently been discovered and was being excavated when we visited it.

I eventually found it possible to drive through the desert cross-country from the bottom of the escarpment via Wadi Rum to Aqaba. This was great fun and passed by some interesting sites, such as rock paintings and circular holes drilled into rocks, thought to be used by an ancient civilisation to make coins. Both these places were well off the tourist map. The scenery, too, was spectacular; in particular, two amazing rock arches. One of these was on the desert floor, quite accessible and relatively safe for people to clamber up and over. The other was several hundred feet above the desert atop a sheer *jebel* on the approach to Wadi Rum.

On one occasion, Toni and I were invited to join a group from the Embassy camping in Wadi Rum. The following morning I was asked to take them to see the high rock arch. As we approached, we spotted a woman waving to us at the base of the *jebel*. Going over to investigate we found a man lying injured on the ground. They were a young French couple and had tried to climb up to the high arch the previous evening, when the man lost his footing and fell. They had been there all night.

Not one of us was medically trained, but we were on our own and miles from any help. We checked that the injured man could move his head, arms and legs and then made a stretcher out of one of our army camp beds. Keeping him as straight and steady as possible, we eased him onto this makeshift stretcher and laid him along the back seat of my Land Rover. Then we crawled to the Wadi Rum police post, where the police summoned an ambulance from the hospital in Aqaba. A few days later we received a bouquet of flowers and a note from the French couple, thanking us for our help. The man had cracked a couple of vertebra, but had been fitted with a brace and they were now en-route to Syria to continue their adventure! Oh to be young!

Toni's mother came out to visit us in May 1994. Although a little frail, we were able to show her around Petra in a pony and trap, as well as taking her for a dip in the Dead Sea. We had also planned for my mother to come out for a visit. However, before this could be arranged she was sadly struck down by another, massive stroke. She died some four months later having never regained consciousness. Of course, my brother, who was also a soldier, and I were granted compassionate leave to return home to see her, which we found very distressing as she was not being properly looked after. Whilst I had to return to Jordan after a week, my brother, Hedley, who was stationed at Supreme Headquarters Allied Powers Europe (SHAPE) in Belgium, was able to get her into a home, where she was much better cared for and thus more at ease. We were also both able to get home for her funeral.

Toni's youngest sister, Pip, visited us with a friend and, in addition to seeing much of Jordan, we took them up to Damascus, where we spent a night at St Paul's convent just outside the city walls. When one of the nuns showed us to our room, I pointed out that I was married to only one of these ladies, to which she replied sternly: "I'm sure you know how to behave in God's house!" I nodded sheepishly.

The visit that will always remain in our minds was when Bishop Michael Kenny came to stay in February 1995. He had been such a tower of strength for Rorie and me whilst we were hostages in Baghdad in 1990. He was his usual exuberant self, bounding with energy and enthusiasm, yet thoughtful and sensitive. When driving towards Petra along the King's Highway we came across a patch of snow in a spot sheltered from the sun. Bishop Michael immediately asked if we could stop, "So that I can make a snowball in the desert." In Petra, he climbed up the rocky hillside beside the monastery – the largest structure in Petra – and walked out onto the roof of the monument to look down on us, making my toes curl!

The following day, we had planned to take him to the ruined Roman city of Jerash, but an American priest in Amman asked if he could take him instead, as he wanted a private discussion with the Bishop. Of course, we agreed. Our day passed uneventfully, but as evening approached we began to get concerned that Bishop Michael hadn't returned. Eventually the phone rang. It was the American Air Attaché, who broke the awful news that Bishop Michael had collapsed and died in Jerash. He had suffered a brain aneurysm. The poor priest who had accompanied him was initially arrested on suspicion of murder. The matter was now being dealt with by the American Embassy, and the Air Attaché asked if he could come round in the morning to collect Bishop Michael's things.

We were stunned; here was the man who had looked the picture of health and was so full of life when we bade him farewell that morning. He was only 57. When we went to gather up his possessions we were struck by what little he had – less than we would have packed for a weekend, let alone a fortnight. This was a truly humble man. His unfortunate companion for the day was so badly affected by Bishop Michael's sudden death and his own subsequent arrest by the police that he became unwell had to return to America.

Being an attaché was an entirely new experience for me. I was now answerable to two government departments: the FCO and the MoD. Both departments had the same overall priorities, but sometimes their approaches to achieving these differed. As my direct boss in the Embassy was the Ambassador, the FCO enjoyed the greater leverage. However, as both the Ambassadors under whom I served were former National Service Army officers, they were very understanding of my position and, with typical diplomatic flair, were able to smooth out potential areas of conflict.

During my pre-tour induction training I had been told that the Ambassador's role was a very lonely one. Thus the Attaché's responsibility was not only to execute his military duty, but also to win the trust of his Ambassador as a potential confidant. Luckily, I was able to establish a very healthy working relationship with both my Ambassadors and our families mixed well socially. One told me – in jest, I think – that the terms 'military intelligence' and 'military diplomat' were oxymoronic! I was never able to convince him otherwise.

Being a member of the Attaché Corps and rubbing shoulders with my counterparts was also truly fascinating. The only potential source of discomfort was that the Iraqi Attaché was a brigadier general, whilst the rest of us were colonels or lieutenant colonels (or other service equivalents). As such, the Iraqi was head of the corps. However, he kept a very low profile and our paths rarely crossed.

Of the non-Arab Attachés, the American, Chinese and Russian were the true specialists, spending most, if not all, of their careers immersed in the Arab world, and they were fluent in Arabic. Britain, however, enjoyed a special status in recognition of our long and close history with Jordan, reaching back to the country's emergence after the Great War. As such, our two Attachés, the Defence, Military and Naval Attaché (me) and the Air Attaché, were the only ones authorised to fly car flags when on official duty. This was a much envied privilege and one which we had to exercise religiously, lest it be withdrawn.

I remember well the sense of insecurity felt by the Russian Attachés when the Soviet Union began to collapse. What did the future hold for them? Would they be out of a job? In the end, the transition to the new Russia worked well for them. I recall the day, during a party at our house, when the Russian Assistant Military Attaché, a lieutenant colonel, told me he had bought a car – his very first! He was beaming with pride and asked me to come outside to see it. It was a Nissan Micra, but to him it could have been a Rolls-Royce!

All the Chinese Embassy staff, from the Ambassador downwards, lived communally in their distinctive Embassy building with its pagoda-style roofs. Only a handful had been permitted to be accompanied by their wives and none had been allowed to bring their children with them. Moreover, none of the wives were allowed out of the compound unless escorted by their husbands.

Their receptions and dinners were held in a huge hall within the Embassy. Wine was served before meals and only in liqueur glasses. I remember the Chinese Defence Attaché offering his French counterpart – a true wine buff, who travelled with his own wine cellar – a glass of Chinese wine and inviting his opinion. Sipping the wine, the Frenchman paused for a while before declaring it to be, "a very interesting wine," much to the delight of his host – and a lesson in diplomacy for me.

The Chinese appeared to have been briefed that the outside world liked ballroom dancing. Consequently, this was the usual after-dinner entertainment, at which they excelled but most of us struggled, except for our Air Attaché and his wife, who really flew the flag for Britain.

On one occasion, however, the entertainment was before dinner. The 'star' was an 80-year-old Chinese doctor, who practised a kind of acupuncture using electricity rather than needles. He started his demonstration by strapping a voltmeter to his waist and connecting it to the mains. It duly recorded a reading of around 220 volts. He then took hold of two bare live wires protruding from the voltmeter to make a circuit and invited a Chinese diplomat to hold a normal electric light bulb about six inches away from any part of his body. Amazingly, it lit up wherever it was held, showing that his whole being was electrified!

At this point, the Romanian Defence Attaché leapt up to try to touch the doctor and see for himself. Horrified, the doctor stepped back, shouting, "You touch me you die! You touch me you die!" Luckily, the Romanian backed off. The doctor then laid two raw steaks on metal strips that were attached to the mains. Grabbing hold of both ends he completed the circuit and the steaks were cooked in less than two minutes!

The doctor then showed how he could, indeed, control the voltage by willpower if given a few seconds. Low and behold, the voltmeter gradually decreased until it was reading zero, even though it was still connected to the mains and the lights around us were still burning brightly.

This, he explained, was how he was able to use electricity in his work and, to prove it was safe, he invited volunteers to join him holding hands in a circle. Before we could stop her, our daughter Zoë joined the circle. He was still plugged into the mains with the voltmeter recording zero. First, he raised the voltage to 4.5 volts – similar to a torch battery. Zoë told us afterwards that this caused a tingling sensation in her fingertips on both hands. He then increased the voltage in stages three or four times, demonstrating that he could set the desired voltage, until suddenly everyone yelled and let go of each other. Finally, he invited a volunteer to come forward to try his form of acupuncture. The gallant Italian Defence Attaché, Danilo, an Alpini, stepped forward. He had hurt his shoulder playing tennis and was thus an ideal subject for such a demonstration. Using the tips of his fingers to administer electric shocks of various voltages, the doctor worked on Danilo's shoulder for about 15 minutes, throughout which Danilo's shoulder twitched uncontrollably as it was bombarded by electrical pulses. He was genuinely impressed with the result, claiming that his shoulder felt much easier.

I was lucky enough to sit next to the doctor during dinner. What little body hair he had on his arms stood erect and his skin was still hot to the touch. During conversation he told me that he had been identified at the age of two or three as someone who could be taught to control electricity through Kung Fu, using his blood vessels as conduits. He had then been trained to use this ability to heal people. Indeed, he was visiting Jordan to see if there was a market for this type of treatment here. Whilst he made an indelible impression on all of us, the Jordanians didn't buy into the concept. I wouldn't blame anybody for not believing what I have just written; all I can do is record what I saw and experienced – my memory backed up by my diary notes written at the time.

The headquarters of the Jordanian Armed Forces kindly hosted an annual party for the Attaché Corps, including our wives. In 1994, our Jordanian hosts elected to hold this event in a Bedouin tent on the shores of the Dead Sea. I had to work late that day so was unable to join Toni on the coach taking everyone to the venue. My intention was to make my own way down later. The weather was fine when I set off from Amman, and on the descent into the Jordan Valley I was waved down by a policeman, who asked if I could give him a lift to his post at the Dead Sea. As we neared the valley floor, the wind suddenly started to pick up and soon we found ourselves engulfed in a really dense sandstorm. My headlights just threw the light back in my face and I couldn't even see the end of the car bonnet.

I knew we were on a raised section of road that was dead straight and level. It crossed a minefield dating back to the 1967 or 1973 Arab/Israeli wars. I asked the Jordanian policeman to keep an eye on the edge of the road on his side, whilst I kept an eye on my side. We crawled along like this until we felt the car suddenly tilt forwards on my side. We were going down the embankment into the minefield. I stopped immediately and suggested that we should get out of the car to give us more chance of seeing or hearing vehicles that might run into us. Taking what shelter we could beside the car, we waited for the storm to pass.

Meanwhile, down at the Dead Sea the storm had put paid to our party. Toni told me it was quite frightening seeing the huge waves on the Dead Sea crashing onto the shore. The water, being so much heavier than normal sea water, made the waves far more powerful and dangerous.

Eventually, the storm moved on. I got the car back onto the road, dropped the policeman off at his post and reached the party venue in time to help with the packing up. It had been quite an experience for everyone, but at least we were all safe. Not to be thwarted, the Jordanians very kindly re-scheduled the party for a later date so that we were not denied this special experience by the shores of the Dead Sea.

The Jordanians always held a farewell dinner for Attachés at the end of their tour, at which the departing Attaché(s) were expected to deliver a farewell speech. When my turn came, I elected to make my speech in Arabic. My ability in the language was inadequate so I sought the help of a retired Jordanian teacher. Having written my speech out in English, I asked her to help me to translate it into Arabic.

I was one of four departing Attachés. We were in civilian evening dress and I had opted to wear my kilt. When it was my turn to take the stand and say my farewells I was able to do so in passable Arabic, a gesture greatly appreciated by my Jordanian hosts. When the evening drew to a close, the Chinese Defence Attaché came up to me and asked to see my script. Seeing it was written in Arabic, he shook my hand, saying: "You are a very clever DA. I never knew you could speak Arabic." I think he was concerned that I might have eavesdropped on some of his conversations over the years. He need not have worried; not only was I not a fluent Arabist like him, but like most 'tankies' (RTR soldiers) I was also quite deaf!

On 2 May 1993 it was the 40th anniversary of King Hussein's coronation as the third ruler of the Hashemite Kingdom of Jordan. The day was marked by the most dynamic and colourful pageant, masterminded by Major Sir Michael Parker KCVO CBE, famous for, amongst other things, organising the Royal Tournament in London. The event took place outside Amman in an enormous arena. Numerous flags, stretched horizontal by a stiff breeze, outlined the perimeter and a massive golden crown topped the performers' main access gate. Before King Hussein arrived, various tribal groups entertained us with traditional dances and music. My diary notes take up the story:

> *2 May 1993*
>
> *King Hussein arrived and as soon as he was seated the pageant exploded into life with a re-enactment of the Great Arab Revolt – very colourful, with people mounted on numerous camels and horses careering about, whilst an ancient 'Dove' aircraft swooped low overhead. This was followed by a mock modern day combined arms battle involving jet aircraft, helicopters and infantry soldiers. Next came an amazing demonstration of continuity drill by 1,000 soldiers and policemen – possibly the largest group ever to perform in this way. They had been trained by a sergeant from the Queen's Colour Squadron, RAF. Keeping up the tempo, an equally brilliant combined musical ride by 41 horsemen and 80 cameleers enthralled us with their skill. They had been trained by a staff*

sergeant in the King's Troop, Royal Horse Artillery. He had never worked with camels before, and the combination of horses and camels performing a musical ride was possibly another world first. Other events included a mass physical training display by 800 schoolboys, an impressive martial arts display by 800 people of the Popular Army – roughly equivalent to our Home Guard – and a superb aerobatic display by The Royal Jordanian Falcons, the country's equivalent of the Red Arrows.

Sadly, due to the restriction on numbers, our wives were unable to attend this spectacle, but at least Toni had been able to accompany me to the dress rehearsal the previous day, which was every bit as spectacular.

There was great excitement in June 1993 when Prince Abdullah, then a serving brigadier in the Jordanian Army, married Rania al Yassin, a Kuwaiti-born Palestinian. We were privileged to be included in some of the lavish celebrations, including a sumptuous banquet in Amman's most evocative restaurant, Kan Zaman. This is a vaulted building that stands at the top of a hill just outside the city. Built 150-200 years ago with stone gathered from numerous nearby Roman ruins, it probably served originally as a *caravanserai*. Some 500 of us dined in the company of Prince Abdullah and his bride to be, together with Princess Muna and Tony Gardiner, Prince Abdullah's mother and grandfather respectively, with whom we were privileged to have become good friends, and all the younger members of the Jordanian Royal Family.

The highlight, however, was the wedding reception held in the grounds of Basman Palace. The entire Jordanian Royal Family stood on a raised dais to shake hands with some 2,000 guests. Also on view was the massive wedding cake – a seven-tier work of art standing eight feet high and weighing almost 800 pounds!

As soon as the Royal Party had greeted the last guest, a Jordanian

Special Forces freefall parachutist dropped from the night sky in spectacular fashion and skilfully landed right on target. Then, spurred on by all our cheers, he sprinted up to Prince Abdullah to hand him the ceremonial sword with which to cut the cake!

Just over a year later, Princess Rania gave birth to a boy, who King Hussein named Hussein. Imagine our surprise and delight when Prince Abdullah invited us the next day to visit Princess Rania in hospital. There to greet us were Princess Muna, Tony Gardiner and Princess Rania's mother, Ilham Yassin. We were later joined by the Crown Prince, Prince Hassan, and his wife, Princess Sarvath el Hassan, as well as Prince Abdullah, the proud father, dressed in combat kit – august company indeed!

Whilst the family visited Princess Rania, we were served a special dessert that is traditionally given to guests to mark the birth of a boy. Then, when the Royal Family had left, we were ushered in to see the Princess. She looked radiant and was as charming as she is beautiful. After offering her our congratulations we were invited to see the little prince next door. He was remarkably quiet and, according to Toni, looked just like his father. We didn't know it at the time, but we were looking at the future Crown Prince of Jordan (Prince Hussein was named Crown Prince by Royal Decree in July 2009). Before leaving the hospital we were each given a silver keepsake inscribed in Arabic as a memento of this happy event.

In 1993, the Muslim Feast of Eid al-Adha coincided with the end of Rorie's academic year at Alexandria University. We decided to combine some of my annual leave with this holiday to drive over to Alexandria and bring him home to Jordan.

We were up and away before dawn on 25 May and saw the eastern skies redden into a beautiful sunrise as we made our way down the main road towards Aqaba. We stopped for a picnic breakfast at Ras al Naqb, the point at which the Eastern Heights plunge down to the floor of the desert, and watched the sun chase away the darkness on the ground far below as it rose steadily into the sky. We reached Aqaba Port just after 9.00 a.m. and joined a multitude of Egyptians going home to celebrate the Eid. Luckily, Colonel Hussein, the Commander of the RJNF, had sent one of his officers to assist us in negotiating all the daunting boarding procedures.

The ferry, a tired looking vessel, was due to arrive at 11.00 a.m., but was two hours late. By the time we set sail at 4.30 p.m. we were some four hours behind schedule. I don't know how many people were aboard, but I just hoped that the Almighty would look after us, as I was sure there were insufficient lifeboats and rafts to cater for everyone. We were the only Europeans on board and, thanks to our RJNF facilitator, were taken straight up to the bridge.

The sea was like a millpond and dolphins played in front of our bows, while flying fish skimmed across the surface to get out of our way. We reached Nuweba just as the sun began to sink behind the craggy *jebels* of Sinai. Thanks again to our RJNF facilitator, our car had been loaded last onto the ferry so was first off. However, unfortunately, he wasn't there to help us navigate the extremely complex immigration and Customs procedures. We were stuck in the port for five hours, being sent hither and thither to get various forms signed by numerous officials, each of whom demanded money for their services. It was well after midnight before we flopped into bed at our chalet in the nearby tourist village.

Next morning, after a hearty breakfast, we set off for Cairo. First we had to get through the formidable mountain barrier inland from the coast. The road snaked through a *wadi* flanked by towering mountains, and here and there we had to avoid debris deposited by the last flash flood. It certainly wouldn't be wise to be on this road in heavy rain, as it clearly became a river!

Once through the *jebel*, the land flattened out into endless miles of sand. The heat was intense. Just after midday we stopped for a bite to eat under the shade of the one and only tree for miles. We then ploughed on until we came to a low range of hills – the Mitla Pass – which was the scene of many a battle in the Arab/ Israeli wars of 1956, 1967 and 1973. The area was still strewn with the detritus of war – barbed wire, defence works, knocked out tanks and unmarked minefields. Signs warned us not to venture off the tarmac.

The Suez Canal lay just beyond the pass, its presence signalled by the sight of a ship seemingly sailing through a sea of sand. I had passed through this canal five times as a child. In those days, the only way across it was by ferry, but now our road led down to a tunnel. However, we were a little unnerved to find the tunnel undergoing extensive repair work. Only one lane was open and vehicles had to queue up on either side to be escorted through in convoy, one side at a time. What was even more worrying, an awful lot of water was falling from the roof as we made our way through.

Cairo must be one of the most frightening cities to drive in, especially if you don't know the way. The Ambassador, Christopher Long, had kindly invited us to stay at the Embassy, splendidly situated on the banks of the Nile. We knew this was to our West, so once we hit the city we headed towards the setting sun. After travelling for some time through this veritable urban jungle, we decided to ask for help and a very kind Egyptian offered to lead us to the Corniche, the road on which the Embassy stood. We had been surprisingly close.

We spent the next morning visiting the Citadel, a medieval fortification built by Saladin in the 12th century to protect the city from the Crusaders. One of the mosques within the fortifications had pillars taken from a wide variety of temples, churches and other buildings of differing architectural periods and styles. No two pillars were alike either in dimension or shape, yet they all worked perfectly together to support the upper gallery. Remarkably, one of these pillars had a Coptic Christian cross engraved upon it.

We returned to the Embassy in time to be taken for a late lunch at a farm owned by a Syrian near the pyramids. On leaving the city, we entered a world of utter squalor travelling for about three miles along the banks of an open sewer. However, when we reached Mr Said Rasic's farm we were transported into a different world. Brilliant white single-storey buildings, breezy verandas and cooling water fountains, both indoors and outside, made this a haven of peace and tranquillity. We found ourselves in very eminent company as Mr Rasic kindly allowed us to 'gate crash' a party that included the British, Canadian (French speaking), Italian and Algerian Ambassadors.

Next morning, having bade Christopher Long farewell, we set off for Alexandria and three hours later arrived at Rorie's apartment block on the city's Corniche. The flat he shared with his fellow Oxford undergraduate was on the seventh floor of the building. It was reached either by a tiny, unlit and often unreliable lift or by flights of stairs in a pitch black stairwell with no means of illumination. The flat, itself, was airy and spacious, and the view out to sea through the plate glass window at the front was stunning – the blue waters of the Mediterranean, brightly coloured boats bobbing at anchor, and larger vessels lying motionless further out to sea. To the West, Alexandria swept round like an embracing arm reaching out to an imposing fortification surmounted by a large Egyptian flag. This was the Citadel and Fort of Qaitbey. Built by Sultan Qaitbey towards the end of the 15th century, it stands on the site of the Lighthouse of Alexandria, one of the seven wonders of the ancient world.

Directly below us, a seemingly endless stream of traffic flowed along the Corniche, its deafening roar given an edge by the constant sounding of horns. Swarms of people, like so many ants, scurried along the pavements, or took their lives in their hands by working their way through the traffic to the other side of the road. Uniquely, this road operated a timed one-way system; cars travelled West until midday, when the direction was reversed. We never did work out how this was achieved.

We found Alexandria to be a vibrant city of constant noise, bustle and good-natured humanity; an environment that excited all the senses 24 hours a day.

Three quite distinct strata of people lived in the city: those that lived on the streets at ground level, finding what shelter they could; those that lived in the buildings; and, finally, those who lived on the flat roofs, some of whom even tended little gardens. All were fiercely proud and, if anything, those on the bottom and top strata formed tighter communities. Rorie seemed to know everyone in his neighbourhood, stopping every few steps to say goodbye and exchange addresses with friends and local shop-keepers as he showed us round his 'patch'. He had certainly taken to Alexandria and had even joined, and competed for, a roof-dwellers' boxing team! He and his Oxford colleague had also paid for the mother of Saidi, the watchman-cum-custodian (*buwaab*) of their building, to have a cataract operation, thereby restoring her sight. They were repaid a hundredfold for their kindness in friendship and loyalty by the family and strangers alike.

On leaving Alexandria, we headed west along the coast for some 75 miles to El Alamein. Meaning 'The Two Flags' in Arabic, this was the scene of one of the pivotal battles of the Second World War. For the most part, the forbidding desert wastes on our left were in stark contrast to the pristine and untrodden sandy beaches and sparkling blue waters of the Mediterranean on our right. Here and there, however, seaside tourist villages were beginning to spring up.

Our visit to the British and Commonwealth war cemetery was a sobering experience. So many young lives cut down in their prime; row upon row of headstones bearing testimony to their sacrifice so far from home – Australians, New Zealanders, South Africans, Indians and Britons in their hundreds, including a large number from my own Regiment. It made us feel very humble, almost guilty.

Yet this place was alive! The cemetery was an oasis of peace and tranquillity in this otherwise unforgiving landscape: roses bloomed under the fierce African sun, bougainvillea bushes added rich colour on the sand between the graves, and the odd tree provided some much-needed shade. Birds had discovered this haven and their carefree song cheered the spirit. We sought out the Egyptian custodian and congratulated him and his colleagues on the manner in which they tended this place.

We didn't have time to visit the German war cemetery a little further along the coast, but visited the museum in which there were exhibits from a number of nations that took part in the battle, including Germany. These helped us to appreciate the see-saw nature of the North African campaign and the significance of the Allied victory at El Alamein.

Hot and sticky after our visit, we headed back towards Alexandria, but turned off as soon as we found a track down to the sea. The beach was empty for as far as the eye could see and the water was an unbelievable aquamarine hue. Gentle waves lapped the glaringly white sands. We plunged in to cool off before the long journey back to Cairo.

Next morning, after a good night's sleep, we set off for Sinai, the Ambassador kindly leading us out of Cairo to the Suez Canal Tunnel road. The contrast between the sheer vibrancy and clamour of Cairo and the still, open desert was both sudden and stark. We were on our own again. Crossing under the Canal, instead of continuing east across Sinai to the Gulf of Aqaba, we turned south, along the far side of the canal and down the east coast of the Gulf of Suez to link up with the road to St Catherine's Monastery.

Set in the midst of the Sinai Peninsula some 5,000 feet above sea level, St Catherine's stands proudly on the desert floor at the base of Mount Sinai.

The journey wasn't all plain sailing. The route took us through the picturesque oasis of Feiran where we got a nasty shock; our way was blocked by youths wielding what looked like pistols. At the time, Islamic extremists were causing trouble in parts of Egypt. Unable to turn round and certainly unwilling to stop, we decided to edge forward, smiling and waving to try and ease the tension. As it turned out, our would-be attackers were a group of youths wielding toy weapons. Nevertheless, they were certainly unfriendly and gave our car quite a battering as we passed by them.

We arrived at St Catherine's just as the sun was setting. The surrounding *jebels* rose majestically around us, their craggy profiles accentuated by the dying rays of the sun. Here and there, rustic crosses stood defiantly along the seemingly inaccessible ridges, marking the caves where hermit monks had lived years before.

There has been an Orthodox Christian monastery in this peaceful, spiritual *wadi* at the foot of Mount Sinai since 323 AD. The site is reputed to be where God spoke to Moses from within the burning bush, telling him to lead his people out of Egypt and into the Promised Land, as recorded in The Book of Exodus. This makes St Catherine's perhaps the oldest continuously lived in Christian monastery in the world. I say 'perhaps', because another monastery in Egypt, St Anthony's, which lies in the desert almost due west of St Catherine's on the opposite shores of the Gulf of Suez, also claims this distinction.

Mount Sinai is also the place where St Catherine of Alexandria's body is said to have been miraculously transported after she had been martyred by the Roman Emperor Maxentius in the 4th century for refusing to denounce her Christian faith. Her presence on the mountain is claimed to have been revealed to one of the monks, who then found and buried her, building a small church at the site. In the 6th century, Emperor Justinian 1 replaced the existing monastery with a massive new structure and St Catherine's body was exhumed and laid to rest within it. This is the structure that we see today. Surrounded by a wall that stands 40 to 50 feet high, it resembles a miniature walled city.

Never in its long history has the monastery been conquered or destroyed. On the contrary, it has enjoyed the protection of Arab and Turkish rulers, the Crusaders, Napoleon and, most significantly, the Prophet Mohammed. A copy of Mohammed's decree for the monastery to remain unharmed hangs in the entrance hall. The monks have always lived at peace with the local Bedouin, a fact emphasised by the presence of a mosque beside the church within the defensive walls. Indeed, the *Bedu* in this area today are the descendants of the families from Anatolia and Alexandria who came with the original monks centuries ago, many of whom then married into the local Jebaliya tribe.

The beautifully carved wooden doors at the entrance of the church are the original doors installed around 15 centuries ago. They were somewhat defaced by the Crusaders, who carved their coats of arms on them, but this was a small price to pay, considering that the Crusaders destroyed most of the Orthodox monasteries in Sinai. No doubt aware of the universal desire to protect St Catherine's, they lived peacefully within its walls for ten years.

Just outside the walls, the monastery had its own small guesthouse and we were able to get a room here for the night, joining some dozen or so other pilgrims. Rorie and I then spent an hour before supper with some local *Bedu*, sharing a cup of tea with them as they sat with their camels around a warming camp fire.

Supper was a very simple affair of rissoles and spaghetti and was eaten communally, 'refectory-style' at two long tables. Then it was off to bed. Our alarm stirred us from our sleep at 2.00 a.m. It was pitch black in the room and there was no electricity as the generator had been switched off. We dressed quickly in readiness to trek up the mountain. Outside the air was pleasantly cool and a star-studded sky afforded some light. Down in the *wadi* we could see the flashes of hundreds of torches and hear the footfalls and murmurings of a vast number of pilgrims making their way up to the monastery and onwards towards the summit of Mount Sinai.

There are two routes up the mountain. One goes straight up via almost 4,000 steps hewn out of the bare rock – the work of a monk undertaking a lifetime's penance. Unsurprisingly, it is popularly known as the Steps of Penitence, or *Siket Sayidna Musa* in Arabic (not a translation). The other route, known popularly as the Camel Route, or *Siket al Bashait* in Arabic (again, not a translation), is much longer but gentler until the final push to the summit, where it joins the 'steps' route. As its name implies, older or tired pilgrims can ride a camel up this route almost to the top, although none were used on the night we made the climb.

We arrived at the top just as the first rays of dawn began to light up the eastern sky across Sinai's rugged mountain tops. As we waited expectantly for the sun to appear we were joined by hundreds of pilgrims, and then, as the sun broke over the distant mountain crests, some fine Italian voices near us burst out in song, followed by some rich French voices further along the ridge.

After soaking up the atmosphere and taking photographs, we set off down the mountain again, retracing our steps on the Camel Route, rather than tackling those daunting steps. Seeing the path in the harsh light of day, we wondered how we had managed it at all – now that we could see the steep gradients and sheer, unprotected drops it was quite unnerving.

We were quite tired by the time we reached our little guesthouse and certainly ready for our breakfast. This was another simple, yet adequate communal affair and much livelier than the previous evening, as everyone shared their experiences of our night's adventure. We then turned in for a nap before visiting the monastery.

In the early days of Christianity, some 4,000 monks lived in Sinai, but when we visited St Catherine's in 1993, it was home to only 14 monks. The monk who showed us around and took us to the Burning Bush came from East London, having grown up in Devon! I carried two letters from our

Ambassador in Jordan for the Abbot of St Catherine's. When I mentioned this to our host, he told me that the Abbot was away. However, after our tour of the monastery, including a visit to the crypt in which St Catherine's remains lie, he took us to have tea with the monastery's Treasurer, to whom I handed over the letters.

After lunch, we headed south across the majestic rugged mountain wasteland we had seen from Mount Sinai at dawn to Sharm Al Sheikh, on the coast near the tip of the Sinai Peninsula. For over 125 miles we saw only one sign of life, a lone group of *Bedu* with a small herd of camels. In contrast, Sharm Al Sheikh initially looked quite inviting, but in truth was a rather haphazard, shabby tourist resort. Developed by the Israelis after the area was captured during the 1967 war, it had been handed back to the Egyptians in 1982 following the Camp David Agreement.

We found a small hotel more in keeping with the Egypt we had been living in – unpretentious, simple and not frequented by overseas tourists. The staff were very friendly and thought Rorie was a Jordanian as he was so fluent in Arabic. Once settled in, we enjoyed a delicious supper outside under the stars.

Next morning, we hired snorkelling equipment and headed a few miles south of Sharm al Sheikh to Ras Mohammed, an utterly desolate, rocky wasteland, devoid of shelter at the very tip of the Sinai Peninsula. The only respite from the scorching sun was the inviting waters of the Red Sea, in which a handful of people were clearly enjoying themselves.

We waded over the rocky shallows to join them at a point where the sea took on a deep blue hue. We were now standing quite literally at the top of a subterranean cliff that fell away vertically for well over 300 feet.

We stepped into the abyss to find the cliff face carpeted in a kaleidoscope of different coloured corals and the sea teeming with fish of all shapes and sizes in every imaginable combination of colours. Most of the fish were tiny and swam amongst the corals, but others were quite large.

One particularly large dark brown fish seemed to take an unhealthy interest in us. It was as large as a man's torso and must have weighted over 100 pounds. Although it looked rather menacing, it did us no harm. Thankfully, we didn't encounter a single shark.

The sea was so buoyant that we really didn't need to swim to stay afloat and we were able to spend a total of almost four hours in the water, marvelling at this magical underwater world. Eventually, we had to drag ourselves away as we had a ferry to catch. Leaving Ras Mohammed we drove up the coast of the Gulf of Aqaba, reaching the tourist village in Nuweba in time for supper.

Next morning, after an early morning dip in the sea and another hearty breakfast, we braced ourselves for the challenges of the day – negotiating the port entry procedures and the ferry crossing. The former were achieved with remarkable ease, thanks to Rorie's fluency in Arabic, and within a matter of minutes we were clear to board. But there was no ferry and we now couldn't leave the port! We had no option but to sit and wait in an enormous open shed, with only the bottle of water we always carried to sustain us in an emergency.

The ferry eventually arrived at 4.30 p.m. and we set sail at 7.00 p.m., our passage illuminated by the soft light of a full moon. The boat was less crowded this time, as we were returning well after the end of the Eid holiday, making the journey up the Gulf of Aqaba much more enjoyable. Just as well, as we were in a very old vessel capable of making only nine knots.

It was after midnight before we reached Aqaba, but there to meet us on the quay was a smiling young lieutenant of the RJNF to ease our passage through Customs. Our original plan had been to return directly to Amman, but this was now out of the question. We therefore made our way to the Petra International Hotel, where, luckily, there was a room available for us.

As next day – Friday – was the start of our weekend, we decided to spend the morning by the sea in Aqaba. Rorie even managed to get two tows behind a ski boat, on the second of which he was passed by none other than His Majesty, King Hussein, skiing in the opposite direction with a helicopter acting as top cover!

After a delicious lunch at our favourite haunt, Ali Baba's, we set off for home, taking the old picturesque road up the escarpment. It was a very hot day with the temperature above 40°C, so we stopped for a quick brew at the top to allow the engine to cool down. We arrived home in the relative cool of the early evening after a memorable adventure to some amazing places, having covered almost 2,000 trouble-free miles through some pretty inhospitable terrain in our trusty old Peugeot.

Whilst Jordan had a surfeit of wonderful places to visit, the allure and proximity of Syria was too good an opportunity to ignore – Damascus (Dimashq in Arabic and generally referred to as Ash Shams in Syria) was only 138 miles away, far closer than Aqaba. However, there was one significant obstacle to negotiate – the border! It took us about an hour and a half to drive from Amman to the Jordanian border control point at Ramtha, and another two hours or so from the Syrian border post at Derra to reach Damascus. But obtaining clearance to leave Ramtha and enter Syria through Derra could more than double our journey time. Still, provided one accepted this as inevitable, the rewards made it all worthwhile.

As a rule, we always drove straight to my opposite number's house in Damascus. As we were driving a Jordanian diplomatic-plated car, we were always tailed by the Syrian secret police – the *mukhabarat.* Initially, we were blissfully unaware of this, but on one trip we decided to divert to visit the ancient ruins of Bosra, famous for its beautifully preserved amphitheatre. As we drew in to the empty car park – we were the only visitors at the time – we noticed another car coming in behind us, out of which four or five men in smart suits and dark glasses emerged and followed us around at a discreet distance. We realised who they were and had to take great care not to point our cameras in their direction, as this would have spelt trouble. That apart, they didn't bother us in any way, but let us take our time before driving in convoy with us to Damascus.

As I sit to write about Syria now, this historic country and its poor people are being torn apart by the twin evils of a merciless civil war and the barbaric actions of a murderous group of jihadist known as the Islamic State of Iraq and Levant (ISIL).

Yet, apart from the 'Big Brother' aspect just mentioned, the Syria we knew in the mid-1990s was a most fascinating country, steeped in history and populated by friendly people. Nowhere was this more evident than in Damascus itself. Arguably the oldest continuously-inhabited city in the world, the capital of Syria offered locals and visitors so much in the way of vibrant souks that fired the imagination.

For us, all these attractions could be found in and around the Souk al Hamidiyya in the centre of the city. As we approached the souk, we came upon the eye-catching building that was the city's station for the Hejaz Railway of Lawrence of Arabia fame. Built by the Ottomans in the early 1900s, the imposing exterior of this building with its coloured glass windows was matched by the grandeur of the main hall within, with its wooden floor and high, beautifully decorated ceiling. Although it no longer operated as a station, the ticket counter was still there and you could even buy train tickets at the 'Deuxième Classe' window, for use at the new station nearby.

At the Souk al Hamidiyya, one can walk along Straight Street – the self-same street referred to in the Bible as '*The Street called Straight*'. Walking along it, we stopped to look down into a baker's shop. It was several feet below the current road surface and the bread was actually being baked on the paving stones of the original Roman road along which Ananias would have walked. His house, where Saint Paul took refuge, is also located in the souk. It, too, is now several feet below ground and has been converted into a tiny chapel. The old city wall, over which Saint Paul was lowered in a basket to make good his escape from Damascus, is also still standing.

Towards the eastern end of the souk lies the magnificent Umayyed mosque. The site has been a place of worship as far back as the second millennium BC. It began as a temple to the Semitic god Hadad, and the Romans then built their temple here and dedicated it to the god Jupiter. In time, Christianity became the Imperial religion and the temple was converted into a cathedral dedicated to Saint John the Baptist. The Arabs conquered Damascus around 630 AD, but the Christians were still allowed to worship in their cathedral, whilst a small prayer house was incorporated into the structure for the Muslims.

This arrangement lasted for about 70 years, by which time the Muslim population had grown so large as to make it impracticable. Caliph al Walid then negotiated a settlement with the Christians, by handing back all previously confiscated places of Christian worship in return for sole possession of their cathedral – an offer, I dare say, they had no option but to accept, but nevertheless, an offer which demonstrated the Caliph's desire to respect both religions.

The cathedral was then largely demolished to build the mosque we see today. Echoes of the past are still evident in its structure. Roman pillars stand to attention in the main prayer hall, which also houses the shrine dedicated to Saint John the Baptist and in which the saint's head is said to be interred. Outside in the massive 'cloistered' compound the walls are intricately decorated in striking green and blue mosaic patterns on a gold background. These mosaics are highly unusual, depicting trees, buildings and landscapes – a vision of Paradise, perhaps – in addition to the usual intricate geometric patterns and Arabic calligraphy that alone adorn other mosques.

When visiting the mosque, Rorie and I wore long-sleeved shirts and trousers, whilst Toni and the girls were sometimes allowed in wearing long skirts, long-sleeved blouses and headscarves. More usually, however, they were issued with all-enveloping black hooded cloaks (*abayas*) which were hot to wear.

The souk, itself, is protected from the elements by a barrel-shaped roof of corrugated iron that is riddled with bullets holes, caused by both celebratory fire when the Arabs drove the Germans and Turks out of Damascus in 1918, and by cannon fire from French fighter aircraft during the Arab Revolt of 1925. In daylight, the resulting pinpricks of light look for all the world like a star-studded sky. The souk is always a seething mass of humanity: the clamour, hustle and bustle, the wonderful aromas in the spice souk, the vivid clash of bright colours in the materials souk, the eye-catching Bedouin jewellery, the shining copper and brass cooking pots and pans and coffee pots and other Arab artefacts all make for an exhilarating, even overwhelming, experience.

One area of the souk is given over to the production of intricate inlaid mosaic boxes. The workers here are all Christians. Living in harmony alongside their vastly more numerous Muslim fellow citizens, they were proud of their heritage in this 'biblical' city. It was fascinating seeing them at work and, apart from buying a number of their products, we were given some rejected mosaic fragments which we put into our photograph albums to illustrate the manufacturing process.

Magnificent silks are woven on looms in the souk, arguably the most famous shop being Tony Stephan's Emporium, which boasted Margaret Thatcher and Nancy Reagan amongst its clientele. Another favourite shop for us was Ghraoui's (pronounced Rhoweys) – a chocolate shop – emblazoned on the front door of which were the words 'Purveyors to H.M. the Queen of England'! We could hardly go wrong here! Contrary to popular belief, I understand that the queen in question isn't Victoria, but Queen Elizabeth II.

My favourite part of the souk was the carpet and rug area. I remember going into one shop that appeared to be a single room, the walls and floor of which were covered with fairly ordinary carpets and rugs of all types and sizes. Seeing nothing that I liked I went to leave, but the owner called me back and asked me what I was looking for. I told him I was interested in buying either a Nain or Isfahan rug. Inviting me to wait a moment, he sent a man out of the shop to fetch some examples from elsewhere – or so I thought. After a few minutes, he reappeared (empty-handed) and said something to the owner, who then pulled back a carpet hanging on the wall to reveal a door. Opening this, he ushered me downstairs into a long, narrow room below ground in which there was an amazing array of the finest carpets and rugs.

Plying me with Arabic coffee, he then proceeded to roll out rug after exquisite rug for me to look at, never, of course, mentioning prices. After about an hour, I had selected three 'possibles', but said I would need to consult my wife before making a decision. I had to wait downstairs until the man above made sure the coast was clear before I could go and find Toni. When we returned we had to go through the same 'cloak and dagger' procedure again and after another hour or so – and more coffee – we ended up with a very nice and reasonably priced Nain.

I visited this shop on a number of occasions. Once I came away with a worn, faded rug, which I was told was a valuable antique. As always, the owner told me that if I didn't like the rug I could exchange it on my next visit. We were unsure of it when we returned to Amman and so decided to take it back on our next trip, which was several months later. True to his word, the owner took back the rug and offered me my money back or an exchange. I opted for a very nice red Afghan rug. Telling me that was insufficient, he invited me to select another rug as well, so I chose an unusual blue and brown Kurdish tribal rug. The drab old antique rug must have been valuable, but I came away with two larger and more colourful rugs that we all preferred, and have enjoyed to this day.

On one of our longer breaks in Syria we decided to explore the western side of the country with Hannah and Zoë. Heading north out of Damascus, we drove through Homs to a small town called Hama, famous for its *norias* – medieval wooden waterwheels fitted with buckets that scooped water out of the Orontes River and carried it upwards to be tipped into channels to irrigate crops in nearby fields. We stopped for a break at a riverside café opposite a group of four *norias*, the largest of which must have been over 50 feet in diameter. As they churned away in the current, a youth hitched a ride on this massive wheel and when it reached its zenith he dived back into the river, a daring feat that I was lucky enough to capture on camera.

We couldn't dally in Hama as we wanted to make Aleppo before nightfall. Aleppo (known as *Halab* in Arabic) vies with Damascus as being the oldest continuously inhabited city in the world and is also Syria's largest city. As we approached, we could clearly see the medieval citadel that stands in the centre of the old part of the city. This massive structure, with its formidable defence works, successfully defended Aleppo against repeated Crusader attacks.

Our destination for the night was Baron's Hotel, the oldest hotel in Aleppo. It had been built in stages between 1909 and 1940. In its heyday it had been regarded as the lap of luxury by the rich and famous, such as Lady Mountbatten, David Rockefeller and Dame Freya Stark. Agatha Christie had stayed here while writing *Murder on the Orient Express*, while Lawrence of Arabia had left proof of his visit there in 1914 in the form of an unpaid bar bill that had been framed and put on display in the reception area.

When we stayed at the hotel in August 1993, it was like going back in time to the 1950s. Dusty old poster-sized advertisements for BOAC, Pan

American and The Orient Express hung from the walls where they had been positioned probably half a century earlier. Parchment lampshades, browned with age, sat upon antiquated lamps in dark recesses in the dining room and an ancient, incontinent dog roamed the ground floor. Of course, there was no air conditioning and nor was there a lift.

However, we had come here for the experience and it was not difficult to imagine how marvellous this place must have been in its glory days. One such clue was the en-suite bedrooms – surely exceptional in the 1940s and 50s – and the gush of water from the taps, instead of the weak dribble to which we had become accustomed at home in Amman.

We appeared to be the hotel's only guests and had been advised not to dine there, but at a café fairly close by. The night was hot and sticky and because there was no air conditioning we had to keep our windows open, thereby letting in the mosquitoes and the noise from the incessant traffic in the street below. And I don't think we were alone in our beds either! All in all, none of us got much sleep but at least we had achieved our aim of staying a night in this once famous old hotel.

We spent the morning in the Souk al Madina (the city market), one of the largest covered markets in the world. Its labyrinthine branches measure over eight miles and are covered by vaulted stone and brick ceilings with numerous square openings to allow for both ventilation and sunlight. Even so, it was still stuffy, and dark enough inside to require electric lighting during the day. All this seemed to accentuate the general hubbub of activity and made for an exhilarating experience.

About midday we drove to Mount Simeon Stylites, about 20 miles northwest of Aleppo. It was here in 422 AD that Saint Simeon, a hermit monk, decided to isolate himself from the world by living on top of a pillar, which was about 50 feet tall and measured some six feet in diameter. Symbolically detached from humanity in this way, he used to preach twice a day to a never-ending stream of people who had been attracted to the site by his bizarre behaviour.

He remained in his 'eyrie' for 37 years until his death in 459 AD, after which a great basilica, reputed to be the oldest Byzantine church in the world, was built over the site. All is now in ruins, including Saint Simeon's pillar, which has been chipped away over the centuries by countless ardent pilgrims intent on collecting relics. All that remains of it today is a large boulder sitting on top of the original plinth – in all, about six feet high.

Fortified by a substantial meal of grilled chicken, we headed westward towards the Mediterranean coast. Our goal was Saladin's Castle, which was in a mountainous area about 18 miles east of the coastal town of Latakia. Our route took us across the northern extremity of the Great Rift Valley that stretches all the way down to Mozambique in south eastern Africa. The lush green-carpeted hills and valleys were in stark contrast to the barren desert wastes to which we'd become accustomed.

We had planned to camp for the night and, as luck would have it, just before we had to leave the main road to head into the hills, we came across a man cooking chicken on a spit by the roadside, then, a little further on, we spotted another man who was driving a tuk tuk loaded with bread. That was supper sorted!

Finding a suitable campsite for the night was more problematic. While it was easy to find a campsite almost anywhere in the desert, it proved much more difficult to do so in this mountainous region covered in trees and prickly undergrowth – we had to beware of snakes and scorpions. As usual, we didn't have a tent – apart from our washing kit, all we ever carried were our sleeping bags, camp beds, water container, spade, a metal door scraper to use as a grill and, most importantly, some powerful insect repellent. Apart from using this on ourselves, we sprayed it on the ground around the perimeter of our cleared area as a deterrent against creepy crawlies.

As darkness fell, and somewhat in desperation, we settled on a flattish area relatively free of rocks and bushes in the lee of the castle ruins. We were totally alone here; no sign of human habitation for miles around, not the slightest sound or even a single pinprick of light visible in the gloaming. Having cleared the area, we set up camp and ate supper looking at Saladin's Castle, spectacularly silhouetted against a glorious sunset. Some of life's best moments come free of charge!

Next morning, we struck camp and went to explore the castle, which dominated the surrounding countryside from its vantage point at the end of a steep-sided ridge. In the relative cool of the early morning we had this magnificent site to ourselves. Its strategic significance was clear; from here it had controlled the former Silk Road and the important trading port of Latakia.

Quite amazingly, a trench over a quarter of a mile long had been hewn out of the ridge by the Byzantines in the 10th century to protect the rear (east) of the castle. It is over 90 feet deep and between 45 to 60 feet wide. Opposite the castle keep, a needle of rock had been left almost intact in the middle of the trench to act as a support for the (long-gone) wooden drawbridge. I say 'almost intact' because the last ten feet or so at the tip of the needle is made up of carefully cut and laid stones, with apparently no mortar holding them together. We were told later that this was a defensive measure; in an emergency the tip of this support could be knocked away to cause the drawbridge to collapse.

This dominant ridge had been a fortified site for over two millennia. Alexander the Great seized it when he reached Syria in the 4th century AD, but it is the Byzantines who are credited with improving its defences. When the Crusaders took possession of the castle at the beginning of the 12th century AD it was known as Saône (Zion). They immediately set about expanding the fortifications to the extent of the ruins we see today. Covering an area roughly the size of ten football fields, it sprawls from east to west along the top of the ridge. Formidable though its defences appeared to be, it was easily overrun by Saladin when he attacked and captured it in 1188.

The Crusaders had occupied the castle for a mere 80 years. They never succeeded in re-capturing it, which is why it is known as Saladin's Castle today. Nevertheless, this was not the last time it was subjected to an enforced change of ownership; in 1287 it was besieged and captured for the final time during an inter-Mamluk power struggle.

The modern day access to the castle is via a series of steps leading up to an entrance in the ramparts on the southern side of the castle. When we visited it, much of the interior was overgrown and difficult to explore, but we did reach the Byzantine keep overlooking the trench. This is a massive structure with walls about 15 feet thick and is the best preserved part of the ruins.

As the temperature rose with the sun, we retreated back to the sanctuary of our air-conditioned car and set off through Latakia and down the Mediterranean coast towards Tartus. For a fleeting moment it felt strange being in Syria and yet driving alongside the Mediterranean. We then ventured a mile or so inland again, on a quite tortuous road, to visit the imposing Crusader castle aptly named *Qal'at al Marqab*, meaning Castle of the Watchtower in Arabic. Crowning a volcanic plug about 1,000 feet above the sea, it dominates its surrounds for miles and its black appearance adds to its forbidding sense of awe. Indeed, it was considered to be so impregnable that Saladin never attempted to attack it.

The formidable outer walls of the castle were more impressive than the interior, which lay largely in ruins, apart from a well preserved Crusader chapel. We didn't tarry here as the sun was now at its fiercest. After a few photographs we resumed our journey along the coast to Tartus, where we were to spend the night. Sadly, the town was a huge disappointment; dominated by a large port and adjacent industrial areas, and there seemed very little evidence of its historical past.

Next day we headed for the jewel of all Syria's medieval castles, Krak des Chevaliers (*qal'at al hisn* – castle of the fort – in Arabic) situated near Homs. Without doubt this was the most majestic and best preserved castle we visited on any of our trips in Syria and Jordan. Yet surprisingly, once again we had it virtually to ourselves. Perhaps sensible people don't visit these sites during the height of summer when daytime temperatures average 40°C.

Originally the site of a Kurdish fort, Krak stands on top of a hill over 2,000 feet above sea level, from where it dominates the plains below. The Crusaders took possession of the site towards the middle of the 12th century and started building the intimidating fortress we see today. Over the next few decades they added to the defences, so that eventually it became a castle within a castle. Indeed, having tested its defences, Saladin thereafter gave it a wide berth. The castle did eventually fall to the Mamluks towards the end of the 13th century, by which time the Crusaders' power was on the wane.

We took our time exploring the fortress, walking up vaulted and cobbled passages, peering into rooms with spectacular views, wandering through enormous stables which once housed hundreds of horses and imagining ourselves feasting in the vast great hall. We also walked on the inner and outer ramparts, quite an unnerving experience as there were no safety rails or protective walls and the drops were sheer. After an exhilarating few hours we ended up in the King's Daughter's tower, which had been converted into a café, to quench our thirst. This marked the end of our whistle-stop tour of Western Syria. After another night in Damascus, we headed home to Jordan.

On a couple of other excursions into Syria we opted to visit Palmyra, or *Tadmur* as it is known in Arabic. Set in the central Syrian desert about 150 miles north east of Damascus, Palmyra was an important settlement as far back as the second millennium BC. It owes its existence in this otherwise harsh and barren desert to the large fertile oasis that lies adjacent to the ruins. Indeed, some historians believe that the Romans gave the city this name, meaning 'City of Palm Trees' when they arrived in the 1st century AD.

The focal point of this ruined city is the Monumental Arch that marks the beginning of an impressive colonnaded avenue – the Great Colonnade – leading at a tangent into the desert. Midway along and to the southwest of this 'main thoroughfare' we saw a number of extraordinary towers standing in a gently rising *wadi*. These turned out to be funerary monuments in an area known as the Valley of Tombs. These strange towers, coupled no doubt with their purpose, lent the area a rather eerie countenance. Some way beyond the Great Colonnade lay a hill surmounted by a castle. This is the Arab fort of Qala'at ibn Maan. It is very much younger than the rest of the ruins and is thought to date from the 17th century.

We had been advised that the best time and place to take in the full spectacle of Palmyra was at dawn from the fort. So this is where we were seated as the eastern sky began to redden next morning. As the sun rose we watched in awe as, little by little, the Monumental Arch, the Great Colonnade and the remainder of the ruins, including the funerary towers, were lit up by a rich red glow.

Of course, we ventured across to the West Bank on a number of occasions to visit Jerusalem and Bethlehem. Such visits entailed passing through the Israeli checkpoint on the western side of the King Hussein Bridge over the River Jordan. We found the armed Israeli officials both brusque and insensitive. On one occasion we were behind a group of nuns, who were clearly experiencing difficulties. As we were about to plead on their behalf one turned to us and asked us to do nothing; they were required to travel regularly between Jordan and Jerusalem and the Israelis never failed to find something wrong with their papers. Eventually, she assured us, they would be allowed through. Arabs were often subjected to body searches and we were upset to see how roughly they were handled, men and women alike. Being British and with diplomatic stamps in our passports we got away pretty lightly.

Until the signing of the peace treaty between Jordan and Israel in October 1994, we were not permitted to take our car over to the West Bank or Jerusalem. My Embassy driver, Auni, would take us down to the King Hussein Bridge, where we boarded a shuttle bus to the Israeli control point on the West Bank. Here passports were checked and we underwent the usual airport-style security procedures, with an interesting addition; if carrying a camera you had to take a photo of the ceiling to prove that it was, indeed, a camera and not an explosive device. Once we were cleared, we used to take a 'service taxi' (a communal taxi that would stop to take on passengers along the way until it was full) to Jerusalem.

Jerusalem's skyline is dominated by The Dome of the Rock. This stands on Temple Mount, along with the Al Aqsa mosque. The western side of Temple Mount incorporates the Wailing Wall, the remains of the wall that surrounded the Jewish temple and a focal point for Jewish worshippers. Located in the Arab quarter of old Jerusalem, this deeply religious historical site encapsulates the close links between the three religions of the book, Judaism, Christianity (in accordance with Jewish custom, the infant Jesus was presented in the temple and later he taught there) and Islam.

We always stayed in the Arab quarter, usually at the rest house run by the Anglican nuns at St George's Convent or, if unable to get in there, a pleasant Palestinian hotel nearby, both of which were only a quarter of a mile outside the Old City's Damascus Gate.

Walking along the ramparts of the city wall we were rewarded with a wonderful view of the roof-tops of the Old City – the mosques and churches clearly identified by their crescent moon-topped minarets and crosses respectively.

We felt more at home in the Arab Quarter. In any case, this was where all the biblical sites were: the Via Dolorosa, the Church of the Holy Sepulchre and, outside the city walls, the Mount of Olives, the Garden of Gethsemane and Golgotha.

We visited Jerusalem on one of the Muslim Eids to see the newly refurbished Dome of the Rock, only to find that the Israelis had mounted a security alert, greatly restricting access to the Old City. I particularly wanted to photograph the re-furbished Dome of the Rock and was also keen to photograph the Garden of Gethsemane, across the valley in front of the city wall. Arriving at the latter site first, we found our way barred by a barrier guarded by an armed Israeli policeman. There were very few people about, so I approached him and, explaining my intention, asked him if I could cross the barrier to reach my desired vantage point some 100 yards ahead. He was an American and seeing that we were virtually alone, kindly agreed to let me pass, on condition that Toni and the children remained behind and I was to come back immediately if he called me. I duly took my photograph and thanked him on returning to the barrier.

We then went into the Old City, where we decided it would be best if I went alone to photograph the Dome of the Rock. Leaving Toni and the children in a café, I went on my way. The first access point onto the Temple Mount I approached was barred, but at least the guards told me where the one and only controlled entry point was. I moved on and, thinking I had reached the correct point of access, approached the guards. Rude and aggressive, they demanded to know what was in my camera case. Telling them that there was no need to be so hostile, I pulled my camera out for them to see, but then one of the guards grabbed it and, holding it above his head, told me to apologise or he would throw it onto the pavement. I had no option. Then, telling me that the access point was the next one along, they bowed mockingly, calling me *Abu Lateef*, Arabic for Father of Politeness.

Of course, we visited Bethlehem to see the 'stable' in which Jesus was born – a cave now located under the Church of the Nativity. The entrance to the church is very low, requiring people to bow down in order to go inside and hence it is called the Door of Humility. A Muslim Arab family held the keys to the church, apparently because in times gone by the various Christian denominations were unable to agree which of them should be the custodian of this historic site.

On one of our visits to the West Bank we booked an Israeli day tour of the Holy Land. As luck would have it, our fellow passengers on the coach were British doctors, who had been attending a medical conference in Eilat, accompanied by their wives.

The tour took us to Nazareth, Capernaum, the Sea of Galilee and the sites of the Sermon on the Mount, and where Jesus was baptised by Saint John the Baptist. This latter site was at the point where the River Jordan flows out of the Sea of Galilee. Our guide explained that this was not the true site, that being several miles downstream in a restricted military zone. We were pleased he hadn't tried to fool us. (I was fortunate enough to over-fly the true site, marked by a shrine, on a couple of occasions whilst on duty.) Near Capernaum, we were shown a point where a walkway had been built out into the Sea of Galilee just an inch or so below the surface to enable tourists, if so inclined, to be photographed walking on water. Our party gave this rather flippant tourist attraction a miss!

As we neared the end of our tour in Jordan, I was gripped with the realisation that, not only was our time in this wonderful country coming to an end, but so, too, was my career in the Army. This filled me with a sense of dread. Aged 55, I was too young to retire and, in any case, still had children to educate. However, having spent 37 years in the Army, mostly abroad, civilian life in Britain seemed an unattractive, even daunting prospect.

To soften the blow, or at least to take our minds off it, we elected to set out on one last adventure before settling down. Having been thwarted twice in our desire to drive home, first from Nigeria (unreliable vehicle) and then Kuwait (Iraqi invasion), we now seemed to have one last chance.

Apart from looking into the procedures for exporting our car from Jordan and driving across so many national borders, we decided to play things by ear. We didn't want to be tied down to a fixed route plan, schedule or hotel and ferry bookings. We also knew we had to avoid former Yugoslavia. At the time, the whole area was unstable – the Bosnian War was raging and the Srebrenica Massacre took place barely a fortnight before our departure.

Mr Abid, the Embassy's 'Mr Fix It', advised us that we didn't require a *Carnet de Passage* for the car as we were travelling through, rather than staying in any of the countries along our route. This advice almost scuppered our adventure in both Syria and Turkey. He also advised us to drive to the Jordanian border using our UK registration plates and then change back to our Jordanian diplomatic plates in 'no man's land' without being seen before arriving at the Syrian border point and then to keep them on until our arrival in the UK. This advice may well have helped us when pleading our case in both Syria and Turkey.

The Embassy honoured us with a really special send-off and we left Amman with heavy hearts on 31 July 1995. Our Peugeot was loaded to the gunwales; not only did it have all our luggage on board, but also Hannah, Rorie and his girlfriend, Gizela. They were going to spend a few days in Damascus before returning home as part of their own adventure. We reached the Jordanian border control point at Ramtha in record time on the newly opened highway, but then ran straight into trouble. Our diary notes at the time state:

> *But the remainder of the day is best forgotten!*

In a nutshell, the officer responsible for clearing the car was on an extended lunch break and there were also problems with both Hannah's and Gizela's passports. Luckily, Rorie's Arabic helped to resolve the latter difficulties.

At one stage, the crowds, the noise and the heat started to get the better of me and I wandered off to the edge of the perimeter, where I spotted a praying mantis. I couldn't recall seeing a praying mantis in Jordan before and certainly didn't expect to see one in this environment. Yet here it was and it seemed totally unperturbed by the chaos surrounding it. I had a 'King Robert the Bruce and the spider' moment. Inspired by this tiny creature, I re-entered the melee with new-found patience and determination and eventually we were cleared to leave Jordan.

As advised, we achieved a quick registration number plate exchange in 'no-man's land' and drove on to the Syrian border control point at Derra. Here, we ran into more trouble. There were new problems with Hannah's passport and, again, the officer responsible for clearing the car was on a break and didn't return until 5.00 p.m. – some two hours after our arrival. When he did arrive he wasn't happy with the car's documentation. Clearly, we did need a *carnet de passage* after all. At first it seemed that we were going to be refused entry but, after much discussion, he said we were to join a lorry convoy and drive non-stop to the Turkish border. I said that wasn't possible, as I was required to call in at the British Embassy in Damascus. Eventually, he agreed to allow us to spend 72 hours in Syria, stopping overnight at Damascus and Aleppo, but not before requiring us to part with a considerable amount of money, of which 60% was to be paid in '*strong money*', which I finally realised was 'hard currency'. We hadn't budgeted for such a financial setback and so had to be rather thrifty from then on.

We knew we would be followed by the *mukhabarat*, so we had no option but to comply with the timings and route restrictions imposed on us, putting paid to our plan to explore eastern Syria along the Euphrates.

We spent the night with my Syrian counterpart and, next day, having completed my business at the Embassy, we spent the rest of the day with Rorie, Hannah and Gizela going around our old haunts in Damascus, including a visit to Saint Ananias's chapel. The new caretaker here was a Sudanese called John, whose family was in Amman. By a happy coincidence, Toni had taught his two children, Winnie and Patrick!

Our last stop was at the old mosaic factory, where we handed over photographs that I had taken on our previous visit. We ended the day with a slap up dinner at Le Meridien Hotel – a raffle prize Toni had fortuitously won at a party in Amman. Then we said goodbye to Hannah, Rorie and Gizela and embarked on the next stage of our homeward journey.

Our next stop was Aleppo, where we returned to the very rundown Baron's hotel. We still wanted to feel the true atmosphere of this historic part of the world, rather than retreat into the antiseptic luxury of a modern hotel. Our reward was another uncomfortable night and a very indifferent breakfast next morning!

As this was almost certainly the last time that we would be in Aleppo, we decided to visit the Citadel. This impressive structure is built on a hilltop, from where it dominates the entire city, and is surrounded by a very deep dry moat. Although the majority of the castle we see today dates from the 12th century, the hill on which it stands has been a defensive site as far back as the 3rd millennium BC.

We clambered up onto the ramparts to gaze down on the city's dusty rooftops, a rather lifeless, drab, beige vista. Yet we knew that beneath the roofs in the khans and souks and along the warrens of walkways there was a rich and vibrant kaleidoscope of colours.

We then set off in good time for the Turkish border post at Bab al Hawr (meaning Gate of the Air or Wind in Arabic). We had been forewarned that if we thought that the crossing between Jordan and Syria was difficult, this crossing was likely to present us with an even greater challenge. In the event, the reverse was true. We appeared to be the only car making the crossing at the time. On the Syrian side, whilst we went through passport control, a very helpful 'Mr Fix It' dealt with all the car's documentation. Of course we had to pay him, but only a nominal sum. Soon we had left Arabia and were on our way to Turkey, the route through 'no-man's land' flanked by hills and marked by ancient Roman ruins.

Our journey almost came to an end at the Turkish side of the border: no *carnet de passage*, no entry! However, after anxious discussions, the Turkish authorities relented. As we were about to leave, they warned us not to use the toll roads – only rich people used these and the traffic on them was virtually non-existent, offering 'bandits' easy pickings. Our car was certain to be targeted, as it was so heavily laden. They also warned us to find accommodation well off the road before nightfall.

On the advice of my opposite number in Syria, we were heading for the small town of Arsuz only a short distance from the border, where there was an idyllic, small hotel right on the beach. Despite not having booked and this being the height of the holiday season, we were given a room for the night with a balcony overlooking the Mediterranean.

Next morning, our route took us north to Iskenderun and then west past Adana, apparently infamous for its car hijackers. We kept to the crowded byways, as advised, and drove for more than 250 miles hugging the coast, initially through rather ugly built up areas, but these soon gave way to beautiful, rugged, forested countryside with mountains plunging straight into the sea. Here and there, the craggy mountain tops were capped by imposing castles – evidence of Turkey's turbulent past. It was when we stopped for a picnic lunch in a glorious wooded area that we first came aware of a constant screeching noise, which at times could be quite deafening. At first we weren't sure what creature was responsible, but then I discovered a large wasp-like insect on a tree trunk to be the source. A huge electric blue/black insect, this was a local male cicada. They were to serenade us throughout our journey along the Turkish coast.

We eventually arrived at the little town of Anamur, with its own magnificent castle – Mamure – that jutted out into the sea. Here we found a delightful little motel right on the beach – our room was, quite literally, a stone's throw from the sea.

It was lovely waking up to the sound of the sea gently lapping on the shore. Soon we were in it, enjoying a quick early morning dip, after which I jogged along the beach to photograph the impressive Mamure castle, a one-time Crusader stronghold, in the early morning light. A massive structure characterised by its formidable walls and numerous towers, it was built by the Romans around the 3rd century AD. Protected by the sea to the south, a flooded moat, teeming with terrapins when we visited, surrounded its land-side perimeter, making it very difficult to attack.

We also noticed a smaller castle, known as Softa Kalesi, perched on top of a steep-sided rocky outcrop a little inland from Mamure castle. We decided to explore this site after breakfast, before the sun reached its full intensity. There appeared to be no obvious path up to it but we came across a young boy at the base of the hill who offered to guide us to our goal.

He set off on hands and knees scrambling up the steep slope in front of us. Somewhat taken aback, we threw caution to the wind and struggled up behind him. By the time we reached the top we were covered in scratches from thorn bushes and sharp rocks, but the sense of achievement, coupled with the magnificent view, made it all worthwhile. Getting down again was even more of a challenge, but the thought of a refreshing swim back at the hotel spurred us on. Our young guide never asked for any money, but was very grateful when we paid him. After all, he had earned his fee.

We then went on to explore Mamure castle, before moving on down the coast. The scenery was stunning, the road twisting through fir-clad hills with spectacular drops down to the sea. We took our time, stopping several times to take photographs as well as for a long lunch break. As a result, we reached the town of Side rather later than planned, only to find ourselves in the midst of a tourist hot spot.

What had looked like miles of inviting beaches on our map turned out to be a solid barrier of hotels, motels and pensions thronging with thousands of people. We had so wanted to visit the old Roman amphitheatre, but couldn't find anywhere to park. Moreover, having been spoilt for the past three years by visiting such sites virtually on our own, we found the crowds quite daunting. Moreover, we could find no accommodation available for 'passing trade'. We were now really into the tourist belt and this, after all, was the height of the tourist season. So we pushed on and eventually found a vacancy in a rather poor hotel at Serik, well inland from the sea and clearly out of favour with holiday makers!

We were on our way early the following morning and, having bypassed the tourist trap of Anatalya, found ourselves driving through magnificent wooded hilly country again. We marvelled at the fresh green fir trees, the contrast with the harsh and dusty deserts of Syria and Jordan enhancing their beauty.

En-route we visited Phaselis, an ancient Roman port that dates back to the 7th Century BC. Now in ruins, it is set in the midst of a glorious pine forest that reaches right down to the sea. By chance, we arrived at opening time and thus had the place to ourselves. We explored the fine amphitheatre, as well as the numerous streets and arches, before succumbing to the beckoning azure waters of the military harbour where, to our amazement, we found ourselves swimming over long-submerged ruins that had been reclaimed by the sea.

Moving on westward we stopped at Demre, on the banks of the River Myros, to visit the ruined Roman city of Myra which had been built on the site of an ancient Lycian settlement dating from the Bronze Age. The first thing that struck us was a number of Lycian rock tombs carved into the vertical cliff face above the river. They were arranged rather haphazardly on top of one another. Their similarity to the carved rock structures in Petra, Jordan, was quite striking. We learned that this was one of two Lycian necropoli in Myra – the river necropolis – the other being the ocean necropolis. To the right of the rock tombs, and rising from the foot of the cliffs, was a massive Roman amphitheatre with colossal stone arches which covered a grand staircase. Unbelievably, we were completely on our own as we explored this amazing site.

To mark our time in Turkey, and also the experience of Myra, we bought a small Turkish rug to take home as a souvenir. Then we were on the road again, heading for what we had been told was a picturesque, little-known fishing village called Ucadiz. The route took us through some magnificent unspoilt mountain scenery on a road that had been built only four years earlier. This new road had changed everything, and Ucadiz was no longer a hidden jewel. The tourist industry's gain was our loss; quaint old buildings and their traditional inhabitants now lived cheek by jowl with shoddy modern waterfront cafés. Brash youths hounded us as soon as we stepped out of the car, offering all manner of bargains and excursions. Disillusioned we pressed on past Kas towards Patara, said to be the birthplace of Saint Nicholas.

Here we again struck gold, in the shape of a delightful, small Turkish hotel, Hotel Akca, which appeared to be run by two charming young girls. Patara is famous for its magnificent sandy beach, a broad expanse of sparkling white sand that stretches along the coast for over 10 miles. It remains so unspoilt because it is an important breeding site for the endangered loggerhead turtle. The entire area has been declared a nature reserve and all development along it is forbidden. Indeed, during the turtles' breeding season – May to October – the beach is off limits to people between sunset and sunrise to ensure that the turtles are left in peace to come ashore and lay their eggs.

Entry to the reserve is by ticket only – a nominal sum – and then the road passes by the ruins of the ancient city of Patara to a car park set well back from the sea. From here, access to the beach is confined to a single designated pathway. Swimming in the sea with its gently shelving bed was wonderful, the only drawback being the complete absence of natural shade ashore to shield us from the scorching sun. However, having lived in the desert, we soon managed to construct a makeshift canopy for ourselves.

After two nights in the Hotel Akca, we headed for Fethiye, just a short drive to the west. This, arguably the most picturesque place along Turkey's Mediterranean coast, boasts a delightful lagoon, a marvellous sand spit and a clear blue sea, all set against a mountainous backdrop. We stopped here to swim in the lagoon and to drink in the scenery along the spit. At its apex, expensive yachts bobbed gently at anchor, whilst holiday makers flew in tandem with experienced para-glider pilots from the mountain tops down onto the beach in front of us.

On the spur of the moment, we decided to head slightly inland to Dalyan to find some accommodation for the night. This turned out to be an inspired choice as Dalyan was a quiet little village on the banks of the Dalyan River and we were lucky enough to find a pension right at the water's edge. Opposite us, the cliffs on the far bank contained another Lycian necropolis, the fascinating rock tombs, reminding us yet again of Petra.

Next morning, our host arranged for a friend to take us in his boat to Kaunos. Way back in the mists of time, Kaunos was an important sea port, but from the 2nd century BC, the bay began to silt up, eventually leaving Kaunos five miles from the sea. We chugged up river to the ruins of the old city and its Hellenistic harbour, which was now inland even from the river. Leaving Toni in a café, I clambered up to the citadel at the top of the highest point on the ridge above the ruins. From here, I was able to see the entire silted up bay with the Dalyan River meandering through it. I was also able to see Iztuzu beach, another protected nesting site for the endangered loggerhead turtles.

Once back in the boat, our guide took us further upstream to the hot sulphur springs and mud baths at Sultaniye, which have been in use for thousands of years. The foul smelling water in the hot spring pool was an inviting 40°C, but we chose to join a crowd of about 100 people at the mud baths instead. Soon we were covered from head to toe in thick, warm mud for the cost of just a few pence.

Our Turkish expedition had been captivating but eventually we reached Kuşadasi, which marked the end of our journey along Turkey's Mediterranean coastline. It was now time to negotiate another border crossing, this time between Turkey and Greece. We had allowed a couple of days to achieve this, as well as book a ferry across to the Greek island of Samos. Next morning, we sat down to what had become our typical Turkish breakfast of olives, feta cheese, sliced cucumber and tomato, watermelon, hard-boiled egg, bread and honey, all washed down with strong, sweet black tea.

Suitably fortified by this healthy meal, I set off for town. I spent the entire morning going from one office to another, but eventually secured agreement to export the car. I was asked to come back in two days to collect the necessary paperwork, as well as our tickets for the ferry, departing in four days' time.

The four-day delay in Kuşadasi suited us quite well as it enabled us to visit Pamukkale, about 100 miles inland to the east where, over millennia, hot springs laden with calcium have turned a terraced mountainside snow white. We set off straight after lunch and before nightfall were happily ensconced in a secluded pension with its own garden and swimming pool fed by the hot springs, at the base of this amazing white spectacle.

We spent the following morning barefoot (mandatory to protect the area) exploring Pamukkale's white terraces and getting coated with calcium in the countless hot water pools they enclosed, along with hundreds of other tourists. The area was so vast that there was plenty of room for us all to enjoy this unique experience at our leisure. The temperature of the water in the pools near the top of the mountain was about 35°C, but was barely above ambient temperature by the time it reached the bottom, so an ascent of the hillside was necessary to enable us, quite literally, to soak in the true pleasures of the site.

That afternoon we headed back to Kuşadasi, via Selçuk, to visit the ruins of Ephesus. Although we were mentally prepared to see something much larger than Jerash in Jordan, we were blown away by the grandeur of Ephesus, especially its enormous amphitheatre, capable of seating 25,000 people on 66 tiered rows soaring up the slopes of Mount Panayir. Unfortunately, a barrier along the upper reaches of the site prevented us climbing to the top tier to get a better view of this ancient city, but at least we were able to locate the epicentre of the stage, from where the echo of our voices came right back to us – even at a whisper.

Ephesus was originally an important trading seaport. Saint Paul is said to have changed ships at the city on his journeys to and from Rome and may even have lived here for a time. However, just as at Dalyan, the harbour around which Ephesus was based gradually silted up and the city eventually died. Today, the ruins are over three miles from the sea.

Although at the time of our visit much of the site was cordoned off and we had to keep to the one designated route, we did manage to see the magnificent facade of the Library of Celsus and the Temple of Hadrian. Ephesus was also dominated by the Byzantine citadel, built around the 6th or 7th century AD on the summit of Mount Ayasuluk. Although we were unable to enter this impressive castle, we reached its massive entrance, known as the Door of Persecution, apparently due to an 18th century traveller wrongly assuming that Trojan War engravings, then on the door, depicted Christians being tortured and killed.

Just below the citadel, we also visited the ruins of St John's Basilica, built by the Emperor Justinian in the 6th century in honour of the apostle to whom Jesus entrusted his mother, Mary, as he lay dying on the cross. Legend has it that St John came to Ephesus after Jesus died, bringing Mary with him. Indeed, there is a small building in Ephesus known as Mary's house. We also saw St John's supposed burial site within the ruins of the Basilica.

Further down the slopes of Mount Ayasuluk lay Isa Bey Mosque, built in the 14th century by Ali al-Damishki, a Syrian architect. A fascinating building, it incorporates stones and columns from the ruins of Ephesus. Indeed, the route through the open courtyard to the mosque's entrance is lined by Roman pillars. We were on our own when we visited the mosque and were just about to take off our shoes before entering, when a gentle voice said: "No need, please come in". It was the Imam – a charming man, who showed us the true, gentle and tolerant face of Islam. Everyone was welcome in his mosque.

After an absorbing few hours, we made our way back to our pension in Kuşadasi. Next morning, I returned to town and was relieved to find that all our documentation to export the car was in order and that we were booked on a ferry to Samos departing early the following morning. I was also able to telephone the Ambassador in Jordan to exchange messages with our children. Thankfully, all was well on that front, and we spent the rest of the day relaxing on a fairly crowded beach.

We were down at the port by 7.00 a.m. next morning. There appeared to be no officials on duty, nor any sign of a ferry. Before we started to panic, we were joined by one other car – from Belgium – and a trickle of foot passengers. We noticed that the foot passengers were being processed first and so joined their queue. We were given a bit of a fright when asked why we had no visas, but were eventually waved through, thanks to the diplomatic stamps in our passports. We were then told to drive our car onto the ferry. "What ferry?" I asked, and the official then pointed to what I could only describe as two very small landing craft – one for each car.

The crossing to Samos took one and a half hours, and our car caused quite a stir on our arrival as the Customs officials had never come across a Jordanian CD plate before. However, we were processed in almost rude haste as an enormous passenger ferry was fast approaching and they needed to clear the quay.

We now needed to find a place to stay, as well as to arrange tickets to island hop to the Greek mainland and then across to Italy. First, we headed out of the tiny town of Vethi (or Samos) and found a delightful pension in the village of Agios Konstantinos. Called Irene, after its owner, it was just a couple of hundred yards or so from a quiet pebble beach, where we spent the rest of the day. By now the sea was choppy with quite big breakers, but the water was wonderfully refreshing. That evening, we enjoyed a delicious meal at a nearby fish restaurant right on the beach. As we ate, we watched two cruise liners sailing by, as fishermen in small boats worked their nets, all against the backdrop of a glorious Mediterranean sunset – a wonderful start to the Greek section of our journey home.

Next morning, we were presented with a small challenge when I went to start the car and found the battery to be completely dead. We were parked facing a wall on a downward slope outside Irene's and our only exit was up a narrow driveway which, to make matters worse, was crossed by a large pipe. A very kind Greek in a small, battered old car offered to tow us up to the road. We doubted whether he could tow our large, heavily laden Peugeot, but he was undaunted. Hauling the car over the pipe almost beat him, but eventually we were on the road and facing downhill. Our Greek rescuer waited until I had managed to get the car started on the hill and then bade us farewell. We drove back into Vethi, where we were able to buy a new battery, before sorting out our tickets for our journey to Italy. We spent the rest of the day lazing on the beautiful Mykali beach near Psili Amos, from where we had to catch the ferry next morning.

We were up and away very early and were surprised to see our ferry, the *Romilda*, already loading when we arrived at the port. We had been advised not to arrive before 7.30 a.m., but in fact that was the ferry's departure time. No sooner were we aboard than she set sail, even before we had climbed out of the car! It was surprisingly cold on deck and we were glad of the advice we had been given to wear our sweaters.

Our journey across the Aegean Sea to Piraeus on the Greek mainland took 13 hours and included stops at the islands of Ikaria, Naxos and Paros, at each of which we were joined by hundreds of bikers and backpackers. It was well after dark by the time we reached Piraeus and found a bed for the night.

Our route next day took us over the Corinthian Canal. This was a spectacular sight, so once we had crossed the bridge we parked up to come back for a proper look from the adjacent footbridge. The canal is four miles long and absolutely straight, and the water surface is 260 feet below its steep-sided walls. As we watched, a small convoy of ships, including a very long cargo ship, slipped slowly through under our feet. We were surprised to see how little space there was between the sides of the ships and the walls.

Amazingly, the first attempt to cut a canal through the Isthmus of Corinth was undertaken in the 1st century AD, at about the time St Paul was writing his letters to the Corinthians! However, it wasn't until the last decade of the 19th century that this dream was realised.

We started driving along the quiet coastal road hugging the northern shores of the Peloponnese and found it to be absolutely enchanting. So much so that when we arrived at the tiny village of Platinos we decided to stop and ask if there were any pensions in the area. There were none, but a woman showed us her self-catering apartment just across the road from the beach. It comprised two bedrooms, a kitchen, with a fridge, and a bathroom, all for the grand sum of about £5.00 per night! It was spotlessly clean and, of course, we grabbed it with both hands.

Next morning we set out to explore the area around us. We had already seen brochures describing a rack railway and a fascinating monastery called Mega Spilaio, which was built into the side of a cliff. The rack railway started from the nearby seaside village of Diakopto and climbed over 2,000 feet into the mountains to the village of Kalavryta, a distance of about 25 miles. We were in luck – having found the station in Diakopto we only had to wait 20 minutes for our train to depart and the subsequent one and a half hour journey was an absolute feast for the eye.

Kalavryta had suffered a dreadful massacre at the hands of the Nazis in December 1943. As a reprisal for the killing of captured German soldiers by Greek guerrillas, itself an atrocity, the Nazis rounded up all the men and boys aged 14 and over in the village, more than 500 in total, and marched them into the hills, where they were mown down by machine guns. The site of the massacre, known as 'The Place of Execution', is now marked by a very moving memorial, the centrepiece being an enormous white cross standing on the stark mountainside and flanked by a flagstaff from which the Greek national flag is flown at half-mast.

We were back in Diakopto by lunchtime and found a quiet spot on a deserted beach nearby for a swim and picnic lunch. Just as we were packing up it started to rain, the first rain we had experienced for four months. It was only a light shower but it was so welcome, as it freshened up the atmosphere.

We were soon heading back into the hills to visit Mega Spilaio. Built around the entrance to the cave that gives it its name, the monastery appears to cling to a sheer cliff face. Founded in the 4th century AD, it has been destroyed and rebuilt on several occasions, the last being at the hands of the Nazis in December 1943, when, apparently, all the monks were executed.

The monastery houses numerous religious treasures, the most important of which is a wax icon of The Blessed Virgin Mary carrying the infant Jesus. It is reputed to have been made by St Luke, the apostle, in 40 AD and depicts Mary cradling the baby Jesus in her right hand. Miraculously, despite the numerous times the monastery has been destroyed or damaged by fire through its long and troubled history, this icon has survived, albeit blackened by smoke.

Nearly 20 miles from Mega Spilaio there was a system of caves and underwater lakes at Kastria and this was where we headed next. The road, however, was very badly damaged and in places proved quite a challenge to our Peugeot. We learnt that this was the result of a minor earthquake that had struck the area barely two months prior to our visit.

The caves run for over a mile into the depths of the mountain, but only 300 yards were open to the public. We had to wait until there were sufficient numbers to form a large enough group before we were led in by a guide. Once inside, the doors were closed behind us to ensure that the temperature within remained at a constant 16-17°C. We walked along a metal platform amongst marvellous rock formations made by the dripping mineral waters over countless centuries – delicate white 'curtains', like silver cascades, stalactites, stalagmites and curious walled pools, similar to those found above ground at Pamukkale.

We were on our way again next day, heading for the port of Patras to catch the evening ferry to Ancona in Italy. This was a state-of-the-art ship – *Superfast 11* – one of two Superfast ferries that had been in service for barely a month. Passport procedures were minimal and there were no Customs checks for us or the car, so boarding couldn't have been simpler.

These ferries lived up to their name, being capable of completing the voyage between Patras and Ancona in 20 hours, as opposed to the 36-48 hours taken by other carriers. Unfortunately, our funds didn't run to a cabin, which would have been sheer luxury, so we opted to use the 'aircraft seats' in the crowded main lounge. The ship swarmed with passengers and soon every deck, every companion way, every corridor was cluttered with bodies, mostly in sleeping bags. Yet when everyone had settled down, we found that we had the rear row of seats to ourselves, so Toni was able to lie across them, whilst I stretched out on the floor at her feet – I know my place!

Once disembarked, our first requirement was to buy a map of Italy, as we had been unable to find one in Greece. Then we headed north up Italy's Adriatic coast to Gabicce Mare, a resort Toni had visited as a child on her family's first package holiday some 30 years before. The place had certainly changed in the meantime: every other building was a hotel, with the result that it was bursting at the seams with holidaymakers.

Our next goal was Venice. The route was rather busy and uninteresting until just beyond Rimini, where my sister, Merrilees, had enjoyed a lovely holiday with a family in the late 1950s. Now looking much like Gabicce Mare, it seemed much less inviting. However, the road beyond ran through a beautiful, naturally wooded area that had been turned into a park. We stopped here for a picnic lunch as numerous butterflies fluttered about in the dappled shade under the trees – a tranquil interlude from the hustle and bustle of the coastal resorts.

We stopped for two nights at the village of Lugo just south of Venice, to allow ourselves a full day in this iconic city. Travelling there and back by river bus, we weren't disappointed – Venice more than lived up to our expectations.

Despite the crowds, we were able to visit St Mark's Basilica and marvel at its exquisite interior, and then take the lift to the top of the bell tower to enjoy a bird's eye view of the city, its canals, peninsulas and numerous islands, all set off by a sparkling turquoise sea. We also visited the Doge's

Palace, with its richly decorated ceilings and large collection of weapons and walked over the Bridge of Sighs, stopping to take in the view on both sides, the last glimpses of the outside world seen by prisoners before being interned in the dungeons beyond.

We ended up walking beside the Grand Canal, admiring the architecture, especially the graceful Rialto Bridge, the canal traffic, including the famous gondolas, and generally soaking up the unique atmosphere of this beautiful place. At one point, we spotted the Union Jack flying over the British Consulate building and pondered at what a desirable FCO posting this must be.

Next day saw us driving right across northern Italy and into France via the Fréjus Tunnel, one of the main transit routes through the Alps between north west Italy and south east France. We found a bed for the night in a modest hotel in St Michel de Maurienne, a small town in Savoie surrounded by mountains. Nearby was the grander Savoy Hotel, where we dined that evening and from where we were able to send faxes to the children and the Embassy in Amman.

After the mad dash along the *autostrada* across Italy the previous day, we decided to take the scenic route into the foothills of the Alps the following day, heading in a roughly north westerly direction and, it has to be said, ending up a little lost in some delightful Alpine pastureland grazed by herds of healthy-looking brown and white cows.

With dusk fast approaching, we needed to find somewhere to spend the night. To make matters worse, for some inexplicable reason I began to suffer one of my panic attacks. They occurred far less frequently now and this little setback was quite unexpected.

We had almost given up hope when we happened upon the Auberge des Tavaillons, set by the roadside completely on its own in an area known as Haut Crêt. It had one room available which we gladly accepted. Because the inn was so isolated the owners also provided a communal-style supper, which was just about to be served. We drifted off to sleep that night to the sound of cowbells just outside the window and by morning I was my usual self again

This was such a beautiful area that we decided not to move on next morning. Instead we went into the nearest town, Lamoura, to buy supplies. There was an excellent information kiosk here where we spotted a brochure on Lés Cascades de Hérrison. They were relatively close to where we were and this seemed too good an opportunity to miss. So, on impulse, we set off to explore them, driving through beautiful Alpine pastures and pine forests to get there.

Having parked the car, we walked a few miles downhill following the Hérrison River, often on very slippery, rocky walkways. Every few hundred yards, we came across a waterfall; there were 31 in total, with drops of up to 190 feet. The pathway actually took us behind the 190-foot fall, giving us a thorough soaking in the process. We took lots of photographs and, despite the weather being rather dour, many were good enough to end up in our album covering the journey.

Afterwards, we went up a rough side track into some really wild country, where we enjoyed a very late picnic lunch. Unfortunately, getting back to the road, I succeeded in grounding the car, damaging the exhaust in the process. It could have been worse – at least I hadn't holed the sump or fuel tank – but we now sounded like a stock-car 'banger' as we made our way back to our auberge at Haut Crêt.

Next morning we set off towards the River Marne via Arbois, home of Louis Pasteur. Then, at the next main town, Dole, we found a Midas garage, where our exhaust was repaired in double quick time. Now we could hear ourselves talking again! Despite our various stops, we succeeded in reaching the Marne by late afternoon. This river had great significance for me; as a cadet at Sandhurst, I served in Marne Company, named after the First World War battle in September 1914 fought in this area. Further on we found a marvellous little hotel, Les Louvières, standing on its own alongside the old Napoleonic canal that runs through the village of Vitry le François, where we spent the night.

We were now nearing the end of our adventure. The next morning, we set off, keeping to the quiet roads, our intention being to reach Calais before nightfall. We stopped for a picnic lunch in the countryside near Cambrai, scene of the battle in November 1917 that saw the advent of the tank as a weapon of war, and the birth of the Royal Tank Regiment.

On our arrival in Calais, we went straight to the ferry terminal to book our journey back to the UK the next day, and then spent our last night in the appropriately named Victoria Hotel. A few hours later we were up on deck gazing at the white cliffs of Dover, just over four weeks after leaving Amman. Journey's end. It was the end, too, of our time in the Army and the dawn of our new life in 'civvy street'.

1. My uncle, Major John H Duncan MC, photographed in July 1950 whilst on loan service with the (Jordanian) Arab Legion from his Regiment, the Royal Scots Fusiliers (RSF)

2. Aerial view of the amphitheatre, Jerash (1992) (Crown copyright)

3. Anglo-Jordanian joint military training was a major aspect of my work in Jordan (Crown copyright)

4. HM King Abdullah II, then a brigadier in the Jordanian Army, in discussion with the British Ambassador, HE Mr Peter Hinchcliffe CMG CVO, on a Jordanian training exercise (by kind permission of the Jordanian Embassy, London)(Crown copyright)

5. Polo was a useful means of fostering Anglo-Jordanian relations. This photograph was taken during a match between the Royal Jordanian Polo Club and the Cyprus Polo Association. The Jordanians won 6-2 (Crown copyright)

6. The Badia Force march past during King Hussein's 57th birthday celebrations in Wadi Rum, 14 November 1992 (Crown copyright)

7. (left to right) Queen Noor, King Hussein, and Queen Sophia of Spain watch the start of the hot air balloon challenge for the King Hussein Challenge Cup (by kind permission of the Jordanian Embassy, London and the Palacio de la Zarzuela, Madrid) (Crown copyright)

8. Hot air balloons take to the skies above Wadi Rum. Being in a Regiment that recruited in the West Country (3RTR), I had been invited to ride in the City of Bath's balloon at the time (Crown copyright)

9. Eid, the *Bedu* who declined to move out of our proposed exercise danger area, roasting coffee beans to make coffee for us when we visited him (Crown copyright)

10. A snowy winter's morning in Amman

11. Like the surrounding hillsides, our otherwise dusty 'lawn' was transformed into a glorious carpet of wild flowers in the Spring

12. At the sea level marker on the way down to the Dead Sea – the lowest point on the surface of the earth (Crown copyright)

13. Jerusalem, depicted in what is, perhaps, the oldest mosaic map of the Holy Land, on the floor of St George's church, Madaba

14. The 'obligatory' photograph of me floating in the Dead Sea whilst reading the newspaper. Toni is also in the picture (top left) (Crown copyright)

15. The first glimpse of the Treasury (*Al Kazneh* in Arabic) one sees just before exiting the Siq

16. An aerial view of Aaron's tomb at the top of Jebel Haroun, Petra (Crown copyright)

17. Oassim, our guide, and Toni photographed whilst having a rest on our way up to Aaron's tomb

18. Taken at the spectacular pageant to mark the 40th Anniversary of King Hussein's reign. The photograph shows the Colours of the Armed Forces taking up their positions, whilst the ever-changing backdrop spells out Allah, Country, King (Crown copyright)

19. Being presented to King Hussein on Armed Forces Day, as Crown Prince Hassan looks on (official photograph included by kind permission of the Jordanian Embassy, London)

20. The marriage between Prince Abdullah and Princess Rania (by kind permission of the Jordanian Embassy, London) (Crown copyright)

21. Saint Catherine's Monastery at the foot of Mount Sinai (*Jebel Musa* in Arabic)

22. Waking up as the sun lights up Saladin's Castle, near Latakia, Syria (1993)

23. The ruins of Palmyra lit up by the early morning sun 1995

24. The recently refurbished gold dome on the Dome of the Rock, Temple Mount, Jerusalem, February 1995

1

2

3

4

6

5

7

8

9

10

11

12

13

14

15

16

17

18

19

20

21

22

23

24

EPILOGUE

Within a few months of leaving the Army I became a management trainer, initially with a company in Edinburgh, where I was given a very good grounding in communication skills training. When that job didn't work out, I was fortunate enough to be offered a job with an IT training company in Oxfordshire, and invited to set up a management training arm for them. This was ideal, both in terms of location and the challenge it presented. My new employers also allowed me to work as a volunteer management trainer, on an as required basis when available, for Médecins Sans Frontières (MSF) with their blessing and support.

Toni gained a Teaching English as a Foreign Language (TEFL) qualification and initially worked in the Regent School, Oxford, teaching English to non-English-speaking adults. Preferring to work closer to home, she subsequently was employed by the local council to help non-English-speaking children in local schools to enable them to cope in the classroom.

Unfortunately, in the Spring of 2011 the department in which she worked fell victim to the austerity measures introduced by the government to deal with the nation's debt. Although she had intended to retire at the end of the school year, this was a sad way to end her teaching career. However, she remains in a local choir, is a volunteer at a nearby high security prison and is a governor on the board of a local primary school.

Rorie successfully completed his Arabic degree and graduated in the summer of 1995. He had made many good friends at Oxford, but was still something of a lost soul. He had aspirations of joining the Royal Marines, but despite passing the rigorous selection process with flying colours, the Royal Marines were concerned about his injured back. He was referred to a specialist consultant who declared him unfit for employment in any capacity in any of the Armed Forces. This was a major blow to his morale.

Determined to make his way in the world, he accepted a job as an IT trainer, in which he proved successful, but he remained rather restless and depressed. Eventually, he became an aid worker, first with a Palestinian aid agency in Sudan and then, from 1999, with MSF, for whom he filled Water and Sanitation (WatSan) and Logistician appointments in Sudan, Indonesia, Sierra Leone and Russia. Some ten years after the trauma of Kuwait he had started to blossom again. He had a lovely Georgian girlfriend, Marina, whom he had met in Oxford, and really enjoyed the challenge of working with an MSF team setting up a tuberculosis hospital in the Republic of Ingushetia, part of the Russian Federation, in the North Caucasus region.

We went to visit him in Moscow in July 2002 and enjoyed a fascinating fortnight in Russia with him and Marina. We all seemed to have turned a corner. Then, on 1 September 2002, he collapsed whilst running in the Moscow marathon. Next day he was flown back to the UK by air ambulance and admitted to the John Radcliffe hospital in Oxford, where he sadly lost his fight for life two days later, on 4 September.

Worth Abbey kindly agreed to conduct his funeral service in their church, just as they had done for his brother, Alex, 12 years earlier. It was another poignant celebration of a young life cut short, attended by hundreds of mourners, including all his former boxing colleagues at Oxford and contingents from both Moscow and Ingushetia, many of whom had never travelled outside Russia before. Rorie's remains now rest in the same grave as his beloved brother's in the tranquil monks' cemetery at Worth Abbey. The two lost souls referred to in his heartfelt poem for Alex had, indeed, been reunited.

After graduating from university, Hannah spent three years as a volunteer nutritionist in the field with MSF, working in Ethiopia, Nigeria and Sudan, where she spent 13 months in the highly volatile war zone of Darfur. This was the very region in which we had experienced such a thrilling adventure in 1982 when visiting Jebal Marra. The mountain was now a Janjaweed stronghold. Indeed, in all probability, the children with whom she had played so happily up at Torra Tonga during that memorable time were now Janjaweed fighters or sympathisers intent on doing her harm.

Hannah married in 2006 and, having gained a Masters in Dietetics at Glasgow Caledonian University, has worked as a dietician for the National Health Service (NHS) in Glasgow ever since.

Zoë followed up her Geography degree at Oxford with a PhD in Geopolitics at the School of Oriental and African Studies (SOAS) in London before joining the Civil Service. A year after Rorie's death, she decided to retrain as a teacher. Leaving the Civil Service, she gained a Postgraduate Certificate in Education (PGCE) and succeeded in getting the first teaching post she applied for. Living in Buckinghamshire, she is currently a full-time mother and a successful watercolour artist.

Toni and I are now proud grandparents to three grandsons in Scotland and two grandsons and one granddaughter in England. Although the tragic loss of our beloved sons, Alex and Rorie, has left a gaping void in the lives of both us and our daughters, it is chilling to realise that there are countless people, especially in parts of Africa and the Middle East, who would gladly swap places with us.